Making Crime Pay

The Writer's Guide to

Criminal Law, Evidence, and Procedure

By Andrea Campbell

ALLWORTH PRESS
NEW YORK

06 05 04 03 02   5 4 3 2 1

Published by Allworth Press
An imprint of Allworth Communications
10 East 23rd Street, New York, NY 10010

Cover design by Derek Bacchus, New York, NY

Page composition/typography by CA Brandes

ISBN: 1-58115-216-7

Library of Congress Cataloging-in-Publication Data:
Campbell, Andrea.
Making crime pay: the writer's guide to criminal law, evidence, and procedure/by Andrea Campbell.
    p.cm.
Includes bibliographical references and index.
ISBN 1-58115-216-7
1. Criminal law—United States. 2. Criminal procedure—United States.
3. Crime writing. 4. authors—Handbooks, manuals, etc. I. Title.

KF9219.8A96.C36 2002
345.73—dc21

2001008077

Printed in Canada

Table of Contents

iii

Thank you, Michael. –Andrea

AUTHOR'S NOTE: *This book is designed to provide information in regard to the subject matter covered. It is not the intent of this book to reprint all the information that is otherwise available to the authors, but to complement, amplify, and encourage reading of other texts.*

The purpose of this book is to educate and entertain. It should not be interpreted as legal advice. The author assumes no liability or responsibility to any person or entity with respect to any loss or damage caused or alleged to be caused, directly or indirectly, by the information and illustrations in this book.

In order to keep the law fresh and compelling, I've used the pronoun "he" as the subject of most actions and directives within this book. The intent here is not to insinuate that crime and criminal acts are exclusively masculine in nature, but it is more disruptive to the narrative to constantly provide for the equivalence of gender by saying, "he or she," throughout the text. If this offends the reader's sensibility, I apologize for the distinction.

Preface

The Drama of Crime

*"No man is above the law and no man is below it; nor do
we ask any man's permission when we require him to obey it."*
—THEODORE ROOSEVELT

Nothing can shake up a character's life more than getting himself involved in a crime or certain criminal acts. For sheer human interest, nothing will capture a reader's dollars quicker than the peril that inherently comes with the distribution of justice—mainly, the law and its procedures. It is compli cated, emotional, and often messy. That's why so many writers use crime and law for storylines. And that's also why so many publishers clamor for the good stuff.

Take a murder, for example: Make it involve a prominent or influential victim, set up a confused crime scene, throw in some mysterious events; then, set it in front of two high-powered attorneys straining at the collar like two pit bulls ready to face off over a bone, and give them a complex venue in which to explore it. For plot points, have the police blunder, let the scientists err, and create a client who is both impulsive and unprepared. Sounds to us like the drama of a crime.

And the great part for the writer is, there are thousands of variations! Provided, of course, they know the detailed ramifications of what life is like, within and without, for all the players. If the writer makes one false move with a statute, applies one incorrect use of jargon, or wends his way into some type of character misrepresentation, his work is sure to wind up as cold and dead as the make-believe victim. The truth is, there are too many experts out there in reader-land. If you try to fudge with the process or don't do your homework and somehow still manage to get published—it will all come back to haunt you—you will get caught.

The smart writer prepares for the journey ahead of time. Because even though criminal courtroom procedure and strategy varies from state to state, the process is still typical, and with a little extra effort, once you know the basics, it will be easier to fit the process into your own fictional jurisdiction. *Making Crime Pay* is here to help you do that. We will winnow down the rules so that you can manipulate them with confidence. Whether you want to shake up a character's life with trauma or help to restore it back toward peace, this is a great place to start.

At a 1987 banquet for the American Academy of Forensic Science members, past president Don Harper Mills astounded the audience with the story of a bizarre death. A medical examiner surveyed the body of Ronald Opus and concluded that he had died from a gunshot wound to the head. The victim had originally jumped from the top of a ten-story building, intending to take his own life. He left a note to that effect, indicating his despondency. But as he fell past the ninth floor, his life was interrupted by a shotgun blast through the window, which killed him instantly.

Neither the shooter nor the deceased was aware that a safety net had been installed just below the eighth floor level to protect building workers. Ronald Opus would have failed to complete his suicide attempt the way he had planned.

"Ordinarily," Dr. Mills continued, "a person who sets out to commit suicide and ultimately succeeds, even though the mechanism might not be what he intended, is still defined as a suicide. Because Mr. Opus was shot on the way to certain death nine stories below, and because his suicide attempt probably would not have been successful due to the safety net, the medical examiner felt that he had a homicide on his hands."

The shotgun blast had come from a room on the ninth floor that was occupied by an elderly man and his wife. They had been arguing, and he was threatening her with a shotgun. The man was so upset that when he missed his wife, the pellets went out the window, striking Mr. Opus.

When one intends to kill subject A but kills subject B in the attempt, one is still guilty of the murder of B. When confronted with the murder charge, the old man and his wife were adamant. They both said they thought the shotgun was not loaded. The old man said it was his long-standing habit to threaten his wife with the unloaded shotgun. He had no intention to murder her.

Therefore, the killing of Mr. Opus appeared to be an accident; that is, the gun had been accidentally loaded.

The continuing investigation turned up a witness who saw the old couple's son loading the shotgun about six weeks prior to the fatal accident. It transpired that the old lady had cut off her son's financial support, and the son, knowing the propensity of his father to use the shotgun threateningly, loaded the gun with the expectation the father would shoot the mother. The case now becomes one of murder on the part of the son for the death of Ronald Opus.

Now comes the bizarre twist. Further investigation revealed that the son in fact was Ronald Opus. He had become increasingly despondent over the failure of his attempt to engineer his mother's murder. This led him to jump off the ten-story building, only to be killed by a shotgun blast passing through the ninth-story window. The son had actually murdered himself, and the medical examiner closed the case as a suicide.

When asked about the truth of this story, Mills told Tracy Thompson, a reporter for the *Washington Post*, "I made it up." Mills claimed ownership of the story, saying it was part of a speech given at the group's 1987 banquet, and he says he did it strictly for entertainment. As to becoming part of an urban legend, Mills said, "I didn't expect it to get on the Internet. So far, I've gotten more than a hundred calls about it." When asked if this surprised him, Mills responded, "No, not really. It's a fabulous story."

And that is the point. By knowing the intricacies of the law and its criminal principles, you, too, can create your own urban legend. This book is set up in a logical manner: delineating the evolution of law, defining criminal law's specific elements, outlining the proper criminal procedure, and finally finishing with law's application. If, per chance, your story does not follow this paradigm, each principle or procedure is covered by its own chapter.

The headings, boxes, and bulleted lists are for speed and ease of use. I have tried to take complicated legal jargon and break it down into its most simple elements, giving you an easy way to begin the "What if" process.

Be sure to check out the appendixes and endnotes, as they hold valuable information in the way of forms, definitions, and additional reference; they are listed in case you decide you would like to read the entire document or the actual criminal case referred to in the text. The writing style throughout is colloquial, in keeping with the title of the book. It is written in regular, conversational language. I hope these techniques help you in all your crime novel endeavors.

Part I: Criminal Law Explained

Chapter 1

The Evolution of Law

The life of law has not been logic; it has been experience.
—OLIVER WENDELL HOLMES JR., *THE COMMON LAW*

We could say laws were shaped on the backs of men—literally, in some cases. In the name of the law, criminals have been beheaded, impaled, burned, flogged, mutilated, and chained to everything from trees to grinding wheels to the oars on great ships. Lawbreakers have also been pressed into service, exiled, and imprisoned.

The criminal procedures used today are fruit from the seeds of long and accepted practices of thought, trial, and error. The beginnings of law and the horrible struggles, war, torture, and inequalities of history paint a glorious if brutal picture. As writers, you will find the foundations of law helpful to know and understand, and the historical perspectives may inspire you to write about another time.

Hail Civilization

When a culture becomes complex enough to support a diverse number of people and ideas, the unity of its inhabitants forms a civilization, which helps to preserve its past, sponsors innovation, and transmits its style and values. Civilization as we know it first emerged some five to six thousand years ago. First, small agricultural villages evolved in the Mesopotamia river valley between the Tigris and Euphrates rivers. Shortly thereafter, communities sprung up in Egypt, around the Nile. These social organizations had more complex rules for conduct than those that guided cave dwellers or the earliest farmers. In fact, the very word "civilization" is borrowed from the old French but taken from Latin *civilis*—relating to private rights, state law, and public right—but with an important distinction: It was for city dwellers only.

In shaping a civilization, the establishment of firm authority required a balance between those doing the governing and those being governed. This practical peace called for certain sophisticated divisions of authority and labor. Specific duties, power, and skills passed down through particular families. Who you were born to pretty much determined your lot in life.

Firm authority required acceptance. Mesopotamia, and later Egypt, had powerful kings and a priestly caste. Seeking social order, the people gave authority to the man or woman who seemed to have some special power, wealth, or ability. In less sophisticated communities, power was handed to the biggest or strongest of men—and in some cases, to men with red hair. Law or formally accepted codes of conduct, were a step-up from the simple customs of village life.

Detailed, recorded law codes tell us how societies controlled relations among their people. The best known is the Laws of Hammurabi, sometimes referred to as the Code of Hammurabi. These judgments were issued by an eighteenth-century B.C. Babylonian king who probably adapted them from older Sumerian and Akkadian law. Hammurabi's laws were engraved on a pillar of stone and related to all aspects of life in Babylonia. Four thousand lines of writing spelled out what was expected from the people: the sanctity of their oath to God, and the necessity of all legal matters and written evidence.

FYI

The cuneiform stone column, which records a long series of the legal judgments published under the name of Hammurabi can be found at the Louvre Museum in Paris, France.

HAMMURABI'S LAW CODE

When Marduk [the patron god of Babylon] sent me to rule the people and to bring help to the country, I established law and justice in the language of the land and promoted the welfare of the people. At the time I decreed:

1. If a man accuses another man of murder but cannot prove it, the accuser shall be put to death.

....

2. If a man bears false witness in a case, or cannot prove his testimony, if that case involves life or death, he shall be put to death.

....

22. If a man commits robbery and is captured, he shall be put to death.

23. If the robber is not captured, the man who has been robbed shall, in the presence of the god, make a list of what he has lost, and the city and the governor of the province where the robbery was committed shall compensate him for his loss.

....

142. If a woman hates her husband and says, "You may not possess

me," the city council shall inquire into her case; and if she has been careful and without reproach and her husband has been going about and belittling her, she is not to blame. She may take her dowry and return to her father's house.

....

195. If a son strikes his father, they shall cut off his hand.
196. If a man destroys the eye of another man, they shall destroy his eye.
197. If a man breaks another man's bone, they shall break his bone.

....

200. If a man knocks out a tooth of a man of his own rank, they shall knock out his tooth.[1]

Lex talionis, the law of retaliation—"an eye for an eye and a tooth for a tooth"—is said to be derived from these early beginnings and is a principle many cultures still adhere to today. In fact, a modern version of Talion law is in effect in the Islamic republic of Iran. Equivalent retaliation takes form in ideology but is practiced in the law—with penalties being proportionate to the severity of the offense, "letting the punishment fit the crime." Today, a person found guilty of theft in Iran could be punished by severing his hands.

One important thing to note: In its implementation, Talion law does not call for retaliatory justice by taking of the perpetrator's eye for one lost by the victim; rather, it limits the victim's legitimate claim to no more than an eye for a lost eye.

Early due process and primitive versions of the trial—a sophisticated treatment of how controversies were settled in ancient western civilization—are illustrated through what we know about Biblical Israel (*circa* 1020–922 B.C.) and a system they had called "trial court at the gate."

Since there was a mix of clans in these communities, certain folkways and mores were taught by one clan to another. Any violations of these beliefs were dealt with by the trial court, at the gate. Trial convened in the morning near the gates to the community, in front of the elders, and before the townspeople left to work in the fields. It attracted an audience and was meant to be public. One of the rights of the accused, the basis for a public trial, began here.

The accuser, who acted as the prosecution, essentially, was the party on the right hand of the justice, with the judge seated in the center. The accused was assisted by a defender who would stand. Death sentences for serious crimes were common, and when the offense warranted stoning, the accuser got to throw the first stone.

There were penalties for false testimony—it usually meant the liar received the same sentence as the accused. Also, as part of the process, no testimony was allowed that was based either on secondhand information or supposition, bringing to mind today's rule of evidence against hearsay. In addition, two witnesses were needed to convict a person of a crime, and this served as the basis for today's theory of corroboration. Plus, if there were a lack of evidence, the accused would take an exculpatory oath; he would call upon God (known as Yahweh) to punish or curse him should he lie.

The people of that time believed that law was an expression of God's commandments and that any violation was a transgression against God. For example, Israeli law commanded that the one who had killed should also be killed. If the blood spirit given to people by God was taken in murder, the law was allowed to take again what rightfully belonged to Yahweh. If no killer was found, a blood sacrifice from an animal was granted to restore balance.

The Age of Laws' Refinement

Two other great Western civilizations helped to shape laws' early beginnings: the Greeks and the Romans. Their attitude toward leadership and law can be summed up in a speech the Athenian leader Pericles gave as a eulogy for his countrymen who were killed during the Golden Age (431–430 B.C.): "Our form of government does not enter into rivalry with the institutions of others. We do not copy our neighbours, but are an example to them."[2]

ATHENIAN JUSTICE: Solon, a popular poet and statesman, was well known for his compassionate work, which made him a towering figure in Greek history. As chief magistrate of Athens, Solon drafted a code that essentially prohibited slavery for indebtedness and class division based on income and property, and granted citizenship to even the lowest peon, thereby allowing men a chance to improve their status economically, regardless of ancestry.

Solon's court of appeals, the Heliaea, consisted of a jury drawn from a lot of six thousand members of the Athenian tribe. With his enactment for more equal citizen participation and responsibility, he pointed the state toward eventual democracy. Three other important contributions from the Heliaea system were: Guilt or innocence was determined by secret ballot; the trial was finished in one day; and the courts relied on the people's contribution and civil action—in other words, it sanctioned the first citizen's arrest.

Some other concepts survived the Athenian law process: filing a complaint, holding preliminary hearings, the notion that the magistrate could dismiss motions or hold them over, and the taking of oath (they also allowed "oath helpers," people within the defendant's family who were sworn in as well). Interestingly, if the defendant had more oath helpers than the accuser, the charges were dismissed.

Also, the Athenians prided themselves on being great orators and perfected the art of the closing argument—summation speeches directed toward the jurists. Other original measures were that monetary fines were imposed as a deterrent to lying; for example, a thousand drachmas were collected from those who pressed false charges. Court penalties included capital punishment, a common remedy, which primarily consisted of drinking hemlock or being thrown into an open pit and stoned. Noncapital punishments included banishment, public degradation, or, in the case of slaves, flogging.

LONG LIVE ROME: A refined system of law and procedure was one of the chief cultural contributions of the Roman civilization. Laws were issued by assemblies made up of citizens who were in the army or who were landholders, and they dealt largely with public issues such as land distribution and military commands overseas. On the other hand, the laws that affected relations between citizens were largely the work of individual elected magistrates who had a limited term of service—one year—and they needed the consent of their colleagues to govern.

Normally, cases came before a judge—again, a private citizen—who relied on the advice of other citizens—called jurists—reputed to know the law. They operated under the adversarial trial process, and the police force was often called in as an investigating element.

Romans distinguished their own citizens from the rest of the other members of the Empire. Natives were subject to civil law—laying the basis for modern civil law—or law applying only to citizens; others were allowed to maintain their own customs, *ius gentium*, or law of other nations. These two laws then, logically, were assigned to two kinds of magistrates: the "urban praetor" and the "traveling praetor."

Eventually, as the powers of authority within the empire grew, the law of custom replaced the law of other nations. Public pressure for codes of law spawned ten bronze and wooden tablets, later to become a dozen etchings called *The Twelve Tablets*. These were fastened to the speaker's stand at the Roman Forum. The word *leges*, which were enactments by Roman assembly, stands for our word "legislation" today. These rules of customary conduct morphed into an issuance called edicts—public orders or decrees. Later, around 130 A.D., officials codified the edicts and leges into one body of law called *edictum perpetuum*, or force of law.

During the height of the Roman Empire, Emperor Justinian created a written summary of laws called the Justinian Code. These collected laws had developed over the course of a thousand years; and with 170 constitutions it became the *corpus juris civilus*, or the Body of Civil Law. This served as the basis for canon law—law of the Catholic Church. Later, in large part due to the church, the canon and common law tied together again to form French Napoleonic Code, which serves today as the influence of a development of law exercised through the Louisiana Purchase, called the Louisiana Civil Code.

PUTTING IT IN PERSPECTIVE: Although these early stories of law give an ordered look to their respective societies, a writer of history must look further for the truth. A well-rounded law researcher and writer would do well

5

to note that Greece was plagued by the lack of law from its early beginnings. One of the most significant episodes in Greek history, the Peloponnesian War, was a civil conflict involving Greeks killing Greeks. When they fought against other nations, such as in another famous conflict, the Trojan War, their enemies were known as barbarians. The expansion of the Greek Empire spawned injustice and was one of the key factors in the advancement of the judicial system.

The Roman Empire hit its height with *pax romana*, the Roman Peace, providing two centuries of solid prosperity. But it, too, was founded on the backs of slaves, and justice for the captive and disenfranchised was nonexistent.

Writer Jump-Start

The dichotomy between slave and free in a land celebrating the height of Roman civil engineering, for one million inhabitants of the most successful city in Western civilization, is a great contrast of humanity. In the midst of great prosperity, Rome was not as great a place to live for the slaves and the conquered barbarians who did all the work. After the death of Augustus (14 A.D.), the empire was preserved by three things: emperors, civil servants and city councils, and the army. The successors of Augustus cared little for those of lower rank. The laws were laws of oppression, if you were not a citizen of Rome. Conflicts such as these make for powerful historical narrations.

Sources of American Criminal Law

The American criminal law, and the subsequent rights of the accused as we know them today, are a blend of two traditions: the common law, which was developed in Saxon England and grounded in customs and precedents; and civil law, which was derived from its Roman antecedents—laws adapted from the earlier efforts used to control human behavior, which survived by means of written and established codes that defined offenses and prescribed penalties for those crimes.

English common law—a tossed salad made up of tribal rules, Roman law, and the customs of invaders and other travelers from France, Scandinavia, and what would later become Germany—influenced our ways as well. In 1066, William the Conqueror, the Norman ruler, imposed his own public mandates on the existing system in order to consolidate his power and authority. Under the royal justices appointed by William, the existing state law became common law—named so because it originated in the customary practices of the realm and was common to all England. And even though common law had its roots in custom and tradition, it evolved through time and through the use of consistent, judicial decision-making.

For this reason, common law is judge-made law. Think of it as a reproduction of a fine antique, one that has been adapted, changed, polished, and buffed to a shine. The whole museum storehouse of common law, then, is an actual collection of decisions handed down from generation to generation.

KINGS AND LAW: Henry I, son of William the Conqueror, made his own contributions to criminal justice and issued *leges Henrici*. One prime example of this, and an idea that has continued to mature since then, was that crimes like robbery and counterfeiting were "against the King's peace." Thus, these offenses became crimes against the state, a precedent for crimes punishable by the state instead of by an individual—a model for crimes of misdemeanor. Later still, King Henry II developed and extended the king's court system and created a jury system called the Inquisition, where a jury panel determined guilt.

They were followed by King John, a serious abuser of power. He increased taxes and governed according to his wishes. This upset the barons—landowners—and church leaders, and they drew up a list of rights for people. In 1215, King John had to sign the Magna Carta. In it were such ideas as separation of church and state, additional rights given to the rising middle class, and a mandate that the king was to seek advice from his barons before enacting any laws.

And, finally for England, King James II, a tyrant king in the late 1600s, was forced to abdicate, and this turn of events helped to produce the English Bill of Rights. As part of these rights, there would be no order for suspending laws without the aid of Parliament, no standing army during peace, free elections for members of Parliament, and no impeachment of the people's freedom of speech.

Therefore, when the "new world" was being settled by English colonists in the seventeenth and eighteenth centuries, they had a basis for law. Later, when the War of Independence had been won, breaking the shackles of English rule, the settlers had their rights to freedom, and a new, American common law system was left to evolve. One man in particular, Sir William Blackstone, helped the new American judges by publishing *Commentaries on the Laws of England*, which illustrated the principles of the common law in an encyclopedic treatment. Blackstone had been a jurist and professor at Oxford, and his effort aided in demystifying English law. The barristers of England were a little put off by Blackstone's seminal effort, because they took pride in offering their services to "discover the law," but his American counterparts found his *Commentaries* to be something of a legal bible.

FIVE SOURCES OF CONTEMPORARY LAW:
1. United States Constitution
2. Acts of Congress
3. State constitutions
4. State statutes and territorial legislature acts
5. The common law

The law of the Constitution is greater than an act of Congress and, when in conflict, can void it out. If a valid act made by Congress clashes with a state constitutional provision, the latter is void. If a provision of a state constitution goes against the statute or law of the same state, the state law is void. If a law of a state or one of its territorial legislatures conflicts with a common law provision, the latter is void.

Types of Law

A writer should be familiar with the different types of law and know what they mean. If your protagonist is a lawyer, he will obviously know the terminology. Described below are the types of law under the umbrella of the American criminal law system:

SUBSTANTIVE CRIMINAL LAW: This is the more formal term for criminal law. The key elements of substantive criminal law are:
- The acts
- Mental states
- Accompanying circumstances or consequences that make up the necessary features of crimes

In other words, it defines the kinds of behavior (acts or omissions) that constitute wrongs against the state and assigns punishments for such conduct. Any references in this book to criminal law are actually references to substantive criminal law.

PROCEDURAL LAW: Also known as "criminal procedure," this type of law stipulates how substantive criminal law should be carried out. These are the steps on how a governing body should proceed in order to enforce criminal law. It defines arrest, probable cause, rights, and search methods—all elements of the law enforcement plan. Based on fundamental fairness and due process, procedural law tells us how evidence should be collected and what rights are guaranteed to the accused.

STATUTORY LAWS: These are laws that are made by state legislatures and Congress. This type of law is most important, because all American jurisdictions have extensive statutes dealing with crimes and criminal law. These laws are put together into codes for sorting purposes and are classified under separate headings. The criminal laws of any state are found under the state penal code. So, to find out how Arkansas defines the crimes of kidnapping, false imprisonment, and vehicular piracy, you would look in the Arkansas Penal Code, as provided in the Arkansas Statutes 5-11-102, 5-11-103, and 5-11-105. State codes are subject to revision at annual legislative sessions.

ADMINISTRATIVE LAWS: Administrative laws are rulings by government agencies at the federal, state, or local levels. For example, an executive branch may set up and give authority to a board of health in order to establish regulations for specific policy areas (in this instance, health standards). Although most of the content of administrative law is not targeted directly at criminal behavior, certain violations are dealt with in criminal courts.

CONSTITUTIONAL LAW: United States Constitution and the constitutions of the individual states dictate this type of law. These, by nature, are supreme over other kinds of law, and the disputes are most likely handled in state supreme courts—and, sometimes, in its final destination (if it gets that far), the Supreme Court. In the event of a conflict, the federal Constitution law is dominant over state constitutional law. The only crime defined in the U.S. Constitution is treason.

PRECEDENTS: This type of law is influenced by the principle stare decisis—"Let the decision stand." Judges use this rule in order to follow what went before in judicial interpretations. This means that judges today accept the decisions made by judges in the past. These principles, or precedents, help them to promote stability and certainty when making legal decisions— although prior decisions are sometimes overturned by the higher authority in a court of appeals, thereby reversing or modifying existing case law.

CASE LAW: Judges may create case law in their rulings on statutory laws. This type of law also applies when they take into account previous rulings and set down, in writing, an opinion of their own.

TORT: A tort is a civil remedy for injury to persons and their property. The injured party may sue for remedy, reparations, or related expenses. Examples of these would be libel, slander, trespassing, and damage from negligence.

Seven Basic Law Principles that Define a Crime

We all have ideas about what we think is inappropriate behavior, but what is a crime in the eyes of the law? Are there basic requirements of a criminal act, a laundry list of wrongs? In simple terms, *yes*.

For a particular behavior to be considered criminal, there are basic conditions that must be met. These factors must all be present and are what the legislatures and courts use to prepare and interpret substantive criminal law. Basically, a crime is *an intentional act or omission in violation of a criminal law, committed without defense or justification and sanctioned by the state as a felony or misdemeanor.* These are the essential ingredients in every crime:

1. Legality
2. *Actus reus*
3. *Mens rea*

4. Concurrence of actus reus and *mens rea*
5. Harm
6. Causation
10. Punishment

LEGALITY: There is an ancient Latin saying, *nullum crimen sine lege*, which means, "no crime without a law." You may also hear it as *nullen crimen, nulla poena, sine lege*, or, "There is no crime, there is no punishment, without law."

> **FYI—**
>
> This is an interesting concept: There can be no crime unless a law exists that has been violated. Examples of this would be the rather recent laws against carjacking, or offenses that are now being defined as "hate crimes."

ACTUS REUS: This term is simply another way of saying "guilty act." Bad thoughts alone do not constitute a crime. Just because you may wish someone dead, unless you take action to bring about that result, it may be sad but it's not a crime. It is important, though, to distinguish thought from speech, because now there are laws that govern that. Also, an agreement to commit a crime is one of the elements required for a criminal conspiracy, which I'll discuss later.

MENS REA: Mens rea means "guilty mind," also referred to as "criminal intent." Proving intent is a hurdle all prosecutors train for. It calls for an assessment of the psychology, motives, and intent of the defendant. The concept of *mens rea* is based on the notion that people have the capacity to control their behavior and can choose between alternative courses of conduct. If a bus driver drives through an intersection without stopping and causes an accident, he will not be charged with a crime if it turns out that his brakes failed and he had done whatever he could to prevent the accident.

CONCURRENCE OF *ACTUS REUS* AND *MENS REA*: This phrase means that the act and the mental state, or intent, work together in time for a crime to be committed. For example, the act and mental state are not concurrent if they are separated by a considerable gap in time.

HARM: Only conduct that is in some way harmful can be considered criminal. The essence of the idea of harm is based on due process. For instance, a criminal law is unconstitutional if it can show no relationship to the matter of injury against its citizens. Harm does not have to be physical, though. In cases of libel, perjury, and treason no physical harm is inflicted.

Just recently, legislatures have expanded harm to include hate crimes and criminal discrimination. A hate crime is an act of violence or property damage committed because of the victim's race, gender, or sexual preference.

CAUSATION: This relates to crime in the same way that a defendant's conduct produces a given result. Only crimes like perjury, lying under oath, or forgery—signing a false name—are defined so that the crime consists of both the act itself and the intent to cause the harmful result, without regard to whether the result actually occurs. The harm that occurs must be similar enough to the intended result that the defendant can still be held responsible.

In some instances, cause is difficult to assess. For example, if A shoots a bullet into B and he dies, we can see through ballistics evidence and the wound that the action and the intent were the cause of B's death. On the other hand, if A shoots B and leaves him on the freeway, and B gets hit by C, who doesn't see him, will A be convicted of B's murder? Only if it can be determined that A's conduct was a substantial factor in bringing about B's death or that what happened was a foreseeable consequence of A's behavior.

PUNISHMENT: Under the American legal system, citizens must not only be warned about what conduct is forbidden but must also be made aware of the consequences of their actions. For this reason, the law stipulates sanctions for every crime.

11

> **Writer's Tip**
> Look to history for great story lines. For example, how about a Roman character, a member of counsel, who has to prove the innocence of his lover? Nothing new there? What if the accused were a slave who worked in the court of the Emperor? And what if a potential heir to the throne, a baby, was killed? Now you've got the beginnings of a dilemma!

Chapter 2

Crimes Defined

Crime, like virtue, has its degrees.
—RACINE, *PHÈDRE*

Would you believe there is an extensive body of law that permits punishment for an incomplete or failed crime? Yes, the offenses of attempt, solicitation, and conspiracy are all inchoate, or anticipatory, crimes. They include any uncompleted activity where the end result would have been, without fail, a crime. So these crimes are a "preparation," if you will. The concept of inchoate offenses was originally created by the courts to give police the power to apprehend dangerous persons who have not yet done the deed, and thereby prevent them from completing their criminal objectives.

Attempt

Of the inchoate crimes, attempt is the most frequent charge. In order for a criminal to be charged with an attempt, certain conditions must be met:

1. The intent to commit an offense AND
2a. A substantial step (also called an "overt act") OR
2b. Conduct that would have been a crime

The state penal code usually gets specific in defining the attempt to commit murder, but a typical statute reads like this one from Florida:

> Whoever attempts to commit an offense prohibited by law and in such attempt does any act toward the commission of an offense, but fails in the perpetration or is intercepted or prevented in execution of the same, commits the offense of criminal attempt.[3]

Solicitation

Solicitation and attempt are different in that solicitation is complete when the request or inducement to do the act is made. In order words, solicitation is
1. The intent to promote or facilitate a crime, AND
2. The instigator's act of commanding, urging, or requesting another to engage in specific conduct that would make up an offense or attempt.

The Gardner case[4] illustrates exactly when the crime of solicitation is performed. Roger Gardner, an alleged contract killer, hired a man named Tim McDonald to kill Alvin Blum for $10,000. Gardner met with McDonald, giving him some expense money, a gun, and ammunition. During their conversation at this meeting, Gardner said he would first kill a man named Hollander, and if that did not create the desired result, then McDonald should go on to kill Blum.

Gardner's attempt failed when he was arrested and charged with solicitation to murder. It turned out that McDonald worked for police as an informant, and his information led to Gardner's arrest.

On appeal, Gardner argued that he did not commit the crime of solicitation because he did not actually direct McDonald to proceed with the murder of Blum, or pay him all the money promised. The Maryland Court of Appeals saw it differently and affirmed Gardner's conviction, saying that "the crime of solicitation was committed when he asked McDonald to commit the murder . . . neither the final direction to proceed nor fulfillment of conditions precedent [paying of the money] was required." The court observed that the "gist of the offense is incitement."

One important distinction of solicitation is this: It does not require direct solicitation of another; it may be done through an intermediary. A Connecticut court also found solicitation to be far more dangerous to society than the attempt to commit the same crime. The court's reasoning? In *State v. Schleifer*[5] the court said that behind it is an evil purpose, "coupled with the pressure of a stronger intellect upon the weak and criminally inclined."

Conspiracy

The necessary elements of conspiracy are:
1. An agreement or what we might call the meeting of the evil minds, AND
2. The purpose or the intent to commit a crime, AND
3. An overt act

Now, the next logical question I can hear your legal mind asking is: What constitutes an overt act? An overt act is any act—not necessarily a substantial act—but anything that indicates the crime is alive and well. It could be something as trivial, but as visible, as writing a laundry list of supplies needed in

13

order to rob a bank. Also, "mere knowledge" of a crime, or thinking bad thoughts, is not enough of a reason to be guilty of a conspiracy, but it may be an interesting way to get a naïve character involved in a story or even to present a vehicle that sends him into hiding.

Now, in the court's mind, conspiracy is a distinct offense, meaning it cannot be melded into other target offenses such as arson, kidnapping, homicide, etc. Overall, judges have expressed their feelings about conspiracy like this: Conspiracy deserves its own attention—is itself a crime—because a group association makes it possible to commit more complex crimes than can be perpetrated by one criminal mind; and crimes unrelated to the original purpose are more likely to happen than what the group first got together to do. This is borne out by the fact that the range of conspiracies cuts across socioeconomic classes in society, a factor that might play out well for your upscale characters who get caught up in someone else's plan.

FYI—Two to Tango

Okay, now that you have this principle about conspiracy's being a distinct offense, here are two exceptions to the rule.

1. There is always an exception to a rule of law; we have to expect it and accept it.

2. Wharton's Rule, named after a famous commentator on criminal law, says that two people cannot conspire to commit certain crimes, such as adultery, incest, or bigamy, because these offenses can only affect its two participants. (I think this has its faults also.)

You should consider some important stipulations about conspiracy if you are going to give it to your prosecutor as a tool, or if you intend to use it in a courtroom scene with dialogue:

1. All acts of one conspirator are chargeable to all others

2. All statements by one conspirator are admissible to all conspirators

3. In a conspiracy, the agreement does not have to be expressed—it can be implied, and

4. It takes two or more. In the eyes of the law, an accomplice's precrime assistance makes a conspirator just as guilty as the person who carries out the actual crime. Plus, a person can be convicted and punished for both the conspiracy and the crime *if* the crime is actually committed

Writer's Tip

missing text

before the movie's release, had been convicted of collaborating with three other perpetrators in the robbery and murder of a widow. Graham's role consisted mainly of helping her cohorts gain access into the widow's home. Graham was sentenced to death and executed in the gas chamber, even though she may not have participated in the actual killing.

Amid debate over the severity of her punishment, two last-minute stays of execution were lifted, making her one of four women ever put to death in California. Susan Hayward won a Best Actress Academy Award for her portrayal of Barbara Graham.

What are some of the things an accomplice, someone who helps the principal to commit the crime, does? For our purposes here, let's assume that Kevin Klever breaks into a jewelry store and steals diamonds. If Naïve Ned is Kevin's accomplice, he may have assisted Kevin by drugging the night watchman, cutting the wires to the security system, or helping Kevin review the floor plan and layout of the store. Even if Naïve Ned were not actually on the scene—if he had, say, rented a U-Haul and left it parked within walking distance of the jewelry store, or if he had agreed to baby-sit Kevin's infant son, Kevin II, while Kevin Klever robbed the store—he is subject to the same charges as Kevin when caught.

An interesting note to those of you who like husband-and-wife criminal teams is that, in the past, common law regarded a husband and wife as one person for most purposes, so the couple could not be guilty of conspiring with one another. But with time and experience, the trend in recent years has been to recognize the separate identities of the spouses. Hello, modern thinking.

And although someone can be guilty of three inchoate crimes, he cannot be punished for all of them—just one. The prosecutor will file as many charges as possible to improve his chances of conviction—sometimes condemned by defense attorneys as "overcharging." This type of practice also serves as a bargaining chip when it comes down to plea negotiation in that the prosecution can offer to dispense with one or more of the charges for the right information.

15

> **FYI**
>
> Although defendants may be convicted of separate charges for the same act, they usually cannot be punished separately for each charge. When a complaint is filed, it may say, for example, that the accused, who stole five computers, is charged with five counts of burglary plus breaking and entering.

Aiding, Abetting, and Hindering

Now, I know you're thinking about certain terms you may have heard used on television or in films, such as "accessory after the fact," or that someone has "aided and abetted," or that someone has "hindered the apprehension" of the perpetrator. Who are these people, what are these charges, and why are they different from conspirators?

AFTER THE FACT: The difference is basically the factor of time, and one might even refer to these offenses as "hidden crimes." Listen to some of the criminal definition: A person commits an offense if, with purpose to hinder the apprehension, prosecution, conviction, or punishment of another for an offense, he carries out any of the following acts:

1. Harbors or conceals the person
2. Provides aid, such as weapons, money, or transportation
3. Prevents or obstructs anyone from performing an act which might aid in the discovery of said person by force or threats
4. Conceals, alters, or destroys evidence
5. Warns persons of impending discovery, or
6. Volunteers false information to police

Do you see the distinction? The help to the perpetrator comes after the criminal act but still affects the crime or the criminal in some elemental way. And a crime is not actually finished until the criminal has reached a place of temporary safety. Perhaps, because by the time an accessory after the fact becomes involved, a crime has already occurred, in most states accessories after the fact face far less punishment than accomplices or their principals.

RENUNCIATION: Okay, so one of your more confused or ambitious characters has gotten caught up in some bad business, and you decide you need a twist. Is there some way to help them "get out of trouble"? Is there a defense for them? I'm glad you asked. And it is a practice more commonly used than you would think. It is called renunciation.

Renunciation is, at the very least, a way to let your character negotiate a better deal with the prosecutor. Renunciation is an active arrangement; it means that the one who strayed will terminate complicity in the commission of a crime *and* will deprive the complicity of its effectiveness or will give timely warning to cops *or* will make a substantial effort to prevent a crime. Maybe your character can even put his own life at stake—that would make for a compelling, redeeming, and distinguishing trait—pointing out the universal fact that we all make mistakes.

STRICT LIABILITY CRIME AND SUPPLIER'S LIABILITY: Before we leave accessory activities, there is another area of aiding a perpetrator called "supplier's liability." Any time you hear about strict liability crimes, these are crimes in which intent is not an element. While *act* plus *intent* equals *criminal liability, forbidden act* equals *strict liability crime*. Offenses that involve no mental element but consist of only forbidden acts or omissions are classified as strict liability crimes. Whereas the Latin term, *mala in se offense* means "wrongs in themselves," *mala prohibita* refers to "prohibited evils" or offenses deemed wrong by the state. This latter type of statute says that if someone does something illegal or neglects to do something required of him without the specific intent of bringing about a harmful result, he is still guilty of a crime.

16

Examples of this would be liquor, narcotics, and food laws; regulatory laws; and traffic regulations. These cases usually involve youthful offenders or matters of public health or welfare.

With supplier's liability, the supplier or "seller" presents goods to the perpetrator, and the supplier has no liability for the "mere knowledge" of the buyer's criminal purpose for the goods unless one or more of the following circumstances are revealed:

1. The seller acquires a stake—receives a benefit such as selling goods at inflated prices
2. No legitimate use for the goods or services exists—the supplier has a directory of prostitutes, for example
3. The volume of business conducted is grossly disproportionate to legitimate demand—for example, a doctor is caught selling Prozac in mass quantities, and
4. The crime that goods are being used for is a felony

Supplier's liability, as a concept for the writer, is a good way to add a plot complication—another "Uh oh" element that a secondary character can get involved in.

Writer's Jump-Start

For a court scene, writers often use "accomplice testimony," such as having an accomplice "roll over" on another conspirator. The truth is, judges have historically been mistrustful of an accomplice who points the finger or shifts the blame to someone else. Because of this inclination, most states have a safeguard rule that a defendant cannot be convicted merely upon the testimony of an accomplice. If your prosecution presents a witness who qualifies as an accomplice, the prosecution will have to "corroborate" that witness's testimony with independent evidence linking the defendant to a crime. You, as a writer, can use this little known fact to your advantage. You can lead readers to believe that a conspirator will get his just rewards because his cohort is turning state's witness. But, actually, you may have to adjourn proceedings when the judge refuses to hear accomplice's testimony, and your prosecutor must then change his tactics in order to search for further truth.

What Is Intent, Anyway?

We've skirted around the issue of "intent." Does it matter what state of mind the criminal was in at the time of the crime? Frankly, yes. State of mind is a major player—the ace in the hole, so to speak, the card used to complete the loaded hand held by the prosecutor—and it is called "intent." Since intent is such a crucial factor to proving someone's liability for a crime, here are the four basic terms pertaining to intent—the mental state, or the state of mind:

1. *Purposeful.* The conscious objective is to engage in a conduct
2. *Knowing.* The person is aware of his conduct, *and* he is practically certain that his conduct will cause the result

3. *Reckless.* Conscious "disregarding" of a substantial and unjustified risk; "disregard" is a gross deviation from the standard of care that a reasonable person would observe

4. *Negligence.* He would be aware of a substantial and unjustifiable risk, *and* the risk must be of a nature whereby the failure to perceive it involves a gross deviation from the standard of care that a reasonable person would observe

Let's take a hypothetical case to explain this sticky wicket. Suppose that the defender, Colt Packer, fired a gun that hit Smith Wesson in the arm. There could be a minimum of four different scenarios to explain the shooting and proof of intent. First, Packer could have fired the gun and hit Wesson accidentally. Second, Packer may have fired the gun intentionally but did not know that Wesson was in the vicinity. Third, Packer may very well have intended to shoot old man Wesson, wounding him after a dispute but not necessarily killing him. And, fourth, Packer may be guilty of attempted murder in that he was trying to prevent Wesson from taking another breath. Four very different versions pose virtually the same result: hitting Wesson with ammunition from a loaded gun. Now, just to complicate things a little further, there is also a legal term called "doctrine of transferred intent." This concept says that when a person intends to commit one criminal act but accomplishes another instead, the law implies that the necessary criminal intent for the second wrongful act is still present. In other words, if the accused intended to hurt one person, and wound up hurting someone else, the intent is still sufficient to make him responsible for the second, unintended victim. In the classic illustration, A aims a gun at B intending to kill B. A misses and instead kills C. A's mental state directed against B is said to be transferred to C, the unintended victim. The only intent left now is for the courts to decide what to do with him.

The Authorities

In chapter 1, we talked about the evolution of law and its historical underpinnings. Before we go much further, we need to get a picture of how the fundamentals of criminal law and procedure look on our United States' family tree. For example, the United States Constitution is at the head of the family; it sets forth the general powers and limits of government and specifies the rights of its individual citizens. The Supreme Court of the United States upholds the Constitution and adjudicates appealed trials concerning issues involving constitutional law specifically. In later chapters, I'll draw simplified court systems and detail their responsibilities so that you will understand the hierarchy at a glance.

On the first tier, or branch, of this tree is the federal government. Our federal government is responsible for defining and punishing federal crimes—you could call them crimes against the nation. Next to this are the state constitutions. These are separate entities that set forth the powers and limits of the fifty state governments, each of which may be distinct from the others.

On our hierarchical chart, within the federal government are the three great powers: the legislative, executive, and judicial branches. The legislative branch is administered by our United States Congress, which enacts laws setting forth the various federal crimes and punishments. The executive branch of the federal government is responsible for enforcing federal laws, prosecuting cases, and supervising punishments. The judicial branch is made up of the federal courts, which help to interpret the laws by deciding particular cases.

These three branches have what's called "the principle of separation of powers." That means that each branch of government must rely on the other for approval—no one power can make decisions without the other. Just to illustrate this tit-for-tat concept: The legislative branch makes laws, the executive branch enforces those laws, and the judicial branch interprets those laws. Now, if the Congress writes a law, the Supreme Court can declare congressional laws unconstitutional. The Congress can also rewrite legislation to circumvent the Court's decisions; and the Senate also confirms the judges and determines the numbers of judges appointed.

The president of the United States can nominate federal judges; he can also refuse to enforce the Court's decisions; and he can grant pardons. The Congress can override a presidential veto of its legislation, and it can remove and impeach a president. The Senate confirms the presidential appointments; plus, it controls the power of the purse and provides funds for the president's programs. And, finally, the Supreme Court can declare presidential actions unconstitutional. That, my friends, is separation of powers!

On the other side of the second tier of authority are the state constitutions. Each state has its own constitution, which sets forth the powers and limits of its own government. State constitutions receive input from their state legislatures, which make state laws (often called state statutes), setting forth their own criminal prohibitions and penalties. There is another section under state constitutions called "state and local government." This body oversees law enforcement, prosecutorial functions, and corrections agencies within that state. And, finally, the third branch is the state court system, which interprets the state laws by deciding particular cases. Each of these entities needs the cooperation of the other in order to operate efficiently.

Criminal? Civil? What's the Difference?

Court cases are fundamentally two types: criminal and civil. A criminal case means that the government seeks to punish an individual for an act that has been deemed by either Congress or a state legislature to be a crime. Consequently, in a criminal case the prosecutor—who is an elected official—

criminal

undertakes and controls the case, not the victim. He will file criminal charges against the offender and does not need the permission of the victim. The prosecutor must prove the defendant's guilt "beyond a reasonable doubt." The defendant, as a result, is almost always guaranteed a trial by a jury of his peers. He also has the option of having a government appointed attorney. Trials are commonly open to the public.

civil

A civil case has different bones. It has to do with a dispute between individuals or organizations and most often concerns either duties or rights that each legally owes the other. The state has a less direct interest (other than peace), and the attorneys are generally representatives of private firms, so the parties in civil cases pay for their own lawyers. Most civil laws address a breach of contract, which means that one or both of the parties involved violated the terms set forth. The injured party is the one who initiates the case.

20

People held liable in civil cases may have to pay damages, give up property, or suffer some other type of remedy. In a civil case, the plaintiff (the one bringing forth the case) only need prove the facts with a preponderance of evidence that the defendant is liable for damages. Only some types of civil cases involve a jury trial. Usually, an "offer of settlement" will negate the need for court.

tort

Now, because you will hear it mentioned, a tort, on the other hand, is a wrongful act that does not violate any enforceable agreement but still violates a legal right on behalf of the injured party. Examples of a tort would be wrongful death or personal injury cases because of either intentional or negligent reasons—including wrongful destruction of goods or property, trespass, libel, slander, or degradation of one's name or standing.

FYI

A person can be subjected to both criminal and civil cases—prosecuted by the state for criminal actions and civilly sued for monetary damages. In 1995, O. J. Simpson, in the most publicized case in history, was prosecuted for the murder of both Nicole Brown Simpson and Ron Goldman and found not guilty. That did not end his trials, however. In an entirely separate case, Simpson was also sued in a civil court for "wrongful death" by the victims' families. At the end of the civil case in 1997, Simpson was found responsible for the victims' deaths and ordered to pay millions of dollars in damages.

Misdemeanors, Felonies, and Infractions

Like people, criminal laws come in an array of sizes and shapes and fit different circumstances. Crimes are separated by their seriousness and, as a consequence, by their punishments. Felonies are the most serious crimes, and, generally speaking, they are punishable by more than a year in prison and fines over $1,000. Examples of felonies are murder, rape, robbery, and kidnapping.

Misdemeanors are less serious crimes and, typically, can be punished by less than one year in jail and fines of no more than $1,000. Examples of common misdemeanors are drunk driving, shoplifting, prostitution, and posses-sion of an unregistered firearm. A unique element of misdemeanors, though, is that the first offense involves less incarceration time, aggravation, and a fine, but the second offense of the same kind can snare someone with felony charges.

Infractions are violations that are classified as less serious than misde-meanors. Infractions commonly involve traffic laws and are typically remedied by a monetary fine. Defendants charged with infractions are not usually eligi-ble for a jury trial. Included in this group may also be municipal laws or offenses called "ordinances." These are rules or laws set up by a particular city or county. A city ordinance may prohibit smoking in government buildings and may uphold so-called blue laws—archaic ordinances—such as "no spitting on the sidewalk." Violators of municipal laws are typically issued fines to pay.

FYI—Wobbler Statutes

Some crimes may be classified by prosecutors and judges as either felonies or mis-demeanors, according to criminal statutes. Such crimes are often referred to as "wobblers." For instance, some wobbler statutes may allow an assault to be charged as a felony or misdemeanor, largely depending on the prosecutor's own discretion. His decision will be based on the severity of the injury to the victim, or the nature of the defendant's intent and past criminal record. Likewise a judge may decide, after hearing the evidence, to reduce a felony assault to a misdemeanor, depending on the circumstances presented.

Suit-and-Tie Crimes

Another relatively new area of crime in the historical scope of all law, white-collar crime presents special problems for criminologists because it is difficult to define, the conduct involved is often elusive, and no readily quantifiable data exists to tell how often it is done. What in the past may have endured as unethical business practice is now redefined as criminal conduct. Plus, other offensive behavior, such as computer crime, does not fit the mold of developed common law and has only become formalized as a forbidden statute in recent years. This slippery genus of law-breaking is usually committed in the course of an occupation or profession and, as such, is thought of as "pinstripe crime," because of the connection with the red "power" tie and pinstriped suit, and is committed primarily by persons in the upper socioeconomic strata of society. As a consequence, white-collar crimes often fall into federal jurisdiction. These may include violation of statutes such as bid rigging, price fixing, money laun-dering, insider trading, and tax fraud. Interestingly, white-collar crimes are frequently defined to include prostitution, gambling, obscenity, and offenses relative to the importing, manufacture, and distribution of illegal drugs. It's these same types of crimes that come under the banner of "organized crime"—but only when they are committed by groups of people who also attempt to gain political influence through graft and corruption while balancing their activities with threats and acts of violence.

If a white-collar crime is prosecuted federally, the violation can be tied to statutes enacted by Congress. These laws will be found in Article I, Section 9 of the U.S. Constitution, which grants the government power over postal, bankruptcy, taxing matters, and problems with regard to domestic and foreign commerce.

Sometimes, a "small fry" gets nicked for white-collar offenses, because he has committed fraud or swindled a target. These contingents operate by using telephone or mail solicitations in order to bilk money out of people by selling "opportunities to buy" unregistered securities, obtain undeserved diplomas, participate in phony contests—or just by generally perpetrating scams, such as would be done with a real estate scheme or fraudulent land sales. And the variety of offenses will continue to grow and evolve in interpretation as electronics takes over more and more of our lives.

FYI:-Murky Waters

In June 1998, in *U.S. v. Singleton*,[6] the U.S. Appeals court ruled that it was illegal under federal law for the government to "purchase" accomplice testimony with a promise of leniency. This decision, made by the 10th U.S. Circuit Court of Appeals, rocked the Justice Department. At issue were the moral and legal underpinnings of immunity deals that would essentially make criminals of the federal prosecutors who offered them. If this ruling had been upheld, it would have had implications for thousands of cases, most recently the convictions of Timothy McVeigh, Terry Nichols, and Michael Fortier, who were tried in connection with the bombing of the federal building in Oklahoma City, which resulted in the deaths of 168 people.

McVeigh was charged with first-degree murder and sentenced to death. A separate jury convicted Nichols of conspiracy, for helping to plan the bombing and collecting supplies—he was sentenced to life in prison. Fortier, another accomplice, received twelve years in prison after pleading guilty to failure to warn authorities of a bomb plot, and to transporting stolen weapons. But, in part, Fortier's lighter sentence was due to his providing crucial testimony that helped convict McVeigh and Nichols.

The ruling was put on hold until the full body of the Denver-based appeals court could decide. In its majority opinion, a twelve-member panel said that "statutes of general purport do not apply to the United States unless Congress makes the application clear and indisputable," that if Congress had intended to overturn the accepted practice, "it would have to do so in clear, unmistakable, and unarguable language." The Justice Department officials were pleased by the reversal, noting that offering leniency in exchange for truthful testimony was "a longstanding, important aspect of the legal system."

The case that stirred this dispute centered on the Kansas conviction of one Sonya Singleton, charged with cocaine trafficking and money laundering. Three judges said that the chief prosecution witness illegally received leniency in exchange for his testimony, violating federal law against bribing witnesses. These same judges did not change their minds with the final vote, which was 9–3.

Writer Jump-Start

We often make assumptions about the criminal justice system that become conventional wisdom, such as: legal counsel always knows best; or, guilt will always be determined by the facts. What if your character's competent legal counsel isn't too bright? Wouldn't he have to take things into his own hands? Perhaps he will need to research the law or become his own detective. Getting your protagonist involved in his own defense makes for good plotting and added suspense.

23

Chapter 3

CRIMES AGAINST THE PERSON

The soul of a murderer is blind.
—ALBERT CAMUS, *THE PLAGUE*

Violent crimes and bodily harm are what people say they fear the most. "Crimes against the person" have a profound psychological aftermath. They affect people as a personal violation, and these feelings fuse themselves onto the victim's thoughts forever (if he lives to persevere). This is an important concept for writers to grasp. The emotional toll on family relations, the loss of income due to attorney meetings, counseling, court appointments, and medical follow-up, plus the loss of time—of being in limbo until resolution—and of needing time afterward to recuperate, make a victim continually aware of his trauma.

Homicide

Though often used interchangeably, homicide and murder are not necessarily the same thing. *Homicide* is any killing of a human being by another. There are some homicides that are justifiably legal, such as the killing of a suspect by police or a killing in self-defense. And there are also vehicular homicides. *Murder*, on the other hand, is an unlawful killing with "malice aforethought." In other words, in order to charge someone with murder, prosecution needs proof that there was premeditation.

Premeditation doesn't mean that the killer acted out because of spite or hate; it means that the killer intended to kill a person—an important distinction. In most states, malice aforethought is not limited to intentional killings but also exists if a killer intentionally inflicts very serious bodily harm, which causes a death, or if a killer's behavior demonstrates "extreme reckless disregard for the value of human life" and results in a victim's death. For example, the perpetrator could have been involved in a dangerous act and demonstrated wanton disregard for other human life on the scene at the time, such as tossing rocks off a highway overpass and causing an accident below.

state defs.

It is important that a writer look up *the particular state's* law for the setting of his story. Some part of the definition may be unique. For example, here is a simplified outline of an Arkansas statute for homicide:

Homicide
Capital murder. A person commits or attempts to commit capital murder if he engages in [one of the seven activities below], and in the course of or the furtherance of that felony, *he causes the death of another* under circumstances manifesting *extreme indifference to the value of a human life*:

A. Limited felony murder:
   1. Rape
   2. Kidnapping
   3 Arson
   4. Vehicular piracy
   5. Robbery
   6. Burglary
   7. First-degree escape

B. Killing of a public servant (listed below) who is acting in the line of duty or performing his job.
   1. Police officer
   2. Judge
   3. Firefighter
   4. Jailer
   5. Prison official, parole officer, or any military personnel

C. A double death: With purpose to kill one, the perpetrator kills two.

D. Killing of a public official: With purpose of killing an elected official, he kills anybody, any time.

E. Life sentence: Under sentence of life imprisonment, he *purposely* causes the death of another after premeditation and deliberation.

F. Contract killing—the hitter: Pursuant to an agreement, he kills someone in return for anything of value.

G. Contract killing—the hirer: A contract killing (agreement) whereby one person enters into agreement to cause the death of another person in return for anything of value.

Capital Murder Is a Class Y Felony: Important Notes in Arkansas Law

•   Conduct must be the proximate cause of death; this means that the victim's death must have been the natural and probable result of the defendant's unlawful conduct

25

- Death does not have to be foreseeable (or intended)
- Death used to be defined as the end of heart and lung function; now, death is cessation or termination of brain activity
- In Arkansas, there are five classifications of homicide, and a capital murder receives the death penalty. The other classifications are Murder in the First Degree, Murder in the Second Degree, Manslaughter, and Negligent Homicide

26

Writer's Jump Start

Say your protagonist belongs to a gang, and they are robbing a small market. She wants to take the money and run. In the process of the heist, though, she frightens the storeowner, and her gun accidentally discharges, killing him. The felony murder rule makes your character strictly liable because she killed him in the process of committing a crime. End of the story? No. A writer used this concept, and Nikita of *La Femme Nikita* was born. Can you do the same? How can you keep your character in the game?

DEATH IN DEGREE FURTHER DEFINED: Homicide and the degree of culpability—in other words, blame—are also somewhat different in each state. Most states classify murder as either "first degree" or "second degree." And the law regards some killers as more dangerous and morally blameworthy than others. Murder in the first degree is willful, deliberate, and premeditated. Now, the period of time required for premeditation does not have to be a long duration—just long enough to consider the gravity of the situation, and it could be as brief as going into the next room to get the Glock.

We've also seen, as in the Arkansas statute above, that murder in the first degree includes any murder in the course of committing a felony. And it only follows that murder in the first degree usually carries a more severe punishment than second-degree murder. Currently, in a majority of states, the ultimate penalty is death. In some other states, instead of capital punishment, sentencing is life in prison without the possibility of parole. Second-degree murder convictions are usually served by a term of years in prison rather than a life sentence, and those convicted of second-degree murder are almost always eligible for parole.

I've also found in the first-degree murder statute here in Arkansas that in the case of a death involving a fetus, the prosecution has to prove that the fetus was viable, and, as of this writing, we believe that constitutes thirty-two weeks. Check out this anomaly in your own state's laws, and you may have an interesting case to build a story on. You could use it to demonstrate an antagonist's previous record; perhaps he "got away with murder" because of this little known pregnancy rule—the louse! That's sure to inflame a lot of your other, more determined characters who set out to seek justice for those who are seldom represented, infants and children.

PREMEDITATION OR SPECULATION: *State v. Bingham*[7] is a case that illustrates the dilemma of deciding whether it is a sound policy to separate out premeditated killings in order to impose more severe penalties than for other murders.

Leslie Cook, a mentally retarded adult living at the Laurisden Home in Port Angeles, was raped and strangled on February 15, 1982. Bingham was the last person with whom she was seen. The two of them got off the Port Angeles–Sequim bus together at Sequim at about 6 p.m. The pair visited a grocery store and two residences. The last of these was Enid Pratt's, where Bingham asked for a ride back to Port Angeles. When he was refused, he said they would hitchhike. They took the infrequently traveled Old Olympic Highway. Three days later, Cook's body was discovered in a field approximately a quarter of mile from the Pratt residence.

27

At trial, the state's expert testified that, in order to cause death by strangulation, Cook's assailant would have had to maintain substantial and continuous pressure on her windpipe for three to five minutes. The state contended that this alone was enough to raise an inference that the murder was premeditated. The trial judge agreed. Therefore, the judge allowed the issue of premeditation to go to the jury. The jury convicted Bingham of aggravated first-degree murder, with rape being the aggravating circumstance.

On appeal, Bingham's attorney conceded that a finding of guilty of murder was justified, but he challenged the finding of premeditation and contended that the evidence was insufficient to support it.

In an opinion given by Chief Judge Worswick, the Supreme Court agreed. There was no evidence presented that proved Bingham had known Cook before February 15 or that he had a motive to kill her. By chance, they had taken the same bus. Judge Worswick said that while it could be inferred that Bingham had raped her, a reasonable jury could not infer from this beyond a reasonable doubt that he had also planned to kill her. There was really no evidence to support premeditation. The case was reversed and remanded for judgment and sentencing for second-degree murder.

MORE MURDER—OF THE SECOND DEGREE: Second-degree murder is a Class B felony. A person commits murder in the second degree if:

    1. He knowingly causes the death of another person under circumstances manifesting extreme indifference to the value of human life; or

    2. With the purpose of causing serious physical injury to another person, he causes the death of any person

Second-degree murder is a killing in which malice aforethought is present, but the premeditation factor is not. This could mean a death resulted from a barroom fight; it could also include parents who abuse children with fatal results.

DEPRAVITY: You will also hear the words "depraved mind or heart" in connection with second-degree murder. An apt example of this would be a case in which the state of New York charged a fifteen-and-a-half-year-old boy with murder in the second degree for reckless conduct that exhibited a grave indifference to human life. In *People v. Roe*,[8] the evidence at trial revealed that the defendant had loaded a mix of live and dummy shells into a twelve-gauge shotgun and pumped a shell into the firing chamber, not knowing whether it was potentially dangerous or not. Then he callously raised the gun to his shoulder and pointed it directly at the victim, stating they would play a game of "Polish roulette," and asked, "Who is first?" The defendant then proceeded to discharge a live round into the chest of a thirteen-year-old, which resulted in his death.

On appeal, the boy's defender argued that it must be shown that his defendant's reckless conduct was imminently dangerous and presented a grave risk of death, whereas, in manslaughter, a much lesser charge, the conduct need only present the lesser "substantial risk" of death.

The New York Court of Appeals held that the evidence presented was such that the defendant had an intense interest in weapons, possessed a detailed knowledge of weapons, and the court therefore reasoned that with this type of information available to him, the macabre game of chance was legally sufficient to support second-degree murder.

FYI

In April of 2001, the House voted on a bill to make it a federal crime to harm a fetus during an assault on its mother, urging action on behalf of "unborn victims." Voted on in previous years, this bill now has the support of the White House. "This legislation affirms our commitment to a culture of life, which welcomes and protects children," said President Bush in a prepared statement for the press in Houston. The bill would apply only to crimes in federal jurisdiction, but about half the states have similar laws. The Supreme Court in 1989 upheld Missouri's version, one of the broadest, which describes an "unborn child" at any stage of prenatal development as a person.[9]

MANSLAUGHTER AND ITS PARTNER, PROVOCATION: Provocation frequently is an ingredient in manslaughter trials. There are two classes of manslaughter under common law: voluntary and involuntary.

Voluntary manslaughter, also known as manslaughter in the first degree, arises when a person is suddenly provoked and kills in "the heat of passion" or extreme emotional disturbance. The words *hate, rage*, and *jealousy* come to mind. Human weakness helps to define voluntary manslaughter in that the circumstances are likely to provoke any reasonable person into action. The killer may act intentionally, but the emotional context prevents him from being able to control his behavior, reducing his moral blameworthiness. It is a Class C Felony under Arkansas law.

A common scenario is the husband who returns home unexpectedly to find his wife in bed with another. One other vital characteristic in this state's law is that "mere words"—such as "You idiot!"—are not sufficient enough to provoke a person to kill. However, informational words—such as "Your husband is sleeping around"—can be considered to provoke extreme emotion and reckless behavior. Intricacies? The law is full of them and, as a writer, you can use these subtle characteristics to your advantage when it comes to the prosecutor's charging your key players.

A person guilty of involuntary manslaughter is one who has shown reckless disregard of a substantial risk; his actions have resulted in death, but these actions grew mainly out of carelessness and not intent. Involuntary manslaughter has also been called "criminally negligent homicide" and is sometimes referred to as manslaughter in the second degree.

In order for the prosecution to assign voluntary manslaughter to the charges, he may have to unearth a defendant's specific intent. On the other hand, in a criminal charge involving involuntary manslaughter, the defendant's intent only need be general in terms of not being partial to the victim. The charging details stem from the defendant's act and surrounding circumstances. Two examples of involuntary manslaughter would be waving a loaded gun around, which results in someone's death, or, as mentioned earlier, throwing bricks off an overpass onto oncoming traffic, which also results in an accidental death.

VEHICULAR HOMICIDE: Road rage and the bloodshed on American highways have spawned many states to enact vehicular homicide as a specific felony, rather than charge an offender with manslaughter for causing a traffic death. An excerpt from the Florida statute reads like this: "Vehicular homicide is the killing of a human being, or the killing of a viable fetus by any injury to the mother, caused by the operation of a motor vehicle by another in a reckless manner likely to cause death of, or great bodily harm to, another."[10]

By using this unique language, the state, in effect, has enabled its prosecutors to secure a conviction in instances in which the state is unable to meet the level of proof necessary for establishing manslaughter. For a character who operates a motor vehicle in such a negligent manner that it causes a death, the writer had best consult individual state statutes for the charges.

Writer's Tip

Research tells us that some typical motives for homicide may include revenge, sadism, personal gain, mental deficiency, self-defense, sex, mercy, fear, love, feuding,

29

contract killings, ambition, rivalry, protecting someone or something, attempt to cover up another crime, jealousy, the framing of another, blackmail, debt, and—probably the least viable and the hardest to demonstrate—thrill killing. For writers, these powerful key words should conjure up a plot point for your story to follow. If you construct your story with one of these motives in mind and continually allow the suspected intent to poke itself into the mind of your detective—the *why, why, why did it happen?*—you will have a reason to drive your character into action and discovery. Investigative brainstorming should always give plenty of attention to motive.

REAL LIFE VERSUS FICTION: When it comes to homicide, fiction is more optimistic than reality. Today in the United States, you will not find a homicide detective who has solved every case like the character in your favorite crime novel. And while the numbers of murders committed has dropped, the rate at which they are solved is dropping more quickly. Statistics tell us that in 1968 police solved 86 percent of all murders. The FBI reports say that homicide solution figures for the year 1998 stood at 69 percent. Cases are getting harder to crack!

Experts provide several reasons for this disparity. More murders today are committed by strangers rather than by spouses or friends. James Fox, a criminologist at Northeastern University says, "Now we have taken the home out of homicide. There is a greater distance between victims and offenders, and the greater the distance, the more difficult it is to solve the crime."

Other, more apparent, frustrating factors continue to complicate cases and leave more and more investigators baffled. Robert Ressler, a retired FBI agent, says that murderers today have become more sophisticated and that killers know more about crime-solving techniques. Also, a lot of the victims of homicide lie on the fringe of society. Coupled together with this "invisible people" problem is the fact that the homeless, runaway, and prostitute victims have lifestyles that make it harder to track their killers. And finally, witnesses today seem more likely to refuse to talk, especially when the offenders are connected to gangs or deal in drugs. Fox says that the good old days of 80 percent clearance rates will probably never return.

FYI

According to the Bureau of Justice Statistics Sourcebook, law enforcement agencies *clear* or solve offenses when at least one person is arrested, charged, and turned over to the court for prosecution. In 1994, the portion of violent crimes—murder, nonnegligent manslaughter, forcible rape, robbery, and aggravated assault—cleared by arrest was 45.3 percent.

OTHER TYPES OF SERIOUS HARM: Homicides can be accomplished by several methods—shooting, strangulation, knifing, poisoning, electrical shock, gassing, vehicular death, hanging, beating, suffocation, and burning. But what if it happens under the guise of something else?

HOSPITAL HOMICIDE: Technological advances in medicine have given physicians the option of using sophisticated life-support systems to prolong life for indefinite periods of time. Along with this comes a burden whose ramifications involve moral, ethical, and religious concerns. A landmark case, In re Quinlan,[11] involving Karen Ann Quinlan, who lay in a comatose state with no reasonable medical probability of regaining a sentient life, tells the tale of parents who requested her removal from life-support systems and were granted their petition. The court said that withdrawal of such life-support systems, under the circumstances, would not constitute a criminal homicide.

But there are other issues and varying judicial opinions as to when, under what circumstances, and by whom, cessation may be ordered for minors and incompetents. And haven't we read stories in the news about people who work in hospitals who have taken it upon themselves to relieve certain patients of their lives? This, too, is a powerful controversy for writers to engage in. Just be aware that there is no statutory or judicial consensus on the viability of—or the procedures to execute—termination. And, also, there is a vast difference between medical personnel who go haywire with their power and those who follow procedures that have been granted in good faith based on competent medical advice and consent of an equally competent patient and family.

Threats and Physical Harm

The assaultive offenses—assault and battery—are commonly used as a pair but are really separate offenses at common law. Under most states' laws, a simple *assault* would include a threat to strike someone with the fist, or a missed punch. Assault also carries two different manners of distribution: An assault is an *attempt* to commit battery or the intentional creation, by other than mere words alone, of a reasonable fear in the mind of the victim of immediate bodily harm. As an example, in a majority of American jurisdictions, the pointing of a gun at another would be an assault, since it places another in reasonable apprehension of receiving a battery.

A *battery*, on the other hand, requires some physical contact with the victim. Simple battery would include hitting or pushing someone, but it could even encompass offensive touching against someone's will, intentionally tripping someone, or a parent or teacher's using excessive force in disciplining a child. Simple assaults and batteries generally remain misdemeanors unless they are perpetrated against public officers like police or firemen, and then they are frequently classified as felonies.

When these offenses are labeled "aggravated," they cease to be called simple, having taken on new meaning. For example, as aptly explained by authors Scheb and Scheb in their textbook *Criminal Law & Procedure*,

> A frequent litigated issue in prosecutions for aggravated assault and aggravated battery is whether the instrument used by the defendant

is a dangerous weapon capable of producing death or great bodily harm. An air pistol, a hammer, a club, or an ice pick—and under some circumstances even a person's fist—have been found to qualify. Courts generally reason that the test is not whether great bodily harm resulted, but whether the instrument used was capable of producing such harm.

Although a completed battery can be committed recklessly, the definitions often require that an assault of either type is evident only if the defendant acted purposely or with knowledge. This next Supreme Court case presents several of these interesting points.

In *Harrod v. State*,[12] the appeals' court needed to decide whether a person could be convicted of assaulting another, if the victim has suffered no harm and was never aware of the alleged assault. The appellant, John G. Harrod, was charged and convicted with two counts of assault. Here are the notes from his first court case—you decide:

A confrontation between John Harrod, his wife Cheryl, and her friend Calvin Crigger occurred on September 15, 1983. Cheryl testified that Calvin Crigger came over to visit when she thought her husband had gone to work; and that "all of a sudden [John Harrod] came out of the bedroom with a hammer in his hand, swinging it around, coming after me and my friend." Calvin ran out of the house and down the steps. Then Cheryl testified that her husband then threw the hammer over the top of their son Christopher's port-a-crib in the living room, and it went into the wall. After this, he reentered the bedroom and returned with a with a five-inch hunting knife and told Cheryl he was gong to kill her and that if she took his son away from him, he was going to kill Christopher. John Harrod then put the knife into the banister near Cheryl's arm and followed Cheryl out to Calvin's car and "went after Calvin, going around and around the car."

John Harrod told his side of the story next, saying that he had missed his ride to work that day and returned back home around 10:00 a.m. Going to sleep in a back room, he heard Calvin's deep voice. He confessed to picking up the hammer, walking into the room, and suggesting that Calvin leave. Cheryl protested, saying he didn't have to go, and John Harrod said, "Buddy, if you want your head busted in, stand here; if you want to be healthy and leave, go." Harrod claims that Calvin just stood there, so he swung the hammer, Calvin moved his head back, and the hammer stuck in the wall over the crib, which was near the door.

The court in rendering its verdict decided that, beyond a reasonable doubt and to a moral certainty, that Mr. Harrod did go after

Cheryl and Calvin, swinging a hammer and missing, wielding a knife and missing, and that he was guilty of two counts of carrying a deadly weapon—the knife and the hammer—and also two counts of assault, one against Cheryl and one against the minor child.

What do you think?

On appeal, the Supreme Court judges dismissed the charge of assault against Christopher, saying that there was no evidence in the record that Christopher was in fact aware of the occurrences in his home on the morning in question. Therefore, there was insignificant evidence to find Mr. Harrod guilty of putting that victim in fear-type assault. And because the trial was erroneous in finding the appellant guilty of an assault on Christopher, they reversed that conviction.

33

MAYHEM: "Mayhem" is an old-fashioned word, but it is still on the books in California. Their statute states: Every person who unlawfully and maliciously deprives a human being of a member of his body, or disables, disfigures, or renders it useless, or cuts or disables the tongue, or puts out an eye, or slits the nose, ear, or lip, is guilty of mayhem.[13]

Originally, the definition of mayhem was "to willfully and maliciously injure another to render him unable to fight." In some states that was changed to include all injuries that disfigure a person. The prosecutor has to prove the offender's intent to maim or disfigure the victim. This type of attack is typically associated with revenge and, in an aggravated case, would be to *permanently disable* the victim, something we often associate with organized crime. Again, a writer should consult his specific state's law, because mayhem may be rolled in with other statutory crimes and referred to as aggravated battery or attempted murder.

STALKING: Times do change, and at the end of the 1980s, police noticed an increase in complaints from persons who were continually being followed, harassed, or threatened. In order to name the language that seeks to describe this type of behavior, they came up with the term "stalking" and noted that the complaints came primarily from women who were targeted by men.

By 1993, several states met the challenges presented by this new nuisance and further defined "stalking," turning it into a crime. The general stipulation is that a person who willfully, maliciously, and repeatedly follows or harasses or makes a credible threat against another is guilty of stalking. The words "credible threat," which showed up in many state law books, have been struck from most of the definitions since being questioned under litigation. Certain other challenges have been made, such as in the Illinois Supreme Court fairly recently, over whether the law held up against a person's right to freedom of speech. The Illinois law still stands, but another attempt at dismantling the statute came from Georgia, who had to decide whether attempted stalking was really a criminal offense at all, and not merely an assault misdemeanor. But the Georgia Supreme Court, in *State v. Rooks*,[14] confirmed that stalking is an offense because such conduct constitutes an attempt to follow, place under surveillance, or contact another person.

Writers interested in using this type of behavior for their characters should also watch for complaints being filed by women and men who nowadays fall victim to relentless e-mail messages. This ceaseless terror (although it may have started as a simple amorous advance) may lead to enactment of new laws, both through federal and state channels.

34   RAPE AND STATUTORY: Rape laws have gone through many versions and incarnations from the times since the common-law scheme as defined in the early English common-law period. Questions about force, consent, gender terminology, and what constitutes the physical act have all been disputed as the decades pass and charges are challenged. Statutory rape, the purpose of which was to protect young women from all acts of sexual intercourse, has also been subject to definition refining when it comes to age limits, gender discrimination, and whether "carnal knowledge" is sexual intercourse or other sexual encounters involving minors.

One of the most significant legal reforms concerning rape came about during the late 1970s and early 1980s in respect to rape shield laws. This enactment precludes presenting in court evidence of a victim's prior sexual activity with anyone other than the defendant. Some state's laws require that certain evidence be first submitted *in camera*—in chambers—for a determination as to whether the evidence of the defendant's prior relationship with the victim is relevant to the victim's consent.

Today, Michigan has a modern, comprehensive law for first-degree criminal sexual offense. The criminal sexual conduct is defined by various degrees; it tells whether it involves sexual penetration or sexual contact and spells it out. Some of its provisions are: Sexual penetration is sexual intercourse, cunnilingus, fellatio, anal intercourse, or any other intrusion, however slight, of any part of a person's body or of any object into the genital or anal openings of another person's body, but emission of seed is not required. In addition, the statute is a gender-neutral offense, which has become a basic reform. It also makes provisions for those people who commit sexual batteries against the helpless, those who take advantage of their family position, supervisory authority, or an offense that occurs between a doctor and his patient.[15]

If, as a writer, you wish to use a rape scenario as your primary focus, in order to provide a complete and thorough analysis, you should also seek to find your state's explanation of spousal rape and whether it carries lesser penalties than the traditional rape statutes. The entire issue was once held together by a universally accepted dictum called Hale's Rule. Lord Hale, a seventeenth-century English jurist, wrote that a husband could not be guilty of the rape of his wife, because: She was chattel belonging to her husband; a husband and wife were "one" and, as such, he could not rape himself; and, finally, marriage meant the wife irrevocably consented to intercourse with her husband on a continuing basis. Unbelievably for the independent women of today, it wasn't until the 1980s that Hale's Rule began to erode, and a writer should still check the specifics of his state.

Writer's Tip

As in all criminal cases, the prosecution bears the burden of *corpus delicti*, proving that the crime has been committed. One common problem in sexual battery prosecutions is the lack of independent eyewitness testimony. It may all boil down to the victim's word against the defendant's, and here is an area a writer can use to exploit the scene for emotion. Police and prosecutors, while being sympathetic, almost always rely on hard evidence—the preservation of semen, pubic hairs, and evidence of bruises in the form of photographs—in order to pull a sexual assault case together. The credibility of a witness is hardly ever more important than in a rape case. Consequently, there are lots of ways to exploit the energy, anger, and the denial of key characters.

MODERN CONCEPTS: Spurred on by social agencies, certain laws have sprung up to define the problem associated with abuse of members of society who either cannot take care of themselves or require protection because of age, disability, or lack of resources. These abusive offenses sometimes show up in state statutes as strict liability crimes—criminal penalties that do not require intent. Child abuse falls under this category and is often referred to as "endangering the welfare of a child." Normally, these offenses would be prosecuted under the category of assault and battery, or under "aggravated" categories of each, but with the rise of neglect and abuse, certain states have child abuse laws covering a broader range of abusive behavior.

Instances of spousal abuse, which would likely fall under the umbrella of the criminal assault laws, are now being set aside by some states for individual treatment and definition, because these new statutes can make for provisions such as an issuance of court injunctions—for example, a temporary restraining order—for those spouses who are subject to domestic violence. Abuse of the elderly can take many forms and will most likely result in physical abuse, neglect, abandonment, isolation, fiduciary abuse, or any other treatment resulting in harm, pain, mental suffering, deprivation of food and services, or continued mental suffering. Regulatory agencies and social workers are usually the ones who encounter abuse of the elderly the most, but, often, procedures will require handling by a civil court. Abuse of the elderly is generally reported to law enforcement and prosecution as a matter of process and has been known to incorporate the citing of one or more of the traditional statutes of assault and battery. Today, some progressive state legislatures have passed bills that call for enhanced penalties for those who commit violence against elderly persons.

FYI

Why would offenses like child abuse, spousal abuse, or even abuse of the elderly make a difference to your novel when you are looking for a major crime to wrap your story around? Because, generally, people who commit crimes have many other problems—family life among them. Therefore, in order to depict their disposition correctly, you need to show some dimension to their behavior. An antagonist doesn't just go down to a bank and blow people away because you need him to, for the story. Rather, a person who commits a crime is most likely burdened by great stressors, such as problems with unemployment, marital discord, and demands from parents; these, when coupled together with character flaws such as laziness, belligerence toward authority, and perhaps a drug problem, all go into the big stew that makes for a pretty dangerous, off-balanced, and unsettled character. Now, you don't have to add in hitting the dog, but, in fact, you just might want to portray the opposite, and show an antagonist's unusual devotion to a dog, for contrast.

LEAVING IS NOT AN OPTION: There are a couple of key differences between false imprisonment and kidnapping. Not all states have laws against false imprisonment. False imprisonment is usually classified as a misdemeanor, but, for example, in Texas, if the restrained victim is exposed to a substantial risk of bodily harm, guess what? False imprisonment jumps into the felony pool. Also, to illustrate the difference between these two offenses, false imprisonment is a restraining offense against a victim, whereas kidnapping is an unlawful taking and forcible carrying away—often referred to as "asportation"—of a person without his consent. Kidnapping is classified as a serious felony, universally forbidden by both state and federal jurisdictions.

There are several ways to paint a picture of false imprisonment, and it is often employed in movies with seemingly no mention or notice. For example, if a policeman takes a person into custody without either probable cause or a warrant, that could be an unlawful arrest, or false imprisonment. What about a storekeeper who detains a customer on the hunch he may be shoplifting but has no reasonable basis for his suspicion? Or how about the employer who holds an employee, using his authority over him, in order to suppress departure for the sake of obtaining information from him? Anyway, false imprisonment is not a commonly charged offense, so you probably won't need it, but know that it has elements of kidnapping, and usually the victim tends to want to take the person to civil court for damages rather than press criminal charges. If you are writing historical novels, however, you may just want to check the statutes of your setting's state for the period you are writing about.

Kidnapping is not simply a felony—it can also have its degrees. And it can jump into federal jurisdiction if, for example, a minor is taken out of one state and transported into another. To begin, it could be labeled "kidnapping in the first degree" if the intent involves one or more of the following:

- The extorting of money or property for the return of the victim
- Restraining a person for a certain number of hours (under a New York penal code it is twelve hours)[16] with the intent to inflict physical injury or abuse the victim sexually
- Restraining a person while in the process of committing another felony
- Terrorizing the captive victim
- Interfering with the performance of a governmental or political function
- Death of the captive during the abduction or before he is able to return to safety

Causing the death of the hostage, committing another type of felony simultaneously, and interfering with a government or political function can add to the severity of the charges.

> **FYI—**
>
> An interesting note: The Federal Kidnapping Act is commonly called the Lindbergh Law, as a result of the case in which the Lindbergh infant son was taken from the home of Charles A. Lindbergh, the man who became famous for making the first non-stop solo flight across the Atlantic Ocean, which earned him the nickname "Lone Eagle." Bruno Richard Hauptmann was convicted of the crime, which made for a spectacular hunt, a multitude of newspaper headlines, and a well documented trial, the result of which was the execution of Hauptmann in 1936.

Another, more recent statute, makes hostage-taking a federal offense, and, to elucidate its description, states that it is a crime to knowingly receive, possess, or dispose of any money or property that has been delivered as ransom for a victim of a kidnapping; or that it is unlawful for a bank robber to avoid apprehension by forcing someone to accompany him. And—one sure thing about violating federal statutes—the manpower and resources available for government operations can be quite overwhelming for the culprit.

For a domestic plot line, much has been written about parents who abduct their own children as a result of a divorce or some kind of custody program. In this type of scenario, one parent seizes the child from its custodial parent and travels to another state. As a consequence, most states have made child-snatching a felony, and one of the stipulations is the government's ability to extradite violators to the state in which the offense took place. There are extra provisions in some states' laws, and an act called the Uniform Child Custody Jurisdiction Act (UCCJA) is enforced in all fifty states. The UCCJA helps to continue jurisdiction for custody in the home or resident state of the child,

37

which means that cooperation between different states and judges is now mostly assured. Be sure to check your individual state's provisions if you plan on using child-snatching as your premise.

TORTURE: There is little written about torture in criminal law books. In his book *Order in the Court*, David S. Mullally defines it as "the intentional infliction of great bodily injury on another." As an example, he refers to a character named Frank, who uses a blowtorch and pliers to burn and peel the skin off another character's face. Mullally's concluding comment about this anecdote is, "Frank is guilty of torture." No argument there!

Since torture is an aberration often associated with serial murder, it might behoove you as a writer to check with your individual state's law for further information as to the statute's elements and punishment.

Chapter 4

COPS AND ROBBERS AND MORE

The loser is always suspicious.
—PUBLILIUS SYRUS, *MORAL SAYINGS*

We often think of crime as violent. But there are other, less demonstrative ways to victimize the unsuspecting. As long as there are people with money and valuables, there will be other people who will try to take the goods for themselves. And this is no less a violation, because it renders the victim more vulnerable and less trusting—it shakes their very sensibilities. This chapter zeroes in on some of those crimes.

The Paper Trail

The justice system is buried in paper. A variety of federal government agencies collect crime-related data and ultimately publish the information in order to respond to issues and to help develop law-enforcement plans. For example, the Department of Justice, the FBI, the National Institute of Justice, the Office of Juvenile Justice and Delinquency Prevention, the Bureau of Justice Statistics, and the Bureau of Prisons each collect data and participate in the distribution of important information about the study of crime.

The FBI also publishes an annual report, *Crime in the U.S.*, in which offenses are divided into categories called "Index Crimes." These eight Index Crimes are included because of their seriousness, frequency of occurrence, and likelihood of being reported to and by police.

The FBI's subsidiary program, Uniform Crime Reporting, is a useful tool. The primary goal of the UCR is to generate reliable criminal statistics for use in law enforcement, and, of interesting note, these are the reports that the average citizen is exposed to through the media—by listening to the radio, viewing television, or reading the daily newspaper. Few laypersons realize that the news reports refer to only eight categories: murder and nonnegligent manslaughter, aggravated assault, forcible rape, robbery, burglary, larceny or theft, motor vehicle theft, and arson. UCR is also used by criminal justice practitioners, scholars, and citizens-in-the-know. Why is this important to writers? Because these reports can provide you with facts, statistics, actual cases, and analyses—and they're all available for the asking. You can read reports at government sites on the Internet or receive hard copies free or for a nominal fee through the mail. By utilizing these services—you can even get e-mail about updates—you will have your finger on the pulse of new legislation and the most current Justice Department and law enforcement thinking. In the Appendixes, you will find listings for a variety of Web sites that provide a mother lode of information.

A redesigned UCR program called the National Incident-Based Reporting System, or NIBRS, was developed in order to expand the reportage, maximize integrity, prevent false clearing of the books (a cooked version of improving police clearance rates), and modernize crime information records. Knowing that these documents exist will add verisimilitude to your story when your law enforcement characters have to file reports, and this knowledge will give you, the writer, inside information into the methodology and current rationale of the various government branches.

Crimes Against Property

Crimes against property cover a broad range of offenses, many of which differ so slightly that every word of a statute defining the crime is vital. Many of these crimes can be called "crimes against habitation" and "acquisition offenses." Huh? Do you know the differences between robbery, theft, burglary, and larceny? Basically, the distinctions include: whether they threaten the owner's enjoyment of property but pose no immediate risk to his safety; whether they involve other interests, such as moving assets; or, as in the case of robbery, whether their perpetrators use physical force. On the other hand, malicious mischief, forgery, and bad checks are unlike the acquisition offenses in that with these crimes, the owner is still in possession of a version of his property upon completion of the crime. However, unique to these particular transgressions, his property is now damaged or impaired in some way. We'll talk about the varied divisions of these and other crimes so that you'll understand more about the vast array of cops and robbers.

IT WASN'T PHONY MONEY: Brian Donovan and Robert Grant were pretty proud of themselves. In a bar one night, the pair was overheard talking about a "helluvan idea" they had of using a phony deposit box. The Massachusetts jury did not have quite the same take on the affair when its members convicted the two of larceny. Evidence introduced at trial showed that they had constructed a phony night-deposit box and attached it to the wall of a building. Looking just like a real depository, the box was fashioned of heavy gauge steel. Seven depositors lost an estimated $37,000 by putting deposits into the phony box. Although the actual box was never discovered, the bar conversation was used against the two in court. Another witness said that Grant had admitted to her that he had robbed a bank using a fake bank box.

On appeal, the Massachusetts Supreme Court[17] rejected the defendants' contentions that certain evidence had been improperly admitted into evidence and ruled instead that the evidence produced at trial was legally sufficient to prove the crime of larceny. Larceny is one of the more clearly defined crimes in common law, although the old-fashioned terminology first used to describe it will sometimes confuse law students. For example, the phrase "caption" was employed instead of the word "taking"; the term "asportation" meant "carrying away"; and the personal property involved had to be "corporeal," which meant it had to have a physical presence. In order to simplify it here, let's use these steps: Larceny consists of taking, then carrying away, personal property of another, with the intent to permanently deprive the owner of the property. Some examples of larceny are shoplifting; theft of objects, parts, or accessories from motor vehicles; purse-snatching; and bicycle theft.

Now, real estate, land, and fixtures cannot be part of the list because the property must consist of tangible items, which can be carried away. Larceny is more easily remembered if you think of it as a crime against possession. Some modern laws have used the term "theft," which makes evident the distinction that items are taken unlawfully *while on the premise lawfully*.

Now we may come upon the question, what is the difference between *grand theft* and *petty theft?* In this sense, *grand theft* is the equivalent of first-degree theft and is subject to more serious consequences. For example, if the property taken is worth more than a minimum amount—it usually involves property valued at $200–$400 or more, depending on the state; the theft of cars—sometimes called "grand theft auto"—and some types of animal-stealing are often classified as grand theft regardless of their actual market value.

FYI—

An interesting question and a popular plot concoction for writers is this: If property is stolen from a thief who has stolen it previously, is it still illegal? Sorry, but yes. Although we sometimes want to take the side of those who steal from stealers (the movie *Sneakers* comes to mind), theft is illegal even if the person from whom property is stolen had no right to the property in the first place.

Petty theft (petit theft) sometimes includes property, usually of a value under $300, that is taken directly from a person but by means other than force or fear. A pickpocket crime would be a good example of this offense. And—just an aside for those who want to use a character with sticky fingers—petty theft, a misdemeanor, can graduate to grand theft and a felony charge if there are prior convictions. In order to make the charge more serious, the prosecutor would have to name the prior conviction on the Complaint or Information.

A favorite question among law students is: When someone finds "lost" property, is it still a theft for the discoverer to keep it? When someone takes control of property without taking a reasonable measure to restore it to its rightful owner, yes, it is a crime. For example, if Charles sees a $100 bill fall out of Marie's wallet, and she is unaware she has dropped the money, and then Charles skates over to claim it, Charles has committed theft. Since Charles knows the money belongs to Marie and since he had a reasonable opportunity to return it to her, he commits a crime by not attempting to return the money. This is called "constructive" taking.

Now, if Charles was skating by and discovered a $100 bill blowing down the street with no one in sight, it's his lucky day, and he would not be guilty of theft if he were to keep it—although it might become the beginning of a story if his windblown bill turned out to be counterfeit and led to other trouble. So, what if . . .

MOTOR VEHICLE THEFT: Motor vehicle theft has become big business, perpetrated by "car theft rings." Thieves pop a door lock to obtain the ignition key code number, and with a portable key maker, they make a duplicate key and drive away with the vehicle in about seven minutes or less. Nissan Pathfinders and Toyota 4-Runners are popular choices, because they are relatively easy to steal.

Where stolen cars once went through a transformation with painting and disguising of ownership, today they are merely transported—taken across state lines and delivered to unsuspecting or unscrupulous car dealers, or shipped out of the country. The United States is fast becoming a supplier of stolen vehicles to Third World countries.

EMBEZZLEMENT AND FALSE PRETENSE: Larceny is known as one of the acquisition crimes. Two others are embezzlement and false pretenses—also known as "fraud." Embezzlement is fraud, which consists of conversion of the property of another, by one who is already in lawful possession thereof, with the intent to defraud the victim (for example, the accountant who "cooks the books" and steals while on the job). The main acquisition element, which makes this offense so successful for abusers, is the "conversion" stipulation. As a consequence, this undertaking is commonly perpetrated by accountants, lawyers, store managers, and treasurers. Conversion could be diverting the money or property intended for the employer to the representative's personal use or working account.

False pretense is acquiring someone else's property through the use of fraud, a slight distinction from the other acquisition offenses. If someone obtains a title to property by means of material false representation, with the intent to defraud the victim, he is guilty of false pretense. There is a double mens rea to the crime of false pretense. The defendant must know that he is lying and must also intend to defraud the victim. This usually means that the property is acquired by means of lies, trickery, deceit, or some type of scam played out by the defendant.

Conditionally, the element of misrepresentation must involve a concern of a past or present fact and not something happening in the future. This key lynchpin of "time" points out the fact that the victim has been scammed so completely that he is not giving up temporary possession to his goods but will give up all of his money or goods to the thief due specifically to the scam. In other words, a thief tricks the victim into voluntarily handing over money or property, usually through a cruel and devastating hoax. False pretense, then, is a prime situation for perpetuating revenge—and a continuing plot device for a character who has been burned.

BURGLARY: Burglary is also referred to as a "habitation offense" by certain criminal justice researchers. A burglary occurs when a culprit breaks into and enters the dwelling of another, without consent, with the intent to commit a felony or steal property. The original common law against burglary was to protect buildings under the cover of night. Today, many states have enacted the statutes proscribing breaking and entering, thereby making the law extend beyond dwelling houses, and eliminating the requirement of night. In addition, some law codes not only specify buildings of any type such as shops, barns, and outhouses—as structures at risk, but even extend to portable units—such as cars, boats, and mobile homes. In addition, the courts have a tendency to liberally construe what *breaking* and *entering* mean. For instance, there is no force required to satisfy the *breaking* initiative. Even going into a building through an open window qualifies. And *entering* can be defined as a hand, foot, or even a finger within the dwelling; just the slightest touch of the toe is enough for a sufficient breaking and entering element. The prosecution does have to prove, however, that a defendant meant to commit a felony or theft inside a building at the very moment the defendant entered it.

FYI—

"Any felony" will often do for the crime of burglary. Even if you picture the typical burglar donning a mask, waving a flashlight, and carrying a sack for the booty—entry into a building with the specific intent to commit any type of felony, whether that includes molesting a child or burning the house down, is sufficient for burglary, and you'd better believe a smart prosecutor will throw everything into the charges. Also, degrees of burglary exist; for example, the danger of physical harm is greatest when a burglar enters an inhabited building, so, in many states, this constitutes a first-degree burglary.

ROBBERY DEFINED: Robbery is the taking, or the attempt to take, anything of value from the care, custody, or control of a person by force, by threat of violence, by actual violence, or by putting the victim in fear. Because of its personal and violent nature, robbery is another crime against person, and, as such, is feared greatly by the public.

A couple of distinctive notes help to define the offense of robbery: Mainly, the force used does not have to be major; a threat of violence is enough, even though the classification between a robbery and larceny is marginal. Also, in some state courts, the force applied or implied does not have to occur simultaneously with the taking. A typical example of robbery is the hold-up of a convenience store at a gunpoint, but it could also be a purse-snatching if the purse is on one's shoulder or if it is during a confrontation.

Writer's Tip

- *Robbery*. Theft plus force, or the threat of physical force, or fear
- *Burglary*. Unlawful attendance or entry with the purpose of committing an offense
- *Theft*. Items taken while lawfully on premises; the exercise of control of another's property or the obtaining of property by deception or threat
- *Larceny*. Taking; the carrying away of personal property of another—the intent is to permanently deprive the owner

FYI—

This temporal relationship to the force of taking is an area for writers to exploit, and many interesting cases have come up regarding both when the force was applied and how much force is required to qualify for robbery. Also, robbery is a "specific intent" crime. The government has to prove that a thief intended to permanently deprive a victim of stolen property. Usually, a prosecutor relies on circumstantial evidence to prove intent and implores the judge and jury to use their common sense to infer a thief's intent from the circumstances. Of course, if police have the actual goods, well, the intent is well met.

As with other crimes, degrees of robbery exist; for example, aggravated robbery, or first-degree robbery, makes for another, more serious, class of crime and punishment. Remember when researching: It is very important to check the law of the state where your crime was committed. For example, under Colorado law, robbery of the elderly or handicapped is afforded the same punishment as the offense of aggravated robbery.[18]

Jones v. Commonwealth[19] is a case with the question of whether the evidence is sufficient enough to support the conviction of robbery. On March 17, 1989, Deputy John Stanton of the Williamsburg Sheriff's Department was transporting Jerry Earl Jones from the Richmond Penitentiary to Williamsburg. The defendant was in leg chains and a waist chain with handcuffs attached to each side. Stanton was driving an unmarked vehicle with Jones in the back and no divider between them.

En route, the defendant suddenly yelled, "Sheriff, don't make me blow your damn brains out!" Stanton, startled and scared, jerked to see what was going on. He observed a metal object that appeared to be the barrel of a pistol. Traveling sixty-five miles per hour, Stanton lost control briefly until he managed to direct the car to a grassy median.

Stanton immediately began to look and feel for his gun, which was missing from his holster, and the car went out of control. Unarmed, Stanton did not get the car back on the road as ordered by Jones, and, in an effort to "wreck" the car and "bail out," he steered toward the guardrail and jumped into the grass. Jones, however, gained control of the car and sped away.

Later, the car was found without a radio antenna, with several hubcaps removed. A "fake gun" was found on the rear seat. Jones was arrested shortly thereafter and indicted on March 20, 1989.

The evidence—the fake gun—was challenged on appeal, but the conviction was affirmed. Judge Bray, who gave the opinion, said, "Stanton was fearful and surrendered the vehicle to the defendant. The defendant then escaped with both the automobile and Stanton's pistol, apparently taken by the defendant while Stanton was in extremity. These circumstances amply support a robbery conviction."

CARJACKING—A NEW BREED OF CRIME: The force of taking cannot be better demonstrated than in the forcible taking of another's vehicle, referred to under a fairly new statutory offense called "carjacking." In February 1993, the first trial under the new federal law—the Anti-Car Theft Act of 1992—was upheld in Orlando, Florida, when three young males were accused of carjacking. They had stolen two vehicles and committed execution-style slaying of two young men, injuring a third. The prosecution built its case on the facts that they were guilty of stealing a car involved in interstate commerce, doing it by force, and using a firearm. The defense lawyers, on the other hand, maintained that although the defendants may have been guilty of some offenses under state law, they were not guilty of violating the new federal law on armed carjacking involving violence. To the aid of the state's case, and as a detriment to the others, a co-conspirator pleaded guilty and testified against the other three. Six hours of deliberation produced a jury verdict that found the three defendants guilty of conspiracy, two counts of armed carjacking involving death, and two counts of using a firearm during a felony. In April 1993, the three defendants were sentenced to life terms, plus twenty-five years. The fourth perp? Well, I don't know his sentence, but he is probably looking over his shoulder a lot.

FYI—

A landlord in Portland, Oregon, had rented a house to a group of college-aged kids. After they left, he cleaned the house and, while he was sweeping, a scrap piece of paper that looked like a map fell on the floor. On the map was an arrow pointing to a bank that had just been robbed. The landlord contacted the FBI, which sent agents out to sift through a large Dumpster nearby. They uncovered thousands of tiny scraps of paper, which document examiners painstakingly pieced together after seven weeks' worth of work.

The evidence that specialists recovered was integral in helping federal agents build their case against the group. The restored paper, with fingerprints, pointed to five bank robberies, the planned kidnapping of Portland's mayor, and the attempted bombing of an army induction center. Four suspects were identified by name from the notes, and three addresses assisted authorities in helping to track down the whole gang. Eight people were arrested in connection with the crime spree, and almost all the evidence came from the trash.

This story, from David Fisher's book *Hard Evidence*, shows how forensic evidence can add drama to a story. Although you may initially think about using bank robbery and several other heinous crimes for the plot, it's the evidence and surrounding story details that make it a crime worth telling.

EXTORTION: Similar to the crime of robbery, extortion is made up of several elements: Obtaining property, by threats, with the intent to obtain the property by fear and coercion. Extortion is often called blackmail, which, by the way, is actually a federal statute—the Blackmail Statute—that reads something like this: "Whoever, under a threat of informing, or as a consideration for not informing, against any violation of any law of the United States, demands, or receives, any money or other valuable thing, shall be fined . . ."[20]

The intimidation used by extortionists is often threats to either accuse a person of crime or expose a secret affair affecting another, and, when these don't work, a threat to cause injury to the person or a member of his family. Once a common theme of motivation running through episodes of *Murder, She Wrote*, "blackmailing" often involved important characters who were seeking to hide some type of past indiscretion, infraction, or family secret— there is a lot of variation on the theme, and a writer can exploit the endless possibilities.

GETTING THE GOODS: Receiving stolen property is a convenient way to get a naïve character into trouble. It is a crime to receive property of another, either knowing that it has been stolen or believing that it probably has been stolen, with the purpose to deprive the owner thereof. So, if an individual recognizes that serial numbers or store names have been obliterated from merchandise, he has a good indication that the goods are "hot." But what if there are no telltale, identifying characteristics? And what if the true owner wants his goods back? And what if . . . well, you can see where I'm going here.

ARSON: INVESTIGATION REQUIRED: Arson consists of any willful or malicious burning, or attempt to burn, a dwelling, house, public building, motor vehicle, aircraft, or property of another. As originally stated in common law, though, setting fire to one's own home was not considered arson. Modern statutes today, however, have extended the offense to include the intentional burning of buildings, structures, and vehicles of all types—frequently, this includes a person's own property. But there are areas to exploit here, and many differences of law opinion. For example, a Michigan court held in *People v. Williams*[21] that to establish the *corpus delicti* of arson of a dwelling house, the state must show not only a burned house, but also that it resulted from an intentional criminal act. The presumption here was that a burned building showed presence of fire, but it could have been accidentally caused.

In *Kennedy v. State*,[22] a Georgia court upheld the conviction on appeal of Henry Xavier Kennedy, saying that a fire in a building belonging to the defendant was incendiary in origin. The case at issue was this: One early morning, at approximately quarter to four A.M., Kennedy's log cabin was reported burning and was eventually destroyed. Investigators found a hot plate with its switch in the "On" position, in the most heavily burned area of the cabin. Investigators also testified that kerosene had been poured around the area of the hot plate, and that is what had accelerated the fire.

Kennedy might have gotten away with it had he not renewed a $40,000 insurance policy a mere five days before the fire. In addition, evidence presented showed that Kennedy's building business had been slow, and even though he had his own evidence of an alibi from midnight until about four A.M., investigators testified that an incendiary device could have been set before midnight.

MALICIOUS MISCHIEF: Malicious mischief is sometimes referred to as "vandalism," and it occurs when a person maliciously inflicts injury on the property of another. With malicious mischief, the real legal issue is how much damage needs to be done to qualify. The courts have generally agreed that if the damage prevents the property from being used as it is used most often, or if the damage significantly diminishes its value, then the injury to the property is sufficient.

In *State v. Tonnisen*[23] the defendant appealed his conviction for malicious mischief. The state produced evidence that the defendant allowed for a tank trailer truck to dump its load of caustic soda all over the road during a strike and employee walkout. In testifying in his own defense, Tonnisen said that he had not put his hand "anywheres in the vicinity of between the truck and the trailer."

Unfortunately for him, a police officer on duty, along with other observant persons, watched the defendant go over to the truck, stick his hand between the truck and its trailer, and pull the hand back full of grease.

47

FYI—
This brings to mind a historical idea called "hue and cry." While waiting for the Danish invasion, Alfred the Great (849–899 A.D.) established a strong system called "mutual pledge." It was developed in order to organize local citizenry into an association for tithing and protection. Alfred instituted the program "hue and cry," which meant that any person who discovered a crime was to give out a hue and cry in order to rally people to catch the offender "red-handed"—with blood on his hands. When the criminal was brought to the tithe chief, the people enforced the sentences of death for murder and of civil restitution, bondage, or servitude for theft. This, then, was the historical basis for the civil code remedy of restitution.

48

FORGERY: Because of the importance of written and printed documents, both federal and state statutes generally classify forgery as a felony. Almost every type of public or private legal instrument in almost all the American jurisdictions is covered by the crime of forgery. It's that important. Also, it is not necessary to show that anyone was actually defrauded by the forgery for the crime to be complete. That said, here are the elements of forgery: the fraudulent making, with the intent to deceive, of a false writing that has apparent legal significance, with the perpetrator's knowing the writing is false.

The Arizona Criminal Code uses the same principles stated above but even goes a step further. It reads:

A. A person commits forgery if, with intent to defraud, such person:

    1. Falsely makes, completes, or alters a written instrument; or

    2. Knowingly possesses a forged instrument; or

    3. Offers or presents, whether accepted or not, a forged instrument or one which contains false information.[24]

Arizona, then, has expanded the offense by including the offering or passing of such a document (which is also referred to as "uttering a forged instrument") in its parameters.

Common examples of forgery and uttering a forged instrument are: signing another's name to an application for a driver's license or to the transfer of a certificate of stock; writing a check on another's bank account without authority; altering grades or credits on a college transcript; printing bogus tickets to a concert or sporting event; altering the amount of a check or note; and changing a legal description on a deed of property. Since computers are being used extensively for forms and applications more commonly today, new statutes proscribing both forgery and uttering a forged instrument need to be updated.

Now, with this area so broadly defined, one would think that presenting a worthless check on his bank account would be a forgery. And, indeed, as commercial banking grew in terms of numbers of customers and transactions, this presented a problem in trying to prove that the accused fraudulently obtained goods. The flip side of the forgery question was: Did he simply miscalculate his checking account balances? In order to cope with this uncertainty, state legislatures created what is commonly called "bad check," or "worthless check," statutes. Texas sums it up nicely in its state law by saying: "A person commits an offense if he issues or passes a check or similar sight order for the payment of money knowing that the issuer does not have sufficient funds in or on deposit with the bank . . ."[25]

In the past, a person who used a stolen credit card or otherwise obtained a card through fraud was subject to the laws of larceny and theft. Due to the widespread use of credit cards, however, many states have enacted laws actually proscribing credit card fraud. Pennsylvania probably has the most in-depth statute and, summarized, it stipulates that a person commits an offense if he:

- Uses a credit card for obtaining property or service and knows that the card is stolen, forged, or fictitious; belongs to another; has been revoked or cancelled; or is not authorized to use
- Makes, knowingly sells, or aids and abets the fraudulent use of a credit card
- Publishes code or numbering to avoid payment for property or services

Offenses Against Public Morality

Criminal justice scholars are always interested in crimes against morality for many reasons. Originally, common law did not address these issues, because they were the domain of the church, were known as ecclesiastical crimes, and were normally tried and punished by the Church of England. Consequently, in the early part of American history, the Puritans, a religious group, made a concerted effort to ensure that all the offenses against morality were criminalized by state statutes in keeping with their beliefs. For the most part, they were successful, although today many of those laws have been revised or removed because there are constitutional limitations to be considered on each of these laws. For example, when talking about the practicality of instituting moral codes, many people believe the aphorism "you can't legislate morality." A prime example of this is illustrated in a landmark case, *Griswold v. Connecticut.*[26] The U.S. Supreme Court struck down a state law that made it a crime for all persons, even married couples, to use birth control devices. Who would have thought that a law like that could ever be instituted, especially since the case law is dated 1965?

Debate will always continue over morality crime, and public opinion about the law changes; but, even so, every state has at least one, if not all, of the following five crimes against morality: fornication, adultery, illicit cohabitation, bigamy, and incest. But because of changing societal attitudes, fornication, adultery, and seduction (the unfulfilled promise of marriage) are rarely, if ever, prosecuted.

49

And what can a writer do with the other crimes against morality? Well, if a character wants to add particular angst to another's life, he can accuse that person of incest or bigamy. Between the cost of proving it isn't so and the insult and injury to character, that additional poke in the eye could add up to a lot of revenge and an extra plot point. So, for those who seek to know it all, incest is a crime that prohibits intermarriage or sexual relations between certain persons of kinship, or "blood relations," such as parents and children, brothers and sisters, etc. And while bigamy still occurs, however occasionally, it is defined as a marriage between two persons when one is already legally married to a third person.

Sodomy, a rarely prosecuted offense, which was described originally as a "crime against nature" in general, includes oral or anal sex between humans and sexual intercourse between humans and animals (sometimes called "bestiality"). While less than half the states retain this offense, you may hear of it when it is incident to a charge of rape and sexual battery. When sodomy is nonconsensual, it is considered a crime against a person, not an offense against morality.

PROSTITUTION, PIMPING, AND PANDERING: Sometimes called the "oldest profession," prostitution is the act of engaging in sexual activity for hire. Today, prostitution is illegal in all states except Nevada, where it exists by local option in some counties, although it is strictly regulated by law.[27] In the past, statutes have been directed at females, but, increasingly, enforcement has come to include males as well. And, originally, the definitive language was aimed almost exclusively at the prostitute, but now there is conviction for the customers and also for those who live off the earnings of a person practicing prostitution. And there is a loophole here: If the statutes are not all-inclusive with respect to pimps, partners, and clients alike, they might be vulnerable to constitutional attack as a denial of equal protection of the law.

Normally listed as a misdemeanor, in Texas it is a serious felony for a person to cause another by force, threat, or fraud to commit prostitution. The federal government has gotten involved in the problem, too, with the Mann Act,[28] which prohibits interstate transportation of individuals for prostitution or for compelling them to engage in immoral practice. The Supreme Court has ruled that the act applies to transporting persons for immoral purposes whether or not commercial vice is involved.

PRIVATE PARTS: Indecent exposure is a misdemeanor offense for persons showing their private parts in a public place. Frequently referred to as "lewd and lascivious conduct," the laws generally stipulate that exposure must be done willfully and in an offensive manner, not by mere accident. Some statutes, such as the one in Florida, have defined that in order for an act to be offensive exposure, it has to "incorporate sensory awareness as well as physical proximity"[29]—a man who was convicted of masturbating in the presence of his thirteen-month-old child had his charges reversed by the state's supreme court. In the court's view, the child did not have sensory awareness.

The sunny state of Florida must have its problems making people keep their clothes on, because there is a statute that prohibits public nudity on beaches and other recreational areas. Arrests under this provision are not common, however, and certain areas are set aside where topless or nude sunbathing is permitted. Perhaps you have a fictional free-wheeling, wealthy character, and you need a vehicle that will show more than his personality—public nudity may be your answer!

JUST WHAT IS OBSCENE?: In the highly expressive 1970s, a high school boy extended his middle finger toward a highway trooper from the back of a school bus. In *State v. Anonymous*[30] the court got to consider whether it was an offense to make an obscene gesture in a public place with "intent to cause inconvenience, annoyance, or alarm or recklessly creating a risk thereof." The court found the rambunctious student not guilty, stating that to be obscene, an expression "must be in a significant way erotic."

Writer's Tip

Obscenity is a great vehicle to use when you need to complicate matters for your character, whether he is a policeman, prosecutor, or offender. It is one of those needling statutes that are hard to define. Literally dozens of cases have dealt with obscenity issues and, more distinctly, with how to define what the Supreme Court has called "utterly without redeeming social importance"[31]—so as not to deny people their right to free speech. There are cases involving nude dancing in clubs, obscene solicitations in the mail, lewd movies and plays, and child pornography. By the way, child pornography, like obscenity, is not protected by the First Amendment to the Constitution.[32] And, be aware, legislation for pornography on the Internet is looming (see chapter 7).

For those who write historical novels, by the late 1800s Congress had made it an offense to mail any obscene, lewd, or lascivious paper or writing[33] and had decreed that the word "obscene" should be treated the same as it had been by common law, which considered obscenity to be public nuisance and punishable as a misdemeanor. Sounds like turn-of-the-century trouble for those who write passionate letters that fall into the wrong hands.

ONE MAN'S VULGARITY:. . . is another's lyric. Profanity is another offense that is hard to uphold. In *Cohen v. California*, supra,[34] the Supreme Court invalidated the "offensive conduct" conviction of a man who entered a courthouse wearing a jacket emblazoned with the slogan FUCK THE DRAFT. Justice Harlan agreed that the litigation over the four-letter word's being litigated was indeed tasteful, but, nonetheless, it was the defendant's right to say it. In order for something to be profane, right now—although watch current news releases, because it is subject to change—the defendant's language must be either "fighting words" or a breach of the peace.

GAMBLING—A ROLL OF THE DICE AGAINST PUBLIC MORALITY: Gambling crept in under the wire of offenses against public morality and sits next to sexual offenses. This may seem an incongruity, since common law did not regard gambling as an offense. Today federal laws and a variety of state statutes and local ordinances make all or certain forms of gambling illegal. Laws regulating gambling come under the police power of the state. And a trip to the U.S. Supreme Court has determined that there is no constitutional right to gamble. Common forms of gambling are craps, bingo, poker, bookmaking, and slot machines. Betting on sports events, horses, and card games is included as well. Since there are so many types of gambling, they are separated by the legal versus the illegal. Buying a lottery ticket in many states not only is legal—it is an important source of revenue for the state, with resources going toward education and other improvements. In the same vein, a common form of illegal gambling is running numbers. In order to play, one places a bet on a number in the hopes that it will match a preselected number for a win.

So, what it gambling? It must consist of these three elements:
1. A valuable consideration
2. A prize
3. A chance

This seems to fit into a lot of categories, including raffles, promotional schemes, local carnivals and fairs, and a variety of games played for prizes. It can be hard to tell the difference between games of chance and games of skill. In order to define the difference for your needs, each individual state statute will spell out the distinction. And, often, the only way to be sure is with court distinction.

Some statutes prohibiting gambling exclude athletics or other contests in which participants must pit their physical or mental skills against one another for a prize. In some states nonprofit organizations benefit from particular forms of gambling that are otherwise forbidden. The paradox continues, because there are states that will allow dog tracks for betting, while an individual may be prosecuted for making a wager on the Kentucky Derby in his own home. Certain pinball operators have had their trade defined for them by an Ohio appellate court, which decided that the outcome of the operation was largely determined by the skill of the user and was therefore not a game of chance.

Breaches of the Peace—Offenses Against Public Order and Safety

State and local governments shoulder most of the responsibility for maintaining public order and peace, the most basic of criminal offenses and those close to home. These criminal acts are different in that they threaten *society's* interests for order and safety. And all these acts have English common law as their source. For example, common law acknowledged the right of the people to assemble peaceably for lawful purposes. However, maintenance of public order was given a high priority, starting with three misdemeanors: unlawful assembly, rout, and riot. The other offenses grew out of the desire to prohibit disorderly conduct and to control undesirable, violent, tumultuous behavior.

ILLEGAL WEAPONS: According to a report by the Center on Crime Communities & Culture, thirty-five states require no registration or licensing for guns. A whopping forty-three states require no permit or registration for purchase of assault weapons. And eighteen states have no minimum age for possession of rifles or shotguns. With statistics like that, you can be assured that illegal weapons are big business—and will provide a lot of work and wreak havoc for your law-enforcement characters. Keep listening to the media, however: the gun debate rages on.

CONCEALED WEAPONS: Some states have statutes making it unlawful to carry a concealed weapon. A concealed weapon is carried on or about a person in such a manner as to conceal it from sight. That makes sense. And story has it that a defendant was properly convicted of carrying a concealed weapon in her purse when the metal detector went off at the courthouse. But, sometimes, it is not as clear as all that. Once, a Georgia appellate court decided that even though the handle of a gun could be seen peeking out of a defendant's pants, the weapon was concealed.[35] And many concealed weapon laws make it unlawful to carry a concealed weapon in a vehicle. Check into this further for some added intrigue.

REVEALED WEAPONS: The term "brandishing a weapon" is an ancient relic of a law meaning that someone draws or exhibits a weapon in an angry or threatening manner. Check your individual state's ruling, as you may have another "nuisance" offense to use in your charges.

DISTURBING THE PEACE: Unlawful assembly and riot is aimed at group behavior, while laws proscribing disorderly conduct encompass both group and individual conduct. To illustrate the distinction, the Indiana Code defines unlawful assembly as "an assembly of five or more persons whose common object is to commit an unlawful act, or a lawful act by unlawful means."[36]

53

To further define the riotous conduct, the statute goes on to say it is "conduct that results in, or is likely to result in, serious bodily injury to a person or substantial damage to property." The conduct itself is held as a misdemeanor, unless it is committed while the offender is armed with a deadly weapon—then it becomes a felony. The Federal Anti-Riot Act of 1968 was spurred on by the high incidence of controversy over the Vietnam War, racial unrest, and other social upheavals experienced in the turbulent 1960s.

Disorderly conduct rides the rails with unlawful assembly, but it is applied to a person who recklessly, knowingly, or intentionally:

1. Engages in fighting or tumultuous conduct
2. Makes unreasonable noise and continues to do so after being asked to stop
3. Disrupts a lawful assembly of persons

54

FIGHTING WORDS: The Supreme Court has ruled on the utterance of fighting words in several cases and feels it is beyond the protection of the First Amendment. In *Chaplinsky v. New Hampshire*, supra,[37] the Court said that fighting words are those that inflict injury, tend to create a breach of the peace, and are not an essential part of the expression of ideas. When profanity is aimed at a police officer, some courts view that type of behavior by a different standard—they feel the officer should know how to handle the situation and, consequently, hesitate to convict. Regardless of the circumstances, the prosecution must establish that these words are intended to incite violence. As writers, you can use these offenses to mix it up when opposing groups get together to hash it out.

HATE CRIMES: As to the growing incidence of hate crime—which is bigotry expressed toward minorities by the use of symbols, objects, or characterizations that cause alarm, anger, or resentment, on the basis of race, color, religion, or gender—some jurisdictions have enacted measures prohibiting hate crimes and have fixed them as misdemeanors. The term "hate crimes" implies a category of bias-motivated criminal acts, from vandalism to murder. The legal definition, as interpreted by several recent Supreme Court decisions, distinguishes between purely spoken or symbolic expressions or hatred, and actual conduct. Words may be verbal pistols, but they are protected by the Constitution. Actions are not. These offenses will continue to change and adapt and must always be weighed against the First Amendment right to free speech. Some states maintain stand-alone laws that allow hate crimes to be prosecuted as separate offenses; others have penalty enhancement statutes that permit the prosecution of a hate crime only in connection with another offense.

VAGRANCY AND LOITERING: Those elites in feudal England sure knew how to control a serf. That's where this business with vagrancy and loitering came from—England. Apparently, the higher-ups did not want their laborers to search for improved working conditions, and, in the same breath, they did not want the idlers to become public charges. So, in order to regulate the economics of the populace, the common law developed a misdemeanor called "vagrancy." The offense normally required three parts:
1. Being without a visible means of support
2. Being unemployed
3. Being able to work but refusing to do so

Get off my bench! . . . Oh, excuse me, but Americans weren't much better, and used the vagrancy laws as broad discretion for taking people into custody in order to control the undesirables or to "shake them down." Since the indigents who were rousted were the most unlikely candidates to realize the unconstitutionality of the laws—how do you proscribe laws for doing nothing?—over the years, there has been terrible injustice aimed toward loafers, alcoholics, derelicts, and tramps. By 1960, the constitutionality of the vagrancy laws was frequently being challenged on the grounds that the laws were vague, that they violated due process of law requirements, and that they exceeded the police power of the states. The courts generally upheld the right of the legislature or the states to define its own terms, however—until much later, when the long awaited blow of vagrancy laws finally showed signs of vagueness to the judges and were struck down. In one Jacksonville, Florida, case,[38] the vagrancy law collapsed because it was too vague and because it served as a vehicle for "arbitrary and erratic arrests and convictions." Incidentally, you don't have to look too hard to see that police still uses loitering ordinances today; it's a convenient excuse to remove suspected drug dealers from the streets.

55

TRAFFIC VIOLATIONS: In the past, traffic offenses such as failure to yield and failure to observe traffic signs and signals were treated as misdemeanors, and people committing them were arrested and required to post bond to avoid confinement pending adjudication. Since the 1960s, these offenses have turned the corner to become civil infractions rather than misdemeanors. As a result, offenders are now given tickets or citations instead of being subject to arrest. And, in answer to the modern day mobility of travel, states have updated their thinking and adopted "model" laws, which make traffic offenses fairly uniform across boundaries. When a driver is stopped for a violation, however, police may observe the driver's conduct and direct a search based on reasonable suspicion, which may further move the police officer's instinct to probable cause and, finally, to an arrest based on the evidence found.

ALCOHOL AND DRUG OFFENSES: There are many different names for driving under the influence (DUI):

- *DWI*: Driving while intoxicated
- *DUIL*: Driving under the influence of liquor
- *OMVI*: Operating a motor vehicle intoxicated
- *OWI*: Operating while intoxicated
- *OUI*: Operating under the influence
- *DUBAL*: Driving with an unlawful blood alcohol level.

All states have attempted to enact laws to keep American roadways free of drunk driver carnage. According to the California Vehicle Code, it is unlawful:

- For any person who is under the influence of an alcohol beverage or any drug, or under the combined influence of an alcoholic beverage and any drug, to drive a vehicle
- For any person who has 0.08 percent or more, by weight, of alcohol in his blood to drive a vehicle[39]

One defendant tried to get around this statute by claiming that the prosecution failed to prove he was "driving the vehicle." In *State v. Harrison*,[40] evidence supported the fact that Harrison was found asleep behind the steering wheel of his car parked on the roadway with the key in the ignition, motor running, and the transmission in drive. The court didn't see it his way and concluded that this evidence established that he was in actual physical control of the vehicle and therefore the evidence was sufficient to prove that the defendant was driving the automobile.

"Standard sentencing" for DUI generally falls along the line of probation, plus fine, plus treatment program and some time in jail. In later chapters, we'll take another look, from a different point of view, at driving while under the influence and at drug use offenses; unfortunately, it's quite common, and if your protagonist is a cop, well, he may see it—or even partake in it—every day.

Chapter 5

Behind Enemy Lines: Finding—and Understanding— Legal Information

The rich rob the poor and the poor rob one another.
—SOJOURNER TRUTH

In this chapter I have laid a trail for you through the maze of the legal process, so that you can come and go at will, confident of finding your way. I do hope that I will have assisted you in tackling research. Since only you can know what it is you're looking for, obtaining the skills with which to investigate will hand you the key to a fascinating and challenging world.

With that goal in mind then, chapter 5 covers the nature and the basics of legal research. To begin, the mindset of a researcher should be like that of an adventurer: know that while seeking out the unknown, you most likely will find a few blind alleys or dead-end situations. Two of the best qualities a writer-researcher can possess are patience and persistence; so it is with the law and legal research.

There are billions of words written on lawful facts and opinions. Seeking and finding information requires a plan, similar to building a cabinet or sewing a dress. To illustrate, I will use the cabinet analogy: you must choose from the French, English, Country, and other categories of design. Next, you find one or two good books on woodworking that will provide you with an overview of the techniques common to that style. Does it, for example, have dentil molding, Queen Anne legs, and mortise and tendon joints? From there, you get more specific and decide on a set of blueprints, learning any unfamiliar terms and making a list of the tools and parts required. Finally, you assemble the components and machinery required, and follow the instructions in the plan.

Researching the law is similar; after heavy doses of labor, if all goes well, you will have something to help your writing, and if you've built the cabinet above, you will also have something to put your law books into! The first and easiest way to research some legal aspect is to ask another person who is most likely to know the answer. Your local prosecutor is an elected official and, as such, may answer your questions or, at the least, direct you to a source. Law librarians are most knowledgeable and can be helpful in pointing out further resources and suggesting ways of using them. (They are also held captive in the correct venue, a most encouraging component; make friends of them.) Courtroom clerks can explain some procedural details, such as providing jury instructions, voir dire stipulations, and court rules. Just be aware that they are also likely to be overwhelmed by the sheer numbers of people who pass through the system or, worse, that they may have to deal with a lot of rude and desperate people—act humble and polite and don't be offended when they tell you they cannot offer legal advice. Criminal lawyers can certainly help—at cost—but their tight calendars mean you will not be a priority, and, once again, research tips are the most you can hope for. And, finally, the Internet is a compelling and exciting medium with which you can explore the vast array of facts and figures awaiting your eye. Online possibilities are endless, though, and it is important for you to know about the tips, trends, and traps of using the World Wide Web.

58

Volumes at Your Fingertips

Let's move on, then, to books. Reliable law dictionaries can explain specific words and unfamiliar terms or just provide you with ideas. Some good volumes are:
*   *Gilbert Law Summaries Pocket Size Law Dictionary* by Gilbert Law Summaries (San Diego: Harcourt Brace Legal & Professional Pubns., 1998)
*   *Dictionary of Legal Terms: A Simplified Guide to the Language of Law* by Stephen H. Gifis (New York: Barrons Educational Series, 1998)
*   *Dictionary of American Legal Usage* by David Melinkoff (St. Paul, Minnesota: West/Wadsworth Publishing Co., 1993)
*   *Burton's Legal Thesaurus* by William C. Burton (New York: Simon & Schuster, 1999)
*   *Black's Law Dictionary*, edited by Byron A. Garner, 7th Ed. (St. Paul, Minnesota: West Group, 1999)

FYI—Two to Tango
Writers, there is a terrific book for finding case stories titled *Homicide: A Bibliography*, by Bal K. Jerath and Rajinder Jerath, 2nd Ed. (Boca Raton, Florida: CRC Press, 1993). This volume represents an exhaustive search of the world's literature regarding homicide. More than seven thousand entries have been compiled from references selected from major indexes in libraries, from outstanding universities, government agencies, the Library of Congress, and other sources.

Legal encyclopedias—alphabetically arranged—may give you more background information, and there are two main national law encyclopedias called *American Jurisprudence* (Rochester, New York: Bancroft-Whitney/ Lawyers

Coop) and *Corpus Juris Secundum* (St. Paul, Minnesota: West Publishing). Both encyclopedias are updated annually. These expensive tomes—multivolume sets that sell for over $2,000—will offer broad-based discussions on the laws in all fifty states. Keep looking and you will find that many of the largest states have their own state-specific encyclopedias as well.

Form books may aid you, especially if you need to see the types of documents that lawyers copy instead of inventing their own legal papers. Inside these books, you will find collections of sample legal documents—mostly fill-in-the-blanks forms for a specific procedural task. Commonly, form books will provide an overview of the procedure required to go along with the form chosen, and additional notes on how to make the document specific by using the most common modifications. Want to see a complaint, a subpoena, a motion document? Look here. One suggestion is to start with a form book that is specific to your state, if there is one. Forms in the *American Jurisprudence Legal Forms* (Rochester, New York: Lawyers Coop, updated annually) are primarily national in scope.

Practice manuals, like the old *CliffsNotes* we used in order to bypass reading the "great literature" assigned in school, give lawyers hands-on information logically organized, covering a specialized area of practice. Don't know how to defend a drunk driving case? Find the practice manual called *Drunk Driving Defense* by Edward L. Fiandach (New York and Chicago: Clark Boardman/Callaghan, updated annually). A second volume, a kind of "bible," *Defense of Drunk Driving Cases: Criminal-Civil* by Richard E. Erwin, et al. (Albany, New York: Matthew Bender, 1963), contains everything an attorney would need to know about handling this specific offense. Practice manuals are available on a variety of topics, such as family law, search and seizure issues, and a number of other subjects. *Prosecution and Defense of Criminal Conspiracy Cases* by Paul Marcus (Newark, New Jersey: Matthew Bender, 1978) details evidentiary matters, constitutional issues, and practical considerations including procedural problems. Another Matthew Bender book that merits attention is *Bender's Forms of Discovery* (Newark, New Jersey: Matthew Bender, annual update); also available on a $2,500 CD-ROM. Matthew Bender Publications and Shepard's Citation Books are now under the umbrella of LexisNexis and have an extensive bookstore, database, and Web site online.

The proof-of-facts CD-ROM, *American Jurisprudence Proof of Facts* by Publisher's Editorial Staff (Rochester, New York: Bancroft-Whitney/Lawyers Coop, 1995), gives detailed discussions of the burden of proof issues in practically every kind of civil and criminal case. The subject index will point you to an excellent general summary of circumstances related to your case.

Law reviews and journals will give you articles about recent legislation, important or landmark cases, and certain legal philosophy as published by various law schools, commercial publishers, and professional legal societies or bar associations. The topics are authored by professors of law, law students, and well known practicing attorneys. You will usually find them in paperback pamphlets; and libraries will often bind them into hardcover editions at the end of a year.

Treatises and monographs are different resources for the law student or writer-researcher who has a fairly good background, because these vehicles tend to provide a much deeper expertise than what is offered in other reference materials. The difference between a treatise and a monograph is one of length. A treatise covers an entire area of law, whereas a monograph either zeroes in on a small portion of a general legal field, is a discourse on a single subject (hence the suffix "mono"), or introduces a new concept. Usually, an author will present much theoretical evidence, so these articles call for both patience and rereading.

60

Textbooks, most of them published by West Group, offer an excellent basic understanding of criminal law and its accompanying procedures. These can be found in campus bookstores, ordered through commercial outlets, or found on the Web. In addition to school books, there is a new self-help book trend in the market for those who wish either to educate themselves with the intent of avoiding the high costs of hiring a lawyer or to use these books' materials as an adjunct to their continuing edification. Nolo Press has a variety of self-help books—the one I most frequently recommend is entitled *The Criminal Law Handbook: Know Your Rights, Survive the System* by attorneys Paul Bergman and Sara J. Berman-Barrett (Berkeley, California: Nolo Press, 1999). This paperback is a highly readable step-by-step guide for anyone interested in the machinations involved within the criminal justice system. Nolo Press also has a fine Web site with a legal encyclopedia, explaining many issues in plain English. You can find the company on the Internet at *www.nolo.com.*

RESEARCH FOR THE DIE-HARD: One of the very best sources for legal research is the book *Legal Research: How to Find & Understand the Law* (Berkeley, California: Nolo Press, 1999) by attorneys Stephen Elias and Susan Levinkind. They have taken painstaking effort in order to offer the reader step-by-step methods for finding material both in hard copy and on the Internet. These methods are similar to small tutorials that walk you through the process by showing what appears on each page of a particular title or Web site screen.

Questions for Plotting Ideas

After you become familiar with certain terms, try to formulate questions in order to help categorize your legal issue. Start with these:

DOES THE SITUATION ENCOMPASS A FEDERAL OR STATE CRIME?: Discussions and the specifics of state law and federal law are commonly found in different books, and for good reasons. Our Founding Fathers were concerned about government's overwhelming power and potential abuse of it, so they created constitutional guidelines. Consequently, most legal research customarily involves state rather than federal law. Congress's power—and the results of its power, federal law—is held to a few specific areas under constitutional direction, so most of the lawmaking decisions are left to state governments. Federal law, as a result, generally affects a broad range of social welfare, health, and environmental questions. There is overlap, though—say, with environmental law as an example, because the government helps to regulate and fund these laws for states too. For crimes under this type of situation, such as kidnapping, you may have to look at both state and federal law background.

Some criminal actions also involve multiple offenses. For example, robbing a bank can involve conspiracy and robbery and possession of a deadly weapon—these are violations against both the state and the federally protected banking administration. Typically, a prosecutor will charge for every possible crime, some easier to prove than others, and the defendant can be prosecuted for violating both sets of laws. Although this may smack of double jeopardy, it is not. The jurisdictions are not the same, though, and usually only one prosecutor will pursue the case so as not to tie up valuable resources from both offices.

61

DOES IT INVOLVE CRIMINAL LAW OR CIVIL LAW?: Criminal law is any type of behavior—a crime—punishable by incarceration and a fine, or both. The party bringing charges is usually the prosecutor who represents the state; the "burden of guilt" is the prosecutor's as well. The defendant may receive the services of a government-paid attorney, and may have the right to a trial.

In contrast, in a civil case, the injured party is the one who sues, usually over rights and duties of individuals and organizations named in the dispute that may have been caused by money damages or the loss of property. The lawyers in a civil case are usually private attorneys who charge a fee for services, and in a civil case the plaintiff must provide a "preponderance of the evidence" in order to collect damages.

DOES IT PERTAIN TO THE SUBSTANCE OF THE LAW OR LEGAL PROCEDURE?: To reiterate the difference between substantive criminal law and criminal procedure, substantive criminal law concerns the definition and punishment of crimes, written and published in order to meet the edict "no crime without a law." Criminal procedure, on the other hand, is interested in how people accused of crimes are to be treated by the criminal justice system.

This is not a matching chart, merely two lists

FYI—

Criminal Law Substantive	Criminal Procedure
Assault	Arraignment
Breaking and entering	Arrest
Burglary	Confessions
Conspiracy	Cross-examination
Disorderly conduct	Extradition
Drug and narcotic offenses	Grand jury
Driving under the influence	Indictments
Juvenile offenses	Jury selection; jury verdicts
Kidnapping	Miranda warning
Larceny	Plea bargaining
Lewd and lascivious behavior	Preliminary hearings
Malicious mischief	Probation; probation reports
Murder	Right to counsel
Rape	Search and seizure
Robbery	Sentencing
Shoplifting	Speedy trial
Smuggling	Suppression of evidence
Tax evasion	Trials
Trespass	Witnesses
Weapons offenses	

What Legal Category Does It Fit?

It will also help your research if you find a subject area for your idea. For example, most law books contain indexes organized by generalized topics such as Motor Vehicles, Traffic Rules, and so on. Under each of these major headings, you will see an alphabetized list of still smaller subtopics or narrower ideas; beneath which are even smaller, more concentrated lists:

Evaluation facility referral

Evidence

Fines and penalties

Alcohol and drug substance abuse courses

Personal injury accident

Sentencing options

(You see how it is narrowing and narrowing until you find the legal description of just what you want.)

Down to the Meat of It

You now have background tools for the idea you wish to explore. You understand the terms, have reduced the jargon to understandable English, and have used any number of general resource materials listed above; you have spent some time thinking about questions that have logical answers, and now it's time to get down to the meat of the issue. If you want to write about criminal law and constitutional matters, the best idea would be to consult a primary source. Say you want to write about a manhunt and a difficult arrest. First ask yourself: What does the amendment say about search and seizure? Remember, all criminal law and procedure comes out of the Bill of Rights. Read the Fourth Amendment.

Next, you need to find statute material and then the applications of that material, or "cases in point." Okay, let's back up to finding statutes or law codes. Federal offenses are defined in statutes enacted by the United States Congress, and state offenses are defined in statutes enacted by state legislatures. Federal statutes are published annually in the United States Statutes at Large. The states have their own volumes, called "session laws," and these include all the new laws enacted in a given session in any state legislature. Later on, these will be merged into the existing laws, which will then be arranged systematically by subject and put into an index.

OUR LAWMAKERS:
* *The U.S. Constitution* has amendments, and interpretations of the Constitution and its amendments are referred to as *constitutional law*
* *State constitutions* and cases that result from them are *state constitutional law*
* *Congress* passes laws called "statutes," which decree *federal statutory law*
* *Federal courts* interpret *federal statutory law* and write opinions that make up a body of *federal case law*; they also decide cases and write opinions about state statutes, but only when the parties before the court are from different states
* *Federal administrative agencies* are created by Congress and staffed by the executive branch, such as the Federal Aviation Administration or the Federal Communications Commission, and they issue regulations that constitute the *federal administrative law*
* *Sovereign Indian tribes* have their own courts and law, which empower the government of tribal law
* *State legislatures* pass statutes, which constitute *state statutory law*
* *State courts* rule on court cases and write opinions, which constitute *state case law*
* *State administrative agencies* (created by state legislature and staffed by the governor's appointees) write regulations, which help to make up *state administrative law*
* *Local city and county governments* pass *ordinances* that become police codes, building codes, health codes, and so on, for small communities and local cities

FINDING FEDERAL STATUTES: One popular source has compiled the federal law—which started out as "bills" presented to Congress—in a series of books, the *United States Code Annotated,* also known as the *U.S.C.A.* (St. Paul, Minnesota: West Publishing, updated annually). *U.S.C.A.* costs almost two thousand dollars and has a topic index, historical notes, and is cross-referenced for ease of use. The *U.S.C.A. Quarterly Supplement* prints statutes a month or two after they have been passed by Congress. Laws typically have labels and numbers describing which house of Congress they originally came from, such as Senate Bill 5 (coded S.5) for a bill introduced in the Senate, or House of Representatives Bill 116 (the shorthand for it is *H.R. 116).*

The *U.S.C.A.* incorporates fifty separate titles that correspond to the text of the Official Code of the Laws of the United States. The primary law source of a federal statute is referred to as a "citation." Citations to federal statutes contain the title of the U.S. Code where the statute is found, and the section number. Title 18, for instance, is titled "Crimes and Criminal Procedure." The codes' annotations provide cursory information, such as one-sentence summaries, historical notes, and cross-references to other relevant statutes.

Here is an example on how to read a citation, which is a reference to any primary law source under the *United States Code Annotated.* The one illustrated below is the Civil Rights Act of 1964.

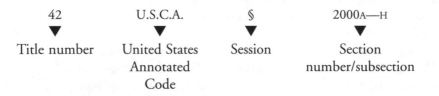

42	U.S.C.A.	§	2000A—H
Title number	United States Annotated Code	Session	Section number/subsection

Other sources you may find useful are two Internet sites that contain the U.S. Code; each is presented in a different way:
* The U.S. House of Representatives Internet Law Library (*http://law.house.gov/92.htm*)
* Cornell Law School at *www.law.cornell.edu/uscode*

STATE STATUTES: State statutes can be organized in a couple different ways, either annotated (containing notes and references) or not annotated (in which case only the text of the statute appears). Legal students most often prefer the annotated versions, which not only convey the actual language of the statute but also provide a listing for significant court cases. State statutes can also be organized into books according to subject matter (such as the "Penal Code" for criminal statutes), title number, or chronology (according to the date each statute was passed). Books that contain collections of statutes usually include an index in the last volume that has directions to the whereabouts of particular statutes according to their subject matter. The word "code" in most instances is synonymous with "law." If you are not finding your topic in the index—say, it involves arrest—try looking under a couple of different headings such as "Search and Seizure" or "Fourth Amendment."

Below is an example of an Arkansas statute for burglary.

Burglary, Residential, Commercial.
5-39-101. Definitions.

As used in this chapter, unless the context otherwise requires:
(1) "Residential occupiable structure" means a vehicle, building, or other structure:

(A) Where any person lives; or (B) Which is customarily used for overnight accommodation of persons whether or not a person is actually present. Each unit of a residential occupiable structure divided into separately occupied units is itself a residential occupiable structure.

(2) "Commercial occupiable structure" means a vehicle, building, or other structure:

(A) Where any person carries on a business or other calling; or

(B) Where people assemble for purposes of business, government, education, religion, entertainment, or public transportation.

(3) "Premises" means occupiable structures and any real property.

(4) "Enter or remain unlawfully" means to enter or remain in or upon premises when not licensed or privileged to do so. A person who enters or remains in or upon premises that are at the time open to the public does so with license and privilege, regardless of his purpose, unless he defies a lawful order not to enter or remain personally communicated to him by the owner of the premises or some other person authorized by the owner. A license or privilege to enter or remain in or upon premises only part of which are open to the public is not a license or privilege to enter or remain in a part of the premises not open to the public. A person who enters or remains upon unimproved and apparently unused land not fenced or otherwise enclosed in a manner designed to exclude intruders does so with license and privilege unless notice not to enter or remain is personally communicated to him by the owner or some person authorized by the owner, or unless notice is given by posting in a conspicuous manner.

(5) "Vehicle" means any craft or device designed for the transportation of people or property across land or water or through the air.

39-201. Residential burglary—Commercial burglary.

(a)(1) A person commits residential burglary if he enters or remains unlawfully in a residential occupiable structure of

65

another person with the purpose of committing therein any offense punishable by imprisonment.

(2) Residential burglary is a Class B felony.

(b)(1) A person commits commercial burglary if he enters or remains unlawfully in a commercial occupiable structure of another with the purpose of committing therein any offense punishable by imprisonment.

(2) Commercial burglary is a Class C felony.

History. Acts 1975, No. 280, § 2002; A.S.A. 1947, § 41-2002; Acts 1993, No. 442, § 2; 1993, No. 552, § 2.

66 State statute locations may also look like this example below:
West's Annotated California Codes, Vol. 51A, § 1524

A typical state statutory citation may appear as follows: "23 Vt. Stat. Ann. § 1185." This citation references Vermont title number or volume number 23, whose source is Vermont Statutes Annotated and whose section number is 1185.

To find state statutes on the Internet, go to:

- Findlaw: *www.findlaw.com/11stategov*
- The U.S. House of Representatives Internet Law Library: *http://law.house.gov/92.htm*
- Cornell University: *www.law.cornell.edu/states/index.html*

STATUTES ARE NOT EASY READING: One of the reasons for the complex writing in statutes is that the work has undergone many drafts by many editors, most of whom use legalese on a daily basis. Another reason is that for every law there is an exception, or many exceptions. Legal research experts suggest that you read the material several times. Be aware of the differences between "AND" and "OR." The "AND" designation usually means that these two factors must be employed together. The "OR" stipulation, on the other hand, means that the conditions must be met by one condition OR the other.

Make an attempt to look up every word that is unfamiliar or that could be construed to mean different variations on a similar theme. If a Latin term such as "prima facie" arises in any of your reading, and you find out that it means "lawfully sufficient," before moving further, see how that definition applies to the rest of the text. Does it make more sense if it means, "the minimum of facts needed in order to proceed"?

Check to see if the other statutes mentioned along with yours relate to the one you are reading. Remember, there is a concept among justice scholars called "strict interpretation." Basically, this means that laws must be interpreted literally—verbatim—and the prosecution (the more knowledgeable source of the law than the defendant) must show that the accused meets all the elements listed for each crime in order for it to stick. And bear in mind that all statutes must be interpreted by judges and lawyers, and interpretations about statutes are almost always subject to varying ideology. By reading the history of a decision and working up to present day, you'll be able to see how the law has evolved through use. Plan on spending some time to backtrack at least one decade, if you can.

If you arrange to let a character argue a case based on a state statute, make sure that you have the latest version. Laws are often updated and revised. In collections of annotated versions, updates are posted in what is called the pocket parts. A pocket part is an add-on version that fits into the hardcover volume. Any changes like additions will be underlined; and deletions will be indicated by an asterisk. If the particular law is still pending, probably the best source for the latest developments will be with your local representative. Call his office and request a copy of the bill (even if you do not have the number of the bill, knowing what the bill is about and who sponsors it should be enough for identification). In addition, your local law librarian might have an amended copy of the latest version called a "slip law."

APPEALS: When the law is applied and the defendant and lawyer find reasons not to accept the decision, they make an appeal to a higher court. The appeals court is not in the position to decide guilt or innocence; their primary concern is to read the transcript of the trial and make a decision about the lawfulness of the decision. Does it violate the defendant's constitutional rights? Is the law too vague to enforce as written? Is there room for more than one interpretation? These judge-rendered decisions are kept and published as case notes. Case reading is fun and interesting in that it tells the actual facts of the case as it came down. Case notes accompany the statutes in annotated codes and also in books that publish cases and materials. A couple of good books housing Supreme Court cases—cases involving constitutional law—and their decisions are:

• *Basic Criminal Law: Cases and Materials*, by George E. Dix and M. Michael Sharlot, 3rd Ed. (St. Paul, Minnesota: West's Criminal Justice Series, 1987)

• *Basic Criminal Procedure: Cases, Comments and Questions*, by Yale Kamisar, Wayne R. LaFave, and Jerold H. Israel, 8th Ed. (St. Paul, Minnesota: American Casebook Series, West Publishing Co., 1994)

In addition, there is a series of books called *Shepard's Citations for Statutes*. These dark red, hardcover volumes provide a complete listing of each time a particular statute or constitutional provision has been referred to and perhaps interpreted by a federal or state court. Legal researchers have a nickname for finding how their statute has been reported; it is called "Shepardizing" a case. In order to use *Shepard's*, you will need to know the exact number (citation) of the statute, and it is helpful to know the year it was passed.

For instructions on how to Shepardize federal and state statutes, I suggest *Legal Research: How to Find & Understand the Law* by Elias and Levinkind (Berkeley, California: Nolo Press, 1999) chapter 9, pages 10 and 11.

THE REPORTER SYSTEM: There are volumes that contain appellate court decisions specifically. These are called "reporters." The National Reporter System includes decisions from the U.S. Supreme Court, lower federal courts, and the state appellate courts. The National Reporter System contains the text of each reported decision plus a brief summary of the decision called a "syllabus" and a section for topics called "headnotes." These headnotes briefly describe the principles involved and are indexed by a series of "key numbers." For example, decisions about first-degree murder are classified under the heading "homicide," and there is a key number for each aspect of the crime. Therefore, homicide with intent to kill in the first degree might be classified as "Homicide 9—Intent and design to effect death."

There is also a series of regional reporters that document decisions of the highest state courts—but not always the supreme courts; the decisions of the intermediate state courts, called appellate courts, are found in regional reporters. Examples of reporters are: *Atlantic Reporter, Pacific Reporter, Northeastern Reporter, Northwestern Reporter, Southeastern Reporter, Southern Reporter, Southwestern Reporter.*

CASE IN POINT:
Case citations have usually five or six items:
• The case name, which is comprised of the names of the plaintiff and the defendant
• The volume number of the reporter where the case is published
• The name of the reporter
• The page number of the volume
• The year the case was decided
• For federal appeals cases or federal district cases, a designation of the circuit is listed; or for state cases the judicial district where the state is located is used

STATE V. ROOKS,	468	S.E.2D	354	(GA. 1996)
▼	▼	▼	▼	▼
1. CASE NAME	2. VOLUME NUMBER	3. NAME OF REPORTER	4. PAGE NUMBER	5. STATE; YEAR

Other Informational Goldmines

I would be remiss if I did not mention a particular Web site run by a friend, defense attorney Kim Kruglick. Kim's pages offer not only a thorough explanation of law and criminal law sources but also a nice section on forensic Web sites. You can find the site at *www.kruglaw.com*.

For much lighter research, check out *www.courttv.com*. And for a glimpse into the legal organizations, there is the American Bar Association at *www.abanet.org* and the National District Attorney's Association at *www.ndaa-apri.org*.

There is a concept called "synchronicity" that comes from Carl Jung, a Swiss psychiatrist who was famous for expounding his views on introversion and extroversion. Jung gave this name to the phenomenon that once someone becomes *mindful* of a subject, the amount of repeat awareness of that subject increases considerably with each new encounter. Now that you have the basics of law research, I hope that you will develop a synchronicity of your own and find law everywhere: in the newspaper, on television, in the films you watch, etc. Your knowledge and mindfulness will make those instances of application—of your writing about the subject—that much more interesting. Good hunting!

69

Chapter 6

Defenses, Justification, and Excuse

*Laws are like spiders' webs: If some poor weak creature
comes up against them, it is caught; but a big one can
break through and get away.*
—SOLON, *LIVES OF EMINENT PHILOSOPHERS*

Ever hear of the "Twinkie defense," the "abuse excuse," or the "insanity plea"? American criminal jurisprudence admits that even though the defendant may have perpetrated the crime he is charged with, the defendant is not necessarily guilty of crime. What one may call "loopholes" are defenses, which, if believed to be true by the jury, must as a matter of law negate the criminal responsibility of the accused. Remember, to begin, the prosecution must prove all elements of a crime—for example, that the accused committed the act; that the act and the intent happened in concert; that there were no attendant circumstances like self-defense, which would cancel out criminal liability; and that the outcome was caused by a criminal act.

Chapter 6 introduces a number of defenses. Both common law and state's law allow the accused to come forward and present credible evidence that such a defense is factually possible.

Allege It, Prove It

In general, a defendant may, and is likely to, plead "Not guilty, Sir" to the charges. In addition, he may offer up a defense—sometimes called a "negative defense"—and the defendant (since now the tables have turned) has the burden of raising some evidence to back it up. That process is called the "burden of production of evidence." Later, when the defense evidence is presented, the prosecution needs to counter the negative defense in order to overcome it. As an example, say, our defendant is charged with manslaughter because he killed a person who forced entry into his home. The defendant asserts that on the night in question he was asleep, and claims to have used deadly force to defend his home. If any evidence proves that he did, in fact, act in self-defense—say, the offender had weapons that showed usage—the prosecution must prove the defendant did not act reasonably. (I see an acquittal here, don't you?) In some jurisdictions, though, innocence gets harder to prove, as the defendant is saddled with the burden of proving self-defense despite the greater weight of the evidence against him, a disadvantage usually referred to as a preponderance of the evidence.

Remember, the most common defense argument is a principle called "the presumption of innocence." Any time a defendant takes charge of his own defense, he will also be taking on many other burdens; and he leaves himself and his witnesses open to cross-examination. For the defendant who chooses to remain silent and to present no witnesses, the prosecution has the burden of offering proof beyond a reasonable doubt—and the defendant can later claim that the prosecution's case was too weak for the burden, even if everything the prosecution witnesses have said was accurate. In addition, the defense attorney can poke holes in the "guilty" argument by cross-examining the prosecution's witnesses, and holes in a witness's testimony make for reasonable doubt.

71

Another very important point and a boon to the defense in both theory and practice is this: If the defense presents no argument, the prosecution is not allowed to comment on the fact that the defendant chooses not to testify or has failed to put on an affirmative case. The risk here, though, is that jurors have a tendency to disregard this rule. The juror's assumption—or first impression, perhaps—is that the defendant won't stand up for himself because he has something to hide.

Did It? Defend It!

A defendant's guilty plea, met with a claim of defense for the act, is called an affirmative, or "true," defense. Lawfully defined, the only true defense arguments are those whereby the defendant has admitted to committing a crime but seeks to avoid punishment based on a legal excuse or justification. Some examples of this kind of defense are duress, self-defense, and entrapment.

In order to give you a clearer picture of affirmative defenses, I'll order them into five different categories:

1. Those asserting lack of capacity: infancy, insanity, intoxication, and automatism

2. Those alleging justification or excuse: duress, consent, necessity, mistake of law, and mistake of fact

3. Those justifying a use of force: self-defense, defense of habitation, defense of property, defense of others, and using force to resist an arrest

4. Those depending on constitutional or statutory rights: immunity, double jeopardy, and statutes of limitation

5. Those attacking government conduct: entrapment, selective prosecution

Of course, it is up to the prosecution to produce evidence beyond a reasonable doubt that negates the affirmative defense.

Writer's Jump-Start

Affirmative defenses make possible the "twist" every plot cries out for. It is the difference between being predictable and adding the element of surprise that readers love. Plus, again, it allows the accused a chance to defend himself, which can become very iffy, very edgy.

Let's look at the affirmative defenses individually for a better understanding of how they work, starting with the lack-of-capacity defenses:

INFANCY: HE'S SO YOUNG!: Under common law, a child of less than seven is assumed unconditionally unable to form criminal intent. This is the basis of the defense of infancy. For this reason, most of these cases are "adjudicated in juvenile court." But the same charge for a child between seven and fourteen is debatable, and some jurisdictions permit the child to be tried as an adult, especially if the crime is particularly heinous. The prosecution, though, must be able to introduce evidence that shows the delinquent child knew what he was doing. How is this done? Well, if the child tried to conceal the crime, bribe a witness, or accuse others of the deed, he is showing his own deliberate hand.

Laws are still evolving as the age of murderers drops and modern statutes differ in their treatment—some have raised the age while some have modified it—but all agree that it's the child's age at the time of commission of the crime and not the child's age at trial that determines the relocation from juvenile court to adult venues.

I Thought I Was Napoleon

In a twist of affairs, all offenders are presumed sane unless pronounced by agreement as insane (although we may not agree with their general assessment). Contrary to popular belief, the insanity defense is not a frequently used ploy, and the accused are not really getting away with anything when it actually works out. Confinement to a mental facility is neither synonymous with a rest home nor like a free ticket to a spa. Any preconceived notions you may have of a mental hospital as a place that houses quaint, eccentric, or dingy people is wholly incorrect.

The original rule for insanity is based on a historical English case and is named the M'Naghten Rule. A man named Daniel M'Naghten suffered from the delusion that he was being persecuted by government officials. In his mind, the best way to resolve this situation was to kill Sir Robert Peel, the founder of the British Police System and the man after whom the term "Bobbies" was crafted. To end his torture, M'Naghten positioned himself outside Peel's domicile and, instead of shooting him, shot and killed his secretary, Edward Drummond. At trial, M'Naghten's barristers argued that their client was insane at the time of the shooting, and the jury agreed. Queen Victoria was outraged by the outcome and insisted that a yardstick for the insanity defense be set. The House of Lords responded with this:

> It must be clearly proved that, at the time of committing the act, the
> party accused as labouring under such a defect of reason, from dis-
> ease of the mind, as not to know the nature and quality of the act
> he was doing; or, if he did know it, that he did not know what he
> was doing was wrong.[41]

As new theories involving mental capacity developed among those who practiced psychology and psychiatry, the rule seemed a bad fit. Since it was based
solely on intellect, it ignored that powerful notion of irresistible impulse, an
emotional concept built on self-control. In other words, this new notion
allowed that there were people who, while knowing an act was wrong, still
succumbed to an uncontrollable desire or the duress of a mental disease,
and committed the act anyway, and therefore should be excused from
criminal liability.

Since this formula did not fit all forms of perpetrators either, the Durham
test came into being: the accused was not criminally responsible if his unlawful act was the "product of mental disease or defect."[42] Now this was a definition a psychiatrist could live with, but the electorate could not, and it was
eventually discarded.

In 1962, the ALI standard, named for the American Law Institute, pro-
posed this version:

> A person is not responsible for criminal conduct if at the time of
> such conduct, as a result of mental disease or defect, a person lacks
> substantial capacity either to appreciate the wrongfulness or his con-
> duct or to conform his conduct to the requirements of law.

The idea of combining both cognitive and volitional capacities as a test for
sanity was adopted by the federal courts and was used as a test for the Hinckley
case, where a man named John Hinckley was found not guilty by reason of
insanity for his attack on former president Reagan.

Congress wasn't happy with this rendition and soon passed the Insanity
Defense Reform Act of 1984 for the federal government. It reads like this:

> It is an affirmative defense to a prosecution under any Federal
> statute that, at the time of the commission of the acts constituting
> the offense, the defendants, as a result of a severe mental disease or
> defect, was unable to appreciate the nature and quality or the
> wrongfulness of his act. Mental disease or defect does not otherwise
> constitute a defense.[43]

An interesting facet of the revised act is that it now provided a clause that stated the "defendant has the burden of proving the defense of insanity by *clear and convincing evidence* [italics mine]." This requirement puts the evidence in the middle as far as strictness, as much as standards can be defined. It is more demanding than the "preponderance of evidence" as required by civil evidence, but still less difficult to obtain than the evidence of the "beyond a reasonable doubt" variety.

74

The state courts remain divided on this issue, and four states currently have abolished the defense of insanity altogether: Montana, Idaho, Utah, and Kansas. One of the more interesting state cases dealing with insanity comes down from a 1983 Maryland decision. A woman named Joy Ann Robey was charged with involuntary manslaughter and child abuse in connection with the death of her ten-month-old daughter Christina. Robey admitted at trial to beating the child severely and repeatedly over a two-month period but pleaded not guilty by reason of insanity. The trial court agreed that she must have been temporarily insane each time she beat the child but that she returned to sanity thereafter. Accordingly, they felt the defendant could not be held criminally liable for the beatings but was responsible for her failure to seek medical care for her child. Robey was convicted of involuntary manslaughter and child abuse and sentenced to three consecutive ten-year terms in prison. Later, her conviction was upheld despite her contention that the trial court erred in holding her criminally responsible after acknowledging that she was insane at the time of the beatings.[44]

Writer's Tip

The insanity defense does not sit well with many people who suggest that a victim who is killed by an insane person is just as dead as someone who is killed by a sane person. Also, many citizens are doubtful of the competence of the psychiatrists and judges who pronounce mental disease and are more uncomfortable still with the connection—or disconnection—between a mental disease and the commission of a crime. Is this an area to exploit for its controversy?

THOSE DARN TWINKIES!: If you are moving in the direction of using mental capability in a story, you will probably come up against the term "diminished capacity." This is a partial defense related to insanity. What it boils down to, if used, is that it can reduce the criminal responsibility of defendants whose acts are the result of mental illness falling short of insanity. In the 1980s, diminished capacity played a pivotal role in an important California trial when a jury accepted a diminished capacity defense and convicted Dan White of manslaughter for killing San Francisco mayor George Moscone and Harvey Milk, an openly gay county supervisor. White brought to the fore the so-called Twinkie defense. His claim was that eating food high in sugar had rendered him temporarily unable to control his actions. The public was so incensed after the verdict that the California legislature outlawed the diminished capacity defense;[45] many other states have done likewise.

I HAD ONE TOO MANY AND . . . The voluntary ingestion of drugs or alcohol does not provide a defense to a criminal charge, but it can serve as a partial defense—that is, if the defendant's intoxication produced mental impairment, enough so that it would render him unable to form premeditated intent, then he might be convicted of a lesser crime. But, similar to insanity, this defense will need to be validated by either medical or psychiatric testimony or both.

A rather interesting case about this concept is found in *Montana v. Egelhoff*.[46] In July 1992, Egelhoff was camping and mushroom-picking in the Yaak region of northwestern Montana. Egelhoff made friends with two other campers and mushroom-pickers, Roberta Pavola and John Christenson. On Sunday, July 12, the three sold the mushrooms they had collected and spent the rest of the day and evening drinking in bars and at a private party in Troy, Montana. Some time after 9:00 P.M., they left the party and got into Christenson's 1974 Ford Galaxy station wagon. Egelhoff was seen buying beer at 9:20 P.M., and the drinking binge continued, Egelhoff recalled, as he and Christenson were "sitting on a hill or a bank and passing a bottle of Black Velvet back and forth."

Officers from the sheriff's department of Lincoln County, Montana, were called about midnight that night in response to reports about a possible drunk driver. They discovered Christenson's station wagon stuck in a ditch along U.S. Highway 2. In the front seat were Pavola and Christenson, each dead from a single gunshot to the head. In the rear of the car lay Egelhoff, alive and yelling obscenities. His blood alcohol content measured .36 percent over one hour later. Near the brake pedal, on the floor of the car, was Egelhoff's .38 caliber handgun, with four loaded rounds and two empty casings. Egelhoff had gunshot residue on his hands.

The defendant was charged with two counts of deliberate homicide, a crime defined by Montana law as "purposely" or "knowingly" causing the death of another human being. The defendant's defense tactic at trial was that an unidentified fourth person must have committed the murders because, he claimed, his own intoxication had rendered him physically incapable of committing the murders or even recalling the events of the night of July 12. Although he was able to present this scenario, the jury was instructed to ignore the defendant's intoxicated condition in determining the existence of a mental state, an element of the offense. The jury decided Egelhoff was guilty and sentenced him to eighty-four years' imprisonment.

Apparently, the Supreme Court of Montana reversed his sentence on appeal when they agreed that the respondent "had a due process right to present and have considered by the jury all relevant evidence to rebut the State's evidence on all elements of the offense charged. . . ." In their opinion, the Montana justices believed the question of whether the respondent acted knowingly and purposely was a relevant issue.

The cornerstone of the case review when it reached the Supreme Court was the due process clause guaranteeing a defendant the right to present all relevant evidence. And, in their opinion, the Supreme Court judges did not disagree with that essential, categorical rule. But, they said, "The accused does not have an unfettered right to offer [evidence] that is incompetent, privileged, or otherwise inadmissible under standard rules of evidence . . . that a defendant's voluntary intoxication provided neither an 'excuse' nor a 'justification' for his crimes. . . ."

With involuntary intoxication, the scenario is much different: The offender may commit a crime as a result of having consumed drugs, alcohol, or a prescription medicine through no fault of his own, and then, if the jury finds that he could not have controlled his behavior, he may be allowed to go free. Of course, the judge and jury must agree, and the weight of the evidence is on the defendant's shoulders.

Since the rules under intoxication can vary widely between states—and change quickly, besides—be sure to check your current individual state statutes before using this as a defense.

Writer's Tip

While we are on the subject of involuntary intoxication, here is a summary of a House of Representatives Bill, H.R. 2130, about the "Date Rape Drug" that recently became law:

Sponsor: Rep. Fred Upton

Related Bills: H.R. 3457, S. 1561

Latest Major Action: February 18, 2000, the bill became Public Law No. 106–172.

Title: An act to amend the Controlled Substances Act to direct the emergency scheduling of gamma hydroxybutyric acid, to provide for a national awareness campaign, and for other purposes. Amends the Controlled Substances Act (CSA) and the Controlled Substances Import and Export Act to provide additional penalties relating to GHB. Adds gamma butyrolactone (GBL) as an additional list I chemical.

I DID IT IN A DREAM: Under the umbrella of the insanity defense, automatism is a stretch for most people to accept, and for that reason it is used infrequently. It requires the jury to believe that an unlawful act is committed because of an involuntary condition like somnambulism—that is, sleepwalking. A defendant in Butler, Pennsylvania, contended in November of 1994 that his condition, a sleep apneas disorder, depleted his oxygen supply so much it caused him to shoot his wife. The jury saw otherwise and convicted him of murder.

76

In one Wyoming case, the court gave a good reason for separating automatism from the insanity plea and its consequences. The outcome, they said, is that, generally, no follow-up, such as institutionalization, is needed with sleepwalking, and that is where sleepwalkers differ from those who are legally insane. Perhaps they had not met the man from Butler, Pennsylvania.

I DID IT BECAUSE HE MADE ME: Duress is another one of those borderline, better-check-your-local-statutes defenses. Also referred to as coercion or compulsion, it is recognized today, although it is used most frequently by defendants who have committed robberies and thefts, or by prisoners who have escaped from custody. Intertwined with duress is also a notion called "the common law presumption," which means that if a wife committed a felony other than murder or treason in her husband's presence, she did so because of his coercion. That rendering has been abolished in most jurisdictions, but, because all things about the law are dynamic, other new affirmative defenses are emerging, some of which have taken root in certain states—for example, the battered woman's defense. In 1992, a California appellate court agreed to a new development in the law of duress: Battered Woman Syndrome. The Battered Woman Syndrome was allowed as a defense in support of a woman who committed robbery offenses out of fear that the man she lived with would kill her if she didn't comply.

77

In another case, *People v. Merhige*,[47] a cab driver used the duress defense rather effectively when he claimed that a gun was held to his head while he was ordered to transport his passengers to a bank, despite his knowing they would commit a robbery. The Michigan Supreme Court believed the cabby when he told them he feared for his life had he not cooperated, and they reversed his conviction.

Writer's Tip

Because of its vagueness, duress could make for interesting plot confusion. Kansas has allowed a person to plead duress as a defense to crimes—other than murder—in which the threat is against one's spouse, parent, child, brother, or sister.[48]

I DID IT BECAUSE I COULD: Generally, we are a forgiving lot. Despite our nature, historically the courts have said that a victim may not excuse a criminal act and, therefore, consent is not an excuse or a defense. There are exceptions, though. For example, with larceny, consent is a defense because lack of consent is an element of the offense. And it may also be true in rape situations, but only where competent adults freely consent before having sexual relations. We also give consent to physicians before we go under the knife, and professional athletes give consent to sports teams' owners when they agree to accept "contact" in contact sports.

I Did It, but Didn't Like It: Different from duress, where the crime has as its source the actions of others, the defense of necessity is defined as the choice between the lesser of two evils. For example, a man with a suspended driver's license, no telephone, and the absence of a neighbor, drove to a telephone booth in order to call a relative to get someone to take his pregnant wife to the hospital. As timing would have it, he was stopped for a broken taillight and then arrested for driving without a license. The Supreme Court of South Carolina[49] ruled in a 3–2 decision that, under the circumstances, the defendant could use the defense of necessity. (I'm sure his wife appreciates that.)

Likewise, Florida gave the necessity defense to a couple who had contracted AIDS and claimed they used the possession and cultivation of marijuana to help them get through their disease.

On another front, in *Commonwealth v. Berrigan*,[50] the antinuclear activists were sanctioned, even though their plea of necessity got them all the way to the appellate court. The necessity defense did not serve their cause, though—after the Pennsylvania Supreme Court heard of their escapade of entering a Pennsylvania factory, damaging nuclear bomb components, and pouring blood on the premises. In fact, other activist activities have not done well, and the Alaska Supreme Court has reoutlined the three steps required for their citizens who want to claim necessity defense:

1. The act charged must have been done to prevent a significant evil;
2. There must have been no adequate alternative; and
3. The harm caused must not have been disproportionate to the harm avoided.[51]

I Did It but I Didn't Know It Was Wrong: The Model Penal Code generally lumps the mistake or ignorance of "fact" and "law" into a single provision, but for our purposes of illustration and because the judicial discussions have a tendency to treat them as separate distinctions when they make rulings, we will take them individually.

You may, in your studies, come across the principle, "Ignorance of the law is no excuse." The demands of society are such that, just because a person claims he may not know he had committed a criminal act, his ignorance does not excuse the crime. But, again, there are exceptions called "the mistake of law." A defendant's honest but mistaken view of the law is sometimes considered a defense. One example is a mistake that negates the specific-intent element of a crime. For example, a person who trusts in the validity of his divorce and who mistakenly takes that situation on faith as being legal—a "done deed"— may not be guilty of bigamy when he marries again.

Certain state's codes also have exceptions to the general rule that a person's ignorance of the law does not excuse unlawful conduct. The Illinois Criminal Code sets forth four circumstances in which a person's "reasonable belief" that certain conduct does not constitute a criminal offense can be used as a defense. The term "reasonable" is the optimum word here, but, simplified, it applies if:

• The offense is defined by an administrative regulation which is not known to the offender (like fishing without a license pending legislation); or

• The offender relies on a law that is later determined to be invalid; or,

• He sets forth into an activity whose illegality is later overruled by an appellate court; or

• He acts in the belief that an official interpretation of a statute or regulation, made by a public officer or agency that is legally authorized to interpret such things, is law.

I DID IT, BUT I MISTAKENLY THOUGHT IT WAS ALRIGHT: An often talked about mistake of fact is a case that occurred one autumn in Mississippi. A group of hunters was charged with the murder of two fellow hunters during the deer-hunting season. A deer camp had a Halloween party and two of the hunters invited were extremely intoxicated. Thinking it would be good fun, they donned a costume made of deer head in front of them and a blanket over their backs, and left for the party. Within five minutes, they got shot and received twenty-three bullet wounds. All of the men who discharged weapons were charged with murder. The defense attorneys alleged their clients mistakenly thought they were shooting at a deer. The jury agreed this was a "reasonable" mistake of fact, clearing them of the criminal responsibility for homicide.

79

I DID IT IN SELF-DEFENSE: Using the defense of self-defense sometimes breaks down to provocation and begs the question, "Who started it?" Although, here, too, there is wiggle room because a person who claims self-defense can strike someone before being hit if, in fact, the evidence supports the conclusion that physical harm was in the offing and that the defendant therefore used force to "prevent" an attack.

This defense tactic means that people do not have to wait until they are actually struck to act in self-defense. And some of the charges that can be vacated vary from battery and assault to assault with a deadly weapon, to manslaughter, and even to first- or second-degree murder. This defense, then, is the linchpin of many mysteries whose protagonist is a "woman in jeopardy"—yes, an entire genre, the woman-in-jeopardy suspense, was built around this concept.

Since self-defense is such an important feature in the denouement of most "private eye" mysteries in which the protagonist must confront the offender in a "face-off" scene (most times our hero has the responsibility of using his wiles in order to overcome the "it's him or me" tenor), we will look closely at the specific elements of self-defense.

The first requirement is that the defendant must believe that force was necessary for his own protection. This belief must be qualified as a reasonable belief, such that a reasonable person in the same or similar situation would have formed the same strategy; and, in some cases, even if the belief is wrong, the defense may still hold. For example, one recent famous case brought forth in 1993 cites the behavior of defendant Rodney Peairs. Peairs, a thirty-one-year-old meat market manager, was charged with the manslaughter of an exchange student from Japan, Yoshi Hattori. In October 1992, Hattori and his American host brother, dressed as characters from *Saturday Night Fever,* lost their way while looking for a Halloween party. When Hattori and his host brother sought their bearings and knocked on the wrong door, they were met by a panicked man who shouted "Freeze!" Hattori's English was sketchy at best, and he apparently did not understand, moved forward, and was shot once in the chest. The Japanese press descended on the town of Baton Rouge, Louisiana, in order to cover the court case's every turn. In trial, Peairs claimed the boys had made a commotion that had scared his wife. As a consequence, he claimed, he grabbed his .44 caliber Magnum with the intent of defending his family. Peairs later apologized for the shooting, saying he didn't have time to think. A Louisiana jury wound up acquitting Peairs and, within the parameters of the law, ruled his fear reasonable and his self-defense lawful.

One other requirement, as established by some states, is that the elements of retreat and deadly force be present. Most courts reject a common law doctrine that requires a person to retreat to the greatest extent possible before meeting force with force. While the Oklahoma law on this principle is clear— "There is no duty to retreat if one is threatened with bodily harm"[52]—the Tennessee Supreme Court has said that a person who can safely retreat must do so before using deadly force.[53] And, again, the exception here is that most courts that follow the retreat rule have also taken on the standard that a person does not have to retreat in his own home.

How much force constitutes a reasonable response in self-defense? The amount depends on the circumstances of each situation, particularly the amount of force a supposed victim is using against the defendant. There are two tests that usually come to support the issue. The first, a more traditional approach, is the subjective standard of reasonableness. This requires that the jury place itself "in the defendant's shoes." The second standard is the objective test, whereupon the jury is expected to place itself in the shoes of a hypothetical "reasonable and prudent person." In general, though, the whole concept has been tweaked somewhat, and what is generally known now as "climbing into the shoes of the victim" has made the subjective argument the more popular standard as a result of a multitude of cases in which women have had to use deadly force against the assaultive or homicidal offenses of men in order to protect their own lives. In homicide cases, one who killed in honest belief that the killing was necessary in self-defense but who exceeded the scope of the legal right of self-defense is generally regarded as guilty only of manslaughter.

This is often characterized as involving an "imperfect" defense, because the defendant's liability is reduced but he is not exonerated. This applies to one who acted before force was reasonably necessary or who used more force than reasonably could have appeared necessary to prevent the threatened harm.

Following the Battered Woman Syndrome of self-defense, there is a rationale called the Battered Child Syndrome, which is the defense of a child accused of assaulting or killing a parent. In 1993, when California charged Erik and Lyle Menendez, ages eighteen and twenty-one respectively, with the brutal murder of their parents, many prosecutors felt the brothers' claim amounted to an "abuse excuse" and that it was undermining the law of self-defense. Should the brothers have been allowed this "imperfect self-defense," the punishment would have been reduced to manslaughter. Despite the highly publicized opinions held by the state, the first two trials ended with the jurors locked into mistrial because they could not agree on a verdict. In March 1996, though, the Menendez brothers were convicted and sentenced to life in prison without the possibility of parole.

FYI—

Using self-defense expands the scope of admissible evidence, evidence that might not be presented in the absence of this type of defense. For instance, witnesses testifying on what would be termed "rumors" are ordinarily not allowed. But a self-defense claim can lead to any information that might point to the defendant's believing his use of force was necessary. So, if the victim were rumored to have been violent, for example, the defendant could then verbalize that belief as part of his testimony.

I DID IT BECAUSE I WAS DEFENDING MY HOME: Sometimes this will be called the "defense of habitation." The historical view on the security of a person's dwelling is demonstrated best by Sir Edward Coke, who said in his *Commentaries*: "A man's home is his castle—for where shall a man be safe if it not be in his house?" In a more recent case adjudicated by the Illinois Supreme Court, *People v. Eatman*, the Eatman court was of the opinion that "he may use all of the force apparently necessary to repel any invasion of his home."[54] This principle is referred to as the Castle Doctrine. Since then, the legality of the use of deadly force to protect one's home has undergone some revision in that the deadly part is justifiable only if the occupant reasonably believes that death or bodily injury will be imminent to himself or to the other occupants of the house or if he believes the assailant intends to commit a felony.

Writer's Tip

Defending one's home holds a lot of promise when it comes to story lines. Great epics and films such as *Braveheart* and *The Patriot*, made famous by defender-hero

Mel Gibson, have both involved the theme of home and loss crossed with war and vengeance, leading to rapt attention and honors from his viewer fans.

I DID IT BECAUSE I WAS DEFENDING MY PROPERTY: Society places a pretty high premium on the preservation of human life, more than on the protection of property. For that reason, the right to use force to defend one's property will not allow the same measures as if you were protecting your home. The use of deadly force in this instance must be weighed against the amount of force encountered. So, for our purposes here, using only nondeadly force to protect real property, personal property, and possessions is acceptable against an unlawful interference. Now, even this usage carries a stipulation: A prior request to desist from interfering with the property must be issued. Of course, if someone is breaking into your car and your warning to stop is either dangerous, useless, or not viable, common sense says, "Let it go." It's just a thing, and you are more important than your property. And if your character does likewise, he will gain more respect than someone who chooses to do something stupid. Of course, if part of the characterization you need calls for stupidity, you have your scenario to show it!

I DID IT TO DEFEND ANOTHER: The defense of defending another follows the same dictum as protecting oneself, and many a court has noted that "what one may do for himself, he may do for another."[55] So, basically, irrespective of relationship, there could always be someone out there (or in your book) who may be available to protect a third person. Just remember: For your characters, the defendant must be faced with a reasonable amount of force, and then, if it turns deadly, the defendant or those the defendant is defending must be in their own home in order to truly justify a killing. And it must be necessary, not retaliatory.

I DID IT BECAUSE I DIDN'T WANT TO BE ARRESTED: When common law was knee-high to a grasshopper, a person had a right to use any force necessary, short of killing, towards resisting an unlawful arrest. This concept was largely the result of unfair English practices, such as arrest without bail, arraignments when hell freezes over, and terrible conditions in jail. In some states, it is still allowed. Over time, though, certain courts have become aware that resistance often begets violence, and the outrage has a tendency to escalate relative to the amount of resisting performed. This defense is an obscure concept—check your individual state statute for its ruling on resistance to arrest.

Now, the right of a private person to use force to effect an arrest is given less credence than that of a police officer, who can do it on reasonable grounds. A "citizen's arrest" and the use of force must be held together by the fact that the offender was committing a felony. And, still, the courts say a private indi-

82

vidual acts at his own peril when using deadly force. In other words, the action has to be the result of a tough, felonious situation in order to rank as a justifiable defense in a court of law.

We can take this one step further: A police officer occasionally requires the assistance of a private individual to effect an arrest. Under these circumstances, the civilian has the same privileges as does the officer. This is reasonable, because it is against the law to resist helping an officer make an arrest when asked. And the suspect's innocence (oops, made a mistake!) will not negate the defense. Model Penal Code is somewhat stricter with who-gets-what-power, in that a private person effecting an arrest and using deadly force must prove that he believed he was assisting a police officer.[56]

[handwritten margin note: Plot idea?]

> **FYI—**
> The Model Penal Code is a collection of documents drafted by a committee of the American Law Institute (ALI), an organization of leading scholars. In 1962, they formulated proposed legislation on a variety of subjects. Even though the Model Penal Code sounds like law, it is not. It is, however, a compilation of general provisions relating to criminal law in the areas of criminal liability, sentences, defenses, and definitions that are available to legislatures that may, or may not, use or adopt them partially. In fact, it has served as the basis for existing statutory provisions in many states.

I DID IT BECAUSE THE COPS TALKED ME INTO IT: Entrapment is a double-edged sword for the accused. Truth is, if the government induces someone into committing a crime, the prosecution cannot punish that person for doing it. However, if the defendant is a doer and wants to plead entrapment as a defense, he leaves himself open for more trouble, because now the prosecution gets to introduce evidence that shows the defendant was "predisposed" to commit the crime anyway. Get it?

I know you do, and your story's character will have a hard time proving he did not want to do the deed. Defendants who claim they were entrapped into committing illegal acts normally have the burden of convincing a judge or jury—by a preponderance of the evidence—that they were induced to do the crime and not just predisposed to doing it. This defense is most often heard of in connection with prostitution or narcotics sting operations.

There are two tests (or schools of thought) that justices use to determine the focus of the criminal intent. The first is called *the subjective test of entrapment*. This presupposes that the defendant did the crime but that what is in question is whether the criminal intent originated because of his predisposition to do it or whether he was induced into action by the police. This means that in order to sustain this as a defense, the defendant would need to show the methods of persuasion police actually used to make a law-abiding person commit a crime.

83

The objective test of entrapment means the court would simply determine whether police methods themselves were so improper that they likely induced or ensnared the person into committing a crime. This circumstance would be evaluated by a judge, not a jury.

Using entrapment is a rather hackneyed approach to plot complication, and making the government a conspirator is nothing new—its officials are often held as conspiring or manipulative. It will be the new twist on this concept that will propel an entrapment-inspired story onto the best-sellers' list.

I'M NOT TELLING IF I DID IT OR NOT: Two years after signing the Constitution, James Madison—who would later become president— came forth with twelve more constitutional amendments. Congress approved ten of them, and these became the Bill of Rights. The significance of the Bill of Rights is that it restricts governments rather than individuals and private groups. The Fifth Amendment has to do with constitutional immunity, the concept that a person cannot be compelled to say anything that might be self-incriminating. The states also abide by this ruling as a result of the Fourteenth Amendment (which incorporates federal laws for the states), but some states have even written similar protections in their own state constitutions. This self-incrimination clause means that a person does not have to say anything in a court of law which may reveal information that later can be used as evidence of guilt and used against him in another proceeding, whether it is a civil or criminal offense, in a formal or informal proceeding, now or in the future. The federal version of this guarantee applies only to natural persons—read this as a "native-born" person—and not corporations. An interesting aside: when O. J. Simpson found himself in civil court, he was impelled to testify—why? he had already been found "not guilty."

USE IMMUNITY: So when a witness invokes the Fifth Amendment— "I refuse to answer on the grounds that it may incriminate me"—the court needs some course of action in order to compel that person to speak. This is achieved by extending immunity to the defendant, which is a grant of amnesty, or we could say "exemption," from prosecution through the use of compelled testimony. This process is called "giving a witness use immunity" and is sometimes referred to as "derivative immunity" as well. Use immunity, though, only bars the use of the witness's testimony against him in a subsequent prosecution. Federal grand juries are authorized to grant use immunity.[57]

TRANSACTIONAL IMMUNITY: Another type of immunity in some states is called "transactional immunity." This is a broader protection than use immunity in that it protects a witness from prosecution for any activity mentioned in the witnesses' testimony.

CONTRACTUAL IMMUNITY: Then there is "contractual immunity." The intent with this umbrella is to prompt a suspect to testify against someone else, thereby enabling the prosecution to win a conviction not otherwise available because of constitutional protection against self-incrimination. This type of immunity is rarely given if other available evidence will result in a conviction. Only the United States Attorney, with approval of the attorney general or certain authorized assistants, is authorized to grant contractual immunity in federal courts. At the state level, such authoritative power is generally approved by the chief prosecuting officer—that is, the district or state attorney.

Diplomatic Immunity: Under international law, there are those who enjoy diplomatic immunity as part and parcel of their political status. A person who serves as part of a diplomatic mission, as well as members of the diplomatic staff and household, is immune from arrest and prosecution. The expectation, of course, is that American diplomats and their dependents and staff members will enjoy similar immunity in foreign nations. This type of immunity is most often found in the political thriller, and, as such, is a powerful tool.

FYI—

The interesting part of immunity is that it allows our government a way to get around the Fifth Amendment. But there is a price to pay, because, granted immunity the compelled witness can confess to a serious crime, and there is nothing that can be done about it. What a great way to introduce a "questionable" deal to get at the truth—but what if the deal is actually worse than the truth?

You Won't Know If I Did It or Not, Because Time Ran Out

All crimes, except murder, have a statute of limitations. By law, that means there is a time limit on the prosecution of a crime. There are no historical criteria stipulating the length for this time limit, but, nevertheless, both the federal government and almost all the states have laws that prescribe certain time limits. There are two reasons for this enactment:

1. It is believed a person should not have to live under the onus of prosecution for a long period of time
2. Proof is absent after a prolonged duration or is, at the least, not credible

According to the parameters of most statutes, the period for prosecution begins when a crime is committed rather than when it is discovered. And the ending of the period is triggered by different circumstances, such as the issuing of an arrest warrant, the return of an indictment, or the filing of conclusive information. A period can also be interrupted—an effect called "tolling"—when a perpetrator is a fugitive or conceals himself from authorities.

Generally, for federal statutes there is a five-year limitation for prosecution on noncapital crimes. The states have varying times, although Ohio (whose standards are the same as many other states) seems to have a rudimentary provision, which says the time limit for a felony other than aggravated murder or murder is six years; for a misdemeanor other than a minor misdemeanor the limit is two years; and a minor misdemeanor holds for six months.[58]

Some jurisdictions do not agree on whether a statute of limitations in a criminal action is an affirmative defense. For it to be an affirmative defense, it must be pled as such; if not, it is considered waived. (Any action either ignored or unused is relinquished.) Other states will differ, though, in that the minute the prosecution files an indictment beyond the designated period allowed by the statute of limitations, the prosecution is barred from proceeding. Can we say "timing is everything"?

I'm Being Picked on, Man

Selective prosecution, also referred to as discriminatory enforcement of statute, is a concept involving directed unfairness of police or prosecution. The claim that a defendant was unjustly charged with crimes because he is Irish Catholic, black, or has his hair glitter-dyed—or simply because "the police just don't like me"—is not a claim of having suffered constitutional violation. Police discrimination is indeed rather imperceptible or abstract in nature. Because of these characteristics, it is difficult to prove that one has been singled out as a result of prejudice. In order to prevail with this defense, the defendant must show that other persons like himself have also been persecuted and that the wielding of power is aimed at people who are different either by race, religion, or gender, or by their use of free speech, which has offended those in command.

In May 1996, a decision based on this notion was decided in the Supreme Court, *United States v. Armstrong*.[59] The defendant, Christopher Lee Armstrong, was indicted for selling "crack" cocaine and other federal charges. Armstrong filed a pretrial motion for discovery or dismissal, claiming that he and his friends were selected for prosecution because they were black. The Court held that the defendants failed to produce any credible evidence that similarly situated defendants of other races could have been prosecuted but were not.

The prosecution showed that its reasons for prosecuting were that "there was [*sic*] over 100 grams of cocaine base involved, twice the threshold necessary for a ten-year mandatory minimum sentence; there were multiple sales involving multiple defendants, thereby indicating a fairly substantial crack cocaine ring; . . . there were multiple federal firearms violations . . . and several of the defendants had criminal histories including narcotics and firearms violations."

The Court agreed that a defendant did have a right to examine documents material to his defense, but it did not give him the right to work product—prosecution strategy—in his own case. Also, the defendant would have had to identify individuals who were not black and who could have been prosecuted for the same offense but were not. And, finally, a newspaper article, which the defendant claimed supported his case, was thrown out because it was based on hearsay and reported personal conclusions based on anecdotal evidence. So, although the defendant had managed to get as far as the Supreme Court, the case was reversed and remanded; in other words, it didn't work.

Nontraditional Defenses

As a writer, you should keep your eyes open for the innovative or novel defenses—they make for interesting, ahead-of-the-curve types of stories. The Battered Woman Syndrome served as an acquittal for many women before it was sanctioned as a viable form of self-defense. When a new defense leads to an acquittal, the appellate courts do not have a chance to intervene, nor do they have the opportunity to evaluate the decision, because an acquittal is the end of the process. In the list below are some of the nontraditional defenses that have been tried unsuccessfully.

• *Religious beliefs and practices.* Some of the issues in this category have circumscribed laws prohibiting religious rites that are dangerous; parents' rights to raise their children according to religious beliefs; failure to supply medical care to children; and certain marriage statutes.

• *Victim's negligence.* A victim's negligence does not negate a crime, and neither does wrongdoing on behalf of the victim; even a victim's forgiveness does not relieve someone of criminal wrongdoing. Your scrambling defendant may opt for this route, but his downfall will be a hard one.

• *Compulsive gambling.* Gambling is out of the realm of defense unless it involves insanity, and pathological behavior does not allow someone to rob a bank.

• *Post-traumatic stress syndrome (PTSS).* Stresses related to armed combat or other symptoms such as blackouts, blocked memory, or outbursts—commonly called "shell shock"—can be introduced to help explain the defendant's state of mind or difficulties adjusting to civilian life. Although these factors will not excuse a criminal act, they may help to mitigate punishment.

• *Premenstrual syndrome (PMS).* Although the changes a woman undergoes during the days close to the onset of menstruation do cause physiological changes, including depression, hormone imbalance, and irritability, they are not a defense of criminal conduct. In Great Britain, though, PMS has been used as a basis to lighten punishment.

• *Television intoxication.* Establishing insanity on the basis of psychiatric testimony with regard to a cycle called "involuntary subliminal television intoxication" is a difficult claim. The evidence must still meet the requirement of the M'Naghten Rule.

• *Pornographic intoxication.* There have been cases, along with academic debate, regarding the effect of pornography on the psyche. So far, it has not passed muster. An appellate court held that acting under "pornographic intoxication" does not permit one to use this excuse in order to mitigate the defendant's death sentence for rape and murder.

• *Junk food or sugar defense.* While the jury may have been affected in the case of Dan White, the former city supervisor who shot and killed the mayor of San Francisco and his aide, this testimony of sugar intoxication has not set a precedence for using the gorging on junk foods as a defense.

There have been cases argued on behalf of a defendant's propensity for violence because of black rage, multiple personalities, the urban survival syndrome, and a chromosome XYY abnormality. Since breaking-edge medical research has indicated that a person's behavior is influenced greatly by his genes, will this assertion be the next possible plea for excuse? Another possible justification is a recent behavior called "wilding." This urban slang terminology has come about after a pack of young men ran amok through Central Park stripping and groping at least four women. The attacks came at the end of a steamy weekend in New York, in which six people were killed and fifty-nine others were stabbed or shot. Will this phenomena be the latest in justification?

PART II: CRIMINAL PROCEDURE AND EVIDENCE

Chapter 7

Search and Seizure,
Then Arrest

A bill of rights is what the people are entitled to against every government on earth.
—THOMAS JEFFERSON, LETTER TO JAMES MADISON

Some information came to light that a man named Rochin was believed to be selling narcotics. Based on this tip, three deputy sheriffs forced open the door of his room. They found him, partially dressed, sitting on the side of the bed, next to where his wife was lying.

"On a 'night stand' beside the bed the deputies spied two capsules. No sooner had the question, 'Whose stuff is this?' come out than Rochin seized the capsules and put them in his mouth." A scuffle ensued, in the course of which the three officers "jumped upon him" and unsuccessfully attempted to extract the capsules from his mouth.

Rochin was then handcuffed and taken to a hospital. Under instructions from one of the officers, a doctor forced an emetic solution through a tube into Rochin's stomach against his will. This procedure is also called "stomach pumping," and the result induces vomiting. The maneuver worked on Rochin in the desired manner, and two capsules were found in the vomited matter. The capsules contained morphine. Rochin was convicted of possessing morphine and sentenced to sixty days' imprisonment. The chief evidence against him were the two capsules.

When officers broke into Rochin's residence, they violated Rochin's right to privacy and his right to feel secure in his home. Police cannot direct a pumping of a person's stomach without violating his personal right to privacy. There are limits placed upon the conduct of police officers and prosecutors. In this particular case, the police were skipping required steps and violating procedure.

The issues presented in Rochin's case[60] are all about "due process," the constitutional guarantee of fairness in the administration of justice. These protections, and certain other rights, are granted under the Bill of Rights and are widely debated every day of our lives and in many situations such as that illustrated above with Mr. Rochin. The police who raided Mr. Rochin's home believed they were doing what was needed in order to catch this criminal. Amendments IV, V, VI, and VIII in the Bill of Rights, along with provisions within the document of our Constitution, are directly aimed at rights individuals are supposed to receive when subject to a criminal investigation, trial, and sentence. The importance of the Bill of Rights is that it restricts governments rather than individuals and private groups.

By the way, what was the outcome for Mr. Rochin? The Supreme Court, under the opinion of Judge Frankfurter, concluded that the police conduct against Mr. Rochin violated the Fourteenth Amendment's due process. He said:

> This is conduct that shocks the conscience. Illegally breaking into the privacy of the petitioner, the struggle to open his mouth and remove what was there, the forcible extraction of his stomach's contents—this course of proceeding by agents of government to obtain evidence is bound to offend even hardened sensibilities. They are methods too close to the rack and the screw to permit of Constitutional differentiation.

Justice Douglas wrote a separate, concurring opinion on this case, comparing elements of it to the Fifth Amendment rule of self-incrimination. He maintained that the privilege against self-incrimination applied to the states as well as to the federal government, and because of this privilege "words taken from lips [of an accused], capsules taken from his stomach, blood taken from his veins are all inadmissible provided they are taken from him without consent. [This] is an unequivocal, definite and workable rule of evidence for state and federal courts."

Only the most confounding cases and fascinating real-life stories reach the Supreme Court. These are the kinds of cases whereby reasonable men in all good conscience can choose to disagree with their states' enforcement of the law. And for a writer, appellate cases can form the basis for an interesting story.

It's true that we live in times of violent crime; although the incidence of violent crimes like homicide, rape, robbery, and assault have gone down in general, more than 80 percent of Americans will experience some sort of violent crime in their own lifetime. According to national polls taken in the last decade, the number-one concern of Americans is crime. For writers, that makes the crime novel one that will always have a market.

Let's think like writers here for a moment. It's a given that we want to feel safe from crime, and, as a consequence, we give great authority to police in order to handle difficult situations. If you asked most Americans whether they would be willing to relinquish their Bill of Rights, you would hear a resounding "NO!" But what about our right to be left alone? What can be searched and seized, and when? This tug-of-war between the desire for security versus the respect for rights is an ongoing question because rights change, and rights change laws. And there are always political forces that seem to stress either favoring law and order or increasing individual rights. This is an area of exploitation for a writer—there are a lot of shades of gray between what we want and how it's attained.

The Constitution sets forth the basic guidelines for the ever-changing balance between the rights of the accused and the rights of society to feel protected. Almost half of the amendments in the Bill of Rights deal with personal rights and civil liberties. Similarly, one of the main principles of the justice system is that it is better for a thousand guilty men to go free than one innocent man to be punished. Since the late 1960s, some law-enforcement and government officials and citizen action groups think, rights have shifted dangerously to favor suspects. Our law system has always been based on the ideal of the presumption of innocence beyond reasonable doubt. But today, after the World Trade Center attack in New York City, where terrorists crashed two American passenger planes into the famous twin towers, rights are in question and the pendulum seems to be swinging again in favor of law enforcement. And now our rights to privacy are also in danger of being usurped. In your stories, look for those differences and create passionate characters to go along with the problems.

Mary Broderick, who is with the National Legal Aid and Defense Association, says that most people believe that the justice system favors the criminal too much. "In fact," she says, "the rights of the accused are a symptom of a society myth—that most persons arrested for a crime are convicted."

Broderick says that law-enforcement officials and judges often send the message that conviction is more important than justice. Society in general supports the idea that the same procedures ought to be followed for everyone who is accused of a crime, whether they are citizens of our country or not. And in connection with the Fourth Amendment, due process protects all persons within the United States—that includes adults, children, citizens, aliens both legal and illegal, persons on parole or probation, and corporations.

But we don't usually think twice about procedural rights, and we almost never realize how important they are until the accusing finger is pointed at us. A story character can believe these myths and face great emotional discord when he finds the system is different than he'd thought.

Writer's Jump-Start

Illustrate the dichotomy between a citizen's desire for security and society's long-standing desire to extend rights, because inevitably those rights will enable some people who are guilty to escape punishment.

As originally written, the Bill of Rights addressed injustice concerning national government only—until the Fourteenth Amendment was written: ". . . nor shall any State deprive any person of life, liberty, or property without due process of law; nor deny to any person within its jurisdiction the equal protection of the laws." Up until then, the individual states were not required to abide by those implied rights.

93

Each amendment was written to address an existing violation of citizens' rights by the British Empire, to prevent abuses by the governing authorities of the United States. The Fifth Amendment, due process of law, is a direct descendant of the Magna Carta, which predates the Constitution by some five hundred years.

The main rights of the accused are spelled out in the Fourth, Fifth, Sixth, and Eighth Amendments. In the Fourth Amendment, suspects are guaranteed rights against unreasonable search and seizure. This sprung up as a result of the abuse of "general warrants by the British Crown." The general warrants statute meant the British government could search anywhere, any time, and for any reason, "as long as the King lives."

The Fifth Amendment works in sync with the Fourth in protecting a suspect's rights. It guarantees that the accused cannot be held without evidence sufficient for trial; it stipulates the right of the accused to avoid self-incrimination and sets standards for the right to remain silent; it says that no one can be tried twice for the same crime and that no life, liberty, or property may be taken with due process of law. This was an enormous gain from what had been operative previously!

In the Sixth Amendment, the right to be represented by counsel and the right to a trial by one's own peers is paramount. It helped to guarantee that the poor would not be underrepresented and thereby made a victim of the courts.

The Eighth Amendment stipulates the right against excessive bail and cruel and unusual punishment with respect to detainment and sentencing.

Lives have been sacrificed to the upholding of these constitutional rights, and lives have been given over to these constitutional rights. The judiciary and interested citizens will debate the rights of the accused for as long as they exist. Because of these passions, you are entering a most engaging debate—where laws can affect a person's life completely, even to the point of death. I hope you will never have to exercise your rights or be on the receiving end of distress, but make sure that your characters do.

Amendment IV: Searches and Seizures

The right of the people to be secure in their persons, houses, papers, and effects, against unreasonable searches and seizures, shall not be violated, and no Warrants shall issue, but upon probable cause, supported by Oath or affirmation, and particularly describing the place to be searched, and the persons or things to be seized.

The word "warrant" in this context means justification and refers to a document issued by a judge or magistrate, which must indicate the name, address, and possible offenses committed by the suspect. In addition, anyone requesting the warrant, such as a police officer, must be able to convince the judge or magistrate that an offense most likely has been committed by this person (this is the basis for "probable cause").

The Fourth Amendment's basic principles are:
* No warrant will be granted without probable cause
* The warrant must describe the place to be searched and items to be seized, specifically
* No unreasonable search and seizure
* Constitutional arrest

Probable Cause

Police will have specific guidelines they must adhere to in order to meet their objective with a constitutional arrest. An arrest, with or without a warrant, needs to meet the requirement of probable cause. Probable cause, in layman's terms, means that the facts and circumstances the officer believes to be true at the time of arrest must be based on reasonably trustworthy information. The area of probable cause is fuzzy, because the probable cause rationale must be more than a "suspicion" but does not have to show proof beyond a reasonable doubt. Some of the criteria for probable cause include:
* Suspicious conduct
* Repetitious pattern of suspicious conduct
* Demonstrated unfamiliarity with the surroundings
* Subject's carrying tools or having difficulty with a vehicle, etc.
* Remarkable activity at an inappropriate time of day
* Activity in a high-crime area
* Known criminal record or profile
* Reaction to police officers
* Failing an encounter or giving demonstrably false responses
* Noncooperation with a request from a police officer
* Nervousness during an encounter with a police officer

- Collective knowledge
- Information from an informant

REASONABLE SUSPICION: The courts have struggled with the meaning of reasonable suspicion, and there are many cases to back up this effort. The nature of reasonable suspicion is certainly related to probable cause, and the analysis between the two has some similarities. Mainly, common sense is used to evaluate the factors of the case. The expertise of the law-enforcement officer is given preference. The circumstances are taken in their totality, so they cannot be so quickly explained away. And the reasonableness of mistakes of fact are taken into consideration, meaning that certainty is not required for either standard.

The difference between reasonable suspicion and probable cause is that reasonable suspicion as a standard is less demanding. Some courts define reasonable suspicion as a fair probability of criminal activity, or, in another way, it can be called *possible cause.*

95

The Affidavit

The next step in the process is to secure a warrant. A warrant for arrest is valid only if it is based on a "complaint" or a document called an affidavit that sets forth certain facts showing both the commission of an offense and the accuser's responsibility attached to it. The information, or the "basis of knowledge," used to secure the warrant need not be trial-ready, though. Information can be obtained from an established confidential informant; it can come from a victim of a crime related to the search; it can be based on a statement from a witness to the crime; or it can come from another police officer. In other words, it can be hearsay that seems reliable!

CONFIDENTIAL INFORMANT: When police officers do not have personal knowledge of the facts, they rely on information from other parties. Hearsay evidence is an "out of court" statement offered for the truth of the matter asserted. Since probable cause may be based on hearsay, confidential or anonymous informant sources other than other police officers—often referred to as "snitches" in the vernacular—are an effective investigative tool. This presents a unique problem: An affidavit based on an informant's tip must meet a two-pronged test, sometimes called the Aguilar-Spinelli test. It must establish the reliability of the informant by showing one of the following:
- "Prior use" and reliability of the informant, meaning the informant must have a good track record with the police, having given reliable information on numerous occasions
- A declaration against interest, meaning the informant describes activity against his own penal interest. For example, he might be willing to say "I bought dope from her," which shows he is criminally liable, too

- Clear and precise details in the tip, indicating personal observation and knowledge of the location of the evidence
- A membership of the informant in a reliable group, such as the clergy, school faculty, etc.

In addition, the affidavit must set forth sufficient underlying circumstances to permit a neutral and detached magistrate to understand how the informant reached his conclusion. This is known as the basis of knowledge, detailing such items as who, what, where, when, and why.

The Magistrate

The judge who issues the warrant must be neutral and detached from the law-enforcement officers and the situation presented. The judge cannot enforce the warrant; likewise, he cannot receive compensation when warrants are issued. The first thing that should pop into your mind: Is he neutral and detached?

Obtaining that warrant follows certain constitutional standards, too; a judge will sign it only if the probable cause is spelled out in writing. At least, that's the way it should be. Realistically, the potential for a problem always exists. A drawing of the warrant picture would look like this:

BASIS OF KNOWLEDGE
The first thing that has to be included in an affidavit:
who, what, when, where, and why.
▼
AFFIDAVIT
An affidavit based on an informant's tip must set forth sufficient
underlying circumstances in order to permit further investigation.
▼
JUDGE
"Probable cause" is required for a signature from a neutral and
detached magistrate, who has to understand how the informant
reached his conclusion.
▼
WARRANT
Describing the place to be searched; describing the things or persons to
be seized; Oath or affirmation that the statements in the request are true.
▼
EVIDENCE
▼
TRIAL COURT
▼
SENTENCING
▼
JAIL / PRISON

Warrant Loopholes

Some jurisdictions allow magistrates to issue search warrants over the phone. The police officer will sign the magistrate's name to the duplicate original warrant, and the magistrate signs the other duplicate original in his possession. On return of the officer's duplicate, the judge will sign it, too, and will file both with the court clerk. This is applied only to emergency situations where time is a critical factor.

Executing a Warrant

First of all, the power to execute a warrant doesn't rest with just anyone. In most states, the person must have a "peace officer" stamp of approval or some similar classification. We can call them the "PPP"—publicly paid police. They could be with the local police, the deputy sheriff, or a member of another investigative agency, and they will usually wear special uniforms and will always have law-enforcement identification.

Describing Characteristics in a Search Warrant

The affidavits submitted by police and ruled on by judges have been shaped by over two hundred years of constitutional experience. It is clear that law enforcement must identify objective suspicions in a living and not rely merely on a hunch (although hearsay is allowed if considered reliable). The information in the affidavit need not be cast in a form that would make it admissible at trial. However, in keeping with the Fourth Amendment, the particulars set forth in all documentation should demonstrate credibility.

PLACE: Even if there is probable cause to search a certain location, the warrant must describe the location with reasonable particularity—it should have a street address, an apartment number, and, for rural settings, a rural mailbox designation or requisite landmark.

THINGS TO BE SEIZED: In theft cases, warrants may contain detailed descriptions or specific brand names of property and goods. For documents evidence, records pertaining to fraud, including tax forms and accounting books, would suffice. And it has always been the case that instruments of crime, such as a gun used in a robbery, the fruits of a crime, such as money, or illegal narcotics where possession is prohibited by law, may be picked up as well.

Timeliness of a Search Warrant

Time is an important factor for a warrant! The best reason for executing a timely warrant is that probable cause may disappear. If the information that is the basis for probable cause is stale, the warrant will not issue. For example,

GARLAND COUNTY CIRCUIT/CHANCERY COURT

STATE OF ARKANSAS
VS

SEARCH
WARRANT

TO ANY SHERIFF, CONSTABLE, OR POLICE OFFICER IN THE STATE OF ARKANSAS.

AFFIDAVIT HAVING BEEN MADE BEFORE ME BY _____
_____ THAT HE HAS REASON TO BELIEVE THAT ON THE PROPERTY
OF _____
_____ DESCRIBED AS _____
_____
_____ WHICH IS LOCATED _____
_____
_____ THERE IS NOW BEING CONCEALED
CERTAIN PROPERTY NAMELY_____
_____ WHICH ARE IN VIOLATION OF _____
_____

I AM SATISFIED THAT THERE IS PROBABLE CAUSE TO BELIEVE THAT THE
PROPERTY SO DESCRIBED IS BEING CONCEALED ON THE PREMISES ABOVE AND
THAT THE FOREGOING GROUNDS FOR APPLICATION FOR ISSUANCE OF THE SEARCH
WARRANT EXIST.

YOU ARE HEREBY COMMANDED TO SEARCH FORTHWITH THE PLACE NAMED FOR THE
PROPERTY SPECIFIED, SERVING THIS WARRANT AND MAKING THE SEARCH DURING
THE _DAYTIME___NIGHT___ AND IF THE PROPERTY BE FOUND THERE TO SEIZE
IT, LEAVING A COPY OF THIS WARRANT AND A RECEIPT FOR THE PROPERTY
TAKEN, AND PREPARE A WRITTEN INVENTORY OF THE PROPERTY SEIZED AND
RETURN THIS WARRANT AND BEING THE PROPERTY AS REQUIRED BY LAW.

THIS SEARCH WARRANT SHALL BE RETURNED TO THE _____ COURT
OF HOT SPRINGS, GARLAND COUNTY ON OR BEFORE THE HOUR OF _____
(AM) (PM) ON THE _____ DAY OF _____, 19_____.

DATED THIS _____ DAY OF _____, 19_____ .

_____
JUDGE

RETURN

I RECEIVED THE ATTACHED SEARCH WARRANT_____,
19_____, AND HAVE EXECUTED IT AS FOLLOWS;

ON _____, 19_____, AT _____ O'CLOCK, _____ M, I
SEARCHED THE __PERSON PREMISES__ DESCRIBED IN THE WARRANT AND I LEFT A
COPY OF THE WARRANT WITH_____

(NAME OF PERSON SEARCHED OR OWNER OR AT THE PLACE OF SEARCH)

TOGETHER WITH A RECEIPT FOR THE ITEMS SEIZED.

THE FOLLOWING IS AN INVENTORY OF PROPERTY TAKEN PURSUANT TO THE
WARRANT:

_____
_____
_____
_____
_____
_____
_____
_____
_____

THIS INVENTORY WAS MADE IN THE PRESENCE OF _____
ANI _____.

I SWEAR THAT THIS INVENTORY IS A TRUE AND DETAILED ACCOUNT OF ALL THE
PROPERTY TAKEN BY ME ON THE WARRANT.

_____
OFFICER

SUBSCRIBED AND SWORN TO AND RETURNED BEFORE ME THIS_____ DAY
OF _____, 19_____.

_____
JUDGE

99

```
                      SHERIFF'S RETURN AND FEES

     STATE OF ARKANSAS      )
                            )
     COUNTY OF _____   )

          I have this _____ day of _____ , 2000, duly
     served the within by arresting the said _____
                                             _____
     and personally handing him a copy of the Information.


                              Service.......$_____
                              Mileage.......$_____
                              Return........$_____
     ATN_____            Total......$_____


                         _____ , Sheriff

                         By:_____ , D.S.


          Return Filed, this ____ day of _____ , 2000.


                         _____ , Clerk

                         By:_____ , D.C.
```

100

during ongoing criminal activity—say, a drug lab operation—a lapse of ten to thirty days is acceptable, if the police believe that the evidence will still be in a particular place. Information older than that will be dismissed. A warrant is allowable if the probable cause is anticipatory, such as waiting for a shipment of stolen goods. And a search warrant can be issued for a future date as long as probable cause exists.

Ten days is about the most a jurisdiction allows for the execution of a search warrant. After a statutory time limit (or the time limit set by the judge) has passed, the warrant is dead; and evidence seized on a dead warrant can be suppressed in court.

Nighttime Searches

The time of day a search warrant can be executed is also a consideration. Slightly less than half the states restrict execution of searches to "daylight" hours absent special circumstances. Most jurisdictions go with 6:00 a.m. to 10:00 p.m. as daylight, and anything after that needs a showing of qualifying factors.

Executing a search warrant in the absence of the occupant has been done, and the lower courts generally agree to let it pass, but judges also make it relevant to consider whether police made an attempt to locate the occupants or not. And, covert and surreptitious entries are constitutionally defective. In ruling on *United States v. Freitas*[61]—allowing secret entry to investigate a drug-lab operation, without any postsearch notice to the occupants—the Supreme Court has said that "the mere thought of strangers walking through and examining the center of our privacy interest, our home, arouses our passion for freedom as does nothing else."

Home Search Warrant

We all have an expectation of privacy within our own homes, the most protected area, and the courts respect that. There is also an expectation of privacy for papers inside our briefcases, inside our homes. For this reason, a warrant is required for home searches and must meet certain criteria, specificity of interest being the main objective for a search. A search warrant can be used to search premises belonging to a person not suspected of a crime as long as there is "probable cause to believe that evidence of someone's guilt will be found." (The key is always "probable cause.")

Knock and Announce Rule

Under federal law, an officer is required to knock and announce on arrival at the place to be searched.[62] The purpose of this requirement is to reduce the potential for violence and to protect the right to privacy of the occupants. Exceptions to this rule are cases of true emergencies and situations in which announcing one's presence would endanger the lives of the officers.

For entry, the officer should wait a reasonable amount of time (which can be mere seconds), anticipating a response. There is also the rationale that, if after giving notice, he is refused admittance or must extricate himself from danger, he may break into premises to execute a search warrant. The notice requirement is also excused if the officers believe the occupants already know they are there, or they hear the sound of "running feet," meaning that stating his authority and the purpose of the visit is a useless gesture.

If a police officer makes a search under a warrant that shouldn't have been issued in the first place, in most situations the search will be valid. In *United States v. Leon*,[63] the U.S. Supreme Court ruled that if the police conduct a search in good faith reliance on the warrant, the search passes, and the evidence is admissible, even if the warrant was invalid through no fault of the police. The court's reasoning was that the purpose of the rule was to curb the police, not a judge, and if a judge makes a mistake, it should not be grounds to exclude evidence.

And an entry by ruse does not constitute a "breaking" that requires prior notice. In other words, if the police officer senses that using his knock and announce stipulation will place him in danger, he may choose instead to pretend he is a deliveryman or even a narcotics customer if the situation involves substance abuse and sales. There is also something called a "no-knock warrant" if there is probable cause to believe there is evidence to be destroyed or a situation that could be harmful to police. In such instances, the court will issue a warrant waiving the "knock" requirement.

The actual execution of the warrant means the police are supposed to present or serve a copy of the warrant to the homeowner or leave a copy with whoever is in control of the property, seize the items listed, and, on return, present the warrant to the issuing magistrate.

Scope and Intensity of the Search Warrant

102

The discretion of a police officer's actions following a warrant is limited by the constitutional prerequisite of specification relating both to location and to the items to be seized. By the same token, the scope and duration of a search relate directly to the neutral magistrate's prior judgment of probable cause, thus limiting the officers' freedom to decide what should be done throughout the search.

PREMISES DESCRIBED: In setting the legal boundaries of a search and in defining the premises of an address, you may come upon a term called "curtilage." "Curtilage" is an old-fashioned French word that means "the area attached to a house and forming one enclosure with it," so we are talking about searching not only the house but also the grounds associated with it. Courts have usually stipulated that this includes backyards, courtyards, and associated buildings on farms and ranches, including one's car or vehicles. But the reverse is not true. If a search warrant grants authority to search a vehicle, that authority will not include entry into any private buildings within the scope of that document.

PERSONAL EFFECTS: A valid search warrant does not have to include specific descriptions of rooms, cabinets, or furniture. In general, a warrant authorizing the search of a premises justifies a search of the occupant's personal effects, especially if they represent plausible places for safekeeping the objects specified in the warrant. For example, if a warrant specifies stolen jewelry, it is not out of the realm of possibility that the item may be found in a coat pocket.

SEARCH THE PERSON, PLUS . . . A warrant can justify the search of a person either exclusively or jointly with the search of a particular location. And when the authorities are searching an individual, this also includes property carried by the suspect, such as a purse or any recognizable personal effect. Now, searching other persons not listed on the warrant, such as visiting friends or someone else on the scene, is not acceptable without probable cause—unless the officer can pinpoint with reasonable suspicion that the onlooker is also engaged in criminal activity. If the police have "probable cause" to arrest a person discovered on the premises to be searched, they may search that person incident to the arrest.

FRUITS OF THE DEED: When executing a warrant, the police generally may seize contraband or any fruits or instrumentality *of a crime* that they discover, whether specified in the warrant or not. A search continued beyond the limitations of the warrant may contain evidence that is excluded and likewise inadmissible in a court of law. If police learn of the location of a weapon through interviewing a suspect who is in custody, that weapon is considered "derivative evidence." If police did not administer the Miranda warning, however, the suspect's responses and any weapon discovered are tainted.

103

LIMITS OF SEARCH IN REGARD TO LENGTH AND DAMAGE: A warrant to search for evidence founded on probable cause implicitly carries with it the limited authority to detain occupants of the premises while a proper search is conducted. The court has a permit for police officers to receive assistance from private citizens if it will allow for a more quick and efficient search. For example, telephone company employees may help to locate certain electronic devices used in surreptitious wire communications. Officers may remain on the premises as long as is reasonably necessary to complete the search—sometimes for hours. If causing damage is reasonably necessary to the search—such as digging a hole where fresh dirt is laid or opening a wall newly patched in order to find evidence within the scope of the warrant— it is justified. However, officers must refrain from tearing up a place and using the warrant as an excuse for destruction. For any wanton destruction that is not defensible, they may be liable for civil damages.

WIRETAPPING: ANOTHER FORM OF SEARCH AND SEIZURE: Electronic eavesdropping, also called wiretapping, is considered to be a search under the Fourth Amendment. In order to get a valid warrant authorizing a wiretap, you must have the following:
1.   A showing of probable cause to believe that a specific crime has been or is being committed
2.   The defendant whose conversations are being overheard must be named
3.   The warrant must describe the nature of the conversation that is to be overheard
4.   The wiretap must be limited to a short period of time
5.   Officers must make provisions to terminate the wiretap when the desired information has been obtained

A return must be made to the court showing what conversations have been intercepted. The surveillance is usually allowed for a thirty-day period.[64]

Emergency Searches

What are the circumstances required for police entering a person's home without a warrant? Who bears the burden of proof of demonstrating emergency circumstances? And what exactly is an emergency?

Last things first.

An emergency situation, or exigent circumstance, provides an exception to the warrant requirement, meaning a police officer can enter a person's home to arrest him without a warrant. Some emergency situations are:

1. Hot pursuit of a fleeing criminal
2. Vanishing evidence
3. Children in trouble
4. Property involving fire
5. Risks to police or public safety

104

HOT PURSUIT: If police officers are chasing down a suspect, it is unrealistic to expect them to get an arrest warrant. Some type of harm may occur, and allowing the suspect to get away would render the warrant meaningless anyway. The "hot pursuit" exception is based on the fact that the suspect knows he is being pursued and will try to either escape or destroy evidence.

VANISHING EVIDENCE: Vanishing evidence is a frequently invoked justification for a warrantless search and seizure and is also called evanescent evidence. Say a police officer checks on an injured motorist and discovers illegal drugs, or maybe an officer rushes into a house where the owner has alerted someone to flush drugs down the toilet. The best example for vanishing evidence can be found in *United States v. Riley*.[65] Police officers had a suspected drug house under surveillance. They observed someone leaving the house with a white bag and followed. This person, Terry Moore, drove to a hotel and made an exchange. Police arrested Moore and found a bag containing cocaine. Moore then informed the officers that a large sum of money, a gun, and another person were at the house. While detailing this evidence, police noticed Moore had a cellular phone. They immediately dispatched nine officers to the house for a bust sans warrant. The entry was justified on the grounds that the evidence could have been quickly and easily destroyed. Evidence that is likely to disappear before a warrant can be obtained could also mean a blood sample containing alcohol or any product that could convey an "urgent need."

The government bears the burden of proof of demonstrating exigent circumstances, and police officers must have an arrest warrant in order to enter a person's home or arrest him absent emergency circumstances or consent. However, the "scope of the search" they use may be limited by the scope of the consent. In fact, there are situations and various rules about expectations of privacy and consent that are worth knowing.

Some emergency circumstances exist in these hypothetical situations. For example:

CHILDREN IN TROUBLE: Officers can intervene if a child is screaming in danger or if they hear shooting from an apartment and they have reason to believe that a child is in imminent danger. Under such circumstances, officers may enter the premises without a warrant.

PROPERTY INVOLVING FIRE: When a building is on fire, firefighters may enter without a warrant in the name of public safety.[66] Former Chief Justice Burger (once as a judge) concluded in *Wayne v. United States*[67] that "the need to protect or preserve life or avoid serious injury is justification for what would be otherwise illegal absent an exigency or emergency."

105

RISKS TO POLICE OR PUBLIC SAFETY: Even in the absence of hot pursuit, there may be controlling factors in which the police or the public would be harmed in the time it takes to obtain a warrant. If so, the police are excused from obtaining one. For example, if officers think there is a threat to public safety, and the risk is substantial—a sniper, a bomb, a shooting spree perpetrated by a disgruntled former employee—they will be excused from the warrant requirement.

Other Warrantless Searches of the Home

A warrantless search is considered constitutional if the prosecution can show by a preponderance of evidence[68] that it was made in accordance with an exception, such as exigent circumstances (these have been discussed above), consent to search, or plain view.

CONSENT DOCTRINE: No warrant is necessary when a consent to search is voluntarily offered, but the consent must come from a competent individual who either owns or possesses authority over the premises to be searched or items inspected. Knowledge of the right to withhold consent is not necessary to establish a voluntary, intelligent consent. The scope of the search may be limited by the scope of the consent. Likewise, the consent may be revoked or withdrawn at any time, and the search must cease. So, if a homeowner gets nervous or antsy about the search, he may change his mind at any time.

The person consenting to a property search must have standing, and a person has standing if he owns or possesses the place searched or if the place searched is his home, whether or not he owns the land. So, for example, an employer cannot give consent to search an employee's desk, and some state courts do not allow parents to give consent to allow police to search a child's diary or a locked storage box in the child's own personal room. High school searches? Yes, the principal is allowed to offer up consent for school lockers, usually in connection with published school rules or when in a violation of law. But in college, students' consent is usually required for authorities to be able search their own dorm rooms and locked possessions without a warrant.

The following is a story of "third-party consent" to searches, *Illinois v. Rodriguez*.[69] Someone suspected of committing a crime may not want to allow police entry to his home for various reasons and will demand a warrant for search; but what if the consent was given by someone other than the accused?

On July 26, 1985, police were summoned to the residence of Dorothy Jackson on South Wolcott in Chicago. Gail Fischer, Ms. Jackson's daughter, met them. She showed signs of a severe beating. Fischer told the officers she had been assaulted by Edward Rodriguez earlier that day in an apartment on South California. "Rodriguez is asleep," she told the officers, and then consented to go there with police to unlock the door with her key so they could arrest him. The police noted that Fischer referred to the place as "our" apartment and admitted she had clothes and furniture there. It was unclear whether she lived there currently or had lived there in the past.

Accompanied by Fischer, police drove to South California. They did not obtain an arrest warrant for Rodriguez or seek a search warrant for the apartment. Once they had arrived, Fischer unlocked the door for police and gave permission for them to enter.

In the living room, they observed in "plain view" drug paraphernalia and containers filled with white powder, which they assumed was cocaine just lying about. In the bedroom, Rodriguez was asleep; some of the same containers of powder were nearby in open attaché cases. Officers arrested him and seized the drugs and related goods. He was charged with possession of a controlled substance with intent to deliver. Rodriguez's lawyer moved to suppress all evidence seized, claiming that Fischer had vacated the apartment several weeks earlier and had no authority to consent to entry.[70]

The Cook County Circuit Court granted the motion. They believed that, at the time, Fischer did not have common authority over the apartment. She was an "infrequent visitor"—her name was not on the lease, and she did not contribute to the rent, was not allowed to invite others in, and did not have access when the respondent was away. The circuit court also rejected the state's contention that even if Fischer did not have common authority over the premises, there was no Fourth Amendment violation if the police reasonably believed at the time that Fischer did have standing.

What do you think? The outcome is below.

The Supreme Court reversed the judgment of the Illinois Appellate Court and remanded it back for further proceedings. Their opinion was based on the theory that "Because many situations which confront officers in the course of executing their duties are more or less ambiguous, room must be allowed for some mistakes on their part. But the mistakes must be those of reasonable men, acting on facts leading sensibly to their conclusions of probability." They said, further, that the Constitution is no more violated when officers enter without a warrant because they reasonably (though erroneously) believe that the person who has consented to their entry is a resident of the premises, than it is violated when they enter without a warrant because they reasonably (though erroneously) believe they are in pursuit of a violent felon who is about to escape.

MORE ABOUT PLAIN VIEW: If an officer has the legitimate right to be in a particular location, any evidence he sees is up for grabs. In order for such evidence to be accepted, its discoverers have to inadvertently (or accidentally) come upon evidence of a crime. The evidence must be in "plain view."

107

SEARCH INCIDENT TO ARREST: There is another commonly invoked exception the police use during seizure that eliminates the need for a search warrant requirement, and it involves searches "incident to arrest." Here, the search occurs at the same time and in the same place the police arrest a suspect. If the arrest is lawful—that is, based on probable cause—the courts have said it is not unreasonable for the police to search a suspect.

In *United States v. Robinson*,[71] the Court held that the police may automatically search any person subjected to a custodial arrest, regardless of the nature or severity of the crime. There is no requirement that they actually must fear for their safety or even believe that they will find evidence of a crime. This concept fostered ideas loosely referred to as the "bright-line rules": The search is based on a need to avoid the endless fine distinctions required of police about making on-the-spot determinations. The theory is that each individual case has unique facts in frequently occurring situations and that knowledge must be considered, relative to the minor intrusions to a person's privacy and the safety of the officer. It also means that a suspect's personal effects are transportable—can be carried off to the jail with him. These objects include his automobile if he is in or near it and, possibly, objects collected from the area of arrest—even an area as large as an entire home or area of business.

Searches in the Public Realm

A person does not have a reasonable expectation of privacy in objects held out to the public, such as:

1. The sound of a person's voice
2. Paint on the outside of a car
3. Account records held by a bank

These are obviously things put out into the universe without restraint. Officers can also use drug-sniffing dogs to ferret out evidence in "public areas." An overheard conversation is also subject to use as evidence, as are points of evidence found, within reason, through the use of flashlights, binoculars, and sound amplifies.

AUTOMOBILE SEARCH: What about someone traveling in a car, and what are his privacy issues within? Are police allowed to search a person's car willy-nilly? Why? And under what circumstances? The regulations regarding automobile searches change according to different circumstances, on grounds quite different from the general consent notion and those other issues that have to do with home privacy concerns.

A police officer who stops a car for a traffic infraction can ask the driver and any passengers to exit the car as a safety precaution. He can also make a cursory check for weapons if he reasonably suspects any one of the passengers may be engaged in criminal activity. However, stopping a car to issue a traffic citation does not allow a full-scale search of either the car or its occupants.

In order to conduct a search, police still must have probable cause to believe that the car contains evidence of a crime. And because it is rare that the danger of a car or something in the trunk of a car could be used as a weapon against police, the rationale of police safety alone does not justify a police officer's search of the trunk. Still, the statistics bear out that most car searches pass constitutional muster, but for a different reason. Why? Because automobiles are mobile.

There has to be an exigency created by mobility. It must be likely that the vehicle will be unavailable by the time a warrant can be obtained. Police know and understand that if they don't look in your trunk now, there is a good chance that whatever was in the trunk will be gone by the time they secure a warrant.

There are distinct stipulations about where they can look. They cannot tear out the seats or open up the glove compartment; they can only search a person's "wing span" worth of reach—far enough for a suspect to be able to stash something under the seat.

But your driver isn't off the hook yet. The police searching his car may have enough probable cause to impound the car. The search of a vehicle under this exception does not have to occur at the time of the stop—they can have it towed to the police department and search it on their own good time. There, they may make a warrantless seizure of property found during a routine inventory of an impounded vehicle. Remember, however, that in a nonemergency situation probable cause is a requirement even for impounding a vehicle and conducting an inventory of its contents.

A DIFFERENT KIND OF SEARCH: MAIL, ENTRAPMENT, AND INDUCEMENT: In 1987, after a jury trial, a small town Nebraska school bus driver was found guilty of violating a provision of the Child Protection Act of 1984 by committing the crime of receiving child pornography through the mail. A few years later, in *Jacobson v. United States*,[72] a ruling came down from the Supreme Court reversing the decision that the sixty-one-year-old Keith Jacobson, a round-faced, gray-haired farmer and bus driver who had lawfully ordered a nudist magazine, was guilty.

The veteran-turned-farmer-turned-bus-driver, who supported his elderly father in Nebraska, had ordered two magazines and a brochure from a California adult bookstore. The magazines he ordered, *Bare Boys I* and *Bare Boys II*, contained photographs of nude preteen and teenaged boys. The contents of the magazines surprised Jacobson, who later testified that he had expected to receive photographs of "young men 18 years or older." But since the young men depicted in the magazines were not engaged in sexual activity, Jacobson's receipt of the magazines was legal under both federal and Nebraska law. Within three months of his charge, though, the law with respect to child pornography changed. Congress passed the Child Protection Act, making it illegal to receive sexually explicit pictures of children through the mail. Jacobson was then the target of twenty-six months of mailings from government sting operators. Postal inspection teams masqueraded as organizations dedicated to sexual freedom.

Finally, after considerable government planning, Jacobson yielded to the temptations of a postal sting called "Project Looking Glass" and ordered a magazine titled *Boys Who Love Boys*. Entrapment is the inducement and, as in this case, it is the active encouragement by law-enforcement officials of an individual to commit a crime not contemplated by the individual, undertaken for the sole purpose of instituting a criminal prosecution against that person. Justice Byron R. White wrote the decision for the majority court, overturning Jacobson's original conviction by saying, "When the government's quest for convictions lead to the apprehension of an otherwise law-abiding citizen who, if left to his own devices, likely would never run afoul of the law, the courts should intervene."

Jacobson's arrest drove him into seclusion for months and cost him his job of driving children to and from school. He wound up serving a two-year probation and completed some 250 hours of community service. Afterward, Jacobson said: "I feel happy, grateful, and humble. It's a victory for all Americans. It means you have a right to be let alone if you're minding your own business and not involved in some kind of criminal enterprise."

Justice Sandra Day O'Connor protested the Jacobson decision and produced a dissenting opinion. Her concern was that the court had introduced "a new requirement" that, she believed, could hamper later drug, bribery, and pornography stings. Government agents often mimic criminal behavior to induce criminals to show their true colors. O'Connor felt that this decision might put a damper on any helpful government sting operations in the future, simply by causing sting officials to worry about creating a predisposition in the suspect.

109

As a practical matter, undercover police work often generates opportunities for crime, and the methodology has become increasingly commonplace. In law enforcement's effort to control drug trafficking, for example, inducement is a significant component in their procedure, demonstrated by the fact that it is the subject matter of many of the Supreme Court cases. "Sting" operations are also employed in investigations involving burglars and corrupt public officials. In the case of burglaries, for example, criminals are often identified as a result of their selling stolen goods to police-operated "fencing" fronts. And, concerning the latter, corrupt public officials are the subjects of elaborate purported bribery attempts, and the results have been documented in some famous cases of abuse of the public trust. An example of this would be an operation called "Abscam," where, in February 1980, an FBI agent posed as an Arab sheik and offered

110   bribes to certain congressmen in exchange for political favors.

In *State v. Sainz*,[73] the New Mexico Court of Appeals adopted this formulation of the entrapment defense:

> When the state's participation in the criminal enterprise reaches the
> point where it can be said that except for the conduct of the state a
> crime would probably not have been committed or because the con-
> duct is such that it is likely to induce those to commit a crime who
> would normally avoid crime, or, if the conduct is such that if
> allowed to continue would shake the public's confidence in the fair
> and honorable administration of justice, this then becomes entrap-
> ment as a matter of law.

The chasm between keeping and preserving a person's rights and wanting to preserve security through enforcement has many shades of gray, where nothing is ever clearly black or white. But when cases such as these, involving surveillance and entrapment, come before the courts, it gets harder and harder to tell who is the criminal and who are the police.

EXCEPTIONS TO THE WARRANT REQUIREMENT ON SEIZING CONVERSATIONS: The Fourth Amendment protects only "legitimate" interests—in other words, if the person has undertaken an illegal activity, there is no legitimate privacy interest. However, since it is not possible to know in advance of the search that a suspect's activity is illegal, certain interests must be presumed and protected before the intrusion takes place. Officers are not allowed to enter a suspect's home and tamper with his telephone simply because they wish to hear his conversations. However, the police are free to use as evidence the testimony of those who have spoken with the suspect on the phone, and any conversations that have taken place in the public realm are up for grabs as well.

Law-enforcement officials often use an "unreliable ear." If an informer has a conversation with the suspect and reports such evidence to the police, the suspect has no basis under the Fourth Amendment to object to the retelling of the conversation as a warrantless search. You assume the risk that whomever you tell things may tattle.

Secondly, there is the "uninvited ear." A speaker has no Fourth Amendment claim if he makes no attempt to keep the conversation private— for example, if he makes calls on a public telephone, all of his words can be used against him in a court of law.

AIRPORT SEARCHES: As you approach the concourse, you see a posted sign that warns: ALL BAGS ARE SUBJECT TO SEARCH. This announcement places passengers on notice that ordinary Fourth Amendment protections do not apply here. Because of increased concerns over airplane hijacking and terrorism, increased security at airports—such as walking through the metal detector, the x-raying of baggage, or the inspection of carry-on items—will become the norm. These are valid administrative guidelines as established by the Federal Aviation Administration, and there is little question that these searches are reasonable.

The Fourth Amendment and the Internet

Because of advances in the communications industry, Congress and our courts continue to consider the suitable parameters of governmental conduct in cyberspace. If law enforcement fails to respect online privacy in its investigative techniques, the public's confidence in government will diminish, evidence will be suppressed, and criminals will elude prosecution. On the other hand, if law enforcement is too timid, cyberspace will become a safe haven for criminals and terrorists to communicate and carry out crime without fear of authorized government surveillance. Certain individuals and groups are using this technology to commit crimes such as threats, extortion, fraud, identity theft, child pornography, and, more importantly, threats to government infrastructure.

The Electronic Communications Privacy Act[74] established a three-tier system by which government officials can obtain stored information from electronic service providers:
1. A search warrant is necessary for the retrieval of unopened communications, such as e-mail
2. A court order is necessary for the examination of transactional records
3. A subpoena is necessary for the search of subscriber information

Cybercriminals often cloak their illegal activity by weaving communications through a series of anonymous remailers, thus creating forged e-mail headers with powerful point-and-click tools readily downloadable from hacker Web sites. Some use "free trial" accounts for limited periods of time, eventually "wiping clean" the logging records that would otherwise provide evidence of their activity.

One emerging concern is the growing problem of online harassment or threats amounting to cyberstalking. One California woman was awakened repeatedly through the night by men knocking on her door, offering to "rape" her. A rejected suitor had posted personal advertisements on the Internet, pretending to be her. The ads contained her home address and telephone number and claimed that she fantasized about being raped.

Currently, the foundation of the cybercrime prosecution program is the Criminal Division's Computer Crime and Intellectual Property Section, known as the CCIPS. CCIPS was founded in 1991 as the Computer Crime Unit and became a section in 1996.

During the past few years, the number of search warrant requests for citizens' online data has gone up 800 percent. The searches typically involve cases ranging from harassment and child pornography to violent crime and fraud. The aim is to discover the identity and tracking activities of subscribers.

Congressional leaders informed of the increase have said they will examine legal standards and develop questions for police. Some of the information Congress will require is when, why, and how police perform electronic searches.

While critics and privacy experts fear abuse of electronic surveillance, the FBI's Thomas Gregory Motta says there is little reason for concern.

The Exclusionary Rule and the Ms. Mapp Landmark Case

On May 20, 1957, someone set off a bomb that demolished the front porch and wall of Don King's house. Three days after the bombing, three Cleveland men drove to a two-family home run by Dollree Mapp. Acting on a phone tip, the three plainclothesmen went to Mapp's, thinking that a suspect connected to the bombing, Virgil Ogiltree, would be there; his car was parked outside. Because Ogiltree never came out, officers became inpatient and knocked on the door to make inquiries. Ms. Mapp answered but denied them entrance, stating that she would not allow them to search without a warrant, nor would she open the door without first calling her lawyer. The men kept the house under surveillance and radioed another officer to obtain a warrant.

Later, a half-dozen uniformed men came back and claimed they had a warrant. Mapp again refused to open the door. They entered the residence by breaking out a pane of glass, unlatching the door, and charging up to Mapp's second-floor apartment. She met them on the landing. "Where's the warrant?" she demanded. Sergeant Delau, one of the officers, held up a piece of paper. Mapp grabbed the paper and stuffed it under her turtleneck. The officers proceeded to cuff her and snatched back the paper from inside her sweater. While searching the residence, officers confiscated some obscene materials—pencil sketches of nude models, and four books—and artifacts for betting equipment. Dollree Mapp was arrested and charged with possession of gambling equipment and obscene materials. The later offense was listed as a felony under a newly amended state statute on pornography. Story has it that by the time Mapp was brought to trial in September 1958, the "search warrant" she had tried so hard to keep had disappeared. (Twenty years later, the arresting officer, Sergeant Delau, would admit that contradictory to his trial testimony, his lieutenant had only obtained an affidavit, a document spelling out the reasons for wanting a warrant.)

Mapp was found guilty on the obscenity charge and sentenced to one to seven years in the Ohio State Reformatory for Women. She appealed, and the Supreme Court of Ohio upheld the conviction. Eventually, in 1961, the U.S. Supreme Court consented to hear her appeal on the issue that the Fourth Amendment's guarantee of the right of people to be secure in their houses, papers, and effects, against unreasonable searches, seizures, and warrants, was in question. In this instance, the police had conducted an illegal search and seizure. Not only had they violated Ms. Mapp's privacy, but the search warrant was issued for a bombing suspect and not for the things they collected. This was really one of the first applications of the Exclusionary Rule, a policy forbidding the use of illegally obtained evidence.

But the story does not end here, and the pendulum keeps moving. In 1984, a bill was passed to modify the *Mapp v. Ohio* ruling. Now it limits the exclusion of evidence under certain circumstances, such as instances in which the evidence was gotten through a reasonable, "good faith" belief on the part of police that their obtaining of the evidence has conformed with the Fourth Amendment. Of course, each state gets to craft its own definitions of what constitutes an "illegal" search and seizure. And, later again, the Supreme Court had another chance to modify an exception to the Exclusionary Rule. In the same year, 1984, they decided on an "inevitable discovery" exception. This means that any evidence discovered in violation of a defendant's rights can be used in a trial if the prosecution can establish that the evidence would have been found in the course of a lawful search.

The rules involving search and seizure are constantly being tested, although, contrary to popular belief, the number of criminals freed by the Exclusionary Rule has been small—less than 1 percent of federal cases have not been pressed due to inadmissible evidence.

EXCLUSIONARY RULE EXCEPTIONS: The Exclusionary Rule is enforced with a "Suppression of Evidence Hearing," in which the judge determines whether it is necessary to suppress the evidence. The exceptions to the Exclusionary Rule are laid out as follows:
1. It does not apply to live witnesses (they can still be compelled to testify)
2. It does not apply to grand juries (they do not determine guilt or innocence—just probable cause)
3. It does not apply to civil proceedings

4. It does not apply when cops act in "good faith"
5. It does not apply to evidence obtained by a private individual (unless the individual is working on behalf of the cops)
6. Excluded evidence can still be used for impeachment (proving a lie)

Stop and Frisk

A Cleveland plainclothes detective, Officer McFadden, observed several men who were standing on a street corner in the downtown area at about 2:30 in the afternoon. He became suspicious of their behavior. One of the suspects walked up Huron Road, peered into a store, walked on, and then started back, looking into the store again and then conferring with his companion. The other suspect followed the same procedure and went through this process some twelve times, as if they were "casing" the store prior to a robbery. They also talked with a third man, and then followed him up the street about ten minutes after his departure. McFadden thought the men might be armed; he followed, too, and confronted the men as they were talking. He identified himself and asked for the suspects' names. The men responded by mumbling something, and the officer spun a man named Terry around and patted his breast pocket. He felt a pistol, which he then removed. A "frisk" of Terry's companion revealed another weapon, but the third man was unarmed, and he was not searched any further.

Terry was charged with possessing a concealed weapon, and he moved to have the weapon suppressed as evidence. The motion was denied by a trial judge, the Ohio court of appeals confirmed it, and the state supreme court dismissed Terry's appeal.

This case eventually wound up in front of the Supreme Court of the United States, and the result is known as a landmark decision. The Supreme Court ruled in *Terry v. Ohio*[75] that in circumstances where dangerous situations are unfolding on city streets, the police need to have an escalating set of flexible responses, graduating in response to the amount of information they possess. The judges agreed that a distinction should be made between a "stop" and an "arrest" and between a "frisk" and a "search," and that police should be allowed to "stop" a person and detain him briefly for questioning on suspicion that he may be connected to a criminal activity. Then, if the policeman is again suspicious that the person may be armed, he should be able to conduct a protective "frisk" for weapons only if he reasonably believes that the person is presently dangerous. The scope of the frisk is generally limited to a pat down of the outer clothing for a concealed weapon. If the stop-and-frisk leads to "probable cause" that the suspect may have committed a crime, the police officer should be empowered further to make a formal arrest that allows for a full search. The judges felt that these further definitive rules to procedure were justified, because the officer's actions amounted to a "minor inconvenience and petty indignity" imposed on a citizen in the interest of effective law enforcement.

Information from the Arkansas Law Enforcement Training Academy has a chart that spells out the difference:

	STOP	ARREST
Justification	Reasonable suspicion	Probable cause
Search	Possibly a "pat down"	Complete body search
Record	Minimal	Fingerprints, photographs, and booking
Intent of Officer	To resolve ambiguous situation	To make a formal charge

115

An Encounter

The courts felt that a distinction needed to be made between an encounter and a stop. If an officer cannot form reasonable suspicion for illegal activity, he cannot stop a citizen, because a stop would be a seizure, which requires justification. But an encounter is a way to engage a citizen and is irrelevant under the Fourth Amendment. Would a person ever feel like he would be free to leave if he were approached by an officer to answer questions? Since the court wanted to develop a system so that officers could conduct a preliminary inquiry without the stigma of a stop, they came up with the Mendenhall Test.

MENDENHALL TEST: These factors help to delineate whether the officer has employed tactics satisfactory enough to constitute a stop:
• *Physical obstruction of movement.* If officers block a suspect's forward movement, their behavior serves as a good indication that it is a stop
• *Show of force.* Drawn guns or any other form of menacing behavior is a convincing indication that a stop has occurred
• *Keeping identification or travel documents.* An officer can approach a person and politely request identification or an airline ticket in an encounter. The person is free to reject that request. If the person honors that request, the officer is not permitted, absent reasonable suspicion, to retain the ID or ticket in order to prolong the inquiry
• *Coercive orders or threatening tones.* Any threat of detention or accusation of criminal activity signals a stop
• *Brevity.* Even polite questioning must be brief; anything in length poses reasonable suspicion
• *Polite requests to consent to search or moving the questioning.* Like brevity,

if a request to search luggage in an airport goes beyond cursory, the consensual encounter takes on coercive factors. Likewise, if an officer politely questions a citizen and then asks for a longer conversation, that is fine, but the minute the conversation is moved to an investigative office, the situation is considered a stop

• *The right to terminate an encounter or refuse consent.* An officer is not obligated to tell a citizen that he has a right to refuse conversation or consent to search, or both

• *Coercive surroundings.* Close encounters on a bus or questioning in a cramped space is not coercive per se; it's when the questioning occurs in an area not visible to the public that the officer's behavior may constitute a stop

Constitutional Arrest

It's the Fourth Amendment that provides the principles for a constitutional arrest. Placing a person under arrest establishes a seizure of the body, obviously because authorities are actually taking away the person's freedom to leave the scene. Defense attorneys will admit there is a big variance as to how suspects are treated, what their rights are, and what is required of them, depending on whether they are under "arrest" or not. Michael Saeger, author of the book *Defend Yourself Against Criminal Charges* says the easiest way for a person to know if he's being detained is to inquire: "Am I under arrest?" He suggests that, as much as a suspect would like to believe that he is not under arrest, until he actually knows, there is no way to determine if he can come and go and no way to decide if he must abide by the instructions given.

Describing Characteristics of an Arrest Warrant

Ordinarily, police officers are required to obtain arrest warrants only when they plan to enter a suspect's dwelling in a nonemergency situation to make an arrest. A warrant for arrest is typically routine, though, when based on an indictment by a grand jury—or when an information is filed by a prosecutor, and a *capias* (Latin for "that you take") requires that some named person be taken into custody. In cases of this kind, a suspect is often not aware that he's under investigation, and law enforcement have more than enough time to obtain an arrest warrant without fear that the suspect will flee. A *bench warrant* is then issued by a court, directing the arrest of the defendant. An arrest warrant usually contains the name of the county and state, the details of the offense, the defendant's name; it commands his arrest, names the place where he is to be brought, is dated with the day and year, and is signed by a magistrate, who includes his full title and authority.

116

FYI—Situations in Which the Police Will Question You

1.   Am I legally obligated to answer a policeman's questions? Basically, no. Your silence is not a crime, and you cannot be arrested for failure to respond.

2.   Why? Because the Fifth Amendment guarantees a "right to silence." (That doesn't mean that police will not try to intimidate you, either—they will!)

3.   If I start to answer, may I then stop the questioning and walk away? Yes. Unless a police officer has "probable cause" to make an arrest, or a "reasonable suspicion" that your conduct is criminal, you may leave. Now, if the officer has information that gives him a legal basis to conduct a "stop and frisk," he can detain you. The best thing to do is ask: "Am I under arrest?"

4.   If pulled over by an officer for a traffic offense, can I be arrested if I don't supply identification? Yes, traffic infractions are generally given "citations"—tickets that specify a court appearance or fine. But if you cannot supply personal information in connection with a traffic stop, be prepared to cooperate.

5.   If stopped for drunk driving, must I answer questions? No. But the officer has the right to put you through a sobriety field test, and an arrest may ensue if you fail.

6.   Do I get Miranda rights before questions? No. A Miranda warning advises people of their right not to answer questions and is only required if someone is in custody and the police want to use the statements later, in court.

7.   Can I be harmed by answering? It's possible. Sometimes, people who have done nothing are still subject to being accused—plus, they may unwittingly disclose information implicating themselves.

8.   If I give false information about a friend, am I in trouble? Yes. When an individual lies to police, he may be charged with "accessory after the fact" (see chapter 2), as an accomplice if he is more closely involved, and, in the case of knowing about a felony beforehand, he could be charged with conspiracy.

9.   Can I talk my way out of a crime? I wouldn't suggest it. Self-incrimination is protected under the Fifth Amendment.

Arrest Without a Warrant

Perhaps you remember an instance on a television show or in a movie, where an arrest was made without a warrant. Yes, that happens, but it is fraught with danger for both the arrestee and the arresting officer. Sometimes states' investigators, and even the FBI, will bring along a local uniformed officer to facilitate arrest. One reason for this is that the officer has to have enough power to "restrain the suspect." As citizens and writers, we need to know and understand that law enforcement will have the willingness to use a billy club, a chemical or electric device, a gun, or some other instrument as aid. But a police officer is also restrained against using too much force, and the amount of force opens up a whole host of risky consequences. But, for now, you recognize the pattern of requirement involved in getting an affidavit and a warrant, and you see that police have certain defined limitations.

FELONY ARREST: Under common law, an arrest made without a warrant must meet certain criteria. If the publicly paid police have reasonable grounds to believe that a felony has been committed, and if they have a particular person in mind, a felony arrest is possible. Also, a misdemeanor committed in the presence of law-enforcement personnel is another reason for valid arrest.

In this case involving a public situation, *United States v. Watson*,[76] a reliable informant named Khoury told a postal inspector that he had supplied a man named Watson with a stolen credit card and had agreed to turn over additional cards at their next meeting, which was scheduled for a restaurant location a few days later. As decided ahead of time, Khoury signaled the inspector when Watson had the cards, at which point the postal inspector arrested Watson without a warrant as he was authorized to do under postal regulations.

The court of appeals held the arrest unconstitutional because the inspector had failed to secure a warrant even though he had admitted having had the time to do so. This error in judgment had bearing on the court's additional ruling that Watson's consent to a search of his car was not voluntary.

Eventually, the Supreme Court reversed the earlier decision made in Watson's case on the grounds that each case should be considered under historical guidelines—that to permit felony arrests only with a warrant or in exigent circumstances could severely hamper effective law-enforcement's capabilities.

Four years later, in *Adams v. Williams*,[77] the Court said: "The Fourth Amendment does not require a policeman who lacks the precise level of information necessary for probable cause to arrest to simply shrug his shoulders and allow a crime to occur or a criminal to escape. On the contrary, *Terry v. Ohio* recognizes that it may be the essence of good police work to adopt an intermediate response. . . . A brief stop of a suspicious individual, in order to determine his identity or to maintain the status quo momentarily, while obtaining more information, may be the most reasonable in light of the facts known to the officer at the time." Indeed, stopping citizens in the course of an investigation is a practice that can be traced back to thirteenth-century England.

One other important right to note about arrest protocol is that if someone is arrested without a warrant, he must receive a "probable cause hearing" within forty-eight hours. Otherwise, his detainment would have no limitations and could feasibly produce dire consequences for the accused, his business, and his family. Without this safeguarding of rights, the enormous power and resources of the state dwarf what the individual accused of a crime can bring to bear. To compensate for this and to ensure a degree of fairness, the playing field has to be tilted somewhat in favor of the accused.

TRAFFIC ARREST: A Texas woman named Gail Atwater faced a new Supreme Court ruling with trepidation. Divided on the issue, the court ruled 5–4 that police can arrest and handcuff people for minor traffic offenses. The authority, they say, proceeds naturally from the right to pull someone over.

Ms. Atwater was stopped by police officer Bart Turek. In front of her small children, Atwater was cuffed and then briefly jailed for failing to wear a seatbelt. Atwater claims that she unfastened herself and her passengers only briefly, to aid them in looking for a distraught four-year-old's lost toy. A police officer saw it differently, claiming she endangered her children and ordering her to jail.

Soon after, Atwater's children were picked up by a friend, while she was taken to the police station. Police took her mug shot, and she was placed in a cell alone, until she posted $310 bail. She later pled no contest and paid the $50 fine. Atwater and her husband decided to file a suit against the city, claiming the arrest had violated her constitutional rights. The Supreme Court negated the need for trial, the case was never carried out, and *Atwater v. Lago Vista*, 99–1408, stands as a valid arrest.

"The question is whether the Fourth Amendment forbids a warrantless arrest for a minor criminal offense, such as a misdemeanor seatbelt violation punishable by only a fine. We hold that it does not," Justice David H. Souter wrote for the court majority. Justice Sandra Day O'Conner took the minority view and said that the ruling "cloaks the pointless indignity that Gail Atwater suffered with the mantle of reasonableness."

HELD FOR QUESTIONING: If circumstances are insufficient to arrest an individual on a criminal charge, there is no power (without consent or special statute) to lock a person in jail for questioning or for investigation, except that a judge or magistrate may be authorized to consign, in a criminal case, a material witness who otherwise refuses to make an effort to appear and testify in court after having been directed to do so.

While our system of justice makes allowances for resisting self-incrimination, there is no immunity that allows a mere witness to refuse to give information relative to the guilt of someone else, unless there is some special protection in the particular case, as there is for the person who is the husband or wife of the accused. Historically, witnesses have always been subject to punishment for failure to give officers—outside the courtroom—any firsthand felony information.

CITIZEN'S ARREST: A store security guard can arrest a shoplifter, the owner of a car can arrest a punk trying to break into her car, and in "extraordinary cases," a police officer can conscript a private citizen into aiding the capture of a suspect.

Many writers will be using a citizen or a private detective to make arrests. It is legal for an ordinary citizen to make an arrest, but there are problems:

There is limited protection for private citizens who make mistakes during an arrest. Most states will recognize a private arrest if:
• The citizen has observed the commission of a crime
• The person arrested actually committed a felony
• A felony was committed, and the private citizen has probable cause to believe the arrested person did it

If a private citizen arrests an innocent person, that private citizen is civilly liable—the charge most likely would be false imprisonment. Now, if your private citizen character uses deadly force, courts will usually be hostile toward that type of service. If mistakes are made here, your citizen may be sued both civilly and criminally.

120

UNUSUAL IN-HOME ARREST SITUATIONS:
• *Doorway arrests.* The courts have waffled on whether, when a defendant answers a door, he is arrested in the home or in public. Some courts have said that if the officer remains outside the doorway and informs the defendant that he is under arrest, the arrest is public—or incident to arrest—and no warrant is needed. However, if the arrest is made after entry, then there is a Payton violation, and the information discovered thereafter is illegally obtained. Best to check your individual state's rulings.
• *Common hallways.* Anyone standing in a common hallway is fair game for a public arrest.
• *Hotels and motels.* As long as the person has a rightful possession of the room, a warrant is needed. The minute the rental period has expired however, the turf designation is *nada*.
• *Homeless persons.* Originally, the courts claimed that a homeless person's claim of violation of warrantless arrest was nonexistent. Increasingly, however, the courts have been sympathetic to the privacy interests of homeless persons and have begun to hold flexible ideas as to what constitutes a home, even if it is within a public area.

FYI

Homeowners arrested outside the house are wise to not ask to go back in to get clothes or feed the dog. Police officers are allowed to make a "protective sweep" of the area following an arrest. This means they can make a "cursory visual inspection" of places where an accomplice might be hiding. If a sweep is lawful, any contraband or evidence of a crime in plain view is okay to take.

Chapter 8

Rights Of the Accused

*The public good is in nothing more essentially interested than in
the protection of every individual's private rights.*
—WILLIAM BLACKSTONE, *COMMENTARIES*

The law of criminal procedure is a unique and uncertain balancing act. It is
best described as a set of conflicting rules the government must follow in order
to maintain law and order, while at the same time protecting the rights of its
individual citizens. This "uncertainty" of procedure is due to the nature of
periods in United States history where the political emphasis shifts. What the
law says is illegal today may not be the same as what the law says was illegal
yesterday. And the future is also up for revision.

Amendment V: Grand Juries, Self-incrimination, Double Jeopardy, Due Process, and Eminent Domain

No person shall be held to answer for a capital, or otherwise infamous crime, unless on a presentment or indictment of a Grand Jury,
except in cases arising in the land or naval forces, or in the Militia,
when in actual service in time of War or public danger; nor shall
any person be subject for the same offence to be twice put in jeopardy of life or limb; nor shall be compelled in any criminal case to
be a witness against himself, nor be deprived of life, liberty, or property, without due process of law; nor shall private property be taken
for public use, without just compensation.

There are two types of juries. A *grand jury* looks at physical evidence and listens to the testimony of witnesses and then decides whether there is sufficient
reason to bring a case to trial. A *petit jury* hears the case at trial and makes a
decision about it. "To be twice put in jeopardy" means a person cannot be
tried two times for the same crime and cannot be forced to give evidence or

testimony against himself. Plus, no person's right to life, liberty, or property may be taken away except by following lawful means, called "the due process of law." Private property taken for use in public purposes must be paid for by the government.

Grand Jury

Grand juries are made up of individuals randomly selected for jury duty. (In my community, they come from the registered voter database.) They are charged with the duty of indictment, meaning they decide from the evidence provided whether the person or persons should be charged with a crime. All proceedings for grand juries are held in secret. Their term of service can be as long as a term of court, which can run from six to eighteen months. There are between fifteen and twenty-three people called for service to a grand jury, and a federal grand jury unit has sixteen to twenty-three people. And while petit juries must have unanimity to convict, grand juries need not be unanimous to indict; federal grand juries require only twelve or more to agree to indict.

The grand jury system and due-process rights (I'll discuss these later) generally are recognized as two of the great "checks"—of the "checks and balances" principle—charged with protecting private citizens from the dangers of an overzealous prosecutor. In the case *United States v. Dionisio*,[78] the Supreme Court proclaimed that the purpose of the grand jury is to stand between government agents and the suspect as an unbiased evaluator of evidence. Thus, in theory, the grand jury should protect suspects from indictments based on unsubstantiated information presented to it by the prosecutor.

Over the years, a build-up of constitutional restraints has been placed on traditional crime investigation agencies. As a consequence, there has been an increase in the popularity for using investigative grand juries. In grand jury proceedings, the suspect of the investigation is not afforded the normal due process rights that a criminal suspect receives at the station house. For example, in a federal grand jury proceeding, a witness must *step outside* the courtroom in order to speak with counsel.

Investigative grand juries have the aid of subpoena power. This ability gives the grand jury the right to require the possessions of the accused to be brought forward. These, then, may be obtained without probable cause, which is a necessary staple for police, who have to use the search-warrant system.

Writer's Tip

There are great possibilities for conflict with the federal grand jury system. I am surprised that more writers do not take advantage of the inequities built into the system, to write about it. The insults to "due process" fairly scream out for exposure. Believed to act as a buffer between the accused and an overzealous prosecutor, the grand jury system really cancels out the constitutional rights of the accused to due process, an open and public trial, and the opportunity to face his accusers; the right against self-incrimination; the right to counsel and cross-examination; and the lack of advisement rights so inherent in police interrogation.

Rights of Persons: Interrogations and Confessions

At one time or another, we've all heard an actor playing a witness tell the judge, "I take the Fifth, Your Honor." What is he asking for? How can someone take the Fifth? Among the many provisions in the Fifth Amendment is the right of protection against self-incrimination. In other words: No person "shall be compelled in any criminal case to be a witness against himself." Since an American trial by its nature is supposed to operate under an adversary system, it implies that the state must prove the guilt of the accused, not just assume guilt. "Innocent until proven guilty" are the watchwords of the American system. Self-incrimination has been expanded by interpretation, however, to protect not only a defendant, but also a witness, in all manner of questioning before a court, grand jury, or coroner's inquest, and in investigations by legislative body or administrative official.

123

This concept is most important when it comes to interrogation. Under the protection of the Fifth, basically, it means that no person can be abused or tortured in order to give up a confession. In the cases of *Escobedo v. Illinois* and *Miranda v. Arizona*, the Court added that to secure the validity of confessions, suspects must be notified of their rights against self-incrimination and have a right to counsel. Because of this, certain hurdles must be removed before any self-incriminating statements can be introduced as evidence:
• The state must demonstrate that the confession was not coerced; defendants' statements should not violate the voluntariness requirement of the due process clause of the Fifth and Fourteenth Amendments
• Incriminating statements may not be admitted if the accused did not have his right to counsel or if the statement was made without Miranda warnings
• The state has to be prepared to show that the defendant knowingly and intelligently waived his rights

WHAT IS AN INTERROGATION?: Commonly thought of as questioning at the station house after arrest, interrogation can occur anywhere. The Supreme Court has defined interrogation as "express questioning or its functional equivalent," including "any words or actions on the part of the police that the police should know are [reasonably] likely to elicit an incriminating response from the suspect."[79]

A judge must determine whether the information demanded might incriminate a witness in the future. He uses the system that if the testimony provides a link in a chain of evidence that might be used to show that a witness himself had committed a crime, it is incriminating.[80]

RIGHTS AGAINST SELF-INCRIMINATION: THE MIRANDA WARNING Remember, this only applies if the person being questioned is in *custody!* We're all familiar with these warnings as read by some of our favorite characters on televised police and law-based programs. But who was Miranda? What did he do? And why do these words mean so much to law-enforcement personnel and, in turn, to those accused of a crime? Entire volumes have been written about the specifics of this case. It unfolds here:

Lois Ann Jameson (not her real name) was on her way home from work at the Paramount Theater in downtown Phoenix, Arizona, when things went wrong. She stepped off the bus a few minutes after midnight, heading toward home, when a car suddenly pulled out of a driveway and blocked her path. The driver dragged her into his car, tied her hands and ankles, and warned her not to move. In an outlying desert area she was made to disrobe, was raped and robbed of four dollars. Later, she was allowed to get dressed and return to the neighborhood where she had been abducted. Phoenix Metro Police were called into the case, and on March 4, 1963, Detective Carroll Cooley began his investigation. Evidence, gathered through the police's vigilant observation of Ms. Jameson's habits, soon led law enforcement to the home of Twila Hoffman, who lived in the nearby suburb of Mesa. They discovered that Hoffman lived with a man named Ernest Miranda, who roughly fit the description of Jameson's assailant.

Checking his work record, they found that he was absent from his job at United Produce on the night of the crime. Further checking uncovered Miranda's rather lengthy criminal record.

Cooley and Wilfred Young went to Twila Hoffman's residence and asked Miranda to accompany them downtown to the police station, to discuss a case they were investigating. At police headquarters, Miranda participated in a line-up and was identified by Lois Ann Jameson. Detectives informed Miranda that he had been identified, and began questioning him in greater detail. Later, the detectives would tell the courts that "neither threats nor promises had been made" to Miranda, who had just admitted that he had raped Jameson and then confessed to a second robbery.

The entire interrogation took a little more than two hours. Officers had used his testimony against him, and it had become self-incriminating, and he wound up signing a confession. There was no evidence of police brutality and really nothing out of the ordinary.

Ernest Miranda's charges were for kidnapping and rape, and he was tried and sentenced to two concurrent (running simultaneously rather than one after the other) terms, twenty to thirty years on each charge, to be served at the Arizona State Prison. It is hard to believe that, less than three years later, Ernest Miranda would be responsible for a landmark Supreme Court decision. And the Miranda warning would create a series of repercussions that would change the standard of police procedure from that time forward. The Fifth

Amendment guarantee resolved in the *Miranda v. Arizona* [81] case provides that a suspect has a right to remain silent; and that he is entitled to an attorney before questioning.

Now, all who are brought into custody are told the following:

You have a right to remain silent.

Anything you say can and will be used against you in a court of law.

You have the right to talk to a lawyer and have him present with you while you are being questioned.

If you cannot afford to hire a lawyer, one will be appointed to represent you before any questioning, if you wish one.

You can decide at any time to exercise these rights and not answer any questions or make any statements.

After the warning and in order to secure a waiver, the following questions should be asked and an affirmative reply secured to each question:

Do you understand each of these rights I have explained to you?

Having these rights in mind, do you wish to talk to us now?

A person can waive his Miranda rights, but the prosecutor must prove that the waiver was knowing, voluntary, and intelligent. The proof is generally to have the accused sign a form.

CONFESSIONS: A confession is an either oral or written statement by a person, which tends to prove the commission of a crime and is self-incriminating. If it's not self-incriminating, it's not a confession.

A truly involuntary confession is not admissible for any purpose. The Miranda warning and a valid waiver are prerequisites to the admissibility to any statement made by an accused during custodial interrogation. An interrogation will be considered "custodial" if the individual is not free to leave.

A confession that has been obtained in violation of a defendant's Miranda rights, but that is otherwise voluntary, may be used to impeach the defendant's testimony if he takes the stand at trial. Even so, it is not admissible in the prosecutor's case to prove guilt.

The Miranda requirements do not apply to a witness testifying before a grand jury, even if the witness is under compulsion of a subpoena.

ERRONEOUS COMMENTS: Miranda does not apply to spontaneous talk not made in response to interrogation. However, cops must give the warnings before they can follow up. An interrogation is not only limited to questioning but also to actions by cops designed to elicit incriminating statements. The question of psychological coercion is looked at in a case-by-case approach.

PRIOR WARNINGS: Miranda requires that all suspects be informed of their rights without considering any prior awareness of those rights; for example, every time you pick someone up, you need to read him his rights. Note that date and time are critical on signed documents.

EXERCISING THE SILENT TREATMENT: The accused has the right to terminate the interrogation. If the accused indicates in any manner, at any time prior to or during questioning, that he wants to remain silent, the interrogation must stop. Likewise, when the accused requests counsel, all questions must stop until he gets a lawyer or initiates further communication.

FIRST CHALLENGES TO MIRANDA: Not long after the development of this new procedure, police officials complained that Miranda rulings placed the rights of criminal suspects over the rights of society. In response, the Court's new philosophy was that law enforcement would be made more reliable if founded on independently obtained evidence rather than on confessions secured under coercive interrogation and without benefit of counsel— this would be the new test for justice. But in 1968, in an attempt to rebalance the rights again, several exceptions to the Miranda ruling transpired. The Omnibus Crime Control and Safe Streets Act provided that in federal cases, a voluntary confession could be used as evidence even if the accused person was not informed of his rights. As a result, even in cases not tried in federal courts, confessions have been allowed in evidence under certain circumstances, such as when public safety requires action.

In the 1980s, there was a slight shift toward restricting a person's rights again. In *New York v. Quarles*,[82] the question was whether a policeman could ask a suspect for his gun before he received his Miranda rights. The court upheld that the procedure for securing the gun was all right, because police were applying a "concern for public safety" in a public place over the rights of the accused. This was a much-needed "first-things-first" issue for protecting police security, many said, and it was extremely important in the minds of law-enforcement officers who were facing new and increasing dangers.

GETTING AWAY WITH MURDER: As a blanket assumption, the theory that criminals are "getting off" because the police didn't read them their rights is incorrect. It is more likely that statements or confessions violating Miranda will be inadmissible as evidence in a trial. It doesn't necessarily mean that the charges against a suspect will be dropped, certainly not if the prosecutor and his investigators have other evidence they can use against the accused. But, still, there are always exceptions. The following is a case that illustrates another result.

Police were investigating a series of purse-snatch robberies in California. One of the victims died from the injuries inflicted on her by her assailant, Roy Allen Stewart. Stewart was caught after he endorsed one of the dividend checks taken in one of the robberies; bank authorities had alerted police of his activity right away. At about quarter past seven on the evening on January 31, 1963, police officers went to Stewart's home and arrested him. On arrival, one of the officers asked Stewart if they could search the house and Stewart replied, "Go ahead." The search turned up various items taken from the five robbery victims.

At the time of Stewart's arrest, police also arrested Stewart's wife and three other persons who were visiting. The four were taken to the jail, along with Stewart, and questioned. Then Stewart was taken to the University Station of the Los Angeles Police Department, where he was placed in a cell. During the next five days, police interrogated Stewart on nine different occasions. On one occasion, Stewart was confronted by an accusing witness; during the other sessions, he was isolated with his interrogators.

Sometime during the ninth interrogation, Stewart broke down and admitted that he had robbed the deceased but had not meant to hurt her. Police then brought Stewart before a magistrate for the first time. The other four people arrested with Stewart were released for lack of involvement.

Nothing in the record indicated that Stewart had been advised of his right to remain silent or of his right to counsel. In follow-up, the interrogating officers were asked to recount their conversations, and no one mentioned that Stewart had been advised of his rights.

In court,[83] the jury found Stewart guilty of robbery and first-degree murder and fixed his penalty as death. On appeal, though, the Supreme Court of California reversed the decision on the basis that Stewart should have been advised of his right to remain silent and his right to counsel. The court said it could not presume, in the face of a silent record, that the police had done the required advisement. The Supreme Court affirmed the decision, clarifying its decision further by saying that "nor can a knowing and intelligent waiver of these rights be assumed on a silent record. Furthermore, Stewart's steadfast denial of the alleged offenses through eight of the nine interrogations over a period of five days is subject to no other construction than that he was compelled by persistent interrogation to forgo his Fifth Amendment privilege."

A RECENT MIRANDA CHALLENGE: Miranda received a new challenge in April 2000. The case was the result of a bank robbery in Alexandria, Virginia, in 1997, in which the alleged driver of the getaway vehicle, Charles Dickerson, made a self-incriminating remark before being told of his Miranda rights. The case focused on whether Congress reversed Miranda with a law from 1968 that allowed voluntary confessions to be used at trial, even when defendants have not been read their rights. The law had never before been enforced, but it was thrust from obscurity with Dickerson. In a 7–2 decision, judges gave a resounding rejection of an unprecedented challenge to the opinion. Chief Justice Rehnquist declared that the Miranda warning is rooted in the Constitution and as such is irreversible by Congress.

127

Double Jeopardy

Since most people have deeply rooted ideas about justice, certain cases and their outcomes seem to inflame their sensibilities. When a person has clearly been framed and is still convicted, we cry out for the right to appeal. And when guilt is as evident as the blood on the black leather glove, we gasp in horror as the defendant walks away from the courtroom a free man.

These are the ideas that law students debate ad nauseam. The movie *Double Jeopardy* explores this controversial idea. In the movie, a woman and her husband are sailing overnight on a new boat they bought. The woman wakes up to find blood everywhere, and her husband is gone. She finds a bloodstained knife and picks it up. In a nutshell, she is later tried and convicted for her husband's murder, for which she spends ten years in prison. Desperate and afraid, she asks her best friend to take care of her six year-old son, who is now the recipient of his father's $2 million life insurance policy.

Later, her friend disappears, and when the woman finally finds this "so-called" friend and talks to her son on the telephone, the husband—who was supposedly murdered—walks in. While on the phone, the little boy says, "Hi, Daddy!" This alerts his mother to the setup between her friend and her husband to get the life insurance money and run away together.

While she is incarcerated, another inmate, a disbarred lawyer, tells her that when she gets out, she can walk right up to the husband, who is already declared legally "dead," shoot him in the face, and nobody can touch her. The rationale behind this is that she has already been tried and convicted and will have served her time for his murder. The question is: Would it be double jeopardy to try, convict, and sentence her again?

DOUBLE JEOPARDY FOR REAL: Another characteristic of the important Fifth Amendment is a clause that says no person shall "be subject for the same offense to be twice put in jeopardy of life or limb." This is our constitutional prohibition against double jeopardy. Basically, it means that if the defendant is found "not guilty" at trial or is placed in jeopardy for a significant portion of the trial, he cannot be tried again for the same offense even if overwhelming evidence comes in later that proves his guilt.

But, as with every other law, there are exceptions here, too. The first exception to the rule is when, with the defendant's consent, the first trial ends in a mistrial. He can be tried again for the same offense in the same courtroom. If a mistrial happens to be declared without his consent, it can be moved forward for "the ends of public justice."

FILING A MOTION: Defendants can only be subjected to another trial if they "file a motion" to move for a new trial. They must typically do so very soon after the jury reaches a verdict. In federal court, new trial motions must be made within seven days and based on newly discovered evidence.

128

Such evidence might be newly procured if a witness for the defendant was out of the country, or fled for some reason during the first trial, or if new DNA testing became available. A request for a new trial by a defendant is considered a "waiver" of double jeopardy rights, and the defendant must abide by the new ruling.

A defendant can be tried for the same offense twice if the first case was dismissed, either at trial or during trial, but before conviction. If the trial was already begun, the dismissal must be based on a reason other than the defendant's guilt or innocence.

Another way to get a second trial is in consideration of either a hung jury (the jurors cannot agree), or when the death or illness of judge, juror, or defendant stalls the trial.

DOUBLE JEOPARDY TIMING: You do know that "double jeopardy" cannot be claimed as long as the "statute of limitations" (period of time following a crime within which a case can be filed) has not run out and there is no one charged. There is no statute of limitations on a homicide (although a "solved" case can be "cleared" or "closed").

Also, defendants are not considered to be in jeopardy until the actual trial begins. Jeopardy attaches once a jury is sworn in or when the first witness is sworn in to testify in a nonjury trial.

As soon as a judge or jury finds a defendant "not guilty" of all charges, the prosecution cannot appeal, nor can the prosecution ask the judge to set aside the verdict and order a new trial. So, in essence, even if the judge and half the world know the decision is wrong—hello, O. J. Simpson—a "not guilty" verdict is final.

If a defendant was convicted and appeals his case to a higher court, he has "waived his claim to double jeopardy" simply by initiating the appeals process. The higher court may, as you know, reverse the conviction based on an error made in the first trial. A new trial will be sanctioned—"The Court remands or returns the case to the court of original jurisdiction for a new trial." This time around, the verdict will be final. But there are always exceptions to the rules, and rules for the exceptions. In the case of appeals, there is one additional consideration: The new trial must be for the "same offense" and not for a greater offense nor a greater degree of offense. For example, a class B felony cannot become a class A felony, namely because each "class" or classification carries with it different extremes of punishment.

UNSATISFIED WITH THE MOVIE?: It is a done deal for Ashley Judd's character in *Double Jeopardy*, but a good friend of mine tells me a prosecutor in a federal court would probably try to get her on another charge if she really killed her husband after her prison term; and, remember, there is nothing that says she can't be sued in a civil court, which is another trial procedure with a different basis of proof—the results of this new civil trial would be remuneration or some other type of restitution.

Of course, if no one knew about the killing, or if they didn't care (such as with a sympathetic detective), or if they didn't file charges (lack of evidence) for the actual death, she is free.

The Due Process, 1960s

The due process revolution of the Supreme Court in the 1960s epitomized the social tensions of the period. A series of constitutional judgments were made that included such procedural issues as a defendant's right to an attorney, the right to exclude evidence seized illegally by the police, the right to a jury trial, and the protection against coerced confessions.

Not only does Miranda speak to the issue of coerced confessions, but it brought to the forefront critical right to counsel issues once again. A basic, fundamental liberty in the American criminal justice system is the right to be represented by counsel—an important notion, because more than 90 percent of all citizens accused of a crime in this country cannot afford to retain counsel. As stated in the Sixth Amendment of the Bill of Rights, which I'll discuss at length later in this chapter, in all criminal prosecutions the accused shall enjoy the right to have assistance of counsel for his defense.

GIDEON V. WAINWRIGHT[84]: Just before dawn on June 3, 1961, a Panama City, Florida, police officer was making his rounds. He noticed that the front door of the Bay Harbor Poolroom was slightly open. Upon investigation, he discovered that the rear window of the building had been shattered, and a cigarette machine and a jukebox had apparently been robbed.

A local bystander informed the policeman that he had seen a man in the poolroom earlier, a man named Clarence Gideon. On the basis of this information, Gideon was arrested and charged with breaking and entering with intent to commit a misdemeanor, which is a felony under Florida law.

Gideon had been convicted and served time for a variety of previous offenses, including burglary and possession of government property. He had escaped from prison, was captured, and served a full term, only to repeat another burglary in a different state. Paul B. Wice says in his book *Gideon v. Wainwright*, "On the surface, Gideon appeared to be a typical repeat-offender, a lawbreaker who started his lawbreaking early in life and continued to have trouble conforming to society's rules. On closer examination, however, Gideon, though handicapped by poor health and a forbidding criminal record, was attempting by the early 1950s to provide for his economically distraught family."

In any event, after the above Florida incident, Judge McCrary listened to the defendant's request for counsel—Gideon argued he was destitute and could not afford to pay a lawyer. The judge denied his application. Under Florida law and the current federal constitutional precedent at the time, the court was required to appoint counsel to represent a defendant charged with a capital offense only, a crime which held the potential for the death penalty.

Unable to muster the forces needed for defense, Gideon was sentenced to the maximum penalty, five years' imprisonment. Still without counsel, Gideon proceeded to teach himself the law and made appeals on his own behalf. Gideon's handwritten appeal, written in pencil on notebook paper, eventually caught the attention of the Supreme Court. Gideon found out from the other inmates that counsel was actually not denied in some instances, but there was no consistency about when it was granted.

This time, Gideon did have counsel when his petition was heard during the 1962–63 Supreme Court term. A successful Washington lawyer, Abe Fortas, was appointed for the case. In its decision, the Supreme Court stated that "reason and reflection require us to recognize that in our adversary system, the accused cannot be assured a fair trial unless counsel is provided for him." The court overturned his conviction. Through his efforts, the Gideon decision extended right to counsel to all state indigent defendants—people who could not afford to hire counsel—facing felony trials, and helped to regulate the right to counsel by defining the question of when it should be practiced. This motion served to bolster the adversarial system, which formed the very basis of the United States' system of justice. It was believed that two advocates battling before an impartial judge and jury would produce facts, and that the resulting verdict would be fairly determined.

Over the years, various rulings pertaining to this principle of counsel have come down. The dramatic outcome for today is that if a defendant was entitled to a lawyer by law, the failure to provide him with counsel is an automatic reversal of the conviction, even without showing any specific unfairness in the proceeding. At nontrial proceedings, though, a defendant must show that he was actually harmed as a result of his denial of counsel.

CIRCUMSTANCES IN WHICH THE ACCUSED DOES NOT HAVE A RIGHT TO A GOVERNMENT-APPOINTED LAWYER:

- Discretionary appeal
- Blood sampling
- Handwriting sample
- Photo identification
- Precharge investigative lineup
- During a parole or probation revocation proceeding
- At a postconviction proceeding where he is served a "writ of *habeas corpus*"—meaning, the person is to be brought forth to court to determine if detention is lawful

CIRCUMSTANCES IN WHICH THE ACCUSED HAS A RIGHT TO GOVERNMENT-APPOINTED COUNSEL: The accused must be granted the right to government-appointed counsel if he is indigent and is in any of the following situations:

• Custodial police interrogation (in custody, held by publicly paid police, in a question-and-answer session)
• Postindictment interrogation: Whether custodial or not, charges have been filed, and cops cannot interrogate without a lawyer present
• Preliminary hearings to determine probable cause—before that hearing can be held, the state must provide a lawyer
• At an arraignment, guilty plea or no
• Postcharge lineup; the lawyer cannot stop the lineup, so his main function is to make sure it's done properly
• Pleading guilty or facing sentencing
• During all felony trials (either a $1,000 or more fined, or a year in jail)
• Misdemeanor trials when imprisonment is actually imposed
• Appeal trial as a matter of right (see below)

An indigent is a person who does not have enough money or property to hire counsel, but it does not mean the indigent is totally devoid of funds. Keep these pointers in mind:

• Any doubts of indigency are resolved in favor of the individual
• Right to counsel includes the right to "effective" counsel
• An ineffective assistance of counsel claimed by the convicted defendant is the most often raised grounds for appeal (if the defendant is successful on appeal, the case is remanded back for a new trial)

TRIAL

▼

LOSE

▼

RIGHT TO APPEAL TO COURT OF APPEALS

(lawyer is necessary)

▼

RIGHT TO APPEAL TO STATE SUPREME COURT

(which can accept or reject case—no lawyer necessary for discretionary appeals)

▼

RIGHT TO APPEAL TO U.S. SUPREME COURT

(which may accept or reject appeal—representation is necessary.)

I DID THAT, AND THEN I DID THIS . . .: By a 5–4 vote, the Supreme Court just recently ruled against Texas defendant Raymond Levi

Cobb, who had been charged with burglary and who, months later, confessed to murdering a woman and her toddler during the burglary. Cobb's appeal was based on his not having been given counsel during has confession of the latter crime.

In 1993, the Owings family home in Walker County, Texas, was burglarized. Margaret Owings and her sixteen-month-old daughter were reported missing, and Cobb, their neighbor, confessed to the crime but claimed to know nothing of the disappearances. After being indicted on a burglary charge and released on bond, Cobb confided to his father that he had killed Owings and her daughter. His father contacted the sheriff's office, and Cobb was arrested. Apparently, he waived his right to be silent and told officers about stabbing Owings during the burglary. After stabbing her to death, he dragged the woman's body to a wooded area and discovered the baby when he went back to the house to get a shovel. Cobb put the baby on the ground near her mother's body, and, he claimed, while he was digging the hole, the baby fell into the pit.

133

Having been charged with a crime, Cobb was afforded by the Sixth Amendment a right to counsel throughout the criminal prosecution. At issue in the Cobb case was whether, as some lower courts have previously ruled, a defendant's right to counsel extends to crimes *factually related* to those for which the defendant has been charged.

In response, the Supreme Court ruled that the Sixth Amendment right is linked only to the specific offense being prosecuted at a given time. Chief Justice William Rehnquist said, "To exclude evidence simply because other charges were pending at the time would unnecessarily frustrate . . . the investigation of criminal activities." He also noted that suspects must still be told of their right against self-incrimination. Those who dissented on the opinion said, basically, that the decision limits what many lower courts had believed was the reach of the right to counsel. The pendulum swings toward law enforcement, once again.

FYI—

A terrific area for a writer to exploit might be the self-representation, or "pro se," defense. The Constitution places a defendant's "free choice" above the need for effective representation, although most lawyers have said, "The defendant who chooses to represent himself has a fool for a client!"

In 1984, the Supreme Court also added on some other factors to self-representation, namely, that a defendant does not have the right to personal instruction from the trial judge, he does not have the right to obstruct the workings of the criminal process, and he may not be represented by another person who is not a member of the bar. Judges sometimes appoint standby counsel, someone who assists defendants who wish to represent themselves.

Rights of Persons in Criminal Prosecutions: Privilege and Confidentiality

If the testimony before the court were based on information the accused told his attorney in confidence, should the attorney be made to admit his client's statements? And what is the difference between *privileged communication* and *confidential communication*? Or is there a difference?

Privileged communications are those protected by law, such as transmissions of information that take place between an attorney and his client, or a priest and the penitent. The person on the receiving end of the information cannot be compelled to divulge the contents of the communication unless the person doing the confiding waives his legal right to secrecy. Likewise, private talks between husband and wife are also privileged; however, in some states, a person is allowed to testify on behalf of a spouse. Some other areas where privileged statements may occur are between police informers and police; physicians, therapists, and their patients; and newspaper reporters and their secret, anonymous sources.

"Confidentiality" carries a different interpretation. Confidentiality refers to an ethical obligation on the part of a skilled specialist to safeguard information given by a client, or clients, in a professional capacity. Confidential sharing has no legal protection in the court, unless it is also privileged communication as well. For example, a marriage counselor ethically would not divulge any statements made to him by his clients. But in the courtroom venue, the information the counselor possesses is not considered privileged, and he will be compelled to tell—or risk a contempt-of-court citation (a remedy of a fine or imprisonment levied by the judge is available for refusing).

Discussing the case in a restaurant can be dangerous for a defendant who speaks confidentially with his lawyer over dinner. He may get more than dessert, he may get his "just deserts"! A loudmouth defendant has no reasonable expectation of privacy in a public place; his confession is subject to eavesdroppers.

134

FYI
A client's statements to his lawyer concerning an intention to commit a crime in the future are not confidential. In an emergency, or life-threatening situations, a lawyer might have to reveal such a statement to the police even before a crime is committed. Likewise, a defendant cannot ask his lawyer to hold onto an incriminating tangible object, like a knife that was used in a stabbing.

Writer's Tip
According to protocol, the defendant who brings his "girl" along to a confidential attorney-client meeting risks losing the privilege of confidentiality. The district attorney might be able to ask the girlfriend about what was said during the conference. I see more than coffee brewing here: Maybe the girl is more than she seems?

Amendment VI: Criminal Court Procedures

In all criminal prosecutions, the accused shall enjoy the right to a speedy and public trial, by an impartial jury of the state and district wherein the crime shall have been committed, which district shall have been previously ascertained by law, and to be informed of the nature and cause of the accusation; to be confronted with the witnesses against him; to have compulsory process for obtaining witnesses in his favor, and to have the assistance of counsel for his defence.

Any person accused of a crime has a right to a fair and public trial by a jury in the state in which the crime took place. The charges against the person must be spelled out, and any accused person has the right to know who his accusers are. The accused also has a right to a lawyer to defend him and to question those who testify against the defense. The defendant's attorney may also call people to speak in favor of his client at trial.

Right to a Speedy Trial

Imagine this scenario.

> For Evelyn Stevens, wife of the murdered subject of this trial, it had seemed like years since she'd last heard those words from police officers, lieutenants Haley and McGrew . . . "Ms. Stevens, it's about your husband, Douglas Stevens." Looking into the mirror this morning at tired swollen eyes and strained nerves, she would swear she'd aged seven years in the waiting.

The Sixth Amendment to the Constitution guarantees all criminal defendants "the right to a speedy and public trial." And while some defendants get trials that they feel are altogether too speedy, the constitutional guarantee really serves two purposes. First, a speedy trial relieves a defendant of the pervasive consequences involved with being accused. If the accused was subject to incarceration, any length of time in jail will seem oppressive—not to mention the drain of personal finances, loss of business, personal anxiety, public scorn, and the weakening of his defense. The second purpose of a speedy trial is to promote society's interest in the prompt disposition of charges. Common, law-abiding citizens are often concerned about proper and timely administration of justice when it occurs in "their own backyard"; they may feel threatened by the unresolved details surrounding the crime—and by the potential for additional harm should the perpetrator be out "on the loose."

One very important note on timing is this: The right to a speedy trial begins to apply its pressure only after the person has been accused—after he has been indicted, has received information about the accusation, or has been taken into custody and under arrest. Because of this stipulation, the right is not violated by a delay in filing charges when such delay might violate the person's other rights. Once arrested, however, the accused is entitled to a speedy trial, even if he is subsequently released and not recalled for a substantial period of time.

The actual amount of time that denotes "speedy" is the judge's call. The conduct of both the prosecution and the defendant must be weighed by a judge, who also takes in additional factors, such as the length of delay, the reason for the delay, the defendant's declaration or denial of his right, and actual prejudice to the defendant. Length of delay alone does not establish a violation of a speedy trial, because unless the delay has been sufficiently long to be prejudicial, there is no need to examine the other relevant factors.

Some states, however, exact specific time limits within which an accused must be brought to trial. Often, they will use the federal guidelines, which are published under the Speedy Trial Act.[85] Two of the federal time limits are:

1. The government must formally charge a defendant with a crime within 30 days of the defendant's arrest

2. The government should bring a case to trial not less than 30 nor more than 70 days after charging a defendant with a crime

Under state statutes—take Florida, for example—a nonincarcerated defendant must go to trial within 120 days, and an incarcerated defendant has a shorter trial-date time limit—90 days. These are not set in concrete and are typically subject to a host of exceptions. Often, both defendants and prosecutors agree to delay proceedings.

The reason for delay is legally significant. If the prosecutor deliberately attempts to delay the trial to his advantage, this weighs heavily on the defendant, and his speedy trial claim is taken seriously. It can, ultimately, result in dismissal of the case. However, if the delay is sustained through efforts by the accused, then the accused will be deemed to have waived his right to a speedy trial.

Of final note, the nature and amount of prejudice coming from the delay is considered in light of the consequences this right is designed to protect. For example, if the delay has created a lengthy or oppressive incarceration, has resulted in the loss of evidence, the death of a witness, inaccuracy of witness testimony, or has increased the anxiety of the accused measurably, a showing of prejudice will be strongly considered by the judge when the time comes for his making a "speedy trial analysis."

Right to Be Present at Trial

In all criminal trials, the defendant has the right to be present during the proceeding from arraignment to sentence unless the right has been waived or forfeited. The Federal Rules state that presence is required at every stage, including the impaneling of the jury, the return of the verdict, and the imposition of sentence. A defendant who voluntarily fails to show up for trial may be tried "in absentia."

A few instances in which continued presence is not required are listed below:

- The defendant is voluntarily absent after the trial has commenced
- The trial is a noncapital case or can be dismissed after the defendant is warned about disruptive behavior
- The defendant is an organization and represented by an attorney
- Or, for a punishment and fine or imprisonment for not more than one year (technically, this is a misdemeanor)
- The proceeding is only a conference or a hearing involving a question of law
- The proceeding simply involves a correction of sentence

137

Generally, though, the courts deem that it is essential to the proper administration of criminal justice that a defendant be present and that the courts should indulge every reasonable basis against the loss of this constitutional right. Of course, if a defendant must be removed from the courtroom for belligerent behavior, the court makes it possible for him to communicate with his attorney until such time when he agrees to behave and return to the court.

Publicity

In addition to the timeliness of trials and presence at trials, the Sixth Amendment also provides that in "all criminal prosecutions the accused shall enjoy the right to . . . public trial."

This right to a trial that is available to the public is grounded in history and the Anglo-American distrust of secret goings-on. The purpose of a public trial is to safeguard against any attempts at employing the courts as instruments of persecution and to keep citizens apprised of actions against its own body politic. There are, however, certain trials that take place as closed proceedings. The judge has the ability to exclude members of the public from the trial if he feels the need arises. One example may be in the case of a rape violation. Another reason to close a trial is if it involves youthful offenders. As recently as 1990, a New York trial case of an investment banker who was mugged was closed to spectators during the victim's testimony, and her name was never printed in the media.

An area of major concern currently exists about whether to bar the media from a trial. The courts have said that even if the government, the defendant, and the judge have all agreed to a closed hearing, that the Fifth, Sixth, and First Amendments could be raised by members of the media. Because of this, rules have been laid down in respect to when the media can and cannot attend a trial. Neither the defendant nor anyone else has a right to require the judge to admit unneeded persons into the courtroom. In addition, if seating capacity is exhausted, exclusion of nonessential persons is totally appropriate.

SEQUESTRATION RULES: Sequestration rules are those which attempt to prevent witnesses from being influenced by the testimony of other witnesses. Witnesses who are sequestered must sit outside the courtroom until called to testify. Normally, they cannot discuss their testimony with anyone else who is waiting. Once excused from giving further testimony, however, they are free to go. Typically, if a defendant's family or friends are going to testify, sequestration rules prevent them from being physically present in the courtroom for much of the trial.

The Jury

138

The primary phase of any criminal trial is the selection of a jury. For the accused, now the defendant, it is probably the most important procedure. The right to a trial by jury is a distinctive feature in the system of jurisprudence, dating back more than seven centuries. The English Magna Carta of 1215 contained the stipulation that no freeholder would be deprived of life or property except by judgment of his peers. Article III of the Constitution incorporates this principle with the following statement: "A trial of all crimes except in cases of impeachment shall be by jury." The Sixth Amendment holds that "in all criminal prosecutions the accused shall enjoy the right to a speedy trial by an impartial jury."

The accused also has a right to dispense with a jury and can request to be tried by a judge alone. These trials are called "bench trials." In some states, defendants must file a request for a jury trial either when they enter a plea or at some time before the beginning of a court term in which a jury would be impaneled. Failure to file constitutes a waiver of the right. In all criminal matters in which jail is a potential penalty, though, the accused have an absolute right to a jury trial.

FYI—

A little known fact called "jury trial penalty" means that sometimes juries impose harsher sentences than a judge might consider rendering. If judges suggest, in an aside or off-the-record conversation, that the defense attorney should opt for a bench trial and save the added time and expense of a trial, the defense should take note of this remark, or his client may pay for the ignorance by having time added onto his sentence.

The primary purpose of a jury is to serve as a check against arbitrary or vindictive law enforcement. In *Duncan v. Louisiana*,[86] the U.S. Supreme Court recognized that juries advance the means needed for a fact-finding process: They are selected by law and sworn in to determine matters of fact and, sometimes, matters pertaining to sentencing in a criminal action. But, in reality, most often, the judge is both the fact-finder and the person who decides what law to apply to those facts. It is almost unique to the American system that ordinary citizens have the responsibility to decide a criminal defendant's ultimate fate. The judge's power—and the power of precedent, or previous law—help him in defining the rules of law and the sentencing guidelines, thus providing him with certain amounts of discretionary authority.

It is important for the accused to know what size jury he is entitled to. Over the years, jury costs have forced states to limit jury size, and in many states, a litigant is likely to get a six-person jury if he is not charged with a felony. Given the choice, the twelve-person panel would be to the advantage of the accused. Since the prosecution needs a unanimous jury to convict, it makes sense that he is more likely to find sympathetic individuals within a larger group. Still, there are states, which provide for less than unanimous verdicts in criminal cases, but they are primarily non–death penalty cases. In such a scenario, for example, conviction could be based on nine out of twelve jurors voting for guilty, and this would be constitutionally valid for that state.

139

Confrontation with the Witness

The young defense attorney's assistant unconsciously pushed his fingers through his thick hair; it was beginning an afternoon curl. He would be the first one to admit he was nervous, and excited—excited at the prospect of actually being able to sit in on the Stevens murder case, excited at the idea of keeping good notes on the prosecution's ploys. He wanted to write a book one day, and this was the stuff of good fiction. And when the prosecution brought in Ms. Gaines, a surprise witness, he thought that Defense Attorney Jensen would cave, but wow! The prosecution's move, even though it had been sprung on Jensen—"We were just able to locate Ms. Gaines, Your Honor,"—did not shake him for a minute. Jensen ended the session with a sigh and the words "This comes as a complete surprise to us, Your Honor. We will need a few days to prepare our cross-examination."

The right to confront witnesses is protected by the Sixth Amendment, an all-purpose amendment for the important aspects of a trial, and this clause is no exception. The confrontation provision serves three purposes. The first has to do with oath, and oath-taking was an integral component in the trials of ancient Western civilization. The oath helps to ensure the reliability of the witnesses' testimony. Secondly, confrontation exposes the witness to further examination by means of the defense's cross-examination. And, finally, it allows the judge and jury a chance to weigh the demeanor of the witness and helps them to discern credibility.

Since the right to confront witnesses was deemed a fundamental right in federal and state prosecutions, it is applicable to state's law under the Fourteenth Amendment due process clause. This right includes the right of the accused to be physically present during the course of a trial. However, as I mentioned earlier in this chapter, the accused can waive this right also by voluntarily absenting himself from the proceedings, which will continue in his absence.

The right to confront witnesses is essentially the right to cross-examine witnesses. Being able to cross-examine witnesses is an important skill to master and one of the more significant tools for the trial attorney. When a witness claims to tell the truth as he knows it, that truth may be tainted because of his viewpoint or exposure. It is up to the defense attorney to bring the truth back to the middle through careful questioning. There are many reasons the answers to questions will be skewed: the witnesses are trying to shield themselves; they may have a desire to get back at the accused; or they may become confused or misinformed, or fail to see the importance of what they say as compared with what they believe. The witness may not want to follow through on the adage of the law principle that states that the accused is "innocent until proven guilty." So, the defense must have some way to separate beliefs from the facts; the defense holds the right to impeach the witnesses' own words or to present an alternate theory to the crime.

OTHER PROTECTIVE MEASURES: Reading between the Sixth Amendment's Lines: There is another part to the confrontation process. For what good would it do to have questions for a person if he doesn't show up? The omission itself could be damaging. The Sixth Amendment holds another expressly provided provision. It is not spelled out—but there should be some way to make the right to confront witnesses part of a compulsory process. There should be a way for the defendant to assure that there is the means to compel someone to come to court, just as the prosecutor has the power to subpoena witnesses on the state's behalf. The defendant must depend on others for this claim.

There are other questions inherent in the trial process, too. What if the trial judge makes threatening remarks that drive the only defense witness off the stand? Or, what if the government decides to deport a witness? The courts have said in *Webb v. Texas* that this tactic of the threatening judge, in effect, prevents the accused from presenting his witnesses and their version of the facts, and it is not allowed. Furthermore, exclusion of crucial defense evidence by the trial judge impairs the right of the accused to present a defense, even where the evidence offered is technically inadmissible under appropriate local rules. For example, in *Chambers v. Mississippi*,[87] the defendant offered evidence that the crime he was accused of was committed by someone else and had an oral confession to prove it. The evidence was excluded on the grounds that it

140

was hearsay under the rules of evidence. The Supreme Court reversed that decision, saying that if the evidence were held back for a substantial assurance of trustworthiness, it would impair the defendant's right to present a defense. And what happens when the government deports a witness? If the deported witness and his testimony were material and favorable to the defendant's constitutional claim for defense, then the compulsory process for right to compel witnesses to testify was violated, and the defense must get another trial.

Authority's Long Reach of Power

As you can see, the Fifth and Sixth Amendments are loaded with promises, rules, and guarantees critical to the rights of the accused. Still, in preparation for an investigation and subsequent trial, the defendant may not fully realize the "imbalance of power." While the prosecution can freely grant immunity and compel witnesses to testify, the defense has no such power; he can only protect himself against third-degree tactics, hope for reliable evidence in his favor, and rely on the wisdom of the judge and jury to sort things out.

141

Amendment VIII: Bail, Cruel and Unusual Punishment

> Excessive bail shall not be required, nor excessive fines imposed, nor cruel and unusual punishments inflicted

Usually, an amount of money is requested by the court to ensure that an accused person will return for his court case and final judgment—this is called bail. The amount of bail or the fine imposed as punishment for a crime must be reasonable, compared with the seriousness of the crime involved. Any punishment deemed too harsh or too severe for a crime is prohibited.

The exercising of this right does not mean that the accused has a constitutional right to bail. The Supreme Court has not declared it to be a "due process right." The accused may be denied bail if the prosecution demonstrates clear and convincing evidence that his release might present danger to the public. Some critics have become clearly upset with this decision, claiming that it automatically negates the presumption of innocence. This is one of the subtle incongruities of the law. Also, the Supreme Court has never expressly said that the excessive bail clause is enforceable against the states via the Fourteenth Amendment. The matter is left up to the individual states. So, although the idea of bail is to ensure the appearance of the accused in court, it is up to the states to define what amount of bail money is excessive. The cruel and unusual punishment clause of the Eighth Amendment is a throwback to the use of excessive physical punishment on prisoners common in early European history. The Supreme Court used this measure to invalidate a provision that prescribed a state death penalty law that had allowed capital punishment in cases of rape.[88]

BAD PRISON CONDITIONS—CRUEL AND UNUSUAL?: The Supreme Court has made it tougher for prisoners to file fictitious lawsuits claiming poor prison conditions. In order to challenge substandard prison conditions as "cruel and unusual," their complaints must meet certain standards. A prisoner must prove that prison officials actually knew about the conditions challenged, and he must prove that, despite the substantial risk to inmates caused by the conditions, the officials failed to do anything about them.

Chapter 9

Men in Blue

Anarchism is a game at which police can beat you.
—GEORGE BERNARD SHAW, *MISALLIANCE*

Citizens generally form their ideas of what police are and what they do by watching popular television shows or reading national newspaper headlines. The operations, size, and capabilities of their own police are assumed to be similar to those depicted on the screen. While these "model" composites are entertaining, they may have little to no resemblance to the function, procedure, and real human beings who inhabit the system in your hometown or community. Each law enforcement agency, whether local or city police, a sheriff's department, state police, or one of the federal law-enforcement agencies, has its own blueprint of hierarchy, jurisdiction, and operating procedures. For this reason, the writer should check out the policies of the agency he intends to write about for information specific to that organization.

Because law enforcement did not spring full-grown from the breast of Lady Liberty, and because some writers may be interested in the historical underpinnings of how men became police officers, a few of the key historical figures who helped to shape law enforcement are featured below. Not to mention that the "historical" evolution of policing has story line that begs fresh retelling.

English Cops of the Seventeenth and Eighteenth Centuries

In early England, every citizen was a police officer and every police officer was a citizen, marshalling other citizens together. With the growth of urbanization, a variety of buildings were grouped together, commerce developed, and town guilds appointed a "watch & ward" brigade to rouse the citizens and protect them from fire and burglaries.

Constables were overseers for some communities, and beadles—minor parish officials—were paid to clear vagrants and preserve the peace at civil functions and within the church. In the late 1600s, certain citizens functioned as private investigators called thief-takers, but their behavior more aptly resembled the bounty hunters of yore. Although they possessed no official status or statutory authority, they received rewards from the crown for their service. Highway robbery was big business, making travel perilous, and in 1693 Parliament offered £40 for the capture of a highwayman, payable on conviction. The thief-taker who nabbed his man also got the robber's assets, his horse, money, and weapons. It so happens that, sometimes, professional thief-takers were themselves criminals.

The Gin Riots, around 1720, were responsible for the modern police. Because inexpensive alcohol was available to the folks of all classes, civil unrest—resulting from binges of drinking, rabble-rousing, and rioting— lasted almost a hundred years. Watch and ward bailiffs got beaten up during these skirmishes and often could not control the situation undertaken. As a consequence, citizens were read the "Riot Act," which was a call for the military to quell the riots. Some believe this was the precursor of our present-day National Guard.

In the early 1700s, a man named Jonathan Wild did just that—he ran wild as an organized crime boss. Operating the largest crime faction in London, Wild controlled robbery, thieves, and fencing. His recruits "turned over" their loot by charging a ransom for it. Wild and his conspirators operated with a free hand until they were met with the effort of Henry Fielding.

Henry Fielding is known as one of the greatest artists among English novelists of the eighteenth century and is credited with the birth of the novel as a literary form. A liberal, Fielding was also appointed magistrate in 1748 and helped to lay the foundation for the first modern police force. The progressive Fielding advocated the release of petty thieves, issued reprimand instead of death for punishment, begged leniency for the poverty-stricken, and pushed for lower sentences. He urged local magistrates to pay salaries to their aids, instituted the publication of crime reportage, and provided pawnbrokers with frequent lists of stolen goods. Among these many contributions, Fielding formed the Bow Street Runners, an unpaid volunteer group, which was established to clean up the Bow Street area in London. The theory of crime prevention sprung up under Fielding's atmosphere of invention, and his core of "runners" espoused swift and fair justice; they were physically strong and able, and they were known for their incorruptible nature. Later, these constabulary features were refined and continued as Henry's half-brother, John Fielding, took over due to Henry's failing health.

Sir Robert Peel was a British statesman who served as home secretary in the 1820s. Known as the "father of modern policing," Peel advocated a partial return to the Anglo-Saxon policy of personal responsibility. In addition, the forward-thinking Peel was also largely responsible for the first salaried bureaucratic police force enacted under the Metropolitan Police Act of 1829. This London force comprised the first formally sanctioned police for order, prevention, and detection of crime. The familiar London "Bobbies" are named for him.

Later, under the tutelage of Charles Rowan, a former military man, and Richard Mayne, an attorney, a legally guided and more formal police force evolved. Some of their changes for "reform" were that forces would be militarily organized with a hierarchy of command; they would utilize a "centrally located" division to be deployed by time and area; there would be appropriate disciplinary procedures for their own, along with strength and moral training; and a distinct, uniform look.

Policing in Early America

August Vollmer, sometimes called the "father of modern police" in the United States, was a chief of police in Berkeley, California, and author of *The Police and Modern Society* (1936). Vollmer presented a paper called "Policeman as Social Worker," which recognized the importance of service. A patrol officer serving under Vollmer, O. W. Wilson, whose career spanned several areas of enforcement and service as chief public safety officer in several European countries, instituted a sound management approach. Wilson's ideas specified a professional police" separate from politics, rigorous selection and training, and the use of technology. Oddly, even though Wilson called for professionalism, he did not like civil service tests and the rules of seniority that, he felt, boxed-in the leadership.

Later, works written by such leaders as Raymond B. Fosdick (*Municipal Police Administration*) and Bruce Smith (*Police Systems in the United States*) stressed holding onto the classic kernels of police management while at the same time promoting a synthesis of action, a succinct division of labor allowing for a narrow span of control and a centralization of authority.

William Henry Parker, a compadre of Colonel O. W. Wilson during World War II and a police officer who rose to captain in the Los Angeles Police Department (1950–1968), discovered irregularities in the police promotion process in Los Angeles. Parker had concerns about personal accountability, which triggered his renewed interest in background investigation for new hires, a particular IQ from recruits, and a thorough psychiatric examination of all his potential officers.

Soon after, another model appeared, providing impetus for the formation of system we have known from 1925 to the present. Called the Human Relations and Participative Management Model, it is a synthesis of the personnel thrust of the scientific model and the democratization of the "team policing" approach.

Hierarchy of Police Power

At the national level, federal criminal law violations are investigated and enforced by the Federal Bureau of Investigation (FBI). Located in Washington, D.C., answerable to the Department of Justice, the FBI is by far the most powerful of the federal law-enforcement agencies. With nearly twenty-five thousand people under its command, including more than ten thousand special FBI agents spread out over fifty-six field offices in the United States and twenty-one foreign offices, it uses its broad powers to enforce over 260 rules under its jurisdiction. An annual budget exceeding $2 billion provides the FBI with the most sophisticated methods in crime prevention and investigation. They contribute a number of services to local law-enforcement agencies, including continued education, database system analyses, and advanced investigation techniques.

Other federal agencies have law-enforcement authority in specific areas. Among them are the U.S. Marshals Office, the Bureau of Alcohol, Tobacco and Firearms, the Bureau of Indian Affairs, the Drug Enforcement Administration, the Customs Service, the Immigration and Naturalization Service, the Bureau of Postal Inspection, and the Secret Service.

Many states have their own municipal agencies, which mimic the role of enforcing specific areas of law, ranging from traffic safety to gambling, from agricultural importation to dispensing alcoholic licenses.

At the local level are county and city law-enforcement agencies. Almost every rural county in America has a sheriff. In most states, sheriffs are elected to office and exercise a great deal of authority as chief law-enforcement officers. In northeastern cities, however, many traditional powers have been granted to state or metropolitan police forces. More than twenty thousand cities and towns have a police department.

Law-enforcement agencies enforce criminal law and, as a consequence, have much discretion. Under the umbrella of this power, law-enforcement personnel can investigate suspicious criminal activity, arrest suspected criminals, and detain arrested persons until their cases come before the appropriate courts of law. Two of the primary assumptions society makes in respect to its law enforcement are that officers should both prevent crimes and maintain order. Altogether, forty thousand federal, state, and local agencies are involved in law enforcement.

Discretion

Discretion is the exercise of individual choice or judgment concerning possible courses of action. The authority to exercise legitimate use of power is the most important characteristic of police action. For this reason, discretion is a significant concept for writers to explore when choosing action for their law-enforcement characters. The authority to use individual discretion marks the crossroads of choice police officers are met with daily. It decentralizes hierar-

146

chy. It allows an officer to act without having to check back with management. It implies trust that officers will act in good faith. To begin, here is a list of "discretionary plateaus"—when internal and external pressures and influences are applied at each discretionary choice level: Should I arrest or not? Will evidence support it? What charges should I file?

DISCRETIONARY PLATEAUS:
- When a citizen reports crime to law enforcement
- When police investigate
- When police apprehend a suspect
- When a prosecutor makes charges
- When there is plea bargain or trial
- With a judge or jury sentence
- When a suspect appeals
- When correctional decisions are made
- When a convict reenters society
- When citizens must accept a convict

147

DISCRETION FOR THE POLICE OFFICER IS EXERCISED DURING THESE TIMES:
- When he determines the seriousness of the crime
- As the victim requires his aid
- When he investigates a suspect's previous record
- When he must consider the time of day and location
- When the law is vague

DISCRETION IS AFFECTED BY:
- Departmental policies
- Public expectations
- Precedents (previous court decisions)
- Current attitudes of the prosecutor and his relationship to the department
- Characteristics of behavior of the offender
- Faith in or disenchantment with the justice system

WHAT THE SUPREME COURT SAYS ABOUT OFFICER DISCRETION:
Recent Supreme Court decisions demand police discretion because
- Police officers are more knowledgeable than the average citizen
- Police are entrusted with badges and must strive to be more honest than ordinary citizens
- Special training and experience enable police to exercise actions not apparent to other people

- Police are constantly exposed to unusual danger and must at all times and circumstances act to protect themselves
- The key to effective policing is to allow officers the use of discretion

ARGUMENTS AGAINST THE USE OF DISCRETION:
- Individual discretion leads to unfair and unequal decisions
- It operates in conflict with rules, regulations, policy, and law
- Police should set the example to follow law to the fullest extent
- Discretion is affected by moods, weaknesses, and values
- It can have serious consequences
- It can diminish accountability

148

Characterizing a Police Officer

Law-enforcement officers, no matter what division or level, must uphold and follow the law in order to obtain proof of guilt and the satisfactory result—a judgment against the perpetrator. Any egregious technicalities against the suspect's constitutional rights give rise to many problems, delays, and even mistrials. Any screw-ups can result in a case dismissal. The drama of dealing with these problems can add verisimilitude and depth to your stories. Just realize that not every mistake leads to a criminal's freedom, and not every encounter can end with a major shootout or body count.

It may help you to portray police officers correctly if you remember that they are, first of all, human beings. Everyday civilians view cops with a skewed perception. He is "the guy who gave me a ticket," or he's someone to complain to about an injustice or the problems with society, as if it's in a cop's power to do something about it. It's a status that calls forth certain clichéd images the media helps to perpetuate through news, books, and movies. The Corrupt Cop and the Stupid Cop stereotypes are usually the staples of any private-eye story or anything involving a conspiracy theme. People in general rely so instinctively on these character types and preconceptions that most of the time they don't recognize their overgeneralizations. It would behoove you, then, to take some effort to give them, the cops, life: Mention personal problems, or talk about how they fight disillusionment. Learn to describe the world they live in with more specificity. Much of their time is spent with other fellow officers and their families. Think about how spending the major portion of their day and night with the dregs of society affects their outlook and demeanor. And just as doctors have their Latin prescriptions, and scientists have their elements, so do police officers have their codes and calls. Using their argot, they are able to communicate with each other in a way that is not clear to the common people around them. And you can use that argot to add dimension to your police characters.

Patrol Officers

The patrol division is the backbone of the agency. Regardless of where police officers come from or end up, they will experience some of what the patrol division offers. As the first assignment, a rookie officer is usually placed with a more senior member of the division, who could be referred to as a "field training officer" or, more colloquially, "coach." The trend in law-enforcement training is toward the use of field-training programs; however, a substantial portion relies on on-the-job training combined with additional classroom instruction.

A new officer is assigned to a particular community in accordance with the personnel needs of the patrol bureau and with the philosophy of the chief administrator. One chief may feel, perhaps, that the new officer should be directly challenged and evaluated, and so assigns the rookie to a high-crime area to accelerate the acquiring of experience. Others opt for a slower approach, putting officers in a less hostile environment before immersing them in a highly charged region. A chief may boast about how his patrol bureau is the backbone of the agency, and then proceed to transfer his best and brightest to other assignments or put them in select bureaus like the detective squad. Obviously, if this continues with any regularity, problems ensue. Such practice will keep inexperienced men, or men with little ability or motivation, in the patrol division.

PEER PRESSURE: An important human factor for the rookie is "belonging," or the peer pressure brought to bear on the new recruit. Pressure from contemporaries is used to uphold loyalty for the profession and can be used as a weapon to sanction someone deemed a "hot dog" or one who may not know about unwritten rules. Treating someone as an outcast and using every chance to get the rebel in trouble are classic ways of manipulating behavior for the "good of the group."

The propensity for conforming as required by the clique does serve its own purpose, though—it helps to bolster the officer against the slings and arrows of the outrageous streets. The loss of autonomous values helps the officer to remember where he stands, a kind of "us against them" mentality, and serves to shield him from an emotional reaction—a reaction which itself is a kind of failing, some cops may argue.

While the chain of command follows a discernible hard line and is referred to as "formal structure," the informal structure that subordinates set up can be used for under-the-table advice, sandbagging, or corruption. In its turn, for the sake of balance, this substructure needs a leader with his own pack of memories.

THE LIFE: Another problem that plagues patrol is the fact that these divisions operate round-the-clock, seven days a week; and the dangerous nights, coupled with an erratic schedule, can take their toll. Consequently, many officers wish to be transferred to other units. In addition to laborious shift-related duties, they must budget time for court appearances and their own family conflicts.

Their days are spent on a lot of rather routine duties or patrol, with the odd occasion to perform community services unrelated to stopping crime. Their hours can pulse from the sleepy marking of time to adrenaline-ridden fear. They are subjected to responding to crimes in progress or to crimes that have been just committed. The potential for physical harm in these particular instances is high.

Also, in order to carry out many of their community responsibilities, they will often be expected to work with less desirable civilians: drunks, prostitutes, petty criminals, child abusers, and others with serious mental problems. Even domestic calls are dangerous because of the unpredictability of entering a volatile situation, of having to confront families with deep-seated psychological dysfunctions.

The status of a police officer on patrol does not convey many apparent rewards—financial or otherwise. They may work for many years without glory, and their service goes relatively unrecognized by their community or sometimes even by their department.

There is a lot of leeway for what activities patrol officers pursue, because there are no hard-and-fast rules. Some departments may require a lot of routine patrol duties and observation, while for others the work could include traffic regulations and citations. Or a day's work might simply mean patrolling a business district to deter burglaries or robberies.

Non–crime-related calls eat up between 80 and 90 percent of an officer's time. Calls for property eviction, animal control, disruption during parties, tenant disputes, and property-line disagreements are a few of these. Attendance at certain civic events may be required to help provide for peaceful assembly, and other event-related duties may be incorporated into their day. Sometimes a summons comes down for benevolent community charity— helping people who are lost, informing loved ones about accidents, delivering blood from one hospital to another, or finding adolescent children.

Preliminary investigations are often begun by patrol officers, since they are, most likely, the first people to arrive at the scene of a crime. They are responsible for preserving the integrity of the area, caring for the injured, and apprehending the offender if he is still in the area. The patrol officer who first enters the crime scene may continue in service by collecting evidence, cataloging and filing it, and preparing the necessary reports. The follow-up can be taken away from him by an investigative unit or it may require him to extend his duties far beyond the limits of his assigned district. Many small departments cannot afford the expense of another office, and the patrol officer may act as a jack-of-all-trades in an extremely small community.

For the nontraditional roles of patrol, there may be groups that perform park-and-walk patrol, bicycle patrol, horse patrol, or golf-cart patrol. These are usually developed within departments that recognize the need for additional interaction between police and community residents and businesspersons.

Police traffic problems are some of the most pervasive problems for law enforcement service. Responsibility for congestion control, traffic law enforcement, and accident prevention has a way of finding itself enmeshed in many other activities. Traffic duty, then, is almost always a shared duty unless there is some type of municipal sheriff's station, traffic bureau, or other office—but traffic duty still constitutes a job for everyone in law enforcement at one time or another.

The Detective Role

Part image, part public relations, part god-awful job, the role of the detective falls victim to a lot of depictions in the public (and media) mind. Some of the historical aspects of the freedoms given over to detectives are often highlighted in books and movies, and, now, there is no failure of police literature to mention that a lot of these stereotypical duties are, today, not quite as "freewheeling" as the public assumes.

Usually, investigators are dispatched after a patrol unit files its reports. There are some simultaneous dispatches, but they are rare, for simple allocation reasons. After receiving the patrol unit's documentation, detectives usually become responsible for developing potential leads, mapping out an investigation plan, and canvassing. The investigator will usually make calls and interview those closest to the victim. Since there are always cases pending, they are given individual priority according to the leads presented, the heinousness of the crime, or the victim's notoriety in the press or community.

Some of the investigator's other duties include reviewing new cases, filling out paperwork, processing prisoners who may have been taken into custody the night before, and making court appearances. A follow-up investigation may require constructing lineups, digging through files and field interrogation records, and filling out more and more paperwork for the prosecutor's office. Usually, huge databases of known offenders and intelligence files are maintained in the investigation office. The larger and better-financed departments have crime analysis bureaus, and others can initiate a special strike force or sting operation, such as buying stolen property in an attempt to identify fences and burglars.

The daily operation includes the review of incident reports, which have been prepared and assembled from the previous day and handed out to the appropriate unit. Assignments may be by crime specialty—robberies and sex offenses, for example. But, often, the reports are given over to the unit supervisor, who assigns his own individuals to the various cases. The first twenty-four to forty-eight hours are critical to a case's solvability.

EVIDENCE TECHNICIANS: Many departments use trained evidence technicians to collect and process fingerprints, blood evidence, and any other evidentiary materials (which can range from hair to paper, wood, or cloth fibers). Some are crime scene investigators, or criminalists. They help to preserve the scene, relay information to the medical examiner, and sometimes check latent fingerprints against those of known criminals.

> **FYI—**
>
> The main point about "operations" is that each police agency is different or distinctive from one another because of certain variables like the size of the district, the population of the town, the needs of the people, the budget, the number of qualified personnel, and the types of assignments. Don't be afraid of calling the law-enforcement agency you are writing about to find out how it works. Most have public relations offices, and officers there will be happy to answer your questions—some will refer you to a specific officer or agent who will help you with details about methodology or procedure. Maintain a resource directory for future reference, and be sure to send a note of thanks to the individuals for their time.

THE SUSPECT'S RIGHTS AND THE COP'S LIMITATIONS: In chapters 7 and 8, I addressed the basic constitutional rights of criminal defendants as they pass through the criminal justice system. These rights set forth the following rules for the police:

- The conduct of police officers and prosecutors is regulated
- No unreasonable or unwarranted search and seizure is allowed
- No arrest except under probable cause is allowed
- No coerced confessions or illegal interrogation are allowed
- No entrapment is acceptable
- A suspect must be informed of his rights under questioning

You have seen in earlier chapters the reasons for these standards of police conduct. Now, I'll discuss the effect these standards have on the various day-to-day activities of our law-enforcement officials.

Surveillance

Much reflection on the part of law enforcement, prosecutors, and the courts in regards to the collection and use of evidence has been crammed down the throat of many who enter the profession—and for good reason. These are vitally important procedures that attempt to link evidence (that must be admissible in a courtroom) with those accused of the crime. Surveillance, which is the act of shadowing, tailing, photographing, or listening in on a suspect, is often used in order to detect criminal activity, obtain evidence, or prevent a crime. As an added bonus, surveillance may also lead to possible accomplices, witnesses, or other evidentiary pluses with which to build the case.

TAILING A SUSPECT: Tailing or shadowing a person can run the gamut from a boring car stakeout to a footrace in order to keep up. A lot of manpower and significant downtime is required of surveillance in this up-close-and-personal manner, so it is reserved for those situations most likely to proffer information. Sources such as "streetwise" informants may point to a lead, or often a perpetrator will return to the crime scene out of anxiety.

ELECTRONIC SURVEILLANCE: These silent and invisible intrusions on the privacy of an individual can take many forms, including the use of wire-taps, highly sensitive microphones, and other electronic devices. Since using electronic equipment skirts the protections of the Fourth Amendment, the Supreme Court has approved the use of searchlights, field glasses, aerial photography, and various other means of enhancing a policeman's power of observation. In the past, lower courts have allowed miniaturized television camera surveillance.

The question of legality is always whether the surveillance methods infringe on a person's reasonable expectation of privacy. If police use binoculars to see what could otherwise be seen through the naked eye, then the use of binoculars as a sensory aid is not a search—the rationale here is that it results in exposure of that information which is otherwise publicly visible. The same goes for the use of a flashlight, microphones, and aerial surveillance.

Police have often used beepers and thermal imaging devices to track the movements of a defendant's vehicle. An electronic gadget that sends out radio "beeping" signals is easily attached to a car. In *United States v. Knotts*,[89] the Supreme Court said that the use of a beeper was not a search in these circumstances because the information obtained pertains only to the movements of the suspect within society.

Thermal imaging devices passed muster because a device that compares the intensity of heat emanating from one object to that of surrounding objects does not constitute a search—using this method, the authorities are able to obtain information without entering the private home of the suspect. Police often use this tool as a means of detecting marijuana plants in someone's house, and the courts have likened it to a canine sniff, which is also not a search (see chapter 7). There is no protectible privacy interest in contraband—through the dog sniff or the thermal imaging device, the police officer really learns nothing about any personal, or innocent, information contained inside.

Despite the fact that the government's extensive use of technology sometimes escapes the reigns of the Constitution, there are still definitive limits on the extent of interception a surveillance officer can employ. Electronic eavesdropping—the use of wiretaps and pagers to listen in on a conversation that is taking place inside a suspect's home—smacks of intrusion. By enacting Title

III of the Omnibus Crime Control and Safe Streets Act,[90] Congress prohibited interception of electronic communications without a court-ordered warrant, unless one party to the conversation agrees to the interception. On sworn application, with considerable detailed information, and for a thirty-day period of time, a wiretap order can be executed.

Currently, there is some question in certain state courts about whether cordless and cellular phone interception is legal. The Florida Supreme Court held that nonconsensual interception of cordless phone calls without prior judicial approval violates a state statute protecting the privacy of communications. They based their decision on statutory grounds, however, so check your individual's territory before using this type of surveillance.

154

BANK RECORDS: There was a case, *United States v. Miller*,[91] in which the government served a subpoena on Miller's bank in order to obtain copies of checks, deposit slips, and other financial statements. This activity was not a search, said the court, because Miller could not have had an expectation of privacy in information he conveyed to his bank. The bank has access to it, so the government could have equal access.

TELEPHONE PEN REGISTERS: A pen register is a device that allows the police to access every number dialed from a specifically targeted phone. Does the owner expect the telephone company not to use this information? Since the caller gives the numbers away freely in making the call, it is not a search for police to obtain these numbers—equivalent government access is okay.

DROPSY: The results of a warrantless search do not justify the means. Dropsy is a slang term for recovering evidence during a search or pat-down of a suspect. Word has it that in order for certain evidence (mainly drugs) to hold up in court, when a police officer is doing a search and finds incriminating drugs that may not withstand judicial scrutiny on Fourth Amendment principles, the evidence gets dropped. Usually, the officers will testify in court that the defendants dropped the contraband before the arrest. When it lands on the ground, it becomes plain-view evidence.

Police and Force of Arrest

There are those who think that police-administered beatings of civilians are inexcusable. With certain media enhancement—say, for example, when a particularly brutal beating comes to light like the one we witnessed in the Rodney King case—the cards are stacked against police methodology altogether. Possibly no aspect of police service evokes more passion or controversy than unnecessarily ruthless beating and the use of deadly force.

A recent survey published by the National Institute of Justice[92] provides some answers. Out of a national sample of nine hundred officers interviewed, the majority of American police officers believe that it is unacceptable to use more force than legally allowable to control someone who physically assaults an officer. And although a substantial majority expressed the view that police should be permitted to use more force, the overwhelming majority did not believe that officers regularly engaged in the excessive use of force. In somewhat conflicting statements, however, almost 22 percent agreed or strongly agreed that officers in their departments sometimes used more force than was necessary. And, in response to the "code of silence" question (keeping quiet in the face of misconduct by others), one-quarter of the sample agreed that whistle-blowing is not worth it, and more than two-thirds reported that police officers who reported incidents of misconduct were likely to be given a "cold shoulder" by fellow officers; and a majority agreed it is not unusual for officers to "turn a blind eye" to other officers' improper conduct.

Most states have laws or police regulations specifying the degree of force used to apprehend violators. Officers are usually permitted to use such force as is necessary to effect an arrest and are not required to retreat from an aggressor. The use of deadly force is authorized when apprehending felons or when such force is necessary to prevent the escape of a suspect who poses a significant threat of death or serious injury to the officer or others.

An officer who kills someone in the line of duty is sometimes charged with a criminal offense. As long as he acted reasonably and was not in violation of the Fourth Amendment, a state law, or some other police regulation, he can use the defense of performing a public function, which is one of the legal safety nets available to police officers.

Police Interrogations

An interrogation under Supreme Court description is "express questioning or its functional equivalent," including any words or actions on the part of the police that the police know is reasonably likely to elicit an incriminating response from the suspect. And Miranda applies only to "custodial questioning."

Of course, interrogation is usually done at the station house, but there is no automatic custody rule for station house interrogation, meaning that if someone is asked to come to the station and answer questions, compliance with the request constitutes a voluntary move on the part of the suspect and does not imply custody. Custody also does not apply when a person is called to testify before a grand jury, or during a normal traffic stop. In other words, no warnings are required before questioning in these circumstances.

Interrogations can take many forms, including subtle psychological techniques. Miranda warnings must be issued, though, and the subject must have either waived those rights or obtained counsel. Miranda is supposed to remove inherent pressures of the interrogation atmosphere, but police do employ techniques of their own.

DELAY TACTICS: Sometimes, a police officer will delay the arrest in order to question the suspect in a breezy, conversational manner, feeling that more evidence will be gained that way. If an officer can convince a judge he was engaged in only general questioning and would have allowed the suspect to walk away when finished, when (suddenly!) information came through that provided probable cause for arrest, police can attempt to evade the Miranda mandate.

Using Silence Against the Suspect

If someone is arrested and chooses not to make the statement "I didn't do it," an officer can relay that information to the prosecutor, who will then ask in court, "Why didn't he tell the arresting officer immediately upon arrest that he really didn't do it?"

CONFRONTING A SUSPECT WITH INCRIMINATING EVIDENCE: In a Florida case,[93] a confession hinged on an officer's claim that he had laboratory reports implicating the suspect. The appellate court upheld a trial judge's order, holding the confession involuntary. The court expressed concern that false documents could wind up in police files as genuine.

PHYSICAL THREATS AND BRUTALITY: If the police obtain information by coercive means, it is not only illegal, but the information gathered through such means is not admissible, even if a Miranda warning was given prior to the confession. Not only that, but if any new evidence crops up as a result of a physical threat or brutality, it is considered "fruit of the poisonous tree" and is equally inadmissible.

PSYCHOLOGICAL COERCION: Actual police brutality is unusual and can be documented with photographs. But if an interrogation takes the form of a swearing or screaming match, it is harder to prove improper conduct. Since judges believe that defendants are motivated to lie in order to protect themselves, they are more inclined to side with police and conclude that no coercion took place.

MUTT-AND-JEFF STRATEGY: Sometimes referred to as the good cop/bad cop tactic, this is the routine where one officer is friendly and sympathetic while the other is rude and aggressive. The objective is to coerce the defendant into confessing to the good guy, and there is good reason to believe it works. The Supreme Court has alluded to the fact that Mutt-and-Jeff is a possible example of impermissible psychological coercion, yet courts have generally ignored the questionable nature of practice.

PUBLIC SAFETY EXCEPTION: Police officers may ask arrested persons about weapons and other potential threats to society without Miranda warnings. This exception allows law-enforcement officers to find out the whereabouts of weapons or dangerous objects, such as bombs, before they fall into the hands of conspirators or innocents.

PROMISES OF LENIENCY: Empty are the promises of leniency. Police may want to recommend a lighter sentence in exchange for the suspect's cooperation during interrogation, but in the end, it is the prosecutors and judges who determine charges and sentencing on the basis of law and expediency.

TAPE-RECORDING STATEMENTS: Anything put on tape is likely to show up again at trial. If suspects are afraid their information will be distorted, though, they can request to be taped or, at least, have a written summary to sign, making the opportunity for police to distort facts minimal.

157

LIE-DETECTOR TESTS: Police officers will often ask suspects to take a lie-detector test to "clear their name." It is often used as a ploy to get confessions, and the officers sometimes falsely tell suspects that they are flunking, so they might as well come clean. These tests are not usually allowed in court, and the credibility of their results is in question. All the same, the results of these tests are often used as grounds for arrest if the suspect is not yet officially in custody.

Identification Procedures

There are specific procedures law enforcement should follow in order to collect further evidence, interrogate suspects, and observe the legal ramifications of identification. There are two types of identification procedures. First, forensic science helps police to match suspects with physical evidence taken from the crime scene. Second, there are a variety of methods—lineups, show-ups, and photographs—to find out if victims or witnesses can identify their perpetrators.

FORENSIC SCIENCE: Even without a warrant, police can require a suspect to give his fingerprints, a blood sample, hair and fingernail samples, and either clothing or fibers. As part of the booking process, his photograph will be taken; he may be asked to provide his voice for tapes and his handwriting for exemplar comparison. The Supreme Court has held that providing handwriting can be compelled because it is not testimony but an identifying physical characteristic.[94] Some courts require "probable cause and necessity" before a blood sample, semen, or DNA may be taken without a warrant. Other courts deem that the more intrusive test of collecting pubic hair must also carry a warrant. The two general requirements that courts across the board agree upon are that these methods be conducted by qualified persons and that they do not violate the constitutional prohibition of compulsory self-incrimination. Typically, situations are considered on a case-by-case basis; the Supreme Court denies any broad rules. Defendants can request their attorneys' presence during testing, but it is not legally required.

LINEUPS: An eyewitness identification method, the lineup usually takes place at police stations or jails. In a lineup, a group, typically of five or six people, is displayed. A victim or witness, who is usually shielded from view behind bright lights or a one-way mirror, is asked to pick out the person seen to commit the crime or noticed at the crime scene. Individuals in the lineup are often asked to step forward, turn sideways, wear certain types of clothing, or otherwise speak or assist the witness in identification. One person in the lineup is the suspect; the others may closely resemble him and are decoys.

The Supreme Court has sanctioned the use of lineups, saying there is no Fifth Amendment immunity against being placed in a lineup for identification purposes; lineups are considered "nontestimonial." Witnesses may be brought in separately or together to view the lineup. The only stipulation is that they do not confer or hear another's choice. If there is an indication of influence, the identification may be suppressed upon a motion or attacked as unreliable in court. Police officers and possibly the prosecutor and defense attorney will be present. Defense lawyers may also bring a private investigator or other employee to observe, as protection against any unfair proceedings. It is a defendant's right to have a defense lawyer present at a postcharge lineup, and the advocate may even take photos of the lineup.

An "impermissibly suggestive" lineup may be:
• The defendant stands out as the only person who resembles the witness's account—there is, for example, only one African-American after the perpetrator has been described as African-American
• Witnesses have been allowed to talk to each other, either before entering the viewing room or when inside
• Only one person is in handcuffs, or a handcuffed person was paraded through the waiting room
• Police cannot resist speaking to the witness—saying, for instance, "Pay particular attention to suspect Number Four"

Judges have standards[95] about whether "impermissible suggestiveness" has affected an identification. These "reliability test" standards include:
1. The degree of suggestiveness—for example, a one-on-one photo is more likely to affect a witness
2. The opportunity to view—for example, coming face-to-face with the suspect versus seeing him from forty feet away
3. Degree of attention—for example, the witness was focused on other concerns or objects at the time

4. Accuracy of the description—for example, if the witness describes a unique physical characteristic, it is likely the specificity is accurate
5. Level of certainty—for example, the courts believe that the more certain the witness is about the identification, the more likely it is that the positive identification has come from sources other than police suggestiveness
6. The time between preidentification opportunity to view and the identification itself—the "mental picture" of a perpetrator fades as time passes
7. Character of the witness—suggests to the judge whether the person is easily led or has a need to pinpoint the crime regardless of the accuracy of her assertions

FYI—

A judge may require a person to submit to a lineup as a condition of granting bail or a release on one's own recognizance. In reality, though, bailed-out defendants are less likely to be called up than incarcerated ones are. A refusal to cooperate may have the effect of making police think the person is hiding something and, as a result, may cause the authorities to investigate the resistant suspect more aggressively.

SHOWUPS: A one-on-one identification procedure, the showup is different in character from a lineup in several distinct ways. Showups occur in police stations, but they may also take place "in the field", for example, a handcuffed suspect may be taken by police back to the scene of a crime—returning, for example, to a grocery store to be identified by the clerk who has been robbed. A showup is most effective soon after a crime is committed. And, although showups are thought to be more reliable because of their immediacy, they are inherently suggestive because they make it obvious to the witness that police believe they have caught the offender. Also, since showups almost always take place before a suspect is charged, the right to an attorney's presence is not guaranteed. On the plus side, prompt identifications help to exonerate innocents rather quickly.

PHOTO IDENTIFICATION: A photo pack is a set of "mug shots" that are shown to an eyewitness or victim in the hopes that a reliable identification will be produced. The presentation should not emphasize one photo over another, and an attorney's presence is not required. In addition, police may display photos, or an individual photograph, to a witness in an attempt to "search for a suspect"—meaning, the police may have no evidence that people displayed in the photos have committed the crime. But the fact that photographs may be mug shots tends to indicate a previous criminal record. Generally, people whose photos are used in this procedure do not know that they are about to become suspects.

Police sometimes try to trick suspects into confessing by telling them they have already been identified in a photo array, even if they have not. Judges usually admit the resulting confessions, despite the lie on the part of the police. And the same restrictive principles apply with photo IDs as with lineups and showups; although the prosecutor is generally required to keep records of what photos were displayed, the absence of those records may prompt the judge to exclude the identification from trial.

On the Road: Crime Detection and Prevention

While the arrest power rule—the latitude police are given with searches incident to arrest—is an empowering one for law enforcement, there are still other times when police may conduct inquiry and search—namely, at sobriety checkpoints, at roadblocks, and on the border.

160

In order to reduce the number of drunk driving accidents, police officers often set up sobriety checkpoints. All drivers must stop briefly at a designated point and are observed for signs of intoxication. The legality of sobriety stops has been challenged on Fourth Amendment grounds, mainly that the police have no probable cause to believe that any driver in particular has broken a law. The courts have upheld these measures as minor intrusion and inconvenience, saying that as long as the procedures are not discriminating and apply to all motorists, the stop is reasonable.

Since roadblocks do constitute a restraint on the liberty of the motorist, they are susceptible to challenge under the Fourth Amendment. Because of their restrictive nature, then, police agencies must take care that they are operated according to guidelines that help to constrain the exercise of discretion by the officers. Often, roadblocks are set up to apprehend fleeing criminals or felons, but, occasionally, they are used to perform checks for safety or for possession of insurance. The methodology requires a minimal duration of stop— somewhere in the area of thirty seconds—and, if the driver appears intoxicated, he is instructed to pull the vehicle over to the side of the road for a license-and-registration check. If indicated, a field sobriety test is administered.

Border searches are considered administrative, and the interest is in protecting American borders and regulating the flow of goods into the country. Since the border search involves national interests, it is evaluated under Fourth Amendment principles but is essentially found reasonable without a warrant or probable cause for suspicion. Customs officials at all border points in Canada and Mexico and on all ships of foreign port stations may stop all entrants for routine investigation, questioning, and limited searches of effects, vehicles, and clothing.

Once a person's vehicle is stopped, the police are able to discern whether the driver is intoxicated or whether illegal goods are being transported in the vehicle. The methods they use to discern suspicious behavior vary according to the nature of the suspected infraction.

FIELD SOBRIETY TEST (FST): Police administer field sobriety tests to drivers they believe may be under the influence of alcohol or drugs. The driver may have slurred speech, a smell of alcohol about him, bloodshot eyes, and an unsteady gaze. The officer typically asks the driver to perform field sobriety tests such as reciting the alphabet—forward or backward—walking a line heel-to-toe, making a one-legged stand or a blind nose-touch. In addition, the officer may conduct blood alcohol tests using a portable machine that analyzes a suspect's breath. This device supposedly measures blood alcohol concentration (BAC). The driver blows into a vial. From the breath, his blood alcohol concentration is computed. Most state statutes use 0.08 or 0.10 parts of 100 as the standard for illegal driving. In most jurisdictions, the driver can request a urinalysis or blood test; these will be conducted at the station house.

P.A.S. III SNIFFER: A driver slows to a stop for a sobriety checkpoint and rolls down his window; the police officer thrusts the illuminated end of a flashlight six inches from his nose and starts asking questions. Impolite? No, a secret test. The motorist is unaware that a tiny, battery-powered device on the end of the flashlight is sucking in his breath and analyzing it for traces of alcohol.

Civil liberties groups do not like the Sniffer, saying it is an invasion of privacy and infringes on the Fourth Amendment protection against search and seizure. Covert use amounts to entrapment, said John Whitehead, president of the Rutherford Institute, a civil liberties group based in Charlottesville, Virginia. Truth is, the constitutionality of the Sniffer has never been tested in court.

Jarel R. Kelsey, president of PAS Systems International, thinks the Sniffer falls under the "plain sight doctrine," which holds that observations an officer makes with his senses do not violate the amendment. The doctrine applies whether the officer collects the air sample with his unaided nose or with the Sniffer, Kelsey says. For daylight use, the company also sells a clipboard containing an alcohol senser.

CRIP KITS: For years, police officers have been able to run quick color tests to determine the possible presence of numerous drugs, such as opiates, amphetamines and methamphetamines, cocaine, crack, cannabis, and LSD found both in the field and at the station house. The Crip kit uses color reactions—with reagent solutions—to identify the drug in question. The same company also supplies explosive-incendiary residue test kits.

Chapter 10

Resume of a Prosecution

The true creator is necessity, which is the mother of our invention.
—PLATO, *THE REPUBLIC*

Assistant District Attorney Henry Cassin was well-studied and pre-pared. His opening statement was neither formal nor wordy. Using a clear, direct, and serious tone, he began by introducing himself and his associates, and stressing how important the jury position was to the state and state justice, and how he appreciated the jurors' time and patience. He talked a little about the criminal justice system's objectives and how the jury played an important part in that process, both historically and today. He thanked the jurors for their appearance, and the subtle effect of this warm-up to the case, we all knew, was to convince the jury that he was a nice man and doing his job. But he didn't hasten to remind us that, as a representative of the state—and the very people sitting in the jury box were the state—he had no compunctions about "[his] dogged interest [being] in securing justice."

A prosecutor is recognized as the legal representative of the state, sometimes referred to as the district attorney or state attorney. Most often, prosecutors are elected officials, and this is a powerful political position, because he is the chief law-enforcement agent within a jurisdiction. Prosecutors instigate criminal charges against an accused person and represent the state at trial.

Prosecutors generally are or have been active members in bar associations, although some may start out with little significant experience in the criminal justice system. Experience as a prosecutor is typically a stepping stone to a higher political office and, for that reason, the length of civil service is rather short, and the turnover in office is quite high.

The role of the prosecutor spans the entire criminal justice process. Prosecutors often have available to them a great deal of resource material that is not possessed by the defense. In addition to the great numbers of people on the prosecution staff, they also have the best "scientific tools" at their disposal; items and artifacts that have been examined by the state or county forensic examiners and scientists to help support their cases. And cooperative police have been known to chase an identified suspect relentlessly and, in the case of killers of police officers, with enthusiasm. The "protect and serve" mentality unfortunately sometimes means a lack of impartiality.

The prosecution's power and influence can be observed at every step in the system:

- *Investigation.* Prosecutors often prepare search and arrest warrants and work with police in order to make sure that investigative reports are complete. They may, upon reports from citizens, initiate their own investigations independent of police, but under a harried metropolitan schedule—possibly two hundred cases or more a day—decisions will be based on a cursory review of the police report and criminal's history.

- *Arrest.* Subsequent to arrest, prosecutors screen their files to determine which cases should be prosecuted and which should be dropped. Police officers usually start the charging process with an arrest or citation.

- *Charges.* Since the prosecutor institutes and controls the case, he may file criminal charges, even if the victim does not approve, or refuse to file despite the victim's desire that criminal charges be brought to bear.

- *Initial appearance.* It is up to the prosecutor's office to ensure that all defendants are notified of the charges against them and that someone represents the prosecutor's office at the first court appearance. The prosecutor can also influence bail decisions. A crucial point for anyone accused of a crime— and this is of utmost importance—is that prosecutors can also discontinue a prosecution by drafting a *nolle prosequi*; this is a formal document entered into the record that declares the state is unwilling to go forward.

- *Grand jury.* The prosecutor is for all intents and purposes the "judge and prosecutor" within the grand jury. He is usually the only major legal officer in the room when the citizens determine whether or not to indict. Plus, the prosecutor chooses what evidence the grand jury will hear and not hear.

- *Preliminary hearing.* Prosecutors establish probable cause and draft *nolle prosequi* where applicable. So, in jurisdictions where there is no "initial appearance," they proceed directly to the preliminary hearing with the formal notice of charges and bail option.

- *Information indictment.* Prosecutors prepare information that establishes probable cause and files a document that obligates the accused to attend trial (referred to as "binding over"). In jurisdictions that use indictment rather than information as premise for trial, prosecutors establish probable cause for the grand jury.

- *Arraignment.* Prosecutors bring the accused to the court to answer to the matters charged in the information or indictment. "Plea negotiations" would normally take place during, before, or after this appearance. Plea negotiation is a process that allows the defendants to plead guilty to a reduced charge or charges.

• *Pretrial motions.* As representatives of the state, prosecutors initiate and participate in the arguments for any pretrial motions.

• *Trial.* Prosecutors are the government's trial lawyers; they are sworn to argue the case on behalf of the state, proving the guilt of the accused beyond a reasonable doubt.

• *Sentencing.* Prosecutors make sentencing recommendations to the judge.

• *Appeal.* Through written and oral debate, prosecutors make certain that convictions have been obtained properly and legally, that they should not be susceptible to reversal by the courts.

164

• *Parole.* In some jurisdictions, prosecutors make recommendations for or against parole when an inmate's records come up for review.

• *Probation and parole revocation hearing.* When a probationer or a parolee violates a condition of probation or parole, he is entitled to a hearing to see whether or not probation or parole will be revoked. Someone from the prosecutor's office may act as an advocate for the state in these hearings.

In Light of the Defendant's Courtroom Procedure . . .

As Dr. Z. G. Standing Bear, Diplomate with the American Board of Forensic Examiners, says,

The problems faced by prosecution and defense are quite different and, some say, tend to even each other out given that each side had advantages and disadvantages. This "game theory" approach in what may be a life-or-death situation for someone accused of crime is understandably often not appreciated by the individual looking at execution or at long, hard time in prison. In many situations, criminal defendants are poorly educated, indigent individuals who may not understand how the "game" is played. On such a playing field, often the innocent go to prison, and the guilty go free, depending upon the skill of the gladiator (lawyer) in the ring.

The presentation of the case for the defense is similar to that of the prosecution in that the defense counsel calls witnesses, directly examines them, and then turns them over to the prosecutor for cross-examination. There are standards of behavior and considerations of procedure that apply to the defense as well as the prosecutor. Briefly, they are:

• *The defendant is not required by law to present witnesses.* Instead, the defense can be based entirely on the evidence and testimony presented by the state.

• *The defendant is not required to give personal testimony.* A defendant's refusal to take the stand cannot be called to the attention of the jury by either the prosecutor or the judge. Any inference that would imply guilt, because of the defendant's lack of testimony, is prejudicial. If he does choose to take the witness stand, though, a defendant faces the same hazards of cross-examinations as any other witnesses.

• *The defense lawyer is not obligated to prove the innocence of his client.* He merely must show that the state has failed to prove guilt beyond a reasonable doubt.

The Work Life of the Prosecutor

"Overworked" and "undervalued" are two words to describe the caseload and rigor involved in the life of a prosecutor. For state purposes, there are generally two types of management for prosecutorial tasks: Segmented prosecutorial function and fluid prosecutorial function.

If an office operates under segmented prosecutorial function, only a certain number of prosecutors perform duties during any one particular stage of the system. In large cities, younger prosecutors fill the prosecutorial role at initial appearance and preliminary hearings. The more senior officials are left to determine whether the facts warrant sufficient evidence in order to give rise to criminal charges; if so, it is up to them to decide what charges will be made. Other prosecution attorneys are in charge of arraignments and pretrial motions. Still others are used as state's trial litigators, the lions of the court. And, finally, in another segment of the office, prosecutors will handle only cases on appeal.

In the other type of prosecutor's system—the fluid office, as opposed to the segmented type—a state attorney will handle a case from beginning to end. More conducive to smaller offices and communities, in the fluid system a prosecutor will take the case from its inception, get involved in investigation, and work it until the case is processed through the system. He will act as the jack-of-all-trades, from warrant to incarceration and even beyond.

In addition to the list of services provided in either one of these office systems, prosecutors must also maintain a certain media image. Since they are elected officials, they may appear in public service announcements on television or radio or present themselves at highly publicized, justice-related media events.

When Prosecutors and Police Butt Heads

The marriage of police with prosecutors is not always made in heaven. Insiders who study the system claim that there is a "cooperation gap" between certain police investigators and their legal partners. Policies between these two offices can prove very different, as well as the priorities one places on them. For this reason, case attrition—when an arrest is made but no charge is ever filed—is not out of the realm of possibility. Another difference that can rub the system raw is the fact that the officer is the one most knowledgeable about the case, yet he usually lacks person-to-person contact with the state attorney. They work different hours, have very different points of view, and do not socialize with each other.

In more practical matters, prosecutors need certain types of quality evidence in order to build a case, and the police may not be able to deliver. Thus, when there is a shortage or screw-up, a plea bargain or dismissal may be the only alternative, which tends to leave the cop quite sore. Another example: If the officer and the prosecutor do not coordinate on witness weaknesses, the defense may make them both look stupid in court. There are many other areas open for conflict between these two—a wise writer would do well to exploit them.

166

Bringing Charges

Prosecutors have what is frequently referred to as "prosecutorial discretion." They look at all the factors of a case, including the criminal's past record, and decide whether to file charges on all the crimes for which the suspect has been arrested or to file charges that are more or less severe than the charges leveled by police initially. In felony murder cases, it is the prosecutor who decides whether the defendant will face the death penalty.

If a crime is a misdemeanor, a prosecutor files an accusatory pleading directly in court. This pleading may be called a "criminal complaint," an "information," or a "petition." With a felony, prosecutors can use the same accusatory pleading format as with a misdemeanor, or they can also rely on an indictment handed down by a grand jury.

Writer's Tip
Sometimes, behavior as defined in a statute can perch on the line between felony and misdemeanor. Such crimes are called "wobblers," and the prosecutor has the discretion to decide which charge to bring. When creating a story, you may decide to use the ambiguity of a situation to add angst to a prosecutor's decision over which way to go.

FYI—
How prosecutors decide to seek the death penalty varies widely. Prosecutors use a wide range of criteria, running from visiting the crime scene to seeking the death penalty for anyone who kills with an axe or knife or in some other grisly way; some others come down hard on multiple murderers. One Oklahoma prosecutor admits to taking the hard line on robbers who kill convenience store clerks, and husbands or wives who kill their spouses in anger.

Ready for Court? Facing the Grand Jury
Several states operate under the grand jury system, which means a prosecutor

must obtain an indictment, also called a "true bill" from the grand jury, in addition to or instead of the presentment he would obtain from a preliminary hearing. The Fifth Amendment carries with it the words "No person shall be held to answer for a capital, or otherwise infamous crime, unless on a presentment or indictment of a grand jury." The Supreme Court has allowed states to deviate from this somewhat, deciding that state courts are not bound by the Fourteenth Amendment as the federal courts are. Just the same, about half the states have constitutional provisions obligating the use of grand juries as either an investigatory or supervisory board.

While defendants are usually warned that they are suspected of having committed a crime, the grand jury prosecutor need not tell the accused that he is a target. As a consequence, suspects may be told only of the general subject matter of the proceeding. In fact, the accused does not even have to be present at the proceeding. And most states do not allow the accused to have counsel with him. In federal situations, a witness must step outside the courtroom to speak with his attorney.

In respect to witnesses, anyone who fails to show under subpoena or refuses to cooperate with the investigation can face possible jail time for contempt. A target witness is given no warnings of any kind, yet, if found giving false testimony before the grand jury, he may be prosecuted for perjury. A contempt order may also be issued for anyone who fails to keep the details of the proceedings secret. The sheer power of the coerciveness of the court's demeanor colors the entire interrogation process.

Burden of Proof

It's been bandied about and used as a title for novels and films, but what is the burden of proof, and who is to judge this elusive concept? The burden of proof is a fundamental legal principle, placed on the prosecutor, who must prove the defendant's guilt *beyond a reasonable doubt*. Remember that the defendant is presumed innocent to start with, and remains so up to the time the judge or jury finds him guilty. The prosecutor's job is to provide enough evidence to convince either the judge or jury that the defendant is guilty.

I have defined crimes, breaking them down into their basic elements. For a refresher on those elements, you can refer to chapters 2, 3, and 4. For example, if someone is accused of a simple burglary, the following factors comprise his crime:

1. He has broken into a building
2. He has entered the building
3. That building is a dwelling
4. The dwelling is not his own, and he has not been given consent to enter
5. His intent in breaking and entering has been to commit a felony or to steal property

If the prosecutor wants the defendant convicted for those charges, he must prove all elements to the reasonable satisfaction of the judge or jury.

Reasonable doubt, it has been said, is not a mere possible doubt, because everything related to human affairs and depending on moral evidence is open to some possible or imaginary doubt. It is that state of the case which, after the entire comparison and consideration of all the evidence, leaves the minds of the jurors in the condition in which they cannot say that they feel an abiding conviction, to a moral certainty, of the truth of the charge.

Other standards of proof are:

* *Preponderance of the evidence.* Civil law uses preponderance of evidence as its standard of proof. A much lower standard than proof beyond a reasonable doubt, one side must merely produce slightly more convincing evidence than the other side in order to win.
* *Clear and convincing evidence.* The clear and convincing evidence standard is higher than the usual civil preponderance but somewhat lower than beyond a reasonable doubt. For an insanity defense, it is up to the defendant to prove it by clear and convincing evidence.[96]

Proving guilt lies at the very heart of a criminal trial. For the prosecutor, whether the defendant "did it" or not is not relevant to his prosecution. What is relevant is the prosecution's ability to produce admissible evidence to prove the defendant's guilt to the judge or jury beyond a reasonable doubt. Evidence is what the judge permits the jury to hear and consider. Evidence may take the form of physical exhibits, such as photographs, bullets, or a black-and-blue face. Answers to questions asked by the lawyers or by the judge are evidence, as is the sworn written testimony of a witness who cannot appear personally in court.

It is generally believed that the prosecution gets to go first in a trial because it has the burden of proof. This may not be an advantage. The prosecution, by presenting its case first, does not know much about the defendant's line of attack. Of course, this temporary setback is remedied by a part of the trial called the rebuttal (see chapter 14 for more on this part of the trial).

Rules of Evidence

In order to give the accused the opportunity to provide an informed defense, the state has a duty to present evidence in the early phases of the case. This presentation of evidence is governed essentially by the "rules of evidence." These concepts are similar to the rules of a game that govern the conduct of the players.

Evidence is made up of legal proofs presented to the court in the form of witnesses, records, documents, objects, and other means for the purpose of influencing the opinions of the judge or jury toward the case of the prosecution or the defense. The rules of evidence control the content of the trial—the kind of information witnesses can provide and the manner in which witnesses testify. Thus, the jury and judge obtain information through a series of questions and answers, instead of through a long uninterrupted narrative.

Evidence rules have evolved through common law judicial decisions. Most judicial evidence rules are written into state statutes; for example, California has the California Evidence Code, which was adapted for the Federal Rules of Evidence (FRE).[97] The FRE now govern federal trials. Nowadays, legislatures have taken over the development of evidence law, but the judges are still the ones who interpret it. With this power, the judge can require more proof before he allows legally admissible evidence.

RELEVANCE: Relevance is the foundation for evidence rules. For a piece of evidence to be considered relevant, some logical relationship must exist between the evidence and the factual issue it is supposed to prove. Like a link in a chain, the importance of any single item of evidence needn't be so strong that it proves or disproves a fact. It's good enough if the piece of evidence establishes proof along with other pieces of evidence.

169

Good examples of this are the *Matlock* TV shows, with Andy Griffith as the country lawyer in the ubiquitous seersucker suit. The defense would always object to Matlock's dramatic and lengthy stories' being irrelevant to the case. Of course, in the end, he was always given leeway in order to prove that this one single piece of seemingly insignificant evidence was the key to the case. The main limitation with relevance is that the connection must be based on reason and logic rather than on bias and emotion.

ADMISSIBILITY: Before evidence may be admitted in court, whether real, testimonial, direct, or circumstantial, it must meet certain legal requirements. In order to evaluate this, a judge may have a witness testify privately, which helps to determine whether the jury should be allowed to hear the same testimony. Information used to determine the admissibility of other evidence is called "foundational evidence" and is conducted in a phase of the trial called a minitrial.

Types of Evidence

Every courtroom assertion made on the part of an attorney must be supported by evidence in order to be accepted as true. While there are instances in which the necessity of hard evidence can be circumvented (these will be discussed next), the body of a court case is founded on hard evidence used to prove statements or assertions made by either the defense or the prosecution. The wide variety of evidence types can be consolidated into four basic roles that evidence plays in proving or disproving a charge: real evidence, testimony, direct evidence, and circumstantial evidence. Of course, both real evidence and testimony can be labeled as either direct or circumstantial.

Real evidence is made up of tangible objects, such as maps, stolen goods, photographs, blood samples or fingerprints, knives, guns and other weapons, and so on. Sometimes, reasonable facsimiles of objects—facsimiles like photographs, reproductions, or videos—may stand in place of real objects for practical purposes.

Testimonial evidence is the statement given by sworn witnesses. In a trial, after opening statements are made, the prosecution calls its first witness. The witness takes an oath, or affirmation to tell the truth. The prosecutor then begins to present evidence by using questions and answers called "direct examination."

Direct evidence refers to the observations of eyewitnesses. Indirect evidence, on the other hand, usually consists of circumstantial evidence.

Circumstantial evidence is information, which tends to prove or disprove a point at issue. Circumstantial evidence may be admissible as a result of being inferred; for example, a forensic technician gives testimony in court that the defendant's fingerprints were found on the drawer that held the murder weapon. It may be inferred that the defendant opened the drawer to get the knife.

These four characteristics are manifested in numerous types of evidence, ranging from bloody gloves to psychiatrists' opinions about behavior. Each of the following is admissible in a courtroom, and you would do well to use such a variety in your own descriptions of a case.

STATE'S EVIDENCE: "State's evidence" is a phrase used for testimony given by an accomplice or mutual associate in the commission of a crime. His testimony usually tends to incriminate or convict others and is provided as the result of a promise of immunity.

EXPERT EVIDENCE: Expert witnesses do not have to have any first-hand knowledge of the crime, and they are not restricted from expressing their opinions. Their testimony is given in relation to some scientific, technical, or professional matter, and they are allowed to speak with authority because of their special training, ability, or familiarity with the subject.

MATERIAL EVIDENCE: Evidence that relates to the crime charged or has a legitimate bearing or effective influence on the decision of the case.

PRIMA FACIE EVIDENCE: Evidence that, in the judgment of the law, is sufficient to establish a given fact, demonstrated clearly "on its face." The phrase may be mentioned in respect to a prima facie case—if a grand jury is convinced by the prosecutor's evidence that a *prima facie* case has been made, the evidence will prevail as proof of facts until it can be contradicted or overcome by other evidence.

SIMILAR FACT EVIDENCE: A very technical law of evidence, similar fact evidence presents facts similar to the facts of the crime charged. For example, the evidence might reveal the pattern of an additional or ancillary crime. To get similar fact evidence into court, however, one must show that the knowledge is both relevant and has probative value in establishing a material issue—in other words, the information must provide proof that this is a crucial or pivotal point. Although hemmed in by not being allowed to show bad character or a propensity to commit crime, a prosecutor may introduce similar fact evidence to show motive, identity, or absence of mistake.

A case involving sexual abuse of children might allow similar fact evidence. In a Wyoming case, a young girl testified against her father, who had been charged with sexual misconduct. Her credibility was then attacked by the defense, and the evidence admitted at trial was inconclusive as to the daughter's physical symptoms. However, the prosecution was able to procure similar fact evidence by putting an older sibling on the stand. The older child testified to a course of sexual misconduct similar to that for which the defendant had been charged. A Wyoming Supreme Court upheld admission of the testimony[98] and, in order to block the possibility of appeal, included in the brief a lengthy footnote showing that about half of the state courts now liberally admit the legality of introducing prior bad acts as evidence in sexual offenses.

NONCHARACTER "BAD PERSON" EVIDENCE: As a general principle, evidence rules do not allow prosecutors to charge someone with a crime and then attack the defendant's character in court—it would be too damning. For example, a jury might convict someone because he is a "bad person" and should be punished, regardless of whether the case presented was a strong one or not. To avoid the rule and still get his licks in, a prosecutor may argue that "bad person" evidence is relevant on a noncharacter theory. For an example of this, a judge might allow a prosecutor more latitude if he were to try to convict a defendant charged with assault and wanted to offer up evidence that the defendant had previously assaulted the same person. Despite the risk of the jury's basing its verdict on its impression of the defendant's character, the judge would allow it to be admitted as noncharacter evidence; such information would show the defendant had a grudge against the victim, making this more evidence of motive. To use the information, the judge would need to issue a "limiting instruction" to the jury, warning its members to not think of this as forbidden character use.

The same tactic is used by prosecutors to introduce evidence of "priors." By using the defendant's past convictions as *modus operandi*, the prosecutor can introduce evidence of methodology, proving that the defendant previously used the method that was almost nearly identical to the one allegedly used to commit the present crime. This approach is similar to fact evidence, but the information in this instance is coming from a previous criminal record instead of from witness testimony or a similar facts crime. Again, the judge would institute limiting instruction in order to differentiate between past criminal charges and what could be called the defendant's "M.O."

WITNESS CHARACTER EVIDENCE: Both the prosecution and the defense are allowed to attack the credibility of adverse witnesses according to the rules of evidence. The only stipulation is that the traits attacked must be concerning honesty. They can offer evidence of past misdeeds or anything involving dishonesty, evidence of deceit given by another witness, and evidence of specific acts such as their dodging the IRS and refusing to pay taxes.

SCIENTIFIC EVIDENCE AND THE FRYE TEST: Because of the evolution of new technology, new procedures and forensic services are becoming available to police at every turn. Evidence realized through scientific and technological discoveries can be both relevant and probative in a criminal case. The only stumbling block is ensuring that the new method can be supported by research.

In the past, federal and state courts followed the criterion that was formulated as a result of the case *Frye v. United States*,[99] in which the admissibility of a polygraph (lie detector) test brought new evidence into the courtroom. Experts in the field were called upon to determine whether they accepted the new scientific technique.

Conflicting interpretations and opinions have come to a draw: Both sides present as many expert witnesses as they think they need to shoot down the other side's experts. Juries are often confused, because both sides' experts can hold honest opinions, which can cause misguided opinions on the part of the jury.

Over the years, the test for scientific evidence has been broadened and modified, such as in a New York Court of Appeals decision that says that the technique's acceptance need not be unanimous—but accepted as reliable.

FYI—

Here is a list of evidence factors that can appear in any case. This catalog is certainly not exhaustive, and you should supplement it with your own findings when you do your research.

- Identification of one seen leaving the crime scene
- Forensic or crime scene materials
- Weather
- Animals
- Wounds
- Weapons
- Motive
- Time of death

- Pathology reports
- Exhibits
- Confessions, excited utterances
- Statements of family and friends
- Statements of police, witnesses, experts, and victims
- Noncharacter "bad person" evidence
- Documents, such as wills, letters, plans, and diaries
- Prior record
- Government and business records
- Electronic surveillance, such as videotapes, cameras, or audiotapes
- Receipts and records of rental or purchase
- Personal habits
- Personal electronics, such as answering machines, beepers, and cell phones

173

Sorry—Inadmissible

There are many things that must not be considered as evidence. For instance, what a lawyer says or claims to have proven is not evidence. Nor is testimony that the jury has heard but that the judge has ordered stricken from the record. Although the task is difficult, the jury must treat all such testimony as though it had never been given. Similarly, matters that a lawyer offers to prove but that the judge will not allow to be presented are not to be considered as evidence. A juror is not allowed to consider any information about the witnesses, parties, or lawyers present, or anything connected with the case other than the evidence seen or heard in the courtroom.

Writer's Tip

Two important factors about certain types of testimony and the prosecutor's responsibility. First, a defendant can never be compelled to be a witness by being called on by the prosecutor unless he wants to. But if he does choose to talk, testifying does not allow him to tell what happened in his own words; it must always be in a question-and-answer format. This process gives the prosecutor a high manipulation factor and can be used to a writer's advantage when conveying trial testimony.

Also, it is rare that a prosecutor will bring forth charges for perjury—lying under oath. It's difficult to prove an actual knowledge of false testimony, so it is not generally pursued. The only times perjury must be charged is when the prosecutor has no choice, such as when a high-profile person lies in full view of millions, on televised court proceedings, or when the media makes issue of it.

Judicial Notice, Admission, Stipulation, and Hearsay

Do you remember my assertion that "what a lawyer says or claims to have proven is not evidence"? Well, just as with all of the other hard-and-fast rules

I've provided for you, there are several methods of getting around this hurdle. Certain types of statements are, it turns out, admissible in a courtroom even if they lack tangible courtroom proof. These statements are called judicial notice, admission, stipulation, and hearsay.

Judicial notice is commonly held knowledge, or what one might call "conventional wisdom." It is accepted without proof by the courts. Either party can ask that judicial notice be taken as evidence without question. An example of this would be agreeing not to require proof that whiskey is an intoxicating liquor, because doing so would demand the testimony of a trained medical technician. So, for expediency, we can dispense with the laborious testimony because we all know what happens when someone imbibes.

Admission occurs when either party willingly admits the truth of any matter during the course of discovery or trial. This frees the other party from the trouble of introducing evidence to prove the matter.

Stipulation is a specific statement asserted by either the defense or the prosecution attorney. During a trial you may hear, "The defense stipulates that the day in question was Sunday, your honor." When both sides agree that particular matters or events are true, no further evidence need be offered. This is yet another timesaving device.

Hearsay is a statement or assertion of conduct that was made outside the courtroom by someone other than the witness and is offered for the truth. In other words, hearsay is knowledge or information the witness acquires secondhand—facts he was told by someone else. The "hearsay rule" governs the admissibility of such statements, determining whether something said by an absentee individual can be heard by the jury. It is not admissible when offered to prove its own truth—"I know the defendant murdered the store owner because John Doe told me he did," for example. Despite this rule, which usually expels hearsay from the courtroom—or despite an objection made by defense—out-of-court statements are often heard by the jury because the rule is riddled with exceptions. To figure out if a statement is admissible, ask yourself, "What is the statement offered to prove"? If the statement is offered to prove something other than its own truth, it may be admissible. Here are some examples of exceptions to the hearsay rule:

• *Dying declarations.* Because people want to believe that a dying person's last words will be the truth, this exception admits into evidence statements made by someone who senses imminent death and presents dying declarations. The dying declaration must be that of the victim, not of a third person.

• *Excited utterances.* The excited utterance exception to hearsay admits evidence statements made under the stress of excitement of perceiving an unusual event. The defining words here are "unusual event." For example, after witnessing a shooting, someone might say to the police "That man with the scar on his face just shot that woman!" and that witness runs away and is never found again. The policeman may testify in court to the stranger's comments.

- *Admission of guilt, or confession.* If the accused tells the investigator that he was at the apartment when the shooting took place, that admission will tie the defendant to the crime scene and may be admitted as evidence. This does not defy the Fifth Amendment protection against self-incrimination because the testimony of the law enforcement officer is that he heard the defendant make the admission outside the courtroom.

- *Assertions of state of mind.* The mental state of a defendant is often germane to his behavior and goes to help prove motive and intent in a criminal case. The assertions of state-of-mind exception admits into evidence accounts describing and characterizing people's emotions, beliefs, and intent, as they may hold influence over other criminal elements.

- *Prior inconsistent statements.* If a witness's testimony varies in some important way from prior out-of-court statements made by that same witness, the prior statements are admissible in evidence. Contradictions or a change of fact, before and after, usually indicate dishonesty or fudging with facts. For example, if an officer observes some type of conduct or writes down a statement from a witness, puts it in his report, and then finds that at trial the statement is changed markedly in fact, the prior statement can be admitted and will usually cast doubt on the testimony.

- *Business and government records.* Since businesses and government offices alike often keep records with some regularity and must rely on them for accurate reports, these documents can be admitted as evidence because they are presumed as trustworthy indicators reflecting regular business practices and activities.

175

FYI—

Although the hearsay rule implies the information is based on an "oral statement," it applies to written statements as well. Statements made in letters, faxes, and business reports, or other documents, may be hearsay or not, depending on their usage. And just as hearsay may be admissible because of an exception, so may the contents of a document.

Plea Bargain or "Negotiated Plea"

Since more than 90 percent of felony suspects arraigned plead guilty, writers should know more about plea bargains. A plea bargain is by its very nomenclature an agreement. The defendant agrees to plead guilty or no contest in exchange for an agreement by the prosecutor to drop some charges, reduce a charge to a less serious offense, or recommend to the judge a reduced sentence that is acceptable to the defense. Bargaining occurs between the prosecutor and the defendant—but it also must be sanctioned by the court—and can take place any time, generally, from the moment a defendant speaks to his lawyer for the first time, right up to the time a jury walks in with a verdict. In fact, it's been said that looking into the eyes of jurors has made more than one defendant choose a deal.

STATE'S ADVANTAGE: Despite plea bargains' unpopularity with citizens, there are several good reasons for the plea bargain procedure: It saves time and gets the matter over quickly; it saves money for the courts; those who are not likely to receive much jail time are processed out of jail; there are fewer problems with prison overcrowding, which results in an increased likelihood that serious offenders will not be let go before their full sentence is served; it lightens the state's caseloads; and it beats the possibility of a jury's making not-guilty verdict.

DEFENDANT'S ADVANTAGE: The principal benefit for a defendant's taking a plea bargain is that he may receive a lighter sentence for a less severe charge than he might get from a judge or jury. Other benefits are: The defendant may be released from jail immediately if certain charges are dropped; quick disposition is less stressful; a less serious offense would appear on record; there is less social stigmatizing with reduced charges; plea bargaining saves on lawyer fees; and less publicity is generated.

VICTIM'S POINT OF VIEW: The benefit to the victim is also substantial in that it moves the situation on rather quickly, with less publicity and stress of a trial. Since there is the chance the victim may feel the defendant was "let off" too easily, many judges and prosecutors consult with the victims before accepting any final pleas. In some jurisdictions, the victim or victim's family can address the judge directly before sentencing takes place in an effort to influence the probation terms or sentencing recommendations. With this new determination, the pendulum is swinging away from the defendant.

FYI—

Certain jurisdictions have enacted mandatory sentencing laws for certain crimes. This movement takes away any discretion on part of the judge to adjudicate lower sentences and is the ultimate deal-breaker. Check your jurisdiction's sentencing guidelines.

Writer's Jump-start

It's not at all unusual that an innocent person will take a plea. Sometimes the pressure of the justice system will make the accused so nervous that, when he is told the judge will be harsher if he goes to trial or that the prospect of losing looks bad, he succumbs to a quick negotiation. In reality, the "good deal" that the prosecutor offers may happen simply because the evidence against the defendant is weak. A case of the power of the state against an individual makes for a very compelling and interesting moral and ethical conflict.

Crimes Leading to Crimes

Once a person is involved in a criminal investigation or in a courtroom procedure—whether he is the accused, a witness, or the prosecutor himself—the possibility of new crime escalates. If your characters do not cooperate with the law once a crime has been discovered, they may find themselves in their own tub of hot water.

PERJURY: The Mosaic Code—the codes from Moses, in the Old Testament—had a stipulation about bearing false witness. Today's federal law[100] has proscribed the elements of perjury as: taking an oath to tell the truth before a competent tribunal, officer, or person in which the law of the United States requires an oath; then testifying or swearing falsely about documents or declarations or contributing as true any material matter which you do not believe to be true. Most states follow this basic principle and have laws against perjury. Difficult to prove, perjury is made more difficult to prosecute by the two-witness rule that predominates in most jurisdictions. Under this rule, the prosecution must prove the deceitfulness of the defendant's statements by living and witnesses or by using the testimony of one witness and corroborating documents or circumstances.

177

If someone makes a false statement under oath, he may recant that statement and tell the truth. Federal law makes a defense exception called recantation for people who decide to "'fess up." Recantation is recognized if the perjury has not substantially affected the proceedings and if it has not become evident that the deception has or will be inevitably exposed. The untruthfulness must be repudiated, which means "retracted" from the prior testimony, and the repudiation must take place before prejudice or damage has occurred.

OBSTRUCTION OF JUSTICE: Any time people interfere with the course of justice, they can be charged with obstructing justice. Many states have laws defining obstruction, and it can take many different forms—giving false information, knowingly giving a false alarm, impersonating an officer, intimidating a witness, tampering with a juror, destroying public records, and so on. Do not forget these charges, as they occur frequently in federal law as well. (These activities are a mainstay in many crime novels.) This is a rather modern statutory development, but it is taken very seriously when the prosecution begins stockpiling charges.

COMPOUNDING A CRIME: A person compounds a crime when he accepts money or something else of value in exchange for agreeing not to prosecute a felony. Any benefit given under an agreement for refraining from initiating or aiding in criminal prosecution is illegal. Indeed, turning a "blind eye" to wrongdoing is considered by some to be just as bad as committing the crime. There is, however, a modern statutory approach to the offense, and many states have designed their own policies.

> ### Writer's Jump-Start
>
> Have a character who needs to save face? A common scenario of compounding a crime occurs when a crime victim whose goods have been stolen agrees with the thief to take back the goods in exchange for not prosecuting. In fact, this could be a great story complication if that arrangement has been agreed upon, and then the really bad guys find out! In some courts, the dismissal of this kind of behavior may be granted because of the restitution to the victim, but writers should realize that an agreement cannot always be reached without prior court approval.

178

A Twist of the State Screw: Forfeiture and Confiscation

Taking a defendant's property as part of a "civil forfeiture" proceeding is actually a separate proceeding from the criminal case. The government takes property that has served a role in criminal activity—a boat that transported drugs or an airplane or "conveyance" vehicle used to transport controlled substances.[101] In 1996, the U.S. Supreme Court held that civil forfeiture is not "punishment," and, as a consequence, the forfeiture does not violate the prohibition against double jeopardy.

Cars that are taken because the owner sold narcotics from them are technically "forfeited" goods; in some instances, it does not matter that the car belongs to someone else. The theory is that the owner has the responsibility to see to it that his property is used only under legal conditions.

There is an interesting case you may want to look up. It concerns a home that was purchased with drug money and taken away as part of a bust. The Supreme Court ruled that, although proceeds traceable to an unlawful drug transaction are subject to forfeiture, an owner's "lack of knowledge" that his home had been purchased with the proceeds of illegal drug money constitutes a defense to a forfeiture proceeding under federal law.[102]

"Confiscation" is the seizure of personal property and usually takes the shape of contraband, or property that citizens have no right to possess, such as drugs, pornography, illegal guns, or illegal cigarettes. This type of property often becomes evidence at trial, and the citizen does not get it back. No one talks about it very much, and word has it that illegal narcotics sometimes find their way back out onto the street, after being taken from the police evidence room. Much of it, however, is destroyed.

It has been found that an entire farm was confiscated because the owner grew marijuana on the land. The sale of the farm for forfeiture reasons puts money into the coffers of the law-enforcement agency that seized it in the first place. Not only that, but a fight against forfeiture is both cumbersome and expensive. This may be an area to explore at greater length—the Drug Enforcement Administration has new civil sanctions, which permit a seizure of drug-related booty without a conviction or even a charge. If the property is seized, no matter the outcome, the owner can contest, but he may never get it back. Most forfeiture victims are not model citizens, but a report by the Cato Institute reveals about half of all people who forfeit property are charged with a crime. The Cato Institute is a nonprofit public policy research foundation headquartered in Washington, D.C.

Fines

The most common form of criminal punishment is the "monetary fine." If you've spent any time in the courthouse, you will see the registrar's office taking checks and assessing penalties (the cash register sings!). Most misdemeanors carry fines, especially for first offenses. Serious economic crimes, as defined by federal law, will also carry quite heavy monetary fines as part of the penalty phase.

179

In state courts, defendants are often required to pay court costs in addition to a sentence of probation or imprisonment. The effectiveness of assessing minimum and maximum fines sometimes seems ridiculous, as the defendants who commit these crimes may also be classified as indigents.

Prosecutorial Standards

It's probably no surprise that the American Bar Association—the largest professional organization of United States lawyers—has a list of standards for criminal justice and prosecutorial function in particular. Conduct such as misrepresenting facts, using illegal means to secure evidence, or employing others to do so, is "unprofessional conduct" and is subject to sanctions.

For a list of the standards, go to *www.november.org/ABAstandards.html.*

Part III: A Walk Through The Criminal Justice System

Chapter 11

Arrest, Charges, and Booking

The road to ruin is always kept in good repair.
—ANONYMOUS

In order to better understand the steps the accused—soon to be the defendant—goes through, we will follow the criminal offender on the descent from arrest to trial. Many criminal justice scholars maintain that if one is processed all the way through the criminal justice system, he will encounter eighteen steps, or processes. In this chapter, we will begin with reporting the crime and move sequentially through the stages leading to the time of the trial.

The Reported Crime

Authorities are alerted to the possible commission of a crime by members of the community, by officers who discover an offense on their own, or by fellow policemen conducting investigative and intelligence work. Studies indicate that less than half of all committed crimes are actually reported. The most dominant offenses in reported crime are theft or destruction of property, crimes involving drugs or alcohol and assaults, and, comprising less than 5 percent of reported crimes, robbery, rape, and homicide.

The distinctions between a major crime (felony) and a minor offense (misdemeanor) are made according to the types of offenses committed and the consequences of committing them. Major crimes, coming up through history, were those that caused serious damage to another person or property. The common law called these "felonies." The punishment was, generally, forfeiture of land, property, or life. For modern times, the felony is punishable occasionally by forfeiture, such as what is done with drug crimes, but primarily, it is punishable by more than one year in jail and a loss of certain civil rights—the right to vote and the right to bear arms, for example. Lengthy jail sentences can be served in a state penitentiary, whereas misdemeanors are usually served in county jails or workhouses or may even result in some type of diversion, such as a boot camp or community service. Generally, those charged with felonies are granted the right to a jury trial.

Misdemeanors are met with punishment of a year or less in jail and, most likely, some type of fine or payment of court costs. To help further distinguish the differences between varying degrees of misdemeanor, many states have other classifications that correlate with the possible amount of punishment. The higher classifications are called "gross misdemeanors," or "high misdemeanors." Those infractions on the lower end of the scale will be referred to as "petit crimes" (hence, "petty criminals"), or "simple misdemeanors." Petit crimes will not generally result in a jail sentence and are usually offenses involving a traffic ticket or some type of disorderly conduct. The trial for a petit misdemeanor is most always conducted before a local magistrate or municipal judge and is relatively swift. Serious misdemeanor trials, on the other hand, are completed with six-person juries. For those convicted of misdemeanors, the right to a jury trial will generally be an option only for those charged with multiple infractions or repeated offenses.

182

Writer's Tip

If initiated by a prosecutor, prosecution for a misdemeanor—a less serious offense than a felony—comes in the form of a complaint. The term "complaint" gives the impression that it is an action taken by an injured party or the victim of a crime. Not so. Although the victim of a crime may be the complainant, the plaintiff—i.e., the person who brings the case to the court for remedy—is actually the people of the state acting through their local representative, the district attorney. Writers should only mention misdemeanors as a matter of setting, they are not serious enough to hang a story on.

The Investigation

The police procedures will vary depending on whether the police are investigating a newly discovered crime, past crimes still open on the books, crimes involving anticipatory offenses or sting operations, or leads stipulated under the aegis of the prosecutor, using his direction and power based on subpoena. For our purposes here, we are using a newly discovered crime, so the first questions will be "Was a crime committed?" and "Who did it?" Police will attempt to answer these questions and collect evidence in order to assign guilt at a potential trial. Investigations may involve one or more of the following functions: locating the offender, interviewing suspects and asking for identification, interviewing the victim and any witnesses, canvassing the neighborhood, preserving and examining the scene, collecting physical evidence, checking department records and files, contacting informants, surveying the scene, and working undercover if necessary.

The Arrest

Arrest is based on probable cause, and the accused is taken into custody for transport to police facilities, charging, and detention. Although interrogation usually occurs at the station house after arrest, it may occur anywhere. Miranda warnings must be given if the accused is subjected to express questioning. For misdemeanors or certain traffic crimes, offenders are issued a citation, which is a notice, signed by the offender, to appear in court. These citations allow the offenders to be released until court date. Some suspects who are given citations in lieu of being taken to jail because of overcrowding or other considerations must go through the booking process within a few days of their arrest. Weapons, contraband, or other evidence will be collected from those arrested.

FYI—

Arrest reports in criminal cases play a huge role in the many proceedings after their initial making. They are used to help determine what charges the prosecutor will file; they influence the judge with how much bail is required; they leave their stamp on the aftermath of preliminary hearings where hearsay evidence is permitted; and they affect the willingness of the prosecutor to plea bargain. Likewise, in a strange twist of fate, arrest reports can also be used to discredit the police officer who testifies in court, a defense strategy also called "impeachment."

For the accused, the onus of arrest is far-reaching: In addition to having an official arrest record, the arrest may have to be reported to employers and any licensing agencies like a state board of medical practices or a professional banking affiliation,

Booking

Upon the arrival of the arresting officer and the accused at the holding facility, booking begins. Booking records provide information about the people detained, and the process creates an official arrest record. It is a highly impersonal process. The name, arrival, and offenses are put into the police log, which is strictly a clerical function, and suspects are reinformed of the charges. Most everything is put into a computer system. The arrested person will then be photographed. The photograph, sometimes called a "mug shot," albeit unflattering, serves several purposes in addition to the most obvious purpose of identification; one other purpose is to document the suspect's physical condition on arrival.

Next, personal belongings such as keys, a wallet, or a purse, are held for safekeeping, and a receipt is furnished. Contraband, evidence, or any illegal substances will not be returned. Rumor has it that police can search the contents of the arrested person's wallet, read any papers on his person, or push pager buttons to discover the names and numbers of people who have contacted the suspect most recently. Check with the agency of your story's locale for the procedure of these specifics.

Taking fingerprints is a regular part of the booking record. Many of today's modernized precincts have dispensed with the messy inking and blotters of old, and the suspect places his fingers and palms on an electronic plate, which scans the fingerprints and automatically logs them with the file (somewhat like a copy machine). Any fingerprint or handprint impressions are also, as a matter of record, entered into a nationwide federal database, which is accessible to local, state, and federal agencies. With the AFIS (Automated Fingerprint Identification System), fingerprints can be compared with the countrywide database in the hopes of identifying wanted suspects of crimes.

In addition to the basics, arrestees may also be required to provide voice, hair, and fingernail samples or to act as a "possible" in a lineup for identification purposes. Necessity and probable cause precede the taking of the suspect's blood without a warrant. Blood samples are usually wanted for the purpose of determining whether the suspect is under the influence of alcohol or drugs; but samples may also be used for a comparison to blood found at crime scenes. Collection of pubic hair or other evidentiary minutiae generally requires a warrant, on the premise that such material is an intrusion of personal privacy.

Courts have generally held that a suspect can be subjected to a "strip search" as part of the booking process. Booking searches are conducted by law enforcement personnel—a woman officer checks female arrestees, and a male officer checks the males—and the searches are circumspect with regard to private body areas.

Generally, a full-body search, including the cavities of the body, can be conducted with a court order by a medical doctor, in a hospital, in order to determine if the person is hiding contraband. Violation of these typical guidelines can result in a civil lawsuit.

Some jurisdictions have allowed the police to use reasonable force to prevent someone from destroying evidence by swallowing it. Police cannot choke, threaten, or cut off air passages, but they may force a suspect's chin to his chest, making it difficult to swallow.

And, finally, the booking process may include health screening for the safety of jail officials and the well-being of other inmates. X-rays used to detect tuberculosis are common, and blood tests for a determination of sexually transmitted diseases are sometimes conducted.

Jail and Prisons

Although the word "jail" is adapted from the French-Norman word gaol, the concept of incarceration has existed for thousands of years. All the ancient civilizations had designated confinement areas. Jails are principally a function of local government. Roughly 85 percent of our jails are operated by counties or some form of local government, but some large cities operate a separate department of corrections.

There are three different types of jails—pretrial detention facilities, sentenced facilities, and combination facilities. The sentenced facility is, logically, where people with sentences serve their time, and they are usually defined as misdemeanants, although a few may house felons with short sentences. If operated by a city or county, a sentenced facility may be called a city or county prison, or a city or county correctional facility. It's interesting to note that no one really knows how many jails there are in the United States. Some administrators count their work farms or work-release centers as jails. Lock-ups used specifically for drunk tanks or drug abusers are often counted separately. The federal agency numbers do not add up against those of the Law Enforcement Assistance Administration, which also does not coordinate with the Advisory Commission on Intergovernmental Relations. One thing I do know is certain: Between 1950 and 1986, the jail population more than tripled, occupying what is approximately between 3,500 and 4,000 short-term facilities.

Correctional institutions, also referred to as prisons or penitentiaries, are operated by the federal government, states, or under the umbrella of private corporations. A few states—Hawaii, Rhode Island, Delaware, etc.—have an integrated jail-prison system. In some major metropolitan areas like Chicago, New York, and San Diego, the Federal Bureau of Prisons operates metropolitan correction centers for people awaiting trial on federal charges. Prisons have different classifications: Maximum, medium, and minimum security (there is a new distinction as well, the "maxi-maxi" prison, which houses inmates with chronic behavior problems). All types of classifications may be used in the same institution and the degrees of security vary by state. The inmates generally have been convicted of felonies, multiple felonies, or extremely heinous crimes.

185

FYI—
The first paragraph in a handout called the "Garland County Detention Center Inmate Rules and Regulations" states: "You are now an inmate within the Garland County Detention Facility. We did not catch you, convict you, nor sentence you; but we are charged with the responsibility of confining you."

JAIL FUNCTIONS AND INHABITANTS: Jails serve four functions: deterrence (stopping), incapacitation (isolating); retribution (punishing), and rehabilitation (saving). In other words, they deter the accused from committing future criminal acts, they segregate the offender from the general population in order to ensure that he will appear at court, they serve as punishment for crimes committed, and, ideally, they foster a change in the criminal's attitude and behavior.

Although originally set up as short-term facilities, jails have had to provide additional functions over the years. Various agencies prevail on the "good spirit" of local jails to provide room for a motley crew; hence, any jail's population includes:
• Pretrial detainees
• Federal defendants held according to the Bail Reform Act stipulations of 1966 (see page 198)

- Witnesses in protective custody
- Convicted offenders awaiting sentencing
- Juvenile offenders (those being charged as adults)
- Indigents, vagrants, and the mentally ill, the latter of whom pose many problems, including being "lost" within the system
- Prisoners wanted on warrants in other states
- Persons on agreement between the state and federal prisons for overflows
- Alleged probation and parole violators
- People who are considered to be detached, disreputable, or offensive persons but who are not criminals (for example, persons who have caused disruption in public areas—harassed other drivers, been accused of public drunkenness—or have presented possible endangerment to others)

186

ADMINISTRATION AND PITFALLS: Unfortunately, administration of jails is an unpopular task, the tail that wags the dog. Usually, jails are the province of county sheriffs—those elected to a position—with no special qualifications; previous law enforcement experience is not required, and no national standards for sheriff professionalism are in place. The pay structure for chief jailers and staff is generally poor, and, in some cases, a transfer to such a position serves as a punishment for officers who have committed infractions, or it is used for disciplinary purposes, making the deputies who run the jails no better than custodians.

Oftentimes, officers have no special education or training, and the budgeting constraints make for poor career opportunities as well as poor conditions. In the past, selection of correctional officers has emphasized physical attributes rather than behavioral or educational skills. In general, jail operations are underfunded and inadequate. Little accountability for jail improvements or upkeep is woven into the system, and sometimes money is diverted to the sheriff's other responsibilities, such as keeping the peace within county lines, assuring that traffic flows smoothly, and buying new patrol cars.

JAIL OVERCROWDING: Much has been said about jail overcrowding just recently. According to *Crime and Justice in America*, "A government report published several years ago notes that 22% of the nation's 621 largest jails (those with a capacity of more than 100) were under court order to either expand capacity or reduce the number of inmates housed, and 24% were under court order to improve one or more conditions of confinement." As a consequence, overcrowding creates tension among prisoners and staff, increased wear and tear on the buildings and equipment, problems with overtime for officers, and inability to meet program standards and services.

JAILHOUSE INFORMANTS: The accused should never assume that his fellow inmate is a friend, confidant, or brother or sister. Incarceration may have many effects on the accused, the least of which is to consider the bunkmate as a "soul brother" or someone who will side with him at being "set up" or put in jail on "trumped up charges." Baring the soul or explaining the details of the case could put the accused into deeper water. The people the accused confides in will most likely be looking for a way out themselves, and the prospect of exchanging information for some type of deal is not out of bounds—they're prisoners, after all! Before your character spews forth all he knows, have him picture his confidant sitting in the witness box, testifying that his cellmate confessed everything to him while in jail.

The Decision to Charge

The initial decision to charge the suspect has begun with the arresting officer. That decision will now be reviewed by both the police authority and the prosecutor. Keep in mind that prosecutorial review is an ongoing process. Simultaneous with this is a procedure called checking the warrant, which means the booking officer will check to see if the arrested person has any outstanding warrants or if he is wanted for other infractions, ranging from parking tickets to murder charges coming from other states.

> **FYI—**
> Some states do have mandates allowing suspects to make one or more telephone calls after being booked. Arrestees often phone their attorneys, friends, and family in order to obtain bail money and advice. And since eavesdropping is not disallowed, suspects should be careful about what they say, because police officers and other administrative officials are sometimes known to monitor calls.

PREFILING SCREENING: Prosecutors can adjust charges, require more evidence, or even release the arrestee, rearresting him at a later date, contingent upon obtaining more evidence. They may interview the arresting officer, and some will insist on interviewing the victim in certain cases.

Some common reasons for the decision not to proceed—also called "no paper" or "nolle prosequi"—are the result of:
- Insufficient evidence
- Witness difficulties, such as loss of desire to proceed, fear of reprisal, or the disappearance of the witness
- Criminal proceedings of other means, such as prosecution given over to another jurisdiction, probation revocation, or pending charges for a different offense
- The interest of justice, meaning prosecution, is not appropriate even though proof of guilt is not the problem

- Anticipated use of a diversion program, such as enrolling in treatment programs, providing restitution, or participating in some other corrections program

JOINDER OF OFFENSES: When a defendant is accused of several distinct offenses arising from one related crime, he is prosecuted jointly for all offenses; this is called "joinder." Two or more offenses may be charged in the same indictment or information. In essence, this unites separate counts or charges for an offense if the offenses charged are the same or similar in character and based on the same act. For example, a thief who steals four televisions in one break-in may face a separate charge for each.

FYI—

In order to process multiple criminal charges jointly or separately, a prosecutor must consider the Double Jeopardy Clause of the Fifth Amendment. The basic test given by the Supreme Court is to determine whether there are two separate offenses and whether each provision of the criminal law requires proof of an additional fact that the other does not. The *Blockberger* test compares the elements of the crimes in question. The applicable rule is that, where the same act or transaction constitutes a violation of two distinct statutory provisions, the test to be applied to determine whether there are two offenses or only one is whether each provision requires proof of an additional fact, which the other does not.[103] In 1980, the Supreme Court reviewed a case in which the defendant was first convicted of failing to slow his car in order to avoid an accident. Later, he was charged with manslaughter arising from the same accident. Vitale,[104] the defendant, was told he would have a substantial claim of double jeopardy. Now, the *Blockberger* test is not the exclusive method of determination for the principle of double jeopardy, and some courts look also to the evidence presented with something known as the "same evidence" test. The criteria here bars a second prosecution based on the same conduct by the defendant that was at issue in the first prosecution. This, too, has come and gone, and the *Blockberger* test is back in vogue. One important thing to remember, though, is that the dual sovereignty of the federal government and the states allow separate trials of a defendant for the same offense.

SEVERANCE: In cases where a defendant can show that a joint trial of two or more charges would unfairly prejudice his prosecution, a motion for a severance of the charges is filed. Trial judges have the discretion in this matter, and it is up to the defendant to bear the burden of proving it. When would this work? If a defendant is willing to testify in one case but does not want to speak to another charge, a severance might be his remedy. Or say, for example, a defendant has two charges—one is being a convicted person in possession of a firearm, and the other is a case of robbery. To support the charge in the firearm case, the prosecution would have to show the defendant's prior bad acts or his prior conviction of a felony. Obviously, such a showing would be prejudicial against his defense of the robbery charge if heard by the same jury.

Filing the Complaint

A fairly brief document, the complaint will set forth a statement that the accused, at a particular time and place, committed specific acts constituting a violation of a particular criminal law. The complaint will be signed by a person, usually the victim, who swears under oath that the factual allegations are true. If a police officer is the complainant, and he did not personally witness the crime but relied on information received from witnesses or others, he will note that the allegations are based on "information and belief." After the filing of the complaint, the accused officially becomes the "defendant" in a criminal proceeding. In felony cases, the complaint serves to set forth the charges only before the magistrate court, because an information or grand jury indictment will replace the complaint as the charging instrument when the case reaches the trial court.

189

JURISDICTION: In order to hear and decide a case, the court must have jurisdiction over the subject matter and the parties to a case. State courts, of course, have jurisdiction over criminal offenses that take place in their state. An individual cannot be tried for a crime unless the court has jurisdiction over that person—the individual must be a resident of the state. Once it has been determined that a court does have jurisdiction over the accused, an arrest warrant, or *capias*, is issued. The term *capias* is used when the prosecutor has already filed the information.

The First Appearance

Once the complaint is filed, the case is put before a magistrate court, and the defendant must appear within a specified period of time. This appearance of the accused has many names: "preliminary appearance," "arraignment on the complaint," "initial presentment," or "preliminary arraignment." The exact timing of the arraignment usually depends upon the custodial status of the accused. If the accused was released on a citation or if he posted a "station house bail," there is likely to be an interval of a few days between the filing of a complaint and the arraignment. On the other hand, if the accused was arrested and put into jail for detention, he must be attended to rather quickly, usually within several hours to forty-eight hours of his arrest. He can be sent to an evening or night court, although most arraignments are conducted as the first business on the court day calendar—heard the first thing in the morning, sometimes starting as early as 8:30 A.M.

In some cases, which involve a plea and arraignment for felony, the case is "bound over" to a circuit court, indicating a type of statute that is out of this court's jurisdiction or level of experience.

Usually, the arraignment will be brief. The accused who has not been released will be dressed in jail attire (in my area of Arkansas, that means an orange jumpsuit); he will be escorted from the holding cell; walked or driven over to the courthouse with either shackles or cuffs on legs, or hands, or both; paraded down the courthouse halls; and made to sit on a bench under the watchful eye of a deputy, or bailiff, or both. If the accused is out on bail, he will appear in a suit, or at least in business attire, with hair cut or trimmed.

190

COVER SHEET

STATE OF ARKANSAS

CRIMINAL INFORMATION

This criminal information cover sheet or the standard criminal information form is required by Supreme Court Administrative Order Number 8 to be completed for every defendant and filed by the prosecutor. The data contained herein shall not be admissible as evidence in any court proceeding or replace or supplement the filing and service of pleadings, orders, or other papers as required by law or Supreme Court rule. Instructions are located on the back of the form.

County **Garland**	District	Case Number **CR-2000-**
Judge	Division	Filing Date
Style of Case		
Prosecutor Providing Information		

Is this an Amended Information? ☐ Yes	Is D being charged as a Habitual? ☐ Yes
If yes, are you	Are multiple D's charged in the information? ☐ Yes
Adding Offense(s)? ☐ Yes	
Dropping Offense(s)? ☐ Yes	
Changing Offense(s)? ☐ Yes	

Defendant's Full Name	Date of Birth	Race	Sex	SID #	Arrest Date

Address (Street, City, State, Zip)	SS#	Driver's License No.
	Arrest Tracking #	Prosecutor's File #

Alias 1	Alias 2	Alias 3

The attached information accuses the above named defendant of the following crime(s):

Code #	Offense	A/S/C	Offense Date	Counts	F/M	Class

```
MC:   99-00000
ARR:  6-20-00
B/O:  Direct
SID:  123456
ATN:  567890
```

IN THE CIRCUIT COURT OF GARLAND COUNTY, ARKANSAS

THE STATE OF ARKANSAS   PLAINTIFF

    VS.   Case No. CR 2000-

JOHN DOE   DEFENDANT

INFORMATION

INFORMATION FOR:

Possession of a Firearm by Certain Persons
Class D Felony
NMT 6 yrs. ADC and/or a fine NMT $10,000.00

191

CODE NO: 5-73-103

    I, GEORGE WASHINGTON, Prosecuting Attorney within and for the
Eighteenth Judicial District of the State of Arkansas, of which
Garland County is a part, in the name and by the authority of the
State of Arkansas, on oath, accuse the defendant, **JOHN DOE (W/M
DOB: 1-6-81)**, of the crime **Possession of a Firearm by Certain
Persons**, committed as follows, to-wit: The said defendant on or
about June 20, 2000, in Garland County, Arkansas, did unlawfully
and feloniously: **possess a firearm, having been previously
determined by a jury or court that he committed a felony, to-wit:
Defendant was convicted in Garland County on 10-11-99 for the
charge of Possession of a Controlled Substance,** against the
peace and dignity of the State of Arkansas.

                         GEORGE WASHINGTON
                         PROSECUTING ATTORNEY

                         BY: _____
                         THOMAS JEFFERSON
                         DEPUTY PROSECUTING ATTORNEY

Filed this _____ day of June, 2000.

                         BENJAMIN FRANKLIN, CIRCUIT CLERK

                         BY: _____
                         DEPUTY

Indorsed Witnesses:

The magistrate will certify the identity of the accused, inform him of the charges, read him his rights, and, as one of the most important functions for the accused, set bail. The following are the standard rights read to the accused during an arraignment:

You have a right to an attorney; if you cannot afford one, one will be appointed to you.

You have a right to a trial by a jury of your peers.

You have the right to not incriminate yourself.

You have the right to a speedy trial.

If you plead guilty, you could be sentenced to death (for a capital case) or serve life in prison without the possibility of parole.

Do you understand these rights?

THE PLEA: For a misdemeanor, the defendant will enter a plea, and the magistrate will provide a sentence, which could include jail time, restitution, diversion to a different program, community service, and a fine along with leveling court costs (everyone pays court costs!). For a felony charge, the defendant will stand together with his attorney and enter a plea—most likely, "Not guilty." After hearing the plea, the magistrate will set a date for the preliminary hearing, give advice on any rules or admonitions about timeliness, and set a cutoff date for motions.

Whether or not he had a bail hearing, a defendant can ask the arraignment judge to review his bail status, reduce the bail, or convert bail to out on the defendant's own recognizance. At this point, the prosecutor may ask the court to raise the amount of bail if it appears necessary to ensure the defendant's appearance once again.

COURT-APPOINTED COUNSEL: If the defendant does not have a private attorney with him, the magistrate will inform him of his right to be represented by counsel; if he is indigent, he will be informed of his right to court-appointed counsel. The counsel right is applicable in all jurisdictions and for all felonies or serious misdemeanors. The magistrate determines whether the defendant is indigent by evaluating a financial statement completed by the defendant. If he qualifies, a public defender—who is usually present in the courtroom in case he is needed—will be assigned to him. The accused will talk to his attorney before entering a plea.

If the defendant decides not to take representation, he will have to sign a waiver. This is serious business, because representation of counsel is based on the Sixth Amendment to the Constitution.

Public defenders are held suspect by many different groups. People generally believe they are not very good, because they are not in private practice but work for the state. Because they occupy a government position, defendants don't trust them. Also, it is thought, the quality of service is determined by the money, meaning, public defenders typically receive a set county or municipal fee, no matter how many hours they put in the case—and their caseloads are deep. More money is available for a capital case, naturally, but investigative work and interviewing is expensive, and usually out of the purview of a city employee's salary.

Some say public defenders are young lawyers trying to gain experience. Others claim they are old dogs, not competent enough to support themselves in private practice. And still others say the public defender's office is simply a stepping-stone to politics, entrance into private firms, or even an easing off into retirement.

Even though public defenders rack up more guilty pleas than private attorneys do, one must consider the type of clientele that is thrust upon them. They handle clients who are often guilty. And they are swamped with recidivists, repeat offenders whose guilt is as obvious as their worn-out prison attire.

193

Or, indeed, the public defender of your story's county may be just starting out. A couple of advantages to having a novice attorney, however, may be that he has the zeal to represent a client to his best ability, and the nature of the young mind is such that the criminal law statutes, rules, and new regulations will be very fresh in memory. Whatever one may think about this misrepresented and misunderstood sect of criminal justice society, the attorneys who represent indigent defendants are sorely needed.

Some common complaints with respect to their inefficiency are that they may sacrifice justice in the interest of cutting their overwhelming caseloads. Others believe they may not be sufficiently independent of the system that hires them—in the day-to-day dealings with either opposing counsel or the judge, they may not want to alienate themselves, offend, or "rock the boat," as most often-heard courtroom adage goes. Even so, public defenders do want a successful case record, and a writer may make his public defender follow whatever route will advance the story. I only suggest that you study the public defender's lifestyle, responsibilities, and clientele before you formulate your character outlines and plot points.

A "conflict of interest" may take the public defender out of the game, so to speak, and the next best option for the judge would be to appoint private counsel from the panel attorney roster (more on this below), or appoint private counsel in general. For instance, if two defendants are charged jointly with committing a crime, it's likely the public defender will not take on both clients, because later each defendant may attempt to assign blame to his partner-in-crime. Or, if the victim is a former client of the public defender, conflict of interest is pretty evident. Since crime has a tendency to repeat itself like a bad penny turning up again and again, this second situation presents a double conflict. The public defender would be sworn to zealously represent his current client's interests over any personal inclinations, plus, he would have to agree to not disclose any confidential information learned through previous dealings . . . too much to ask for.

There is something called a "don't peek" policy among public defenders, which unofficially states that a public defender will not use information or any prior evidence against a former client. The term "don't peek" refers to his keeping his honor by not looking into old public defender files for damaging information. The judge has an interest in accepting such promises from a Public Defender, a fiscal incentive. It will almost always be less expensive to appoint a second public defender than it will be to seek out a private attorney for indigent representation.

In states that have not set up public defender offices, there will be panel attorneys, sometimes referred to as "assigned counsel system." Panel attorneys handle most of the criminal cases in a kind of round-robin way. They are pooled from a group of private attorneys who devote either part or all of their practice to representing indigent defendants at government expense.

The assignment of a private counsel or panel attorney also has its benefits and its drawbacks. A lawyer who is pulled out of private practice to defend an indigent client may have fees that are too small to cover his expenses and will not want to exhaust himself or his staff to further the investigation. On the other hand, if he is a defender of right, a crusader, he may go broke trying! Another disadvantage of private counsel's service is that there is no guarantee that an attorney from a pool will have the necessary experience if his background lies primarily in corporate law. This means that your newbie will have to "study up" quickly in order to hold his own, a compelling underdog characterization. Since the private attorneys, too, make a living from billable hours, yours may look for solutions of expediency to the detriment of his client because he is paid a flat fee by the state. The benefits of private counsel are the amount of resources he has access to, for example, research staff, cameras, phone service, etc. So many ways to go.

Here, too, if you are choosing a panel attorney for a character in your story, spend some time researching both the pros and cons of this type of representation. It can aid your story more than you realize.

Bail

Apart from the obvious desire to get out of jail quickly, the accused person has a better chance of aiding his defense counsel if he is "on the outside." While out on bail, he can help locate witnesses, puzzle out details, and confer with counsel without the inconvenience and stigma a jail cell carries. During this interval of freedom, the accused can also pursue gainful employment (a plus in the eyes of the court) and take care of family responsibilities while awaiting the disposition of criminal charges.

Getting a pretrial release is commonly referred to as granting bail. Bail comes in the form of cash or its equivalent, called a bail bond, that is tendered

HOT SPRINGS BAIL BOND COMPANY, INC.
540 Ouachita Avenue
Hot Springs, AR 71901
(501) 321-9100
Fax (501) 321-2164

STATE OF ARKANSAS
COUNTY OF _____

CITY OF _____

CASE NUMBER _____

BAIL BOND

XX_____ _____

_____, hereinafter referred to as the Defendant, being in custody, charged with

Item 5 - defendant

the offense(s) of _____

and having been admitted to bail in the amount of $ _____

Now __HOT SPRINGS BAIL BOND COMPANY, INC.__ does hereby undertake and guarantee that the Defendant will appear before the Court designated below at the time indicated, and further guarantees all subsequent appearances before any court having jurisdiction, including appearances relating to appeals and on remand, until the Defendant is lawfully discharged or upon rendition of final judgement has surrendered himself in execution thereof. If the Defendant fails to perform any of these conditions, we will pay and forfeit to the _____ court of _____
(County or Municipality to be Inserted)

the sum of $ _____

In Witness Whereof I have hereunto set my hand and seal this _____ day of _____, 20 _____

Approved: _____

Defendant: _____

Defendant to Appear In: _____

Address: _____

Municipal Court, City of _____

City, State, Zip: _____

Municipal Court, County of _____

Phone: _____

At _____ A.M./P.M. on _____, 20 _____

Surety: __HOT SPRINGS BAIL BOND COMPANY, INC.__

_____ County Circuit Court

Attorney-in-Fact (agent) _____

_____ County Chancery Court

on NOTICE TERM _____

Power of Attorney

Authority for:	Item 1	Item 2	Item 3	Item 4	Power
		Not valid for bond in excess of	Not valid if used after	Date Issued	Number AA _____
To act as Attorney-In-Fact – State of Arkansas		250,000.00	12-31-2005.		

			Insert Bond Amount Void if Not Completed
DEFENDANT			
SOCIAL SECURITY #:		DATE OF BIRTH:	$

Know All Men By These Presents:

SECTION 1 __HOT SPRINGS BAIL BOND COMPANY, INC.__, a incorporation does hereby make, constitute and appoint the party as set forth in Item One (1) above as its true and lawful Attorney-in-Fact with full power and authority hereby confirmed to execute on behalf of the said Company, as sole surety only subject to the limitations as herein set forth, Bail Bonds, in Judicial Proceedings, whether criminal or civil, appeal bonds or any other kind of appearance bond in any State Court, county Court, or Municipal court and in all U.S. Federal Court on behalf of the above named defendant.

SECTION 2. That the authority of such Attorney-in-Fact to bind the company shall not in any event exceed the amount set forth in Item Two (2) above on any one bond and the said Attorney-in-Fact is hereby authorized to insert in Item Five (5) the name of the person on whose behalf this bond is given.

SECTION 3 This power is not valid unless used on or before the date set forth in Item Three (3) above and can only be used once.

SECTION 4 The authority of such Attorney-in-Fact is limited to appearance bonds and cannot be construed to guarantee failure to provide payments, back alimony payments, child support payments, fines or wage law claims.

SECTION 5 __HOT SPRINGS BAIL BOND COMPANY, INC.__ does make, constitute and appoint the above named agent its true and lawful Attorney-in-Fact for and in its name, place and stead, to execute, seal and deliver for and on its behalf and as its act and deed, as surety, a bail bond only. Authority of such Attorney-in-Fact is limited to appearance bonds and cannot be construed to guarantee failure to provide payments, fines or wage law claims on behalf of above named defendant.

SECTION 6 IN WITNESS WHEREOF __HOT SPRINGS BAIL BOND COMPANY, INC.__ has caused these presents be signed by its Proprietor and its corporate seal to be hereinto affixed (if applicable) on the date set forth in Item Four (4) above.

SECTION 7 DO NOT ACCEPT A POWER OF ATTORNEY WHICH BEARS ANY ALTERATIONS, ERASURE OR INTERLINEATION.

_____
CONTROLLING AGENT

Statement of Bail and Payment Received

HOT SPRINGS BAIL BOND COMPANY, INC. 540 OUACHITA AVENUE, HOT SPRINGS, AR 71907 (501)321-9100

Date _____ Agent _____ Bond # XX _____ _____

Arrestee: _____
Last First Middle DOB: _____

Date & Time of Arrest: _____ A.M./P.M. Date & Time of Release: _____ A.M./P.M.

Court: _____ Appearance Date & Time: _____ A.M./P.M.

Charges: _____

Amount of Bail: _____

Premium: _____

Collateral: NO ☐ YES ☐ Collateral Receipt# _____

Filing Fee: _____

Arrestee _____

State Fee: _____ $10.00

Agent _____

TOTAL: _____

Co-Signer _____

Amount Paid: _____

Co-Signer _____

Balance Due: _____

by the defendant in exchange for release from jail and continued liberty until the conclusion of the case. From the court's viewpoint, bail is a financial incentive for defendants to show up for all court appearances. Most state statutes or court rules have provisions for bail, and the amount generally follows a schedule, but the court is the ultimate decision-maker as to who gets bail and how much. The criteria used to determine whether the defendant is eligible for bail is typically based on the prior convictions of the accused, his character, employment history, and ties to family and community. These factors are weighed against the heinousness of the crime, which could also be called the nature and scope of the criminal charges.

TYPES OF PRETRIAL RELEASE: There are generally four types of pretrial release: personal recognizance, release to the custody of another, posting an individual bond, posting a surety bond. Being released on your own recognizance is akin to pulling the get out of jail free card in Monopoly. Sometimes called O.R. Release—own recognizance release—this type of pretrial release is no-cost bail. To get one, the defendant signs a written promise to appear when needed as required. Even though no amount of money is exchanged, the judge can place conditions on the defendant, such as meeting with the parole officer regularly or refraining from the use of alcohol or drugs. Some communities have O.R. officers who will help the court decide who gets O.R. by running a check on the defendant's background and current activities.

In special circumstances, the magistrate may decide, with encouragement from defendant's attorney, to release the person into the custody of some responsible person, usually the defendant's attorney himself, but it can also be a priest, private counselor, or some other designate.

Posting an individual bond puts the defendant in the position of posting an amount of cash or other security of his own in order to guarantee all future appearances. And posting a surety bond is similar in that the magistrate sets an amount of bail, the defendant signs the bond, which is a type of insurance that he will appear, but the company granting the bond is required to pay the court the amount of bond. After a forfeiture of bail (read this as a failure to appear), any amount over $50 is reported to the bondsman, and he has 180 days to adjust the forfeiture. Adjustment can be accomplished by the bondsman's appearing in court. The bondsman must bring with him either valid notice that the defendant is dead or physically ill and unable to appear in the time allowed, or the defendant himself, who should be prepared to provide a good reason for the failure to show up on time or who will allow himself to be turned over to the court and, subsequently, the police.

SHOW ME THE MONEY: The courts will accept cash or a check for the full amount and, if it is in the vicinity of $1,000, some defendants will pay their own way. For others not so fortunate, surety bonds purchased from a bail bond seller—referred to as a bail bondsman—mean that the defendant can purchase that same $1,000 bond at about 10 percent, or $100. And it's important to note that bail bond sellers often refuse to do business with someone who lacks collateral. Collateral is real property, such as a house or car, that can be used to cover the bond seller's loss should the defendant "fail to appear" in court—also called "jumping bail." The bondsmen are hard-wired to the system, however, and can collect by hiring a bounty hunter, also called "skip tracers," someone to either collect the goods or bring the defendant into court. When a surety employee promptly produces a defendant, it can usually recover any money forfeited to the court because of the defendant's failure to appear, which is ample incentive to "get their man!"

Bail bondsmen accept the persona that depicts them as agents of justice, and they act as if they do the court system a big favor in finding criminals and bringing them back to justice. In reality, many people believe this is a myth. Those who advocate bail reform argue that the interest of the bail bondsman is in retrieving fugitives not for justice reasons but strictly for the financial gain. They believe the system cultivates abuses, such as fee splitting, bribery, and the "fixing of minor cases"—turning them into something more than they are for the bond. Reformers also contend that bail bondsmen have undiminished powers of arrest and custody, and that the corresponding loss of civil liberty for the accused is worse than what is constitutionally acceptable by police officers. Reformers claim that, in a large number of cases, the bounty hunters who look for bail jumpers are simply criminals themselves. They go on to explain that the bail bondsmen's system of enforcing the law means that bail jumpers are often shackled for long periods of time and beaten. Furthermore, no matter what happens, the defendant is still out the 10–20 percent interest; this form of strong-arming tends to put the accused under pressure to obtain the money he owes by illegal means.

197

FYI—

Many people think the bondsman has stuck his neck out for the defendant, but the truth is, the court-demanded payment of bond is made by an insurance company. So the bail bondsman is not really dipping into his own personal assets to pay, and the risk is spread out among all bail bondsmen in the form of an insurance policy.

Some states' courts offer court-financed bail. Sometimes described as a hybrid between posting full cash bail and buying a bond from a private seller, under the hybrid system the defendant pays a fee of 10 percent directly to the court. Collateral may or may not be required under these circumstances. The major difference between this and the surety company system is that when the defendant fails to appear at a required hearing, he will be rearrested, and, usually, a new criminal charge of bail-jumping will be tacked onto the previous offenses listed on the complaint. Writers can use this minimum-pay-flee-and-rearrest process for their most disreputable criminal characters, also known to the rest of us citizenry, as reprobates.

A CHARACTER'S BEST FRIEND: Those defendants who are brave enough to represent themselves may also try to convince the judge to lower the bail or release them on O.R. They will have to assert certain facts to get it, however, and here are some of the factors they can use to prove they are worthy.
• The defendant—"It's just *me*, Your Honor"—does not pose a physical danger to the community (if the crime is especially grisly, this will not hold up)
• The defendant does not have a criminal record and has shown up at all required appearances
• A family member or employer is available in order to illustrate close family ties and employment (as to whether the character witnesses demonstrate satisfactory stability—well, that is for the writer to have fun with)

198

FYI—

"Hurt them in the pocketbook," the cop replied. One of the reasons police tend to report the most serious criminal charge possible—provided the facts support it—is that it hurts the accused in the pocketbook. Escalating a misdemeanor to a felony charge, for example, by taking a small amount of marijuana and classifying it as "possession with intent to sell," means the bail schedule will jump up accordingly.

THE SKY'S THE LIMIT: The Eighth Amendment to the Constitution, which is about our rights against cruel and unusual punishment, has a clause that states: "Excessive bail shall not be required." The Supreme Court has made it clear more than once that the purpose of bail is not to raise money for the state, and it is not a way of punishing the accused, but it does leave to the discretion of individual states the decision of how much to charge and the terms of enforcement.

FEDERAL LAW APPEAL AND BAIL: The Federal Bail Reform Act of 1966 asserted that the defendant in a federal court was entitled to bail pending appeal, unless there was reason to believe that any condition of release would produce a failure to appear. The act didn't last. The Bail Reform Act of 1984[105] put the burden of the presumption of bail entitlement right back onto the defendant. Now, before granting bail pending an appeal, the court must find, basically, that the defendant is not likely to flee, that the appeal is not for the purpose of delay, that the appeal raises a substantial question of law or fact, and that the final decision in a new trial is likely to result in a reversal.

Preliminary Hearing

A preliminary hearing should not be confused with the initial appearance. A preliminary hearing has several other names, such as "probable cause hearing," "preliminary examination," "PX," or "prelim." Generally held within ten days of arrest, the preliminary hearing is the next scheduled step in a felony case and is conducted in the courthouse. It is directed only when the defendant has pleaded "not guilty" at the arraignment. The Supreme Court has ruled that when a warrantless arrest is made, a preliminary hearing is constitutionally required to determine the adequacy of an information, meaning the formal accusation by a prosecutor. At a prelim, the judge will decide whether there is probable cause to bind the accused over for a trial. A kind of minitrial, most states provide for open hearings in semi-adversarial fashion. If the state still uses the grand jury system, sometimes called an "indictment jurisdiction," the case is bound over for a grand jury hearing instead.

Coming before a judge only, the preliminary hearing provides an independent—read this as *neutral*—judicial review of the prosecutor's decision to prosecute. Check the laws of your character's state to figure out exactly what type of system it uses. In some states, preliminary hearings are held in every criminal case. In others, they are only used for felony cases. In still others, the defense may have to request them. On the other hand, the defense may decide to waive his right to a preliminary altogether, which is not uncommon. A substantial percentage of defendants, about 30–50 percent, choose to waive their hearings because they intend to plead guilty and know they will go straight to trial.

The objective of a preliminary hearing is to screen out and guard against unfounded prosecution, which stands to harm the accused unjustly and which clogs up the court calendar with weak cases. There are usually three possible results of a preliminary hearing. Most often, the defendant is "bound over," or instructed to attend trial, and he will be adjudicated on the original charges. Or, the judge may opt to reduce the charges if the evidence is weak, and the defendant will be charged with a lesser crime. And about 5–10 percent of cases undergoing prelim hearings result in dismissal.[106]

The preliminary trial is a nutshell version of what the trial will be like. The prosecutor starts by calling witnesses who will testify to what they saw or heard. If the prosecutor has a witness who balks at testifying at a trial, he will bring the witness into the preliminary because this is another way of preserving his testimony. It is all taken down as a matter of record. At this time, he may introduce certain pieces of physical evidence. He will never present the whole case, reserving some witnesses and other types of evidence for the trial; rather, he shows just enough to convince the judge that the trial should go forward. The burden of proof in a preliminary hearing is reduced to "probable cause that the defendant did it," so the evidence proving each criminal element is minimal.

The procedural rules of evidence in this hearing mimic what's given in a real trial, such that the witnesses cannot give opinions and that the defense may both cross-examine and object to testimony. Hearsay evidence, though, is often a staple at preliminary hearings—relying on the testimony of the arresting officer or his arrest reports is acceptable.

Writer's Tip

Even though your defendant character will want to participate heartily at the preliminary hearing, he and his attorney need to bide their time. Cross-examine a witness or two to try to figure out their weakness, alright, but don't let them present their evidence! Conventional defense strategy advises against helping the prosecution prepare for trial by presenting its witnesses and subjecting them to cross-examination at this pretrial stage. This is a chance to hear the prosecutor's case and prepare an approach to thwart it. At this stage of the book, the writer should show his characters feverishly preparing their defense.

200

When the preliminary hearing is over, the judge signs his name to the complaint, and the prosecutor files his information. Defendants may be free on bail or, if not, can request bail again at this hearing. (They may get it if the case just presented is not as bad or as strong as first reported.) If the court system in the jurisdiction is multileveled, the defendant can be arraigned a second time. In most instances, however, the parties will now either proceed to some type of plea offer and negotiation, or, if the prosecution is unwilling, the case awaits the trial phase.

FYI—

Be aware that the preliminary hearing can be a substitute for a trial if both the prosecutors and the defense attorneys agree to "submit on the record." This means the disposition of the case rests in the decision of the judge and not a jury, because the defense has either waived the defendant's right to a public trial or opted out of jury trial for other reasons. Sometimes, the prosecutor knows he's fighting a losing battle, and instead of facing a poorly executed trial, he will decide to put it into the judge's hands. In the other extreme, the defense may realize the defendant's goose is cooked, a guilty verdict is all but written, and the defendant simply accepts that it's the end. If he's more hardheaded than that, the defendant may ask that his attorney submit on the record in order to move the case right onto appellate court, making this a short-cut route to continued hope.

Grand Jury Review

Even though all American jurisdictions still have the option of authorizing grand jury screening of felony charges, it is mandatory only in those areas that require an indictment, which is a charging instrument issued by a grand jury specifically. Currently, slightly less than half the states require a grand jury indictment for at least some classes of felony prosecutions. Nevertheless, in several of these "indictment states," prosecution by indictment is ordered only for felonies dependent on the most severe punishments, such as life imprisonment and capital punishment. In the federal system, all federal offenses require a grand jury indictment unless it is waived by the defendant. If an indictment is delivered, it will be filed with the general trial court and will replace the complaint as the accusatory instrument in the case.

Writers, remember: For the defendant, the grand jury process is always a frustrating, dangerous, and foreboding question mark. Because of its closed screening, the prosecution is the only side able to put forth evidence. The defendant has no such rights and may not even be present. The secretive atmosphere surrounding this process, and the incongruity for the defense in terms of due process, can provide a great device for foreshadowing events to come.

Typically, the jury consists of twenty-three people, but in smaller jurisdictions, there may be as few as twelve people—and some will require only a small majority to indict. Will seven private citizens find the evidence compelling enough to proceed? More likely than not, they will. Grand juries refuse to indict in only 3–5 percent of the cases presented before them. They are generally the prosecution's darlings.

Other Possible Scenarios for the Accused

The following present a few other niggling details that may or may not affect your characters, but are certainly worth knowing.

SUMMONS: In cases such as minor misdemeanors, traffic violations, or motor vehicle infractions, the offender is simply issued a summons. In many cases, the person can waive his court appearance by paying a predetermined fine. If a court appearance is required, it is typically resolved by the defendant's entering a plea, by the taking of evidence, and, finally, by the rendering of a verdict right then and there by a judge. Defendants can always provide their own counsel, because the expense is probably not worth it, especially when you consider that a summons usually walks hand-in-hand with some type of fine or court costs.

VENUE: Venue is often confused with the terminology and meaning of "jurisdiction." It need not be. The venue refers to the place of the trial. In fact, Article III in the Constitution tries to make that distinction for us. It states: "Trial shall be held in the State where the said crimes shall have been committed; but when not committed within the State, the Trial shall be at such Place or Places as the Congress may by law have directed."

There are Federal courts in all fifty states, as well as federal territories. A federal offense is normally tried in the particular district where the crime was committed. State courts often take in two or more counties and, like the federal mandate, offenses completed in those counties are held in that particular state court. But sometimes the federal jurisdiction will overlap that of the states if, to cite an instance, the crime was perpetrated and committed in both territories; for example, as with a kidnapping. In the past, the conflicting courts have resolved these types of jurisdictional uncertainties according to the precedents set.

EXTRADITION: If you have a suspect that flees the state—seeking asylum—you may have a candidate for extradition. Extradition is the demand, or surrender, of an individual accused or convicted of an offense within that territorial jurisdiction, whether it be a state or a country. To fulfill extradition, the offender must be brought back to the jurisdiction from which he has fled, in order to be adjudicated. Any hearings in a country providing asylum would be for identification purposes only. Be aware, though, many countries will not return someone if the crime carries the death penalty. Likewise, some other countries will not extradite someone who is accused of committing a crime that is not a crime in the asylum country. There are various extradition treaties, and the smart writer would need to consult with the individual jurisdictions before proceeding. Generally, if the crime is quite serious, most countries will try to cooperate. If the extradition is agreed upon, a law enforcement official will travel to that country in order to escort the return of the offender.

Most states have adopted the Uniform Criminal Extradition Law, which sets out procedural rules for handling interstate extradition and transport. Congress has enacted statutes for this in accordance with Article IV, Section 2 of the Constitution.[107] Usually, the governor of the asylum state issues a warrant for the fugitive's arrest. The person sought as a fugitive can contest the extradition—with a petition for a writ of *habeas corpus*—by returning to a court of law in the asylum state and challenging whether in fact the petitioner is the person charged or attacking the method of the proceedings. Under this umbrella, the judge would seek to determine release but would not take on the issue of guilt or innocence.

BENCH WARRANT: An arrest warrant issued by a judge, the bench warrant is usually the result of the defendant's showing up previously in court and then failing to show again at a later time as ordered. This "no-show" behavior angers the judge, and issuing a bench warrant is usually how he deals with it. It is cause for rearrest.

IN THE CIRCUIT COURT OF GARLAND COUNTY, ARKANSAS

STATE OF ARKANSAS   PLAINTIFF

VS.   NO: CR 2000-

JOHN DOE   DEFENDANT

BENCH WARRANT

The State of Arkansas, to any Sheriff, Constable, Coroner, or Policeman, in the States:

YOU ARE COMMANDED forthwith to arrest **JOHN DOE (W/M DOB: 1-6-81) address unknown**_____

(Bond:_____)

and bring him before the Garland County Circuit Court to answer an information in that Court against him for the offense of __Possession of a Firearm by Certain Persons, Class D Felony_____

or if the Court be adjourned for the Term, that you deliver him to the Jailer of Garland County.

The Defendant is to be admitted to bail in the sum of ____

_____

Dollars ($_____) [secured by cash professional surety property with surety's affidavit signature Clerk's 10% deposit]

The undersigned finds reasonable and probable cause for issuance of this Bench Warrant from.

__XXX__   Sworn affidavit of ____(arresting officer)_____
           dated ___6-20-00_____.

_____   Sworn Violation Report of the Garland County Circuit
           Court Adult Probation Office dated _____.

_____   Probable cause finding by Hot Springs Municipal Court
           after hearing, dated _____.

_____   Opportunity for probable cause hearing in the Hot
           Springs Municipal Court, Waiver and thereafter, bound
           to the Grand Jury.

_____   Other: _____
           _____

DATED this _____ day of _____, 2000.

                              _____
                              CIRCUIT JUDGE
                              18th Judicial Circuit East
                              State of Arkansas

203

Chapter 12

Juvenile Justice

Youth is quick in feeling but weak in judgment.
—HOMER, *ILIAD*

Damion, a three-year-old in diapers, managed to wiggle free of the two older girls, one a five-year-old and the other aged six, when they pushed his face into a muddy puddle, in back of Grandma's house. Then the girls decided they could do better. One of them ran into the house and came back with a pillow. They put the pillow over Damion's face, and one girl straddled the boy, while the other sat on the pillow until Damion stopped struggling once and for all. Damion was pronounced dead before he reached the hospital. It was just around eleven o'clock on a hot Sunday morning.

Investigators and police eventually concluded the girls "intended to kill Damion with the pillow," according to a spokesperson for the Riverside County Sheriff's Office in California. He went on to say, "We really don't have a motive."

District Attorney Grover Trask commented that as the California law is written, children under fourteen can be charged only if there is clear proof that at the time of committing the act, they knew its wrongfulness. It is clear the criminal justice system is not prepared to do anything with little girls, five and six years old. Most states consider children under age seven to be legally incapable of forming *mens rea*, that is, guilty mind, which is necessary to be morally guilty of a crime and thus subject to criminal punishment.

Research is telling us that aggression in children is escalating and is taking place at earlier ages. Studies indicate that anywhere from 7 to 25 percent of preschool and early school-age children meet the diagnostic criteria for a scientific-sounding disorder called "oppositional defiant disorder" (ODD), or, in other words, conduct problems akin to aggression, noncompliance, and defiance. Clearly, the Justice Department and current legislation within all states have not prepared for these developments. The current policy is to agree with child-development experts who contend that children of that age cannot understand the irreversibility of killing. One innovative training program called "The Incredible Years Parents, Teachers, and Children Training Series" is designed to prevent, reduce, and treat conduct problems in children aged two to ten and has been adopted by hundreds of youth-serving agencies in forty-three states. We can only hope more programs such as this will address this particular and often startling cause for concern.

Juvenile Delinquent—Whose Concept Is Correct?

"Variance" is a term used to describe the actuality that no one seems to agree on what exactly juvenile delinquency is, when the criminal justice system should get involved, or to what extent. As a consequence, a juvenile is any person below the specified age that any given jurisdiction uses to define an adult. It varies from state to state, and while eighteen years old is the most common age for an adult, some states may be different.

Through their work, many police officials believe juvenile delinquents are youngsters who are impulsive, immature first-time offenders who, very likely, will get a break. Other police officers, many of whom have extensive juvenile experience, believe that juvenile delinquents are those involved in a series of antisocial acts, who do so as a result of personality disorders and who will usually be repeat offenders and the most likely to be processed into the criminal justice system.

School counselors, on the other hand, often see the day-to-day behavioral patterns of their troubled and troublesome students—to them a juvenile delinquent is someone who is either unable or unwilling to respond effectively to school rules and teachers' demands, instead creating altercations. For those who work within special education, a juvenile delinquent is often a mentally or physically handicapped or disabled person whose dissident behavior is the result of the school system's putting struggling students into situations where they are unable to compete; hostile or frustrated, such students strike out against the rules that have inhibited them.

The notion of a juvenile delinquent child as perceived from the viewpoint of parents and siblings is a child who is "out of control" or incorrigible; he does not obey parents' or guardians' demands, defying the reciprocal exchange of home life in general.

The official juvenile delinquent legal viewpoint is one of paternalism: An underage offender who violates the law shall be placed in the hands of the courts, which take on a parental role in their own right. This court paternalism is rooted in history and stems from a legal concept called *parens patriae*, meaning, "parent of the country." The philosophy behind it is that parents are merely custodians of the child, and it is up to the juvenile and family courts to uphold the ultimate responsibility for its minors and minor offenders.

And, finally, social services organizations see a child who has been petitioned through the system for breaking the law as a JINS, a juvenile in need of supervision. Or, such situations may reveal FINS, families in need of supervision. In other words, "juvenile delinquency" is an obscure term and means different things to different states, communities, and individuals.

Cruel History

Two thousand years ago, the Code of Hammurabi, one of the first written surviving codes of law, had over three hundred legal provisions pertaining to the family and its young. There were edicts about witchcraft, wages, and loans, with a particular reference to the motto "The strong shall not injure the weak." *Lex Talionis*, a social order based on individual rights, formalized into law a legal practice referred to as the "law of retaliation." Rebellion against the father was not tolerated —decree and punishment number 195, for example, said, "If a son strikes his father, they shall cut off his hand. During Western civilization's heyday and Ancient Rome's period of greatness, society was primarily patriarchal, and the father of the family exercised unlimited authority and corporal punishment. He was the absolute owner of the whole household—which included children, land, other property, animals, and slaves—and if a child was unwanted, he could be sold into slavery. This, in turn, influenced Anglo-Saxon common law. In thirteenth-century England, the tenet of *parens patriae* was spawned. This meant the king was the father of his country and an overseer of the behavior and property of minors. This entitlement policy sanctioned the right of government to take care of minors and assume the role of parents; the state could take children away from their parents for any number of reasons.

The Hospital of St. Michael was the first institution for the treatment of juvenile offenders. The hospital had work areas and cells for resting; the pope's stated purpose for the facility and its inhabitants was "For the correction and instruction to prevent idle and injurious behavior so that they may become useful to the state when taught." The poor juvenile behavior of the medieval period closely resembled that which can be seen today with juvenile delinquents— bad language, drinking, sexual trysts, and severe school attendance problems.

SEVENTEENTH- AND EIGHTEENTH-CENTURY CHANGES FOR YOUTH: During this era families moved from an extended family structure back into a smaller, nuclear family. Marriage was at that time based on love, but parents were still hard disciplinarians, and children were held to a rigorous standard of behavior. An emergence of boarding and grammar schools provided a distinct regimen for children in order to prepare them for adulthood. This curriculum included intellectual and moral training, while restricting physical movements and activities. "Flogging" from teachers was an accepted practice, and this system was sanctioned by upper classes until the nineteenth century.

A children's court movement signaled the appearance of laws for more state control over children. English poor laws called for the appointment of church wardens and overseers, appointed by the justice of the peace, which allowed for poor kids to be apprenticed as servants—throughout their minority years. These laws served as the advent of the poorhouse and the workhouse. The masters of the business industry within the county had authority over all tasks, and punished children severely. Incarcerated young apprentices were often placed in workshops of isolation, which were precursors for a classification of our penal system today.

The Chancery Court of this time protected property rights under the umbrella of patrial supervision. This meant that under protective order of the king, children could be taken away from parents (but it was essentially used to "control the parents"). This type of coercion fixed on lower-class families, and it was said to be for the protection of the young and incompetent citizens whose behavior fell short of serious crime.

207

In the United States, from approximately 1646 through 1824, the Puritans stressed moral discipline for their children, discipline that was strictly enforced by the governing authorities of the colonies. A child's behavior was often seen as evil, and parents were responsible for controlling their property, their child, and their child's spiritual development. In the mid-1600s, Stubborn Child Laws sprung up, which required children to obey their parents or be whipped in public by their parents. Other neighboring children were required to attend the public beatings and executions of their peers, probably an attempt to further control them.

The Child Protection Laws became popular in 1639. Although the concept sounds like one of merit, the laws were full of hypocrisy and largely symbolic in nature, because families still beat their children as they pleased, and child labor was integral in helping to support the family.

THE NINETEENTH-CENTURY CONCERN FOR YOUTH AND SOCIAL REFORM: The Society for Prevention of Pauperism was an organization formed by a group of rich New York women early in the 1800s. The social reformers under its banner focused on the needs of the underclass and attacked taverns, brothels, and gambling, while advocating considerable "moral training" of children. Later, all sorts of movements were lumped together, and the activists were called the "child savers." Child savers were usually moralist groups, people who felt that poor children presented a threat to the moral fiber of America and must be controlled, or they would hasten the destruction of the nation and the economic system. The child savers' lobbying influenced state legislature so much that, in turn, the states created laws committing runaways and delinquents to the same institutions that included those who were deemed out of control: insane asylums.

The New York House of Refuge ran from 1823 to 1825 and was created by the Society for Prevention of Pauperism. This was the first place established in order to take crime off the streets and place the youth into a family-like environment. The New York House of Refuge took in vagrant kids and status offenders—whose conduct was illegal because of age, such as underage drinking. It was run like a prison, with rigid schedules, discipline, and separation of sexes. There were so many runaways by 1860 that twenty more programs shot up under this model. The institutionalization of deviant, delinquent, and dependent children was in full swing. New York philanthropist Charles Brace was instrumental in forming the Children's Aid Society in 1853, which provided temporary shelter for neglected children in private homes and became the forerunner of today's concept of foster homes.

In 1838, the Pennsylvania Supreme Court said the right of a parent was not inalienable; rather, it could be transferred to another or taken away. In *Ex Parte Crouse*—meaning, in this case, partisan communication with one party to discuss someone who is absent—the court claimed the right to retain custody over a twelve-year-old girl because her father was poor, although she herself had committed no offense. She was taken to the Philadelphia House of Refuge. This special treatment was justified legally by the power of the state to act in *loco parentis*—in place of the parents—for the purpose of "protecting the property interests and the person of the child." Children were seen as helpless, in need of state intervention, and the family was considered to be a major cause of juvenile delinquency.

Finally, in 1899, in Cook County, Illinois, the first juvenile court[108] was formed, establishing a separate legal system for children that used reform and rehabilitation as its ideology. Although it was a bona fide court, its proceedings were dramatically different from adult court operations. The court's primary purpose was to help the wayward child become a productive member of society. Determining guilt or innocence by using the rules of evidence was not of principal importance. The aim was prevention and rehabilitation of behavior and character, not punishment. Disposition of all cases was based on the child's special circumstances and needs. This was the first time the courts would look at the individual and assess his background; judicial decisions in this setup were often aided by social workers and psychologists.

In 1900, the Progressive Reformers of Cook County, Illinois, undertook a ten-year study of juvenile court cases. Through their research and interviews, they concluded that the girls coming before the court were largely there as a result of morality issues or loose behavior and that most of the youths brought before court were the children of poor immigrants.

TWENTIETH-CENTURY PHILOSOPHIES IN LIMBO: Until the late 1960s, jurisprudence in the juvenile court system worked under a philosophical bent that provided assessment, rehabilitation, and a protective nature like that of the parent for the juvenile. Finally, though, experts began to recognize that this model did little or nothing to affect or prevent delinquency. Juvenile court hearings were conducted in an informal atmosphere with a different set of words used to describe criminal situations. Any testimony and background information for a case was introduced without regard to rules of evidence and was usually provided by counselors or child behavior experts. In addition, the juvenile was denied many of the constitutional rights commonly given over to adults, such as representation by counsel, confrontation with one's accuser, cross-examination of witnesses, and the right to invoke the privilege against self-incrimination.

Judges, with the help of social workers, psychologists, and psychiatrists, would determine facts: Who is he? How did he become this way? What can we do to help him? Focusing on the offender and not the crime, this courtroom procedure had a clearly diagnostic feel. Some of the major considerations given weight to the situation went to the environment and physical well-being of the youth; the resulting course of action was to prevent, rehabilitate, and counsel. Youngsters were not criminals, but juvenile delinquents. They were wayward children in need of assistance. The court took on the role as super parent until about 1967.

In *Kent v. United States*,[109] sixteen-year old Morris Kent was arrested for housebreaking, robbery, and rape. At the time, in 1966, juveniles were under the jurisdiction of the District of Columbia Juvenile Court. Their statute, though, said that Kent could be transferred to U.S. District Court. After he was admitted to a receiving home for children, Kent's mother, his attorney, and a social worker discussed the possibility that the juvenile court might waive its jurisdiction. After a week's detainment, there was no arraignment and no hearing. Kent's lawyer arranged for a psychiatric examination and a motion requesting a hearing on the waiver. The juvenile court judge ignored the motion and directed the trial to be held under regular proceedings in criminal court. Kent was indicted by a grand jury, found guilty of housebreaking and robbery, and not guilty by reason of insanity for the rape. He was sentenced to a period of thirty to ninety years on his conviction. On appeal, Justice Abe Fortas of the U.S. Supreme Court said that the guiding philosophy of the juvenile system under *parens patriae* had not been fulfilled and that youngsters were getting the worst of both worlds. They were not only denied rights normally accorded adults, but they did not receive the care and treatment promised under the *parens patriae* doctrine. He wrote, "Under our Constitution, the condition of being a boy does not justify a kangaroo court." From then on, the Supreme Court set up criteria concerning a waiver of jurisdiction. What courts needed to consider before transferring a juvenile to adult court were:

- The seriousness of offense
- The nature of the offense in terms of violence and willfulness
- The question of whether the offense was committed against persons or property

- The merits of the complaint
- The desirability of a trial
- The sophistication and maturity of the juvenile
- The juvenile's record and previous history
- Protection of the public and the likelihood of rehabilitation

Plus, the decision must be determined by the offender's amenability to treatment, the court's grounds to believe the complaint, and a statement of the reason for waiver.

In another case, fifteen-year old Gerald Gault was sentenced to a correctional school for six years, until age twenty-one, for making lewd phone calls.[110] The Supreme Court of Arizona claimed it had followed an "implied" due process in the juvenile courts. Reasonably, if the courts had been adjudicating an adult, the sentence would have been a $5–$50 fine and less than two months in jail. The Arizona court did not explain the charges to Gault, did not allow him to confront his accuser, and did not allow him counsel. The U.S. Supreme Court, in hearing his appeal, took exception to this and said that the courts had violated the family's rights and that the juvenile court system should use more common sense with its sentencing. The sentence was reversed.

WHERE WE ARE TODAY: Under the influence of Kent, Gault, and others, the juvenile court was transformed. Congress passed the Juvenile Justice and Delinquency Prevention (JJDP) Act in 1974, which established the Office of Juvenile Justice and Delinquency Prevention (OJJDP) within the sheltering arms of the Department of Justice. Plus, the juvenile court system now has two distinct facets: an adjudication phase, which accords juveniles the same due process rights as adults, while still omitting the public trial requirement; and a disposition phase, in which, following a determination of guilt, a treatment or rehabilitation plan is drawn up.

Also, today, the juvenile justice system exists in all states by statute. And juvenile court is simply another division of general jurisdiction, similar to a superior court. Most of the nation's twenty thousand police agencies have a juvenile component. There are thousands of juvenile police officers, juvenile court judges, juvenile probation officers, and juvenile correctional employees, whose collective salaries account for hundreds of millions of dollars. Some of them are professionals, some are part-time social workers, and some have no certified training—it is a varied and unusual heterogeneous crew of people and interests. The juvenile justice system of today still provides a legal setting in which youthful offenders can account for their wrongs and receive official protection and assistance. Services include community diversion and mental health programs. The courts also have jurisdiction over those children who are neglected, abandoned, or abused. There has been a movement referred to as the deinstitutionalization of status offenders, which means youths who are caught running away, in truancy, partaking in incorrigible behavior, or acting under curfew violation are not necessarily subject to detention or confinement.

Police still need probable cause to search and arrest a minor, but public officers—quasi-parental figures, like school officials and counselors—do not need probable cause to detain, search a minor, or check property kept in a school backpack or locker.

What Juveniles Do and Why

Identified in state statutes are twenty-five acts that apply to juvenile delinquent behavior, including those referred to as status offenses. Problems with truancy, smoking, underage drinking, or sometimes even carrying beepers are some of the examples of status laws. Basically, it boils down to what a particular community will tolerate, because all states list crimes committed by juveniles that would not be crimes if they were committed by adults. It is behavior that disturbs, or "is offensive." Sometimes the language within different state codes is ambiguous, but status offenses basically constitute behavior that state law generally forbids for people under a specific age.

Through research studies, juvenile experts have come to a consensus about what creates a juvenile delinquent. Some of the more common theories of the cause for juvenile delinquency are boredom, hopelessness, personality disfunction, parental influence or the lack of it, the complexity of life, and fear of the future.

Juvenile Justice Process

There are generally six components within the juvenile justice process:
1. Intake and investigation
2. Detention
3. Court
4. Probation services
5. Rehabilitation services
6. Aftercare

INTAKE AND INVESTIGATION: The juvenile justice process typically begins with the youngster's encountering the police as the result of just being out and about. Police involvement can be prompted by serious offenses, disturbances, or status offenses. Because youth tend to move in groups, their congregating can become the object of complaints. Of course, reports often come in from parents and school officials, and law enforcement receives more referrals than any other agency.

Although police discretion seems haphazard to many people, police are predisposed to help, and their power of discretion—sometimes called "street corner" or "station house adjustments"—often come in the form of reality-

211

planned diversions such as community clean-up or some type of other social service. Alternatives to formal charges are common. To that end, the basic procedural options of the police officer upon his first encounter with a juvenile are to warn and release with no report; to release and prepare a report; to call parents to come and get the child with no charges filed; to locate an agency for help, such as a community-based social service agency or a welfare agency; or to proceed with formal charges, transporting the juvenile to juvenile hall or a shelter and processing the offender through the juvenile court system.

DETENTION: As part of the screening, if law enforcement has filed a petition, parents are notified, and the youth is officially referred to juvenile court. One of the first decisions to get through is one of jurisdiction. Three requirements must be met: The youth must be within the age of jurisdiction for juvenile court—in Arkansas it is ages ten to eighteen; the youth must be involved with an act covered by state law; and, because of the times, there has been an increase in demand for hard evidence to be presented by police—*prima facie* evidence, or evidence of youth's involvement adequate enough to establish a fact. Also, as a general rule—unless the screening determines that the youth is a threat to himself, others, or property—the primary issue now is whether a juvenile should remain in custody and stay at a detention facility, or be returned to the home. A detention hearing, also called an initial hearing or an arraignment, is what is used to determine whether to remand the child to a facility or return the child to home.

The procedures for the initial hearing are just recently being modified, because the juvenile court system is applying a more adversary methodology, which is focused on conviction instead of on the offender, more like the traditional screening role assumed by a prosecutor with an adult. Officials study court reports, interrogate youths as to their previous history, and conduct a school inquiry with either a cursory look at or a full-blown investigation of school records. The officials then ask the juvenile for a plea. If the child denies the allegation of delinquency, an adjudicatory hearing or a true-type trial is scheduled. In the event of extraordinary circumstances, a juvenile who commits a serious crime may be transferred to an adult court instead of being adjudicated.

Various procedures are made possible through an initial hearing. These steps permit the court to screen out its own intake on jurisdiction and social grounds; for example, a particular social environment may dictate that the child needs to go someplace else, perhaps for a medical evaluation. The juvenile court system has tremendous power and can actually remove a child from his parents for days, months, or years.

Intake screening provides an immediate test of jurisdiction; it makes clear contested areas before an actual court proceeding and answers any questions the defense or defendant has. It also serves to cull out cases deemed too petty for juvenile court. The exposure an initial hearing offers also provides a mechanism for referrals to other agencies. Plus, intake screening is the best way to discover the attitude of the parents, the child, and other involved persons. And these preliminaries are engineered with the objective of saving time and limited resources. Finally, intake screening helps local government control the courts' caseload.

ADJUDICATION: Adjudication is what is normally referred to as the trial process, only in juvenile court terminology. The judge will have already solicited the juvenile's "plea" in the initial hearing, and this adjudication is usually the place to ascertain the facts, double-check the outcome, and add any further information pertaining to the case. At this stage, the juvenile is given many of the same privileges and guarantees entitled to adult offenders, such as representation by an attorney (either state-provided or otherwise), freedom against self-incrimination and involuntary confessions, the right to both confront and cross-examine witnesses, and, in exceptional situations, the right to a jury trial. Different states have different ideals regarding rules of evidence, and some exert powers including finding out the competency of witnesses, discussing various pleading options, and entertaining certain pretrial motions. In closing this session, the court—read this as a juvenile court judge—will render a judgment, often called a disposition.

213

FYI—

Adult system	Juvenile system
Criminal	Delinquent child
Crime	Delinquent act
Arrest	Take into custody
Halfway house	Residential facility
File a complaint	File a petition
Warrant	A summons
Jail Detention	
Arraignment	Detention hearing, or initial hearing
Reduction of charges	Substitution
Trial	Adjudicatory hearing
Guilty	Involved
Plead guilty	Agree to a finding
Sentence	Dispositional hearing
Parole	After care
Incarceration	Commitment
Prison	Youth development center, boot camp, training school

Court Procedure

Adult	Juvenile
Trial is public	Juvenile court is private
Juries	Only nine states provide juries
Probation officer assigned upon conviction	Probation counselor assigned early on
Right to bail	No right to bail
Penalties clearly defined	Broad range of discretion
Records are permanent	Records are destroyed (expunged, physically destroyed)

PROBATION: The probation plan is tailored to each individual, and, generally, it is not specifically written in a book but falls within court guidelines. Juvenile probation officers are held responsible for the development and implementation of a "trial period plan"—we could think of this as an experimental plan. The two major approaches to juvenile probation services are a hybridization of social work and probation, with an emphasis placed on the protective parent role; or, instead, an outline of probation services or diversion, for the protection of the community. The final stage in probation may as well call for a crystal ball—the probation officer tries to foresee future problems and comes up with preventative measures to keep the youth out of trouble.

A juvenile probation officer is a character with many layers. Usually manned by social workers or child psychologists, they are charged with the responsibility of knowing a little about everything; creating social studies investigations, writing diagnostic reports, and making decisions involving a child's life. As a consequence, they analyze six important areas in a juvenile's world: peers, family, neighborhood, school, value system, and attitude, which must be brought together in meaningful report. Any decision here has a profound effect on a child's current existence, lifestyle, and future. Someone this influential is bound to be an interesting character.

Juvenile probation is based on supervision, and treatment has three main elements attached to it:

1. *Surveillance.* Keeping in touch with the individual, making him aware of his responsibilities and promises to the court, and giving assurance to the child that says "Society is aware of your situation and is interested in you."

2. *Casework services.* Attempting to determine the extent of the problem between the juvenile and his family. Analysis makes use of every available community service, deciding what organization is best for the child's development; this is a complicated stage—families usually don't want someone messing in their lives.

3. *Counseling.* Bringing service and surveillance together by mobilizing everyone's energies to solve a problem or series of problems for both the par-

ents and the children, the counselor enables them to turn in a different direction. The minimum goal of probation is to prevent delinquent behavior.

In order to do this, probation officers wear many hats: They must be social diagnosticians who identify factors that cause delinquent behavior. They need to develop and implement programs to eliminate delinquent behavior and to prepare the juvenile and his family for the outcome of detention or other remedies. Probation officers must have and pass on adequate information so that a referral to a social agency can be a successful alternative. Most importantly, they need to make this social study a positive experience for the child and the family based upon the key philosophy of social work, which is to strengthen relationships.

The probation officer also has to be a controlling person in order to meet the ultimate goal, which is to restore the juvenile's freedom from his restrictive status. The officer must simultaneously convince the child on the front end that the goal is to "free you" but that it can only be accomplished through a combination of control and help—the child must recognize socially accepted standards and socially accepted controls.

The most common difficulty at this stage is denying the delinquent child access to other delinquent social relationships. How far does one go in restricting his friends, in restricting his jurisdiction, in restricting his activities? As an agent of change, a good probation officer maps out possible relations to both the court and the community. He must identify what can be done to bring the change about, but the unique problem here is that judges in the juvenile courtroom are case-conscious and don't often see the child's problems at the same ground level as a probation officer sees them.

REHABILITATION SERVICES: The emphasis during the rehabilitation phase is on the treatment and individual needs of the juvenile, and the best interest of the child is paramount. Often there is a referral to social service so the family can become part of the process. There is much discretion in decision-making at this point. The child may be placed in police community prevention programs with a limited use of detention, waiver, and plea bargaining. The use of indeterminate sentencing at the disposition may have taken place, with institutional care only as a last resort.

AFTERCARE: Most jurisdictions have incorporated a program of juvenile aftercare or parole. If the child has been institutionalized and paroled, he will be placed under the supervision of a parole officer. This means that he will complete the period of confinement in the community and receive assistance from the parole officer in the form of counseling, school referral, and vocational training.

215

Diversion

There are many alternatives to the formal application of the petition. Diversion, sometimes called "early delinquency intervention," attempts to redirect the juvenile from the juvenile justice system. The idea behind diverting minor offenders from the formal justice process and handling them in a nonpunitive, treatment-oriented fashion has focused on certain groups—youths committing minor noncriminal acts and first offenders. A juvenile can be diverted at any stage of the process. Diversionary programs are numerous and take the guise of boot camps, community service, special schools, institutional counseling, or vocational opportunities. Counseling is a major component.

216

Juvenile Court Controversy

Although the ultimate goal of the juvenile court system is to help, care, and protect a child offender, there is much controversy. People wonder how the court can assume responsibility beyond its resources. Typically, as in almost any system, there is not enough time, staff, or money. The juvenile court cannot fix a failing educational system, it cannot fix a broken home, it cannot take the place of the formal social community such as used to be available in neighborhoods of the past, and it cannot handle serious and violent offenders.

Conventional wisdom says there are many weaknesses in the juvenile court system: Its laws are vague and unclear; its judges and staff are socially directed rather than legally minded, and the workers hold social degrees rather than specific law degrees; many employees work part-time; and staff members are often undertrained and incompetent.

Critics point out that the juvenile court system's focus on the rights of kids is weakening the seriousness of major offenses and that juvenile court fosters a belief in such kids that they can beat the system; for example, gang leaders often use youngsters to run their dirty work because they know the juvenile, if caught, will get off. Also, many pundits wonder if incarceration is such a good idea for someone so young. They claim that more than half go through the system, and, the longer they are jailed, the more they are corrupted. Some opponents of the courts even hold onto a popular social belief that says a juvenile has a better chance of turning out okay if he doesn't get caught.

Children as Victims

According to reports prepared by the Office of Juvenile Justice, juveniles are twice as likely to be victims of serious violent crime and three times as likely to be victims of assault. Between 1908 and 1997, nearly 38,000 juveniles were murdered in the United States. Many victims were quite young, and child-protective services have received reports on more than 3 million maltreated children. In 80 percent of these reported cases, the alleged perpetrator was a parent. The United States has a poor record when it comes to child victimization.

MISSING CHILDREN: Juvenile services are often the venue for many different groups of needy children. A list and a description of each group follows:

• *Runaways.* Life on the streets looks good but usually only temporarily; females comprise almost half of the total numbers. (Two-thirds are between sixteen and seventeen years of age.) They have left parents or guardians without parental consent; not all of them voluntarily want to leave home; and a large majority are running from abuse, some estimated fifty thousand per year.

• *Throwaways.* Children who are pushed out, they may be perceived as too troublesome to parents or ignored, they come and go as they please.

• *Walkaways.* Most juveniles in this growing category leave because of an unbearable situation or parental abuse. Typically, it is not reported because parents know where the kids are. Parents and guardians either don't care or are resigned to the situation; the children may live with friends or relatives. If not for economic reasons, they would be gone from family entirely.

• *Abducted children.* Out of four hundred thousand children per year, many are abducted by parents or family members. But there are also a number of stranger abductions. Children taken by parents are usually the victims of a couple who are divorced or separated. Sometimes the mother or the father simply fails to return the child after a scheduled visitation period. Girl victims account for 75 percent, nine in seven is found.

• *Lost or injured children.* Injured or trapped, these children didn't intend to run away. This usually happens under extraordinary circumstances, but daily occurrences, such as being lost in a park or wandering away from the neighborhood, also cause this problem.

217

The population of homeless children is comprised of all the groups listed above, but it is most applicable to runaways or to those who have been exiled from a family group. Typical runaways are victims of multiple abuses and are most likely unemployed or unemployable. They have no plans and are vulnerable. Despite this, they may seem cocky or defensive. Juveniles in this category are usually frightened and do have potential but fall through the cracks. They do not "feel important" to their families and, as a consequence, learn survival tactics of the street and get involved in criminal activities.

For these children, various public and private organizations have set up runaway shelters, halfway houses, and crisis centers. Frightened kids may go to these places on their own, but in many cases homeless youths are brought by the police to these safe havens. And, most times, law enforcement expect to see the kids back on the streets. Juveniles will often run away from a shelter if they think they will be sent home. Unfortunately, the typical policy of such shelters is to return them to their home, helping to foster a chronic runaway syndrome.

In response to the problem of missing children, the government has instituted various laws and services. Specific leads you may want to research follow:

- Missing Children Act of 1984
- Missing Children Assistance Act: 1984
- National Center for Missing and Exploited Children: (800) THE LOST.

Profile of Today's Troubled Youth

Lieutenant Willie McCoy has invested more than twenty-one years in law enforcement, bringing himself up through the ranks. McCoy has done it all—patrol, traffic, bike patrol, and liaison. He is often asked to speak to various groups and is a key member of the Hot Springs, Arkansas, Police Department, working on public and community relations as well. A tireless advocate for children, he even works at the local Boys Club and has won national awards for his efforts in preventing and subduing youth gang activity. He holds a bachelor's degree and has lectured at numerous schools. Below is a list McCoy uses to show his listeners the difference between a school offense in the 1940s and a typical school offense today.

Top offenses in the year 1940	Top Offenses Today
1. Talking out of turn	1. Drug abuse
2. Chewing gum	2. Alcohol
3. Making noise	3. Pregnancy
4. Running in the hall	4. Suicide
	5. Rape
	6. Robbery

OTHER FACTS AND FIGURES ASSOCIATED WITH JUVENILES: Teen suicide: 5 percent have tried, and 12 percent have come close. Typical reasons for suicide attempts are:

- Adolescent adjustments to responsibilities and life
- Drug abuse
- Peer pressure
- Inability to get along with parents

Number-one reason a child is removed from the home: poverty
Two main reasons for forming or joining a gang: poverty and racism

GANG LIFE: Definition of a gang: a group of three or more with

- A turf or territory
- A unique name
- Identifying mark or symbol
- Regular gatherings
- Engagement in criminal or antisocial conduct

Gang life is glorified in "gangsta rap," a venue in which criminally bent propaganda reaches impressionable youth by the millions. Antisocial encouragements found in this type of rap music include violence, degradation of women, promiscuity, drug use, verbal profanity, disregard of police authority, racism, and general anger and rebellion.

A Juvenile Detention Center

Sergeant Bill Livingston hadn't always worked with kids. He was in manufacturing and automotive work and earned a degree in agricultural engineering. He has worked for the Garland County Sheriff's Department as a bailiff and is now an instructor at the County Juvenile Detention Center in Hot Springs, Arkansas. Livingston says the juvenile detention facility has certain standards, and its key responsibility to juveniles is to protect their rights, to take care of them, and to train them further. "Everything works according to our guidelines," says Livingston.

The center where Livingston works opened November 25, 1996, and has admitted well over three hundred juveniles. Just recently, the center began operations under court order to detain and house truancy offenders. The sergeant says that there are three major differences between the adult and the juvenile systems; these differences have to do with confidentiality, intake approvals, and punishment. "In our facility, punishment is interactive, met with one-on-one counseling," says Livingston.

WHAT DOES IT TAKE TO BE A CASEWORKER AT YOUR CENTER?: "It's an education every day, but the number-one thing is to be open-minded, to listen and respond to their needs," says Livingston. Forty hours of juvenile certification, conducted at the facility, is required in order to work there, and that includes 140 hours of continuing education every year just to remain certified.

There are minimum three people on each shift, and the house has a maximum of twenty kids. (The community population is 36,000-plus.)

Changing behavior, building relationships, and instilling self-confidence

219

in the children are the center's objectives. Juveniles are restricted from activities for acting out. The personnel often go one-on-one with the juveniles, listening to each one, and they do not ridicule or correct them in front of anybody else. "We ask them, 'What do you think would be appropriate to do?' They ask, 'Are you going to turn this [poor behavior report] in to the court?' It's amazing what we can get out of them when they are apprised of the situation," says the sergeant.

GETTING PROCESSED: There are seven thousand square feet in the detention center's main building. A "sally port" is engineered in order to allow an arriving vehicle to enter the building. Weapons are placed in a gun locker before entering (unless allowed by the sheriff.) They shackle one hand of each juvenile and, if needed, cuff them together, then do a pat-down. It's unlawful to take pictures of juveniles, so no typical mug shot is taken. Males do male body searches, females do the female searches, and, according to Livingston, they try to "touch the body as little as possible."

Paperwork is completed, and the new arrivals have their first contact with the intake officer. Livingston says they start building a relationship with a medical history report and try to determine whether the newly admitted are potential suicide victims. They ask parental-type questions, and the intake process takes about an hour and a half, allowing for communication and explaining to the juvenile what is about to take place.

Arrivals then shower and delouse. The staff washes their clothes for reissue; if they've not been to court, they can wear street clothes. When they go to court, they wear green hospital garb, and if they're sentenced, it's orange jumpsuits. (Detainees, the ones dressed in orange, do not get the same privileges as the others.)

Every night, all residents' clothes are washed by staff. "We do all the janitorial service ourselves, everything. The first hour is the most critical time. . . . They cry, and are sometimes scared to death."

ROOMS AND RULES: The control room is visually monitored twenty-four hours a day. It allows the staff to see confrontations and signs of gang-related behavior (which is not tolerated). There are closure system locks for all the doors. The outside doors are always locked, and one must have credentials to come through. The intercom system is always on. "We listen to what's happening in sleeping rooms, and others cannot enter. Anyone approaching must have a picture ID and be family members or guardians," says Sergeant Livingston. No purses are allowed in the facility.

Families visit in one of two visitation rooms, during specific hours: 5:00–7:00 p.m. Monday through Friday and 5:30–7:30 p.m. Saturday and Sunday. The staff encourages family visits, which technically should last fifteen minutes, though employees don't rush them. There are holding cells and one rubber room. The holding cells are used only for the incorrigibles who need to be placed in isolation. The rubber room is for those who demonstrate threats of harm to themselves or to others—if a youth ends up in this room, he's probably exhibited suicidal behavior or has been suffering the ramifications of drug withdrawal. Each location is monitored every five minutes.

In the barracks are sleeping areas, which accommodate one to four people. A staff member stays in the barracks area with them. There is a small library. All personal property is taken and put into a milk crate. The only items the inhabitants get to keep are: one religious reading, soap, towels, linens, shoes, and clothes. The facility provides all their hygiene items.

Staff members are on walkie-talkies at all times, and Livingston says it is amazing what it does for the youths' behavior to have an adult interacting with them constantly. There are TVs in each barracks, but inmates can only watch religious shows, learning programs, and Nickelodeon (approved shows only). Sometimes they'll see a sports event, as a special occasion. Each area has a telephone, for collect calls only, which is off-limits after 9:00 p.m.

An outdoor recreation yard exists, and the staff occasionally does a mesh wire check for contraband. At least one staff member is present for every five residents who go outside, and the entirety of the outdoor recreation area is on monitor.

Rooms for specific activities include classrooms—juveniles have a required, year around school curriculum, with classes credited toward their high school diploma; a conference room, where youths can avail themselves of counseling through the Department of Youth Services, which is state-funded and accessible twenty-four hours a day; and a room where residents can write letters (letter-writing is allowed only in this room).

"By law, juveniles can only be told to clean their surrounding area, and they don't leave the facility except for the doctor, dentist, and going to court. And we don't want them to like it well enough to come back."

Juveniles must go to court within seventy-two hours of arrival in detention. And, of course, they can be bound over to a circuit court and tried as adults. Livingston said, "We had one in for murder. The Department of Youth Services in Little Rock sent the juvenile to us because they do not have enough facilities. People are on waiting lists, and they don't have anywhere to put them. Fifty percent of our visitors come from five other counties."

When asked about the work, Livingston said, "I'll tell you our goal. Our goal is to keep juveniles out of the big system. That's what's important."

Chapter 13

Preliminaries

Life is just one damn thing after another.
—ELBERT HUBBARD, *THOUSAND AND ONE EPIGRAMS*

A defendant is someone you don't want to be, but he is someone your readers will not be able to get enough of. A defendant is someone who has been formally charged—by either the prosecutor or the grand jury—with committing a crime. His defense is information meant to show why he is not guilty. His defense attorney is the person who speaks and acts on his behalf, his legal champion, a counselor who will use all his resources to see that the defendant receives a fair trial. The defense attorney's objective is to win cases. His very livelihood and reputation depends on his ability to present a better case. The reality of a criminal trial, and the script of what is "true to life," occupy a position and viewpoint that is relatively different from the scheme of what is generally portrayed on film or in a novel. In any given year, less than 10 percent of suspects apprehended for serious crimes go through the formal steps of a criminal trial. No matter. The drama of pitting a man against the law in a struggle for either his freedom or his life is one of the most compelling scenarios in fiction. It's been the grist for stories since man first raised his hand to kill, and it will be a story line as long as time continues. In this chapter, we will look at the criminal process through the eyes of the defendant and the defense attorney.

Locking Out the Prosecution?

In addition to the arrest and search powers of law enforcement, the courts have allowed searches of businesses. A search warrant is still required, of course, but the general attitude is that a business holds a lesser privacy interest for the defendant, and written records reflecting regular business and government activities are admissible in court. A crime writer must be careful, though—a search of a newspaper office or a television station must follow certain protocol because of the First Amendment's guarantee of free expression and media's vehemence in protecting it.

Also, the prosecution is not allowed access to the defense attorney's office because of the attorney-client privilege, which applies to all his clients' files. If the defense counsel were involved in other criminal activity, however, a search warrant with specific and narrow delineations as to what items could be recovered is allowed.

Defendant's Pretrial Rights and Procedural Standards

In the course of reading this book, this message appears several times. But, once again, commit these items to memory; as I discuss preparation for trial, it is essential that you understand the rights of your story's accused:

- To be informed of charges
- To remain silent
- Writ of *habeas corpus*
- Prompt arraignment
- Benefit of legal counsel; if indigent, attorney provided
- Reasonable bail

Furthermore, there are procedural rules that apply to every trial. We have discussed each of these points in earlier chapters, but a quick review of them will help you use this chapter more effectively:

- It is up to the state to convince a judge or jury that the defendant is guilty. This is tied into the concept of "burden of proof."
- The prosecution has to prove the elements of the crime to meet its burden of proof. Look to the statute to find the elements.
- The strength of the proof must be "beyond a reasonable doubt." This has no definitive wording—it simply means that the jurors must be convinced of guilt to a "moral certainty."
- The defense does have to prove a notion called "affirmative defenses." For example, if the defense claims the defendant is not guilty by reason of insanity, the defense attorney may have to provide statements from doctors, or other evidence of instability.
- An innocent defendant runs the risk of hurting his case if he testifies on his own behalf, but he does have the right. Some common reasons against testifying are: The jury may not like the defendant's demeanor; on cross-examination the defendant is sworn to tell the truth; it opens up the possibility to show something incriminating in the defendant's past; and it gives the jurors an opportunity to weigh the prosecution's story directly against the defendant's story.
- The defense is allowed to cross-examine the prosecution's witnesses.
- A trial cannot usually be conducted in the absence of the defendant. If

he voluntarily fails to show up, however, the case may move forward "in absentia."
• Judges can prevent the media from televising a trial.
• Every jurisdiction has statutes that specify time limits for moving cases from the charge stage to trial.
• The defendant has a right to know the evidence against him.

Writ of *Habeas Corpus*

This is a petition sent to the court to seek a remedy against an illegal arrest. In Latin, it means "You must have the body," or "Bring the body forth." Technically, it is an application for discharge. The police are to bring the person into court and determine if he is being held improperly. If the court decides in the accused person's favor, he may have cause to bring a civil suit or civil action for either false imprisonment or violation of civil rights. And there could be remuneration in the form of damages. Then, too, if this proves to be the case, the arresting officers may be subject to criminal liability of their own, especially if excessive force was used during the arrest.

Pro Se or *Pro Per*

Self-representation is a tricky proposition, but some will do it. "Pro se" ("for himself"), "*pro per* defendant" ("for the defendant"), or even "in propria persona" ("in one's own proper person") are all acceptable ways of describing a client who is representing himself. The best-known example of this is the high-profile case of Colin Ferguson. Ferguson, dubbed the "Long Island Railroad Killer" by the press, was tried in 1995. Despite the fact that he was facing life in prison without the possibility of parole for gunning down six commuters on the Long Island Railroad, he insisted on leading his own parade.

The judge ruled that Ferguson was legally capable of participating in his own trial, but there were many who saw it as a complete folly and a cruel blow to the survivors of the attack. The jury held up in defiance of Ferguson's often long, rambling dissertations of unintelligible babble, just long enough to convict him on all counts after a quite brief deliberation.

Right to Counsel

The Sixth Amendment's framers wanted to ensure that criminal defendants could be represented at trial by their retained counsel. Under English law, attorneys were prohibited from appearing on behalf of defendants in felony cases. The Sixth Amendment reversed this rule and made counsel's assistance available to all who could not afford to hire a lawyer.

The primary responsibility of the defense attorney is to represent his client, who has the constitutional right to counsel. If there is one credo most defenders live by, it is the ritualized speech most often heard: The rights of the accused were designed to protect the innocent, and if the guilty are freed as a result of some technical issue, then that is the price that must be paid in order to ensure that the scales of justice remain balanced. And, today, it almost goes without saying, defendants facing criminal charges often need a lawyer to assist them. The law and its procedures are confusing, and the tasks required to facilitate fairness require a level of expertise most criminal defendants do not have. In order to understand the nature and consequences of the proceedings against him and to be able to navigate the intricacies of courtroom operations, a defendant needs someone from inside the system.

According to an article by Meredith Halama, a graduate student of the University of Illinois, Urbana-Champaign, subtle shifts have reduced a criminal defendant's right to counsel. She criticized a 1995 decision by the Supreme Court of Louisiana that introduced hairsplitting distinctions in order to permit police to interrogate a suspect alone after he was indicted. Now a clerk for U.S. District Judge James F. Holderman, Halama says the Supreme Court needs to "strike an appropriate balance between obtaining reliable confessions and safeguarding fundamental rights."

An interesting twist on the legal representation guarantee lies in the case *Caplin & Drysdale, Chartered v. United States.* Apparently Caplin & Drysdale used illegal monies and collateral to fund their defense. The Supreme Court said that the right to retain counsel has a major qualification in that, if the defendant has the ability to pay, fine—he may do so. But the defendant in this particular instance had his assets forfeited constitutionally as a result of illegal activity, and had no right to offer them in payment for his attorney.

A second override on this qualified right of chosen counsel rests with the prosecutor's right to object to the defendant's appointing counsel who has a potential for a conflict of interest. A trial judge can disallow representation in such cases, even if the defendant has asked to proceed with his retained counsel of choice and take his chances.[111]

The Supreme Court adopted a two-part test to determine when a person can receive counsel—*what* events are covered in regard to the term "criminal prosecution" and *when* counsel can actually enter the picture.

First, the event must be an "adversarial judicial proceeding," meaning a proceeding marked by the appearance of a prosecutor and a judge. Filing a charging document, such as a complaint or an information, is enough to start the proceeding, and counsel can continue to be present during the arraignment and certain other appearances. Second, the proceeding must qualify as a "critical stage," meaning, any trial-like event, including a preliminary hearing, a post-indictment lineup, a guilty plea negotiation, and a sentencing hearing.

Since there are always exceptions to the rules in law, sometimes defense counsel can be appointed for a noncritical stage according to due process. For instance, counsel may be required to appear at parole or probation revocation hearings—and this is judged on a case-by-case basis. Such exception is made when there are substantial reasons for not revoking (canceling) a convict's parole or probation; the lawyer's appearance is sanctioned because the reasons for release may be complicated or difficult to present without counsel.

Also, the defendant has a right to counsel when the *first* appeal from a criminal conviction is presented. An indigent defendant would need the assistance of someone who is law-savvy in order to present an effective appeal, which generally calls for combing the records, preparing the arguments, and looking for loopholes. A condition of *per se* due process is that the courts expect defense counsel to provide "effective assistance" on this first appeal. There must be something concrete with which to bring the case up for review. In order to not pursue frivolous functions and tie up the resources of the courts, if defense counsel believes the reevaluation of the case has no merit, he can request permission to withdraw. He would file a brief, often called an Anders brief.[112]

226

Ethical Problems of Defense?

The American Bar Association has defined the defense attorney's job as representing and defending the client to the best of the attorney's ability and doing everything possible, within the Canon of Ethics, to ensure that the client is acquitted. Let's explain it another way. Say, for example, the attorney were to hear something he did not want to hear—an admission of guilt, perhaps. As an officer of the court, he is bound to reveal his client's admission to the district attorney, except for the fact that the client-attorney relationship of confidentiality would forbid him from doing so. The only way defense counsel can divulge something the defendant says is if the defendant gave him express permission.

For the defense lawyer, the premise is and always has been that a defendant is not guilty until a jury says so. A lawyer is not required to believe his client. Perhaps, if he is troubled by the guilt of a defendant, a good way to continue would be to tell himself that his client may be protecting someone else or has an irrational need to confess. Also, he may actually believe—per his training and oath taking—that a guilty man deserves his due process just like any other citizen. Whatever methodology he uses, it is the defense attorney's job to come up with an alternate scenario of the crime if he can, to explain the evidence in another, more compelling way. He does not have the job of proving anything—that is the prosecution's job.

And, often, a defense attorney will suggest to his client that he not attempt to tell his side of the story—that he is not, and never will be, obligated to do so. If he knows the defendant is guilty, he will keep him from testifying because of two reasons. First, he would be allowing the client to lie under oath, and he would not do that—he would not be part to perjury. And, two, the defendant's testimony would leave the defendant open to cross-examination and impeachment. All that is needed to make the trial an "adversarial process" is for the defense to demystify and debunk the prosecution's scenario. If the defense lawyer is good enough at providing an alternate version of the prosecutor's scheme, only one member of a jury is needed to believe that new version, to turn things around in favor of his client. The defense attorney is not bound by any moral or ethical code other than whatever he can do for his client.

No one may really know the truth. The prosecution may put forth the testimony of someone who is lying. He is not allowed to do that knowingly, but if he presents such testimony as bona fide evidence, which he believes to be true, he, too, is doing his job.

Defense Counsel Functions

According to the American Bar Association (ABA), the defense attorney, much like the prosecutor, performs a multitude of functions while representing a client throughout the entire criminal proceeding. He must:

227

- Represent the accused immediately after arrest in order to provide advice during interrogation and to ensure constitutional safeguards during pretrial procedures
- Review police reports and conduct further investigation
- Interview the police, the accused, and any other witnesses in order to find additional evidence
- Discuss the unfolding events with the prosecutor with the intention of gaining insight into the strength of the case against them
- Represent the accused at all bail hearings and plea negotiations
- Prepare, file, and argue various pretrial motions
- Prepare the case and an alternate scenario for trial
- Participate in jury selection
- Represent the accused at trial
- Provide advice and assistance at sentencing
- Determine and pursue a legitimate basis for appeal
- Present written or oral arguments for appeal

Criminal Defense Costs

A private defense attorney is an expensive proposition. An attorney will set his fees according to the likely complexity of the case, his level of experience, and geography (the cost of living is different in different regions of the country, and so will be the subsequent fees). Since no standard legal fees exist, they are based on whatever the market will bear. Obviously, a murder trial will cost more than a misdemeanor offense, and if the suspect if famous, the trial could cost millions.

Criminal defense attorneys will typically charge by the hour, called a "billable" hour, or by the case. In addition, some hidden costs may be passed on to the defendant, such as fees for copies, subpoena fees, filing fees, and any extras incurred with, say, the footwork completed by a private investigator or other subcontractor services. People retaining lawyers often feel intimidated by hourly fees, especially if the case becomes unusually complicated. They feel it may give the attorney a reason to spend more time on a case than it requires, or work slowly because of the advantage the clock affords.

Case billing means a lawyer may charge by the case, according to the offense. Say, for example, it is a drunk driving charge; a lawyer may have a set charge of service fees for defendants charged with this crime. A retainer is a portion of money that is paid "up front." It is the equivalent of a down payment on services. Perhaps the client will pay in advance for twenty hours of the lawyer's time. That amount will be set against the bill, and the accused will receive regular statements outlining the balance until it eventually reaches zero, when negotiations of money will need to begin again.

Contingency fees are most commonly used in civil litigation, such as personal injury cases, in which the client stands to receive an award if the court so decides. The lawyer's fee will be a percentage of what monies are recovered for damages, so if the client recovers no money, the attorney won't, either. Contingency fees do not apply in criminal cases and are disallowed and considered unethical by the ABA.[113]

228

Writer's Tip

Want to really add angst to your main character's life? Lawyers who are hired and are members of a firm have a tendency to delegate work to others. For example, a law student may be asked to conduct legal research, an associate lawyer may be told to handle the pretrial conference, and a paralegal might pinch-hit in preparing the defendant for trial. Of course, for the defendant it may make the costs less expensive (if the novices charge less), but he would need to get used to a lot of different faces and the frustration of a changing hierarchy.

Law Office Setting

The size of the firm plays a huge role in the setting of your defendant's story. Whether the defendant has a quiet wait in the lobby or a near run-in with coffee-slinging businessmen from Singapore depends on the type of firm he chooses.

First, we'll explore the legal mall that is the large law firm. It is probably located in a high-rise with an upscale address, and its roster reads like a collegiate-elite alumnae newsletter: everyone's from Princeton, Yale, Harvard, or Stanford. There are the young startups in the basement, checking research. Midlevel, top-dog-wannabe attorneys are working the minor nuisance cases en masse. Upper-level counselors are hitting the streets on their way to court to file and argue motions. And, finally, the senior-level partners are romancing the big-money corporate, insurance, and foreign government clients with offshore accounts. The surroundings are plush with oriental carpets, large wooden or leather doors opening on paneled rooms with wing chairs, mahogany desks, art, and oh, those glorious, expensive legal books ringing the walls.

There may be dozens of secretaries—with their own hierarchy—mailroom clerks, telephone operators, receptionists, and computer technicians all tucked away on floors with less fancy carpeting and more efficient décor.

Then there are the medium-sized types of law offices. A more close-knit group, they have a well thought-out division of labor—this way to insurance, family court here, personal injury through the white door, and estate planning by appointment only. The areas of expertise are all over the board, and the twenty to fifty members either choose their own areas of focus or are assigned to work for a partner. Medium-sized firms are busy places with more utilitarian surroundings than those of bigger firms. Their décor tends to be more modern; floors are oak or painted, and the walls don a trendy color that denotes competence. Smooth round edges and the occasional plastic (but still tasteful!) edge offer a nouveau look for the up-and-coming. Not as quiet as the uptown place: Phones ring, and secretaries are typing and talking, checking calendars and the food cart as it passes through the foyer. Everyone is working, and the place is abuzz; the salaries are lower, but these attorneys are closer to their clients than the biggest fish are to theirs—the clients of medium-sized firm tend to stay around for years.

The littlest firms are, of course, the most intimate. Numbering from three to up to twenty, these firms hire lawyers that are probably friends from college or, at least, legal contemporaries. A little more laid back, these firms make the typical lobby wait a quiet and friendly one. Even though there is a sophisticated phone-and-intercom system, you may hear the county attorney beckon his aid from the small conference room at the end of the hall. An air of camaraderie exists throughout, and the hustling, independent, sole-practitioner days are either a long-ago, unfulfilled fantasy, or a thing of the past.

Lawyers at Lineups

Sometimes, the police will make an effort to push through a lineup before the suspect has been charged, in order to circumvent the appearance of the suspect's lawyer. If the accused asks the police to delay long enough to get a lawyer to show up, the request may be granted; some agencies even have attorneys on "lineup duty," a twenty-four-hour client service.

Not only will the attorney's presence be an assurance to a first-timer, but lawyers often bring cameras or a blank seating chart in order to make sure the procedure is on the up-and-up. Knowing who the witnesses and other suspects are can add invaluable details to the defense case. The lawyer at lineup will also keep an eye open for any questionable behavior on behalf of the police, such behavior as coaching a witness, having the attendees dress differently in a manner that might set them out from the pack, or giving subtle signals. A wise defense attorney will also watch for clues to witness credibility, noting comments to the effect of "It was pretty dark and I was distracted," or "I can't tell,

229

he was wearing a cowboy hat," or "I was coming around the corner, forty feet away. . . ." He can use those statements later on in court.

In addition, while witnesses might not want to speak with an unfamiliar attorney who has just approached them on the street, the presence of the police in a safe environment may make them more apt to consent to an open interview or answer questions in this cooperative setting. Then, too, if they are nervous, they may divulge some clue or attitude that may prove helpful to the defense later on.

By the way, any refusal to cooperate in a lineup by the defendant is considered circumstantial evidence of the suspect's "consciousness of guilt."

Lawyers at Arraignment

230

The arraignment, which is usually held within forty-eight hours of arrest, sets the arrangements for everything that follows. Remember, during an arraignment, the suspect becomes the accused or the defendant, and is presented with the charges against him. The defendant can then apply for court-appointed counsel. The defendant's plea is asked for, and, if the defendant offers a not-guilty plea, the judge sets a schedule for either a pretrial conference, a preliminary hearing, a hearing on pretrial motions, or the trial date itself. After the schedule has been set, any unresolved bail issues are answered in regards to setting bail, raising or lowering bail, or releasing the defendant on O.R. (Own Recognizance).

A defense lawyer may use the tactical advantage of either trying to delay the trial date or, in other cases, pushing it through at the first available moment. The advantage of delay is almost always in favor of the defendant. Why? Because the passage of time increases the likelihood of witnesses' forgetting what they've seen or heard. Law enforcement believes that important cases must generally be worked right away. The first forty-eight hours of a case are critical. After that, the potency of evidence starts to diminish, the crime scene becomes polluted, and prosecutors may lose evidence. And because of factors that cannot be controlled—such as human nature itself— people will have a tendency to lose interest and momentum.

The extra time also allows the defendant to clean up his act. He can receive counseling, find employment, or otherwise establish a course of behavior more favorable to the courts. And he can seek out other witnesses. If released on bail, he can literally makeover his appearance by dressing more appropriately (in a coat and tie) for court appearances, getting a haircut or restyling, and shaving facial hair. The defendant's counsel can choose to formally delay the preliminary hearing by filing a motion to postpone the event, using a document called a "Motion for Continuance." This type of motion can also be made orally and involve a simple rescheduling. Or, at the preliminary hearing, the defense may call for a "waiving of time," giving up the right to a speedy trial in hopes that it will encourage a delay between the crime event and the trial.

In some instances, however, the defense may wish to speed the trial through the courts. A perfect example of that is the 1995 O. J. Simpson case, when Orenthal James Simpson was charged with the murder of his wife, Nicole Brown Simpson, and another, unrelated individual, Ronald Goldman. Simpson's defense team pushed for an early adjudication of this case so that the prosecution was unable to rally all the component people and evidence together and prepare and present an especially complex case in a timely manner.

Another good idea for the defense team is to construct a logical, believable story. They must be able to weave in the evidence and create a scenario that the prosecution and, later, ordinary people—the jury—will accept. This story will obviously run counter to the prosecution's theory of what happened. The defendant and his attorney will have to put their heads together prior to plea-bargaining in order to counter the charges with a strong defense, to dispute the alleged motive by using a counterclaim of some sort.

231

Preliminary Hearing

Remember, preliminary hearings are the best way to get a preview of the trial. And, in order to get one, the defendant must plead "not guilty" at the arraignment.[114] Here, the judge decides whether there is enough evidence to move further. He can also reduce the charges and even dismiss the case. Judges find these hearings to be the perfect opportunities to wield their judicial review authority, often a plus for the defendant.

The defendant's biggest gain from attending this event (even though he most likely will lose, and the case will go forward) is the opportunity to be privy to the other side's evidence for the first time in a legal context. The defendant and his counsel must listen very carefully to any witness stories put forth at this time, because any variation in the telling at trial is cause for impeachment. There is also an opportunity for the defense counsel to vigorously (or politely, depending on the tact) cross-examine prosecution witnesses. The defendant should make notes: How are they holding up? Do they sound credible? What do you know about them that is going unsaid and that may help your case?

Most importantly, some states have rules of evidence whereby defense lawyers are required to object to inadmissible evidence during a prelim; otherwise, they may not be able to assert the right to object to that evidence later at trial. In the absence of such a rule, however, the defense may opt to remain silent and let the prosecution think it has a strong case, only to derail that case, ridden with inaccuracies and misinformation, later in court.

Plea Bargain

At least 90 percent of felony suspects arraigned plead guilty or no contest, so that means that less than 10 percent of criminal cases actually end up in trials. The deal involves an understanding that the accused agrees to plead guilty in exchange for either a reduction in the number and severity of charges or a promise on behalf of the prosecutor not to ask the judge for the maximum penalty for the offense charged.

Since most prosecutors overcharge—that is, they file more charges than they expect to explain and win on—this tactic also gives them more power at the bargaining table. Because there is more to give away and because, most likely, the prosecution would not have been able to demonstrate those charges to the court, the state loses little by reducing the number of charges. Most defense lawyers know this and take it into consideration before they let their client-defendant cry uncle.

If the prosecutor feels confident about pursuing the case, and the defense sees no alternative, the defense attorney may suggest his client make a deal for a lower sentence. Otherwise, they will have to face a judge who may have a tendency to administer the strictest sentence. And, since any outcome under a jury-held trial is always unforeseeable, a plea bargain does allow some control over the result.

In all jurisdictions, plea negotiations need the approval of the trial court to go through—in certain areas, judges participate directly in plea-bargain discussions. The "invited judge" practice is supposed to ensure that the parties agree jointly on an equal and quick resolution, but many courts feel that the presence of the judge may unduly influence the defendant and the outcome, making the presence of a knowledgeable defense attorney all the more important. Another issue of note: One contingency with accepting a plea is that the defendant must accept the plea on the basis of his guilt. If he pleads guilty while still maintaining his innocence, a judge does not have to approve the transaction.

And, finally, there is another instance regarding mandatory sentencing laws that affect plea-bargaining tactics. In some states, judges have no say over what sentences they can impose, meaning a bargaining chip is sorely missing from the game regardless of how they feel. So, unless the defense attorney can finagle a reduction in charges, the defendant may have to take his chances with the jury after all.

The Competent Client

The defendant who helps his attorney present the most effective defense possible is a competent client. Such a client shares the responsibility of defense by understanding the attorney's role and ethical duties, by participating in important case decisions, and by following through on appointments with counselors and supporting activities that display rehabilitation. It would be in the client's best interest to attend court sessions similar to the one awaiting him in order to learn from a real procedure. He can use it as an example, noting the demeanor and dress of witnesses, along with any other details that either impress or turn off the jury.

Defendants should not try to play "second-chair" to the attorney, but instead, they should learn as much about their charges and those charges' previous interpretations in order to see and understand local statute variations and sentencing.

Competence to stand trial is a complicated issue depending on more than just the defendant's current comportment. If, at the time of a trial, a defendant's sanity is in question, other measures must be taken; a defendant cannot be put on trial if he suffers from a mental disease. The defendant needs to be able to understand the proceedings and to assist in his own defense. If not, a judge will hold a hearing and take evidence concerning the defendant's current competence. As mentioned previously in the information about the insanity defense, the defendant has the responsibility of proving incompetence by a preponderance of the evidence. If the judge determines the defendant unstable, he will be placed in a mental institution until his sanity is reestablished. At that time, a trial will be held.

233

Writer's Tip

Much can be made of an unstable defendant by the writer looking for a unique angle. The defense of insanity is a relatively rare plea, and doctors make little use of the idiom "insanity," except for law-related purposes.

Lorena Bobbitt, for example, could have gone to jail for twenty years for cutting off her husband's penis. Instead, as one physician put It, "She broke from reality last June 23 and was unable to control her impulses—the definition of temporary insanity." Over forty-eight witnesses testified on her behalf, filing one by one to the stand, many with alarming accounts of John Bobbitt's having beaten, punched, kicked, and choked his wife. He was ruthless, often breaking down doors to get to her, or dragging her by the hair. The verdict in her case: not guilty by reason of temporary insanity.

Proximate Cause

Proximate cause, sometimes called attenuation, is a term most commonly associated with homicides. If there is a lot of gunfire in your novels, you may need it. You may also hear it defined as the "legal causation."

A defendant will raise homicide causation issues when something interjects itself into the chain of events linking his action and the death of the victim. For example, in *State v. Hall*,[115] Hall, an inmate at an Arizona prison, beat Robert Phillips with a pipe. Phillips remained unconscious for ten days. Phillips then began making medical progress, and continued to do so until about twenty-seven days after the attack, when he suffered a pulmonary embolism in his lungs and died. Hall was prosecuted for intentional murder. Despite his argument that his actions did not cause Phillips's death, he was convicted. The facts showed that Hall intended to cause Phillips's death and did so. Hall may have not intended that Phillips's death occur as it did (from the embolism), but this does not mean that causation is lacking. Legal eagles use the "but for" test here, meaning that "but for" the accused person's actions, the harm would not have happened.

But suppose a victim was only slightly injured by the defendant's bullet to his shoulder, and the victim later died in the hospital as a result of the hospital's negligence, another intervening cause. The perpetrator would likely be charged—not with his murder, but with a lesser offense, such as assault with a deadly weapon.

> **Writer's Tip**
>
> You can add tension to your crime story by using proximate cause. Say your main character is charged with homicide, but he is sure his bullet is not the one that killed the person he shot. Your readers will wait with baited breath, wondering how you're going to save your protagonist from this most serious charge. In order to save his butt from long-time sentencing, you can stage a re-creation of the crime to prove your character is not a killer.

234

Defense-Speak: Depositions and Other Pretrial Investigation

Since it is in the defense's best interest to investigate its own case, there are some techniques for gathering evidence in preparation for the trial. Interviewing prosecution witnesses through deposition is one such technique. Sometimes referred to as the compulsory process, this is tied into the Sixth Amendment guarantee.

In most jurisdictions, interviews are possible through a subpoena, which is a court order compelling the witness to attend an interview and answer questions in order to prepare a deposition. Most commonly used in civil cases, the deposition is a record of testimony, given under oath, and transcribed into a booklet for use. The process is expensive for the defendant, because not only is the attorney's time required for the development of questions and the interview, but the court reporter also receives a fee for the takedown and transcription.

By using depositions, the defense can find out what prosecution witnesses think, how credible they are, whether they are able to connect with people in expressing their beliefs, and whether the testimony rings true or differs greatly from previous testimony (facts established at the preliminary hearing). By studying these testaments, the defense team can develop a tactic that will poke holes in the prosecution witnesses' testimony at trial.

Finally, a deposition can preserve the testimony of an infirm witness or someone who may not be available for trial. It can also be issued to inspect the minutes of a grand jury proceeding, and finally, it might be used to disqualify a judge based on various grounds, including a relationship to involved parties and demonstrated bias.

It is completely legal to speak with and interview prosecution witnesses *prior to the trial,* as their testimony is not controlled solely by the prosecution. It is up to each individual witness to agree to be interviewed, however. The defendant himself should make no attempts to contact the victim, who may interpret contact as a threat, possibly causing the defendant to lose his bail and face other criminal charges as a result. His attorney should make all arrangements for contact in this instance. And although prosecutors, by rule, cannot advise their witnesses to keep to themselves, they will often tell their witnesses, "You are not required to talk with the defense."

If the defendant cannot obtain interviews through deposition, he can hire a private investigator. Provided the money is there, a private investigator will find and interview reluctant witnesses for a fee, often charging between $75 and $150 per hour for his services.

235

Finally, there is the subpoena *duces tecum.* These three magic words can compel uncooperative people or offices to cough up their records, documents, or objects. A subpoena *duces tecum* is relatively easy to get; it is comprised of prestamped forms, and the defense attorney needs only to fill in the blanks to generate a court-ordered directive.

Defense Strategy

Communication between the defendant and his attorney helps to establish the "account" of events from the defendant's viewpoint. The attorney is not expecting to fabricate a story to present as evidence, but the defendant's telling of the story—the actual account—may differ markedly from what the prosecution has said. For example, fingerprints at the scene can be explained away in any number of ways, such as that the defendant had been there the week before, had performed some service for the victim, or had even come in to use the phone. The defendant may have tried to remove himself from the premise before the criminal activity took place. If the defendant had claimed that he had an "alibi" and was out of town at the time of the crime, his account of what he was doing adds credence to his story.

In essence, the ultimate defense strategy grows out of, but is not the same as, a defendant's version of events. The theory of the case will include such high points as moral culpability and the defendant's attitude toward crime. All of these factors must be pieced together with provable facts and hard evidence.

Confidentiality

Because of the rule of confidentiality between the defendant and his lawyer, only certain things need be relayed to the prosecution in preparation for a trial. Normally, the prosecution will know if the defendant's version hangs on an alibi or an insanity defense. The identities of defense witnesses and their written statements are divulged, and the general outline of the case is imparted early, in the event a plea bargain is possible. One very important rule to note here is that the defendant's version of his story, as relayed to his counsel, is the one he must stick with. Any alternate version from the first would constitute perjury if submitted in court. Ethical rules forbid a defense attorney from calling witnesses who, they know, will perjure themselves. Now, this does not mean that the story will not be modified by other important details or even some inaccuracies; it does mean the story cannot be a continual infringement against professional ethics. But the ethical conduct of a lawyer character is up to the writer to develop, and the moral principles of counsel can be tested, can even fail. Lawyers are not sworn in and are not under the same oath as their witnesses are—food for thought.

Pretrial Discovery

236

Every jurisdiction has a procedure in which the prosecution has to tell the accused what evidence it intends to use against him. This is information included in pretrial discovery. The accused may have to make a motion—a written request—or file a pleading to obtain it, or the prosecution may just turn it over for the asking.

The file should include the names of witnesses, their addresses (this part is optional), and any prior criminal activity on their part. Also, a list of documents or other exhibits to be used against the defendant as evidence in court will generally be in the discovery, including hard evidence, such as fingerprints, bullets, photographs, and specimens taken from the body. All types of statements made by the defendant, either oral or written, should be provided. And all the reports prepared by prosecution experts who have conducted examinations of the evidence, any type of physical or mental analyses, and other scientific tests or comparisons, must be turned over.

The defendant should take this process seriously because the prosecution is also obligated to turn over any evidence it has that might either establish the defendant's innocence or point to other options, the latter referred to as "exculpatory evidence." How could that be? Maybe something turned up accidentally, or maybe the police failed to follow another path that has recently come up.

Due Process Right to Tools (Indigents)

Aside from the right to counsel, the court has confirmed that certain types of technical support must be available for an indigent's counsel. For example, in order for a defendant to have adequate access to the appellate process, a trial transcript must be provided by the state. Indigent defendants also have the right to receive the basic tools of adequate defense at trial, including expert witnesses if they are necessary for an effective presentation.

Motions

Motions can be made before, during, or after a trial. Some are more confusing than others, but, basically, the motion is a procedure, whether written or oral, requesting the court to make a ruling with regard to most any legal issue surrounding the case. In extremely complex cases, a motion could consist of a written brief, something that raises intricate legal issues that only a judge can respond to fairly.

Motions are ordinarily a three-step process. First, the defense attorney must give notice that an adversary motion will be made. A written notice called a "Notice of Motion" is prepared and then filed with the court, and another copy is presented to the prosecution. Inside the notice are papers, which state what specific request the party is asking for; an explanation of facts for the request, usually in the form of an affidavit; and the legal basis for the request, usually in a document referred to as the "Memorandum of Points and Authorities."

The next step is a hearing of the motion, during which each party has a right to present its oral arguments with the express purpose of getting the judge to agree to its side. The judge will decide either to uphold—sustain—or to deny the motion.

237

This meeting can take place in the judge's chambers, or it can be avoided if the prosecutor calls for a new court date or some other calendar matter. This would be called "stipulating" to a continuance, whereby the written stipulation would be filed with the court, awaiting the approval of the judge in order for the request to take effect, allowing the prosecution or defense to dodge yet another meeting.

Finally, the judge may make no immediate ruling but rather "take the matter under submission," meaning, he will convey his ruling in his own good time, whether that be the next day, the next week, or even months later. Or, the judge can ask the requesting party to make further written arguments to simplify a complex situation.

FYI—

It would behoove your counsel character to be preparing briefs *ad nauseam*. To begin, a motion made as a legal brief carries more weight simply because the preparation is more exhaustive than that of a simple oral declaration of need. Judges often like to read these arguments and consult other records of precedence before deciding. And, finally, the defendant will have a record of the motion, should an appeal somewhere down the line be needed.

If motions are deemed to be frivolous documents, though, and viewed as tying up both the good nature of the judge and the time of the court, His Honor can fine the offending party. This is not a defense tactic to be abused.

COMMON PRETRIAL MOTIONS:

• *Motion to modify bail.* Even if a judge has already set bail, new circumstances may bring to the judge's attention the need for a reduction, which may vary from the standard measure.

- *Motion to dismiss.* If there are mistakes on the document used to charge the crime, a defendant can attack the improper complaint with a "Motion to Dismiss Complaint" filing. A correct complaint specifies all the elements of the crime, the defendant charged, and the authority making such charges. Technically, the failure of the complaint to allege all these elements could result in a dismissal if not for the fact that prosecutors use templates and often toss out the defective forms. In addition, the state's team is usually allowed to amend the mistakes, so motions of this nature are unlikely to work. However, if it is a motion to dismiss based on double jeopardy, granted immunity, or some other violation, it will be taken in for more careful review. Also—a loophole—if the prosecution fails to refile erroneous charges within the time period specified for the "statute of limitations," the charges may be dismissed.

238

- *Motion for bill of particulars.* This filing is used in order to learn the basis of the formal charge the defendant faces. Upon granting a motion for bill of particulars, the judge will order the prosecutor to specify with particularity just what the defendant did wrong. The return of a document like this helps the defense plan a strategy, but it is usually unnecessary because defense counsel is, as a matter of course, given a copy of the police report and other essential paperwork.

Writer's Tip

A writer, if he wants to portray a stubborn or exceptionally hard-bitten prosecution, may use a motion for a bill of particulars to illuminate an existing problem between the prosecutor and the defense attorney on another level.

- *Motion to reduce charges.* This is an uncommon filing, since the preliminary hearing is already in place for the judge to decide whether the prosecution's felony case is sufficiently supported by evidence. Still, this motion may be used if circumstances change substantially or if new evidence comes up. Plea bargaining, based on either an equitable exchange of information or a confession, is typically the vehicle used for reduction of charges after the preliminary hearing has occurred.
- *Motion for a change of venue.* A jury trial is most often conducted in the county where the crime took place. If there is adverse publicity in the county or if finding unbiased jurors proves too difficult, a motion asking for a change of venue is requested. For the defendant, a change in jurisdiction is not always the best move. What if the case goes to a less desirable location? The distance may put the defense attorney far away from his office, and it may be a stretch for the defendant's family and friends to attend. In addition, away from defense counsel's home base, court costs may be higher. Something to think about, however, is that the O. J. Simpson's case may have had a markedly different outcome should the trial have taken place in

its original jurisdiction of Brentwood, California, instead of in South Los Angeles County.

• *Motion to strike a prior conviction.* Oftentimes, records of conviction have many mistakes. Prior "bad rap sheets" can have a negative connotation when it comes to sentencing. Defendants with "priors" are usually handled more severely and, as a consequence, may be faced with more serious charges. Judges also sentence repeat offenders much more harshly. Also, if a procedural irregularity such as a denial of counsel took place in the prior case, leading to conviction, the defendant would not want that record to reflect on his present circumstances. A motion to strike a prior conviction" would be a positive move. The judge would then strike the information—instruct the prior record to be disregarded, in all manner and form.

• *Motion to preserve evidence.* This is most often used for perishable evidence. It will force a prosecutor to keep evidence safe long enough for the defense to obtain its own experts and run its own tests. The motion to "preserve evidence" would most likely be used for evidence on blood alcohol tests and drunk-driving offenses.

239

• *Motion to disclose identity of a confidential informant.* It is in the defense attorney's interest to find out if the prosecution is relying on the testimony of a government informant. If so, an attack on the informant's credibility is an option, as well as finding out if he is an active participant in the offense. If he is a "paid informant" or has something to gain by testifying against the defense client, knowledge of the mercenary nature of his role provides the defense with a way to curb the damage done by such testimony. The judge's decision to grant the motion is based on balancing the public's interest in the free flow of information to the police against the defendant's right to prepare a defense free of bias.

• *Motion to examine the police officer's personnel file.* Similar to the motion to disclose identity of a confidential informant, the benefit of this motion is one of distraction. If the police officer's personnel record contains reprimands for planting evidence, racial prejudice, or excessive force, his credibility may be at issue and stands to weaken prosecution's case. Note: The motion to examine the police officer's personnel file is a difficult one to obtain, as you can well imagine the state's reluctance to unmask its own staff's weaknesses.

• *Motion to suppress evidence.* Evidence obtained illegally cannot be used in a criminal trial. Such evidence is called "exclusionary evidence." And evidence that has been taken as a result of the exclusionary evidence—fruit of the poisonous tree—is also illegal. If the motion to suppress evidence comes through, an evidentiary hearing is scheduled. The details of the motion will be brought forward, including all charges pertaining to Fourth Amendment grounds of search and seizure, and a granting of the motion will undermine the government's case considerably.

• *Motion in Limine.* Used once the trial has begun, a motion in *Limine* ("at the very beginning") renders evidence inadmissible *before* the prosecution introduces it. By using this motion early on in a trial, the defense can prevent the jury from ever hearing it. A critical move, a motion in *Limine* must be timed perfectly, or the judge would have to issue an order to the jurors to "disregard" the evidence as stated. If I said the evidence involved a "white bear," do you know how difficult it would be to forget the white bear? Another point, this motion action may trigger another legal brief called a "Memorandum of Points and Authorities," a document that describes the legal basis for a request.

• *Motion to suppress confessions, admissions, or other statements made to police.* Since the accused is constitutionally protected from giving involuntary confessions, the way to bring the violation of this right to the attention of the judge is to file the motion to suppress. A number of related questions can arise as the result of defense's seeking this motion, such as whether the confession was obtained in violation of Miranda rules or under self-incriminating conditions imposed by the police or prosecution.

• *Motion to suppress a pretrial identification of the accused.* If a lineup or showup process was impressively suggestive to a witness, the lineup and ensuing identification would be in violation of due-process standards. This motion would be used to generate an inquiry into the practices of police during pretrial identifications.

• *Motion to sequester witnesses.* The defense can request that witnesses be physically barred from the courtroom. They must sit outside and cannot hear another witness's testimony until it's their turn to testify. The reasoning here is that the prosecution witnesses will not have the benefit of hearing anybody's else's words, and at the very least it will frustrate or irritate them. They will surely not be influenced by what others say. They can be kept out from all phases of the trial, such as jury selection, arguments of the counsel, and other witness examinations.

CHAPTER IX

CRIMINAL PROCEDURE

Introductory Note: These forms are based in some instances on the Rules of Criminal Procedure and in some instances on the editor's perception of types of motions which might be employed in certain situations. Some of the forms may go beyond the present status of Arkansas criminal practice. The forms are entirely related to criminal defense practice. The drafting of an information or an indictment would be keyed to the particular offense and the facts relative to it.

_____

1. MOTION TO QUASH THE INFORMATION.

_____, Defendant herein, moves the Court to quash the information for the following reasons:

1. That the defendant _____, is charged with the offense of _____

2. That at the first appearance held before the Honorable _____, on _____, 19 _____, probable cause for detaining defendant was found to exist.

3. That the prosecution, at the first appearance, did not establish probable cause and established only the following facts: [Describe]

4. That the prosecution has failed to establish or allege the following essential elements of the offense charged: [Describe]

WHEREFORE, the Defendant, _____, prays that the Court quash the information.

Respectfully submitted,

_____

Attorney for Defendant

_____

2. APPLICATION FOR CHANGE OF VENUE.

_____, Defendant, petitions the Court for a change of venue and in support of such petition states:

1. That the Defendant, _____, is charged with the offense of _____

2. That the minds of the inhabitants of this County are so prejudiced against the Defendant that a fair and impartial trial cannot be held in this County.

3. That attached hereto in support of such allegations are the affidavits of _____ and _____, two credible persons who are qualified electors and actual residents of this County and who are not related to the Defendant in any way.

4. That this Court has the authority and discretion to change venue pursuant to Arkansas law.

WHEREFORE, the Defendant, _____, prays that the Court grant this petition and issue its order removing this case to [specify desired jurisdiction].

Respectfully submitted,

By: _____

Attorney for Defendant

Address: _____

157

NOTE

See Arkansas Statutes Annotated §43-1501 et seq.

————————

3. MOTION TO REDUCE BAIL.

———————————————, Defendant, for his motion to reduce bail, states:

1. That the Defendant is charged with the offense of ————————————.

2. That a pretrial release inquiry was conducted by [judicial officer], on ——————, 19 ——————, at which time such judicial officer set bail in the amount of $ ————————— to insure the appearance of the Defendant in Court.

3. That such bail is excessive taking into account all facts relevant to the risk of willful nonappearance by the Defendant, including the following:

   (a) Defendant has been a resident of the City of —————— for —————— years.

   (b) Defendant has been employed at ————————— as ————————— for ——————years.

   (c) Defendant has strong family ties to the community in that defendant's [parents] [family] [husband] [wife] [children] reside at —————————.

   (d) Defendant's reputation, character and mental condition are good.

   (e) Defendant has no past history of failure to respond to legal process.

   [(f) Defendant has no prior criminal record.]

   (g) ————————— and —————————, who are responsible members of the community, are prepared to vouch for the Defendant's reliability.

   (h) Defendant is not charged with a serious offense and the apparent probability of [conviction] [the likely sentence] reduces the risk of nonappearance.

WHEREFORE, the Defendant prays that the Court grant his motion to reduce bail.

Respectfully submitted,

By: ————————————————————

Attorney for Defendant

Address: ————————————————

————————

4. MOTION FOR DISCOVERY.

———————————————, Defendant, for his motion for discovery states:

1. That the Defendant is charged with the offense of —————————.

2. That the prosecuting attorney is obligated to disclose to defense counsel the following material and information which is within the possession, control, or knowledge of the prosecuting attorney:

   A. The names and addresses of persons whom the prosecuting attorney intends to call as witnesses at any hearing or at trial;

   B. Any written or recorded statements and the substance of any oral statements made by the Defendant [and —————————, Co-Defendant];

   C. Those portions of Grand Jury minutes containing testimony of the Defendant;

   D. Any reports or statements of experts, made in connection with this case, including results of physical or mental examinations, scientific tests, experiments or comparisons;

   E. Any books, papers, documents, photographs or tangible objects, which the prosecuting attorney intends to use in any hearing or at trial or which were obtained from or belong to the Defendant;

   F. Any record of prior criminal convictions of persons whom the prosecuting attorney intends to call as witnesses at any hearing or at trial;

   G. The substance of any relevant Grand Jury testimony;

H. Whether, in connection with this case, there has been any electronic surveillance of the Defendant's premises or of conversations to which the Defendant was a party;

I. The relationship to the prosecuting attorney of persons to whom the prosecuting attorney intends to call as witnesses;

3. That the prosecuting attorney should disclose and permit inspection, testing, copying, and photocopying of any relevant information regarding:

A. Any searches and seizures resulting from a warrant to search the premises at [address] issued on [date] by [court] and executed on or about [date];

B. The acquisition of a statement from the Defendant on or about [date] at [address] by [law enforcement agency].

4. That the prosecuting attorney should disclose to the defense counsel any material or information within his knowledge, possession, or control, which tends to negate the guilt of the Defendant as to the offense charged or which would tend to reduce the punishment therefor.

5. That this Court in its discretion may require disclosure to defense counsel the following relevant material and information which is material to the preparation of the defense: [List relevant material and information] [to be used when discovery is discretionary under Rule 17 of the Arkansas Rules of Criminal Procedure].

WHEREFORE, the Defendant, _____, prays that the Court grant his motion for discovery and order the prosecuting attorney to disclose the material and information described herein.

243

Respectfully submitted,

By _____

Attorney for Defendant

Address: _____

NOTE

See Rule 17, Arkansas Rules of Criminal Procedure

---

5. MOTION FOR JOINDER OF OFFENSES.

, Defendant, in support of his motion for joinder of offenses, states:

1. That the Defendant is charged with the offense of [specify offense] in Docket No. _____, and is charged with the offense of [specify offense] in Docket No. _____.

2. That both offenses are within the jurisdiction and venue of this Court and are [based on the same conduct] [arise out of the same alleged criminal episode].

3. That the prosecuting attorney has sufficient evidence to warrant trying both of the offenses at the same time.

4. That the ends of justice would be served by joinder of such offenses.

WHEREFORE, the Defendant, _____, prays that the Court grant his motion for joinder of offenses.

Respectfully submitted,

By _____

Attorney for Defendant

Address: _____

NOTE

See Rule 21.3, Arkansas Rules of Criminal Procedure.

---

1. That the Defendant is charged with the offense of _____.
2. That the prosecuting attorney plans to call (number) witnesses to testify in this case.
3. That in order to insure that such witnesses may not hear the testimony of other witnesses, the witnesses should be excluded from the courtroom.

WHEREFORE, the Defendant, _____, prays that the Court segregate the witnesses in this case.

Respectfully submitted,

By: _____

Attorney for Defendant

NOTE

See Arkansas Statutes Annotated §43-2021.

_____

20. MOTION TO SUPPRESS EVIDENCE.

_____, Defendant, for his motion to suppress evidence states:
1. That the Defendant is charged with the offense of _____.
2. That the Defendant is scheduled to be tried on _____, 19 _____.
3. That the prosecuting attorney plans to introduce evidence, namely [describe evidence], seized in violation of the Defendant's constitutional right to be free from unreasonable searches and seizures under the 4th and 14th Amendments to the United States Constitution [and in violation of Rule _____ of the Arkansas Rules of Criminal Procedure] in that:

[A. The evidence seized was not subject to seizure.

B. The seizure was based on the authority of a search warrant issued _____, 19 _____, by [issuing judicial officer], and the issuing judicial officer was not authorized to issue warrants.

C. The seizure was based on the authority of a search warrant issued on _____, 19 _____, by [issuing judicial officer], and on the record before the issuing judicial officer, there was no reasonable cause to believe that the search would discover the individual or things specified in the application for the search warrant.

D. The seizure was based on the authority of a search warrant issued on _____ 19 _____, by [issuing judicial officer], and the warrant was invalid for failure to describe with sufficient particularity the place to be searched or the persons or things to be seized.

E. The seizure was based on the authority of a search warrant issued on _____, 19 _____, by [issuing judicial officer], and the warrant was executed on _____ 19 _____, at approximately [time of day], a time not authorized therein.

F. The seizure was based on the authority of a search warrant issued on _____, 19 _____, by [issuing judicial officer], and the scope of the search by which the things seized were discovered exceeded that authorized by the warrant.

G. The seizure was based on the authority of an arrest of Defendant on or about _____, 19 _____, and the arrest was invalid.

H. The seizure was based on the authority of an arrest of Defendant on or about _____, 19 _____, and the search by which the things seized were discovered, or the seizure, was not authorized.

I. The seizure was based on the consent of _____, and the consent was not voluntary.

J. The seizure was based on the consent of _____, and such person was not authorized to give consent.

K. The seizure was based on consent, and a warning required prior to such consent was not given.

L. The seizure was based on consent, and the scope of the search by which the things seized were discovered exceeded the scope of the consent.]

WHEREFORE, the Defendant, _____, prays that the Court grant his motion to suppress the evidence.

166

Respectfully submitted,

By _____

Attorney for Defendant

NOTE

See Rule 16.2 and Comment thereto, Arkansas Rules of Criminal Procedure.

---

21. MOTION FOR CONTINUANCE.

_____, Defendant, moves the Court to grant a motion for continuance for the following reasons:

1. That the Defendant, _____, is charged with the offense of

2. That a continuance is needed for the following reasons: [Describe]

3. That [specify number] continuances have been previously granted for the following parties: [names].

4. That manifest injustice would result by requiring the trial of this cause to commence as scheduled.

WHEREFORE, the Defendant, _____, prays that the Court grant continuance for [specify time needed].

Respectfully submitted:

_____

Attorney for Defendant

---

22. MOTION FOR RELEASE OF PRISONER FOR FAILURE TO BRING TO TRIAL.

_____, Defendant, for his motion for release, states:

1. That the Defendant is charged with the offense of _____.

2. That such charge was filed on _____, 19 _____.

3. That the Defendant was committed to a jail or prison in this State and has not been brought to trial [before the end of the second full term of Court from the date the charge was filed] [within nine months from the date the charge was filed].

WHEREFORE, the Defendant moves that he be released on his own recognizance or released on order to appear.

Respectfully submitted,

By: _____

Attorney for Defendant

NOTE

See Rule 28 and 30, Arkansas Rules of Criminal Procedure.

---

23. MOTION FOR RELEASE OF BAILED DEFENDANT FOR FAILURE TO BRING TO TRIAL.

_____, Defendant, for his motion for release, states:

1. That the Defendant is charged with the offense of _____.

2. That such charge was filed on _____, 19 _____.

3. That the Defendant was held to bail, or otherwise lawfully set at liberty, and has not been brought

Stipulations

The term *corpus delicti* is Latin for "the body of the crime," and means that, before going further, the prosecution must show a crime has been committed. Often, this phraseology is used incorrectly, making people think that the *corpus delicti* has to do with the body of a victim. But, indeed, murder cases have been won without a corpse. It's rare, but it has happened.

For the charges to be made, the *corpus delicti*, or basic elements of the crime, are "stipulated." Stipulations are a kind of shorthand. A stipulation is a fact agreed upon by both the prosecution and the defense; it is to be accepted by the jury without further proof. For example, if the prosecution has called the medical examiner in to testify, the judge would stipulate that the medical examiner is, indeed, an expert on both death and the cause of death.

246

Other Defense Strategies

In addition to hiring a private investigator, taking depositions of prosecution witnesses, and developing a plan of action, the defense has the option of bringing in its own scientific experts to review the work of forensic lab technicians and others. The cost associated with expert witness testimony is prohibitive, meaning it may be very expensive and out of the reach of defendants with moderate incomes. Keep this in mind. A defendant may be forced into doing his own photography (of the crime scene); his own documentation (gathering records or other court documents); and providing his own safety net (either someone to substantiate an alibi or others interested in equal treatment) in order to save his own skin.

ALIBI DEFENSE: This is a classic practice, consisting of evidence that the defendant was somewhere other than the scene of the crime at the time it was committed. Although subject to a poor connotation—jurors may be loathe to accept an alibi—it is a viable confirmation of innocence and, with corroboration—someone to affirm the alibi—the best piece of evidence possible. If there is no corroborating testimony to support the prosecution's accusations, the prosecution has the burden of proving on its own that the alibi is irrelevant or false.

CHARACTER WITNESSES: Putting a character witness forward to testify to the strengths, disposition, and positive traits of the defendant may backfire on the defendant instead of helping his case. Evidence rules allow that anyone testifying as a witness can be attacked as to their credibility, past misdeeds, or honesty. Because of this cross-examination right, a witness testifying for the defense must be of truly exemplary character. Note: Due to the sharp increase in sexual crimes, assaults, and molestation against children, may states have enacted legislature that allows a new type of character evidence; this new rule gives prosecutors the right to offer proof that defendants charged with sexual crimes have committed previous sexual infractions.

HYPNOTICALLY ENHANCED TESTIMONY: Hypnotically enhanced testimony is an area of expert testimony that has yet to gain credibility, and its admissibility in court in questionable. An early 1980s Maryland court admitted such evidence; later, in an altogether different case, the California Supreme Court did not. The Utah Supreme Court once published an exhaustive opinion and took a look at the overall status of the law at the time, but decided that any testimony regarding anything recalled from the time of a hypnotic session forward is inadmissible as evidence.

Around the same time, the U.S. Supreme Court qualified its position and held that to exclude hypnotically enhanced testimony when it pertained to a defendant's testifying about her own posthypnotic recall violated her constitutional right.[116] Most of the other courts have now taken this position.

Ineffective Lawyers

Under the Sixth Amendment, a claim can be made which involves the habeas review of certain claims that there has been ineffective assistance of counsel. It is a fundamental right given to criminal defendants that they should receive counsel that assures them a fair defense throughout the trial procedure and provides them with a legitimate player in the adversarial process. The ineffective lawyer has shown a deficient performance, with prejudice, and has failed to uphold the standards of competency in an evaluation called the Strickland review.[117] The elements of competence in Strickland are that effective representation should entail both a reasonably thorough investigation and a reasonably competent presentation of the defendant's case. Some examples of incompetence:

• A lawyer "fails to prepare"—fails to contact witnesses, interview the primary witnesses, and complete required paperwork. Such a failure is a possible demonstration of prejudice, causing a significant problem for the case.

• The defense counsel is "appointed late." Another possible manifestation of prejudice, late appointment—sometimes so late that the case has already reached trial—would keep the counsel from being able to prepare adequate defense or a cogent closing argument.

• There is evidence of a "material misrepresentation" by a lawyer, which "induces a guilty plea." For example, an attorney solicits a guilty plea in order to clear his caseload, regardless of the defendant's wishes.

• There is "conflict of interest." Such might be demonstrated if two defendants, tried in the same case, share an attorney who favors the needs of one client over those of the other.

• The defense counsel shows "failure to know" the law. When a lawyer takes on a case beyond his level of expertise, his work could result in a gross neglect of the knowledge required to represent the case, yet again resulting in prejudice.

• Counsel demonstrates a "lack of experience," or youthfulness, resulting in gross negligence and prejudice.

With all of these scenarios, the defendant must show that his counsel's error resulted in a prejudicial trial. In other words, as long as the adversarial nature of the trial has been preserved, the defense attorney is deemed effective. Simple disappointment with the outcome of the trial doesn't qualify.

Contempt

I mention contempt here because people who are accused of a crime have a tendency not only to mistrust the system but to rail against it by speaking out. The offender of the court is called a contemnor, and his outburst is a crime. Conduct that interferes with the orderly functions of the court or the administration of justice (say, acting boisterously during a hearing), that embarrasses the court, or that degrades a judicial officer is punishable under contempt.

Criminal contempt has two different classifications—it's either direct or indirect. Direct contempt is disrespectful behavior that takes place in the courts. An interruption or any hindering of proceedings is considered contemptuous.

The indirect contempt order, sometimes called constructive contempt, is comprised of acts that take place outside the courtroom but that serve either to denigrate the court or to ignore the court's instructions. For example, if a juror were instructed to avoid the media, and he were then to decide to speak out on television, he would be intentionally committing indirect contempt.

Chapter 14

ANATOMY OF A TRIAL

For who can be secure of private right,
If sovereign sway may be dissolved by might?
Nor is the people's judgement always true:
The most may err as grossly as the few.
—JOHN DRYDEN, "ABSALOM AND ACHITOPHEL"

Everything has been building up to this point. All the information presented previously will come together at this junction. The criminal justice system, consisting of three parts—police, courts, and corrections—is decided upon in court, heard under this umbrella. The findings made here will significantly alter what happens for each component and the people involved in criminal conduct: law enforcement, the victim, witnesses, the jurors, counsel, and the defendant.

The authority given over to the courts is established by legal limits called "jurisdiction." Jurisdiction is competent standardized local, state, or federal law, invested with the power to punish, try, and sentence the accused for the crime committed.

You are summoned to court. Here, you will see the legal machinations of the adversarial process. Here is where the drama of decisions and testimony can change a life forever.

Exactly What *Is* State Jurisdiction?
The United States has a dual court system. There are state courts and federal courts. I'd like to make things easy and tell you about the standard state court system, but there is no generic court system in the United States. Even the name designation varies. While supreme courts are usually thought of as the courts of last resort, in New York the name "supreme" is assigned to the main trial court, while its New York Court of Appeals is the state's court of last resort.

To begin, we'll start with the state court system and a simplified three-part hierarchy to help explain jurisdiction. First, there are courts with limited jurisdiction, such as municipal courts, small claims courts, traffic courts, and justice of the peace. These lower courts have the least amount of power. Most often, misdemeanors, rather than felony cases, will show up here. Sentences are typically less than one year in jail, plus a fine of not more than $1,000.

Because of the jurisdictional limitations, no exact records of the proceedings are needed. These courts can also include family court, probate court, and juvenile court. There is no trial process at this level, and there exists an informality in proceedings not seen in the higher courts. It was once common practice to appoint to these courts magistrates with no formal training and little judicial attitude. Typically, the police report acts as the prosecutor, and the accused defends himself. Speed is the watchword.

250

The next level holds courts of general jurisdiction, the primary venue for trial courts in the criminal justice system. Sometimes called circuit court, district court, state court, or county court (the designations vary from state to state), these courts have the power to try and bring major criminal cases to an end. This is the original jurisdiction for felonies, and it also serves as a court appellate jurisdiction for misdemeanor convictions that have been adjudicated in the lower, limited court.

And lastly, there are the courts of appellate jurisdictions. Sometimes called superior court, appellate court, district court of appeals, or state supreme court, depending on the state, these are the appeals courts in the United States. They deal specifically with questions of law arising from the trials and handle appeals coming from the courts of general jurisdiction. In other words, they answer questions about constitutional or legal violations.

LOWER COURTS: Starting at the bottom and working up, the lower courts are ones with limited and special jurisdiction. Numbering over thirteen thousand across the country, they handle all minor criminal offenses—also called petty crimes or misdemeanors, such as traffic offenses, drunk driving, petty theft, and violation of community, county, and city ordinances.

TRIAL COURTS: Because each state has its own independent judicial system, it can be tidy and streamlined or extremely complex, depending on its state constitutional structure. One thing is certain, however: These state trial courts handle more than 90 percent of the criminal prosecutions in the United States. As courts of general jurisdiction, they are the lowest courts of record at the state level.

Some systems within larger communities provide for separate criminal and civil divisions. A few have chancery or equity tribunals specifically for estate or property dispositions (probate courts), and others have domestic relations courts. Only important civil litigation shows up here, and persons accused of crimes governed by a *de novo* trial—crimes heard and tried for the first time—answer for their deeds here. If an appeal is possible, they will be bumped up to a higher court for a hearing.

Occasionally, these trial courts may serve as appellate courts for cases that started out in courts of limited jurisdiction, usually civil in nature.

INTERMEDIATE APPELLATE COURTS: These types of courts often use a panel of three or more judges to review the case presented. The facts of the case are not in question; they are looking for judicial error. Since an appellate court cannot typically reverse the factual findings of the trial court, the judges are working from transcripts and oral arguments. Usually, if an immediate appellate court refuses to hear an appeal, the court's ruling is the same as upholding the lower court's decision.

251

The intermediate appellate court is a more contemporary institution and has locations in thirty-six states, providing relief for overburdened state supreme courts and acting as the court of last resort for a majority of appeals that come up from the courts of original jurisdiction. Other state appellate courts travel *en banc*, meaning, all the judges of an appellate court come together at various locations to hear oral arguments in a case.

COURTS OF LAST RESORT: Each state has an appellate judiciary court, and it is commonly called the state court of appeals, or sometimes is referred to as the [*fill in your state name*] Supreme Court of Appeals. It represents the final authority in issues involving state law. In almost every state, the court is established through the state constitution, and its judges are most often elected. An extensive background of law and law practice is one of stipulations for a judge candidate.

The state court of appeals is similar to the way the U.S. Supreme Court relates to lower federal courts. However, in states that do not have an intermediate appellate division (like Mississippi), the judges of the state court of appeals are not allowed to choose which cases they decide to hear.

Following a loss at the state supreme court level, the only other alternative to going on is to get a hearing from the U.S. Supreme Court. The nine Supreme Court judges have the final word in determining what the U.S. Constitution requires, permits, and prohibits in the areas of law enforcement, prosecution, adjudication, and punishment. Usually, only those cases involving constitutional law go forward; it is a difficult weeding out process, and fewer and fewer appellate court cases reach the U.S. Supreme Court every year.

Federal Court Hierarchy

The difference between federal and state courts is in what they are allowed to hear. Federal courts deal primarily with federal laws or laws made by the

Senate, which govern all the country and which were established under legislative powers expressly granted to Congress by the United States Constitution. Since the Bill of Rights guarantees certain liberties to the American people, any violations of those rights are a concern for the federal courts.

A four-tier federal system has the U.S. Magistrates at the bottom, followed by the U.S. District Courts, then the U.S. Court of Appeals, and, finally, the U.S. Supreme Court at the top. The federal system also includes military law for the armed forces and has exclusive jurisdiction over other federal affairs, such as the federal banking system, the Bureau of Printing and Engraving, the U.S. Postal system, and international trade. Any crimes committed on federal or tribal grounds are also tried in federal courts, sometimes called "U.S. territorial courts."

252

U.S. MAGISTRATES: Not actually a court system, U.S. Magistrates, formerly called U.S. Commissioners, are federal judges who assist the district courts and handle duties such as hearing misdemeanors, setting bail for more serious offenses, reviewing civil rights petitions, and issuing search and arrest warrants.

U.S. DISTRICT COURTS: Created by the Federal Judiciary Act passed by Congress on September 24, 1789, district courts today number over ninety. These are tribunals of original jurisdiction, and the U.S. District Courts typically try noncriminal, or civil, cases under federal law. Some examples of these are patent rights, copyright violations, postal problems, bankruptcy, and those actions prohibited by Congress as criminal and punishable by the federal government.

Each state has at least one territorial district to delineate the district court boundaries. Some larger states have more than one; for example, Texas and New York have four each. District court judges who are nominated by the president are confirmed by the U.S. Senate and appointed for life. Most districts have at least five judges, and some have up to twenty-four. A single judge conducts the trials in the lower tribunals, except in cases that involve the constitutionality of national or state statutes.

FYI—

In recent years, there has been a boom in *habeas corpus* jurisdiction of U.S. District Courts. Inmates who have been tried, sentenced, and confined in and by state courts are contesting their incarceration by state authorities. This type of postconviction remedy is allowed under federal law. The prisoners must contend that some aspect of their federal rights has been violated.

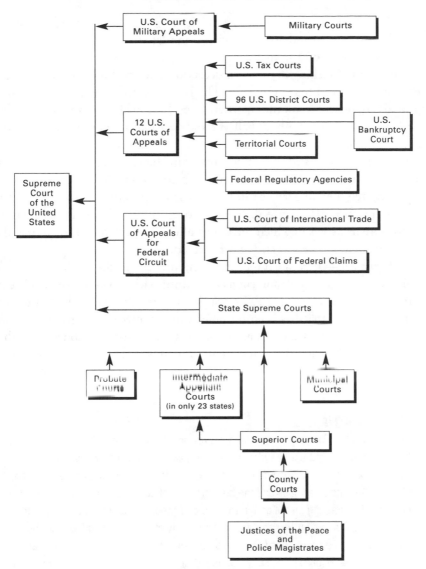

THE U.S. COURTS OF APPEAL: Hovering above the U.S. District Courts and the U.S. Magistrates, are the U.S. Courts of Appeal. Next to them, we could group the specialized federal courts, and the U.S. Supreme Court is at the top (see diagram) Any contested decision of a district court is handled here. Like their state counterparts, U.S. Courts of Appeal accept no new evidence. Decisions are based upon the original transcript of the case along with possible oral arguments.

The number of judges authorized to sit in on each district ranges from six to twenty-eight, but, normally, three adjudicate a case. There are twelve U.S. Courts of Appeal, each with a jurisdiction over a particular geographical area called "judicial circuit."

U.S. SUPREME COURT: The U.S. Supreme Court is the court of last resort for all courts, and its powers are mandated by the Constitution. In 1996, more than 7,600 individuals and companies went "all the way to the Supreme Court," seeking to overturn decisions made by lower courts. The justices that year agreed to hear only 84. The issues ranged from physician-assisted suicide to indecency on the Internet. They are usually issues that will affect large numbers of people. About half of these decisions are announced, with the justices' opinions fully published. For the rest of the unheard cases, the lower court decisions will stand. An important point here: A Supreme Court decision that reverses or overturns a defendant's conviction or sentence does not necessarily free the appellant or impose a lighter penalty. Instead, the Court remands or returns the case to the court of original jurisdiction for a new trial. In those rare instances in which the Court allows the defendant to go free, the case is considered to be reversed and rendered.

254

The justices—there are nine of them, to help avoid a "tie vote"—are appointed by the president and subject to confirmation by the Senate. One of the members is the chief justice. The Supreme Court considers itself a discretionary court, and that has been borne out over the years as fewer and fewer cases receive hearings. Cases usually proceed to the Supreme Court through a writ of *centiorari*, which is an order sent to the lower courts instructing them to prepare records so that the Supreme Court can decide if the law has been correctly applied.

Writer's Tip

There is a controversial book written by a former Supreme Court law clerk, Edward Lazarus, which might help a writer to get the inside skinny on how the Supreme Court works. The book, *Closed Chambers*, describes infighting among justices and clerks during the late 1980s and the politicization of certain issues. Lazarus has been criticized for violating an obligation to keep court matters confidential. However, David Garrow, a law professor at Emory University in Atlanta, read Lazarus's book very carefully and says *Closed Chambers* contains little that was not already available from other books and the late Justice Thurgood Marshall's papers at the Library of Congress.

Far more revealing is another excellent book about the Supreme Court and its history, *A People's History of the Supreme Court* by Peter Irons.

Federal or State?

Sometimes a person will commit an offense involving both state and federal statutes. A common example of this is the assault on an FBI officer. If the officer was on duty, the federal courts want to punish the assailant. If the assault took place in the state of Ohio, the state courts may want to charge the perpetrator with assault and battery as if he were one of the state's citizens. If the crime is especially heinous, such as was the Rodney King beating, the offenders (in this case, police officers), were subject to both courts' charges. Some other federal offenses may be terrorist behavior, such as bombing a federal building (Timothy McVeigh); robbing a bank (which is a federally funded entity); environmental pollution; counterfeiting money, and so on.

Courthouse as Setting

Even though much of the work completed in courthouses is both solemn and serious, courthouses in large metropolitan areas can be bustling, confusing, and noisy. A lot happens out in the halls, and many people in the elevator look nervous and scared.

Often located within a community in the center of town, courthouses may be venerable looking and have pillars, stairs, or large cement blocks holding up their principles. And almost every downtown worker will know where it's located.

Once inside, visitors will find a reception area, a directory, or guards at the main entrance. Some courthouses have taken measures against violence and disruption, and many are equipped with magnetometers or other devices used to detect metal or metal objects on people entering. Occasionally, guards will spot-check visitors' briefcases and ask to look inside packages or bags. No search warrant is needed for this, and judges can request a search of anyone acting suspicious.

In addition to the rooms where trial proceedings are held, there will generally be other courthouse employee offices, holding areas for prisoners, rooms where the press convenes, jury assembly rooms, a law library, and temporary rooms for other court-related activities. The best way to enter any room in a courthouse is to be observant and nonobtrusive. The spectator area is always behind the prosecution and defense tables, somewhere in the gallery. And no one is allowed to enter the gated area, often referred to as "the bar," or the area surrounding the judge.

Writers who want to study the process or find out what goes on at various proceedings should call the courthouse clerk's office to determine the schedule and ask about being a visitor. One note, though: Check just before you leave for the courthouse; things can change so rapidly and often that even jury members usually have to call in the night before to find out if their presence is required.

The R Rulings

Judges make final rulings and, coincidentally, they all begin with the letter R. For example:

• *Remands.* This means a case is returned to its court of original jurisdiction for a retrial; it also means the defendant is returned to custody.

• *Reversed and rendered.* When the case is reversed and rendered, the defendant goes free. Reverse rulings in two-thirds of cases are due to "right-

255

ness" and involve specific issues the court wishes to address; most of the time, they involve constitutional questions.

When the Supreme Court reaches a majority decision and rules on a case, its rule becomes "precedent" that must be honored by all lower courts. The application of precedent in the legal system is a giant wielding of power for the Supreme Court. Its influence helps to shape the everyday operating procedures of the police, corrections departments, and other trial courts.

Courtroom Personae

Many different people with different responsibilities serve the courts or are the key players in cases. Briefly, here are their positions:

256
• *Defendant.* The accused. His guilt or innocence rests with the criminal justice system, the police, the courts, and corrections. If acquitted, the defendant will go free and may not be tried for the same offense again according to the Fifth Amendment guarantee against double jeopardy. If found guilty, the defendant will lose his liberty and, perhaps, even his life.

• *Defense attorney.* A lawyer or group of lawyers who will defend the accused. They make sure the defendant receives a fair trial and will use all the powers and resources at their disposal to free their client. Those who work with the public defender's office often represent indigent clients and face seriously crowded court calendars.

• *Prosecuting attorney.* The person representing the state who brings charges against the defendant. He has a lot of discretion and power in that he can reduce the charges, offer a plea bargain, or pursue prosecution to the full extent of the law. His office commands much respect.

• *Judge.* Also called "magistrate" or "justice," the judge acts as an impartial referee or arbiter. Judges conduct hearings and make rulings on any pretrial business, the filing of motions. It is up to the judge to decide what evidence will be allowed into court. He can confer "expert" status onto those who provide forensic science testimony, and he will rule on all questions regarding substantive law and procedure. A judge will also give the jury instructions and answer any questions for them during the proceedings. Judges sentence defendants in situations absent a jury and establish instructions for jurors during trial.

• *Court clerk.* The court clerk handles all the paperwork and documentation, such as issuing subpoenas, safeguarding evidence, handling business forms and fines, and keeping track of all case records, also called case files— file folders with all the pertinent documents needed for public record. He also keeps track of the dates and times for trials on a court calendar, sometimes referred to as the "docket." His office is located conveniently close to the judge's chambers, and he answers questions on behalf of His Honor and sometimes handles his court calendar. The handyman for judicial paperwork,

? see p. 260

the court clerk will maintain the roster of jury members, call roll, and keep track of who has been selected for *voir dire* questioning, and who will get paid for their service. If a defendant fails to show, the clerk may assist the judge in preparing a bench warrant for his arrest. Occasionally, the clerk will be put in charge of marking, admitting, and controlling evidentiary material.

• *Court reporter.* An employee of the court who takes down testimony using a stenotype machine or recorder. Every word is recorded, and, later, transcripts of each day's proceedings become an official record of the trial. Usually, there is some type of signal to alert the judge to the fact that testimony may not be heard, or, if two people are speaking at once, the process may need to be slowed or reviewed. Electronic technology has replaced some court reporters with audio or video recordings or computer-generated hookups for on-the-spot courtroom monitoring and recording.

257

• *Bailiff.* The court's policeman and peacekeeper; the bailiff is responsible for safeguarding all who appear in court and prevents the defendant from escape or misconduct. He is also known as the arbiter of etiquette and language. A recent trip to municipal court found the bailiff admonishing a visitor for his watch's sounding off every half hour. He can remove anyone he deems disruptive. The bailiff may also signal the proceedings by issuing the crier's archaic invocation of "Oyez-oyez-oyez, all stand, the Honorable Judge Simon Wheedel for the court, the proceedings are now in session." He is graphic to the courtroom attendees that a performance is about to begin and takes the trial across a threshold into a consecrated space. Later, he will also help to shepherd visitors and jurors to where they belong, making sure they do not encroach on the judge's bench or counsel's table. He will also respond to any questions and responses from the jury room, whether summoned by a buzzer or a knock.

• *Court police.* Usually, and often in high-profile cases, there will be additional uniformed and armed police or a peace officer assigned to court duty.

• *Jury.* A community composite of registered voters, licensed drivers, or some other such system is called in for jury duty on behalf of the state. A jury consists of twelve men and women—usually along with two alternates, in case of illness of a principal juror. Jurors promise to listen to the facts and testimony and then render an impartial and fair decision based on the law's guidelines.

• *Witnesses.* Attendees who are sworn in to tell the truth, witnesses will provide additional information and evidence according to their own knowledge of the events of the case. There are two other types of witnesses: character witnesses, who attest to the character of the accused, and "expert" witnesses, who give opinions regarding medical, scientific, or specialized evidence.

• *Court interpreter.* Language translators whose services depend on court demands. They can be called in on an "as needed" basis to interpret and explain court proceedings, interviews, or any other court-related events, including the deciphering of language-specific documents.

• *Law clerks or research attorneys.* These are usually employed by the judge. They may be law students who are waiting to take the bar exam or full-time, licensed attorneys providing a service. Often, they review motions and pleadings and help to prepare paperwork submitted to the court for review. If further research or precedents need looking up, the law clerk is at the ready.

• *Clerk of the court.* A behind-the-scenes employee who works under the direction of the judge to handle administrative duties in regards to courtroom function. The court clerk will hire and prepare reports on personnel, coordinate caseloads, and help with accounting.

• *Jury commissioner.* This person may be appointed by the judge to oversee all duties required insofar as putting together a jury, compiling jury lists and rosters, reviewing requests for postponement from potential jury candidates, and keeping the registers full by issuing jury duty summons and managing the daily operations needed to handle jury availability.

258

The Basic Trial Rights of Criminal Defendants:

• Speedy and public trial before a judge or jury
• Impartial jury selection
• Trial venue free of prejudice, fear, and outside interference
• Freedom from compulsory self-incrimination
• Adequate counsel
• Freedom from cruel and unusual punishment
• Appeal convictions
• Freedom from double jeopardy

The Court

"All rise. The Honorable Judge Simon Wheedel presiding," the sober-looking court bailiff recited. The buttonholes in his khaki shirt were spread open like smiles, fighting to hold back a midriff that looked like a roasting wiener splitting its casing on a hot grill. He was wearing a gun that'd make any little kid's eyes pop open with keen anticipation—a personal-sized cannon wrapped in a black leather holster.

The judge opened the door to the usual fanfare: All in the courtroom were jostled out of their stupor, out of their seats, and onto their feet in homage. Then Judge Wheedel swept in, wearing a stereotypical flow of black Antron nylon, like an aging Zorro sans mask. The justice has flyaway, thinning, red, curly hair, if there were such a combination, and when he applied pince-nez glasses on his nose behind a prodigious hump, his countenance was severe.

I was fixed on the court reporter to the judge's left, my right. She was a big-boned girl, blond, with full pink lips that came to rounded points, like rose hips with the little dips in them. Soon those lips were hidden behind the cone of silence. As the proceedings go on, the court reporter dictates a word-for-word account of everything uttered, by anyone, into this soft mask. It's connected to machinery with a cord like a curly umbilical, and the private receiver that envelops her mouth is contoured to fit over the lay of the cheeks. I'm not sure if the tape gets transcribed later or what happens if she has germs from a terrible cold, but once the drama starts, you never so much as see a tooth from her again.

259

This hypothetical court scene describes what, for many of us, is an unknown alternate world. In legal vernacular, a court is the location where a trial is held, but it can also mean the body holding the trial, and the presiding judge. That is precisely why people often say that "the court is handing down a decision."

It is important for the accused to know what type of court he will be tried in, what the parameters of the court's power are, and what the charges are. The charges will be written out in a document called the "complaint." If there have been grand jury proceedings, the charges will be written out in a similar document known as an "indictment." Those accused of a crime have a right to a copy of this complaint or indictment. Even though it may not make much sense or may be embarrassing to hear read aloud, the accused can insist the judge read it at the first appearance and explain it to him.

The Jury

"In the matter of the State of Ohio versus Derrick Borehead," the clerk called out, "the charge being one count of murder in the first degree with special circumstances. A plea of not guilty has been entered."

"Are we ready?" Judge Wheedel asked, peering over the top of his spectacles from one table to the other.

The people at both tables stood up. "Ready for the prosecution, Your Honor," Assistant District Attorney Henry Cassin said.

"Ready for the defense," attorney Jensen declared. His assistant, a young man with thick hair and generous eyebrows was shaking his head in the affirmative, bobbing his head all around like a fake toy terrier in the rear window of a car.

"Good," the judge said, "Let's impanel a jury and get underway."

A *venire facias*, also referred to as an "array," is a writ summoning the jurors to court.

The number of people who received a letter from the county to report for jury duty must be winnowed down. As the prospective jurors report in, the bailiff will take their juror summons—usually an official letter or jury ticket—and check off their names. They will generally be seated together along the back of the courtroom. After they are assembled, the bailiff instructs jurors that there will be no more talking, eating, drinking, or otherwise casual behavior in the court. He calls the court to order, and the judge enters and takes his seat at the bench.

JURY SELECTION: In the beginning of the thinning process, members of the venire are sometimes asked questions in open court, to determine their general qualifications. If they do not understand and speak English, they may be dismissed. Other reasons for dismissal are health problems, poor hearing, or any personal hardship that might keep them from returning. They must be citizens of the state. Certain states will disqualify a convicted felon from jury duty. In addition, most lawyers and doctors are automatically exempted from the jury in order to continue with the service of their clients and patients, respectively.

His Honor will introduce himself and thank the civilians for responding to their civic duty call. He will explain that they will be asked questions and that they should answer carefully and truthfully so as to find an impartial jury panel. The bailiff administers an oath, and the jurors respond "I will," or "I do."

After reading a short summary of the case, the judge introduces the attorneys and the parties involved—he may read a list of the witnesses—and gives a guesstimate as to the length of time expected for the trial. Afterward, the clerk, who has put all the jurors' names into a bin, mixes the container and pulls them out much like lottery numbers. When a juror's name is called, he marches to the jury box and stands there until all members are selected. The attorneys are carefully watching this procession, making note of any outstanding or inconspicuous characteristics or attributes, as much as one can tell from body language, dress, and demeanor.

Each side in a case is given a list of the potential jurors. There are perhaps 120 names on the original call-up list, so an initial examination of them is difficult. A much smaller percentage will be represented in court on the day of the trial through attrition, and nearing the end of the term of service, the numbers will be smaller still. From this pool, fourteen names (twelve jurors and two alternates) will be drawn at random from the attendees. This first batch will undergo a *voir dire* (pronounced VWAR deer) examination by the judge and the attorneys for both sides.

Voir dire, French for "to speak truly," is the questioning of the jurors by both opposing attorneys. The process is meant to ferret out those who will in their administration of duty act fairly and remain unbiased beyond any reason. The prosecution and the defense are each allowed a specific number of "preemptory challenges," the ability to remove prospective jurors from their duty with no explanation given. They usually work from numbered charts.

There exists a constitutional check on the use of preemptory challenges by the prosecutor. The Supreme Court has upheld the use of preemptory challenges to exclude jurors by reason of racial or other group affiliation in isolated cases, such as *Swain v. Alabama.*[118] Later, Swain was struck down as condoning discrimination against minority groups when the Supreme Court ruled again in a case involving a black defendant named Batson, whose lawyer established a *prima facie* case of racial discrimination in selection of a petit jury on the basis of a prosecution's use of preemptory challenges.

261

Jurors can also be removed for "cause"—this occurs when some fact is disclosed which would make the prospective juror unfit to serve. Some common reasons for removal may be: if there is a relationship between one of the jurors and a witness; if there are conscientious objectors when it comes to alcohol, religion, or guns, which would render a prejudice; or if the potential juror is a member of a specific race or ethnic group of which someone involved is a member.

In cases involving a capital offense, such as murder, jurors are often subjected to complex questions about their attitudes toward the death penalty. A juror who could never vote to put a defendant to death is likely to be excused for cause, as is one who would always vote for death for any defendant convicted of murder. People generally have very definite feelings about the death penalty, and the absence of moral or religious convictions in favor or against, plus an open mind is essential.

Some typical questions that a defense lawyer might ask a jury member are:
• Do you recognize the defendant or have you ever had any business dealings with the defendant?
• Is anyone in your family affiliated with the court, law enforcement, or a member of the Bar Association?
• Have you read the publicity associated with this case?
• Can you follow the judge's instructions to remain fair and impartial in this case?
• Do you have any strong feelings about the defendant or the explanation of the case thus far?

Since picking a jury may be one of the most important elements of winning a case, many lawyers have both strange and sensible ideas about their choices. Along with intuition, some of their "less studied hunches" can prove ridiculous or even superstitious. A few of the more common perceptions surrounding jury selection are that older people are more tolerant and, as a conse-

quence, may be more indulgent. Females are thought to be harsh with sentencing other females, whereas college-educated females under the age of thirty-five are thought to be defendant-friendly. And because most law-enforcement employees feel that blacks from inner-city developments have built-in prejudice toward cops, many defense attorneys believe that as well. Certain groups are labeled as "too intelligent," so writers, editors, and publishers are looked at with caution (thanks!).

Jo-Ellan Dimitrius, a jury consultant, has worked on over six hundred jury trials including Rodney King, McMartin Preschool, and the O. J. Simpson case. "Each courtroom is a microcosm of life," she writes, "filled with anger, nervousness, prejudice, fear, greed, deceit, and every other conceivable human emotion and trait. There, and everywhere, every person reveals his emotions and beliefs in many ways."[119]

262

Writer's Tip

Often, jury consultants use what's called "focus groups" in order to see how potential jurors may react if this or that fact were brought to light, or if thus and so were true. Very little has been written about this process, and some additional research might net some writer a very good subplot scenario for a new criminal novel.

SWEARING IN: The jurors have been whittled down to the twelve regulars, along with two to four alternates just in case. The judge will ask that they not discuss the case outside of the jurors' room, avoid all media—either reading, listening, or speaking to—and not take it upon themselves to visit or view the crime scene.

They will then take an oath to show up, pay attention, and render a verdict based on the evidence presented. When court is in session, they will sit in a specially provided "jury box," located within short walking distance of the witness box so as to better hear the testimony, usually to the left of the judge and the judge's bench. No one goes near the bench, including attorneys, unless asked to come forward or to "approach the bench."

SEQUESTRATION AND OTHER NOTES: Sequestration is used for high-profile cases so as not to allow any tampering with the jurors or their opinions. Based on a judge's decision, the jury and all alternates will be escorted to a hotel, where rooms and meals will be provided, away from any publicity or incoming phone calls.

And since the jurors are supposed to listen very carefully to the evidence as presented by prosecution and defense in court, many trial judges have avoided allowing jurors to take notes. In recent years, however, the notepad rule has changed, and judges do allow notepads and pencils, provided the jurors leave them behind at night before adjourning and returning home.

Often the jurors will be able to ask questions of the judge during deliberation by presenting them to the bailiff for disposition.

Opening Statements

We've come to the trial's beginnings—the centerpiece of this book, if you will—and now you are going to find out what is exactly meant by the term "adversarial proceedings."

The jury has been impaneled. The trial opens with a reading of the indictment or information. It is time now for the prosecutor to give an opening statement. (The prosecution goes first in most states.) This is his opportunity to present an overview of the case to the jury. He will most likely introduce himself (and any staff accompanying him) again, and, after these niceties, he will explain the charges—the major elements of the crime—describe the crime the defendant is alleged to have committed, and point out how the state will prove its case against the defendant "beyond a reasonable doubt." In addition, he may mention what witnesses he is going to call to testify for the state, along with what evidence will be presented. One very important point here: What is said during opening statements is not evidence. The prosecutor may say something like "You will hear the defendant's next-door neighbor tell you she saw him enter the house angry on the night in question." Now, if state's witness does not show at a later date, the defense can use that opening statement against the prosecution in his closing argument by saying something like "and the prosecution failed to deliver the evidence promised by the defendant's neighbor. Why is that?" thereby setting up some doubt. This is a very unique game of hint, gesture, and verbal communication, and all must be carefully observed lest the attorneys dig themselves a hole they can't get out of later.

In his opening statement, the prosecutor may even explain the rules of evidence somewhat—talk to the jury about foundation evidence, hearsay evidence, and its relevancy—a type of quick-course in court semantics. He may also reiterate the judge's instructions and remind the jury of its duty to deliberate and decide the case based on the evidence—not on emotions, not on the look of the witnesses, not on speculation, but simply on the evidence presented.

By going over these specifics, the prosecutor is trying to establish rapport with the jurors, educating them as to the lawful requirements needed for assigning guilt and making sure they are able to follow the case. In essence, he is setting forth a dramatic art; there's a story to tell the jury, and the evidence has to be selectively turned into a believable plot. Like a good movie, each scene that the state unfolds will disclose some piece of the story that the audience needs to learn in order to make an effective decision. One thing the prosecutor cannot do, however, is promise evidence he cannot deliver. And, in regards to rules of evidence, he may not make references to any evidence he knows is inadmissible, and he may not make reference to the defendant's prior criminal record. (Remember, everyone is presumed innocent until proven

263

guilty, and, for the prosecution, that means proven beyond a reasonable doubt—the state has the burden of proof.) It is not unusual for the prosecutor to describe fully what "beyond a reasonable doubt" means. For example, he may say something like,

> Reasonable doubt means that the state's account of the crime, supported by testimony and evidence, must convince you that it is the most plausible, the most reasonable recreation of the case involving the murder of ———— on ———— by ———— using ———— in an unlawful manner and with intent. The account must convince you that our evidence, witnesses, and artifacts fit the facts and leave no reasonable doubt that the defendant committed the crime. It does not mean "no doubt whatsoever." It does not mean our version must be the only possible scenario, because, after all, we were not there. A shadow of a doubt can always be raised by a skillful defense attorney—perhaps it was all a plot made by the defendant's enemies, for instance. Don't allow their story version to cloud the evidence.

For writers, professional rules of conduct dictate that the prosecutor must not be argumentative in the opening statement, as he is just trying to orient the jury to the proceedings, and he will make no disparaging remarks against defendant's counsel. Be sure your scene reflects that premise. Then the prosecutor should thank the jurors for their attention and patience, and sit down.

Now, the defense counsel is entitled to present his opening statement. He may decide to counter what the prosecutor has just said, or, at the very least, stop his momentum. It is his choice. It is typically a good move to get the jurors' minds back to square one by reminding them the defense counsel has another version of the events and that his facts will bear out what really happened. He may indicate that the weakness of the state's case will soon come to light, preparing them for another version.

In no state is the defense attorney compelled to make an opening statement, however, and he may opt out of doing so and decide to make his opening statement at the beginning of the defense's presentation of the case.

FYI—
Either side can request that the witnesses be excluded from the opening statements so that the oration does not affect or influence them.

Presenting the Evidence

We talked about rules of evidence in chapter 10, also exploring such terms as "real evidence," "direct evidence," and "circumstantial evidence." But before we move on to the next stage of a trial, let's refresh our memories on some other terms so we will be in complete command of the obstacles that must be overcome for evidence to be admissible.

- *Foundation.* Foundation evidence is what must be secured in order to present something as reliable. For example, for a document to be admissible, the writer of the evidence must be authenticated before it can be used as truth.

- *Relevancy.* Relevancy has to be evidence that relates in a material way to the fact; for example, it must be something that either proves or disproves a disputed fact and has some real connection. Say, the prosecution wants to prove that Terrell Moore was driving drunk when he hit poor old Mr. Geezer. The state wants to offer up a witness that will testify that Terrell is a member of a street gang. This would not be relevant, unless the prosecution can prove that part of the gang's initiation is to commit a hit-and-run.

THE WHOLE TRUTH: It would be naïve of us to think that witnesses have not undergone preparation. It is a poor and incompetent attorney who does not take steps to prepare his witnesses for what is, what may be, and what may come up. The attorneys will know how to frame their questions in order to elicit the types of response that will most likely help their case. They will not encourage deception and cannot "tamper" with witnesses, getting them to change their testimony or their particular slant. That is illegal.

When an attorney does prepare his witness, however, he must be extremely careful about what he asks for, because the defense attorney can question the witness about what was discussed in preparation. Unlike the privilege between an attorney and his client, there is no client-attorney privilege between a witness and the attorneys.

All witnesses will be sworn in to tell the truth on the witness stand. If they have a religious objection to the procedure, they will be asked to affirm their testimony. They will generally raise their right hand, with their left on a Bible (or some variant—Moslems have the Koran, for example) and declare "I do," in response to "Do you solemnly swear that the testimony you give as evidence is the truth, the whole truth, and nothing but the truth, so help you God?" (Occasionally the words "so help you God" may be omitted, but the effect is the same—check with your local jurisdiction.) This is also a legal warning, so to speak, that if the truth is not told, the witnesses will make themselves vulnerable to perjury charges.

FYI—

The Federal Rules of Evidence are flexible on the question of oath, specifying that witnesses be required to declare their allegiance to the truth, by oath or affirmation, a process calculated to awaken the witnesses' awareness of their duty and of the seriousness of the justice system. The possibility of prosecution for perjury is rare, and it is not high priority because it is difficult to prove actual knowledge of falsity. In high-profile cases, however, prosecutors feel compelled to file charges if witnesses speak falsely.

PRESENTATION OF THE STATE'S EVIDENCE: The opening statements are over, and now it's time for the presentation of the state's evidence, also called the "Prosecution's case-in-chief." The first witness is sworn in, and the prosecutor begins a presentation of evidence by direct examination. He will attempt to prove everything he asserted in his opening statement, and a wise prosecutor will time his most important evidence to come early in the morning, when the jurors are fresh and at their most attentive.

Remember, if you are creating dialogue for a court scene, the format for witnesses is very strict. Testimony will only emerge in a question-and-answer format, not in unbroken narrative, rambling stories, or opinion. The attorney will generally establish who the witness is, his occupation, background, or qualifications (these bits of information are especially important when questioning an expert witness), and how he is involved in the case. After these preliminaries, the prosecutor will inquire as to what the witness saw, heard, did, or found. Questions typically follow the *who, what, where,* and *when* variety, excluding the *why,* which would be more speculation than fact. The prosecutor is trying to establish the chronological order of events leading up to the crime or to establish each and every element of the case.

LEADING QUESTIONS: Inquiries that inherently suggest to the witness how he should answer will most likely be objected to. An example of this would be the prosecutor's asking his witness, "Didn't you hear two shots?" Leading questions are considered to be a form of testimony on the part of the attorney, who, of course, is not allowed to testify.

However, if the prosecution calls a witness, and the witness's testimony helps to incriminate the accused, the witness is considered by the defense to be a "hostile witness." When the defense attorney later cross-examines such a witness, he can ask leading questions. And these leading questions are so pointed that the questioner does most of the talking during the questioning; the witness is subjected to answering only *yes* or *no* in response. The defense might say, for example, "You won't deny to this jury that you had just been to the doctor and your eyes were dilated, sensitive to light, and you were more than a hundred yards away from the scene of the crime, would you?"

ARGUMENTATIVE QUESTIONS: Some questions don't just ask for information. These are argumentative questions and are sometimes referred to as "badgering the witness." Derisive questions, such as "You don't expect the jury to believe that, do you?" are typical. Defense can object, or the witness can turn the tables around, making the prosecution look rather foolish—"I am not looking to convince the jury, I am just telling you what happened."

Writer's Tip

A wise attorney will never ask questions he does not know the answers to if he is not prepared to deal with "surprises." Knowing that, to add suspense or a twist into your plot, you can have a witness change his testimony drastically from what was discussed during investigation or in preparation for trial. The prosecutor may then have to ask for a recess, in order to take in what he has heard, regroup, and go on to Plan B.

THE ABA WEIGHS IN: The American Bar Association has specific rules of conduct, along with published standards, for both the prosecution and defense function. Within its writings about the prosecution's presentation of evidence, it states:

> A prosecutor should not knowingly offer false evidence, whether by documents, tangible evidence, or the testimony of witnesses, or fail to seek withdrawal thereof upon discovery of its falsity.[120]

267

The ABA carries additional requirements as well, stating that prosecutors should not bring inadmissible evidence, ask legally objectionable questions, or make other impermissible comments or arguments. They cannot allow tangible evidence to be displayed, which would prejudice fair consideration, unless there is a reasonable basis for its admission in evidence.

The false testimony stipulation is strict, and the only exception is if the prosecutor is taken by surprise when someone pulls a fast one; he is still obligated to see that it is corrected, even if it means scheduling a new trial.

The inadmissible evidence statement is an interesting one. The ABA believes that the "mere offer of known inadmissible evidence or asking a known improper question may be sufficient to communicate to the trier of fact the very material the rules of evidence are designed to keep from the fact finder." In other words, in their airing, comments made cavalierly or "off the record" do damage which cannot be undone. The showing of evidence before it is formally offered for admission is also grounds for trial dismissal (whereas it may have been okay to present that evidence at a later time in good faith). Remember, a defendant has certain constitutional protections concerning the prosecution's use of forced admissions and confessions and other evidence that has been illegally obtained. The Bar suggests that an immature or inexperienced lawyer confer with senior members before trying to introduce hints about inadmissible evidence. To sum it up, anything unduly inflammatory is verboten.

EXPERT TESTIMONY: Expert witnesses—people who have special training, education, or experience—give testimony pertaining to their areas of expertise, whether they be medical examiners (who will speak of the autopsy), the evidence technicians (who may talk about evidence collection) or forensic lab technicians (who could explain DNA and its individual characteristics). In high-profile murder cases, the procession of forensic experts can entail the entire criminalistics community—forensic pathologists, crime scene technicians, fingerprints experts, blood splatter analysts, trace evidence lab technicians (who deal with hair and fiber analyses), firearms specialists, and so on. Unlike other testimonials, expert witnesses are supposed to give their opinions based on the facts as they know them. They will often refer to published reports, information provided by other witnesses, or their own written reports.

OFFERING EXHIBITS: An integral part of examining witnesses, offering exhibits is an extremely important visual backup to testimony. For what is the talk of a gun without the instrument to look at, and how are we even supposed to know that that particular hole was made by a bullet, otherwise? How good is a verbal walk through the scene, when a map or diagram could show the logistics so much more effectively, and, better still, prove that the scene was not contaminated by false evidence? A document might clearly indicate the intent of the offender, or it may wind up as exculpatory evidence if it is a letter of love. Anything other than words needs to be offered as exhibits, and this is a four-step process, the ignorance of which may render the material inadmissible.

The first step is to have the object marked as an exhibit; usually this happens sometime before a trial begins, although sometimes it is done during the trial. To "mark" the exhibit, a tag or some type of stick-on paper will be attached to the evidence, along with an identifying number or marker. (This is another argument for chain-of-command, meaning, knowing who had the evidence before. All persons who have handled the materials are potential witnesses.) Usually the court reporter will attend to this process.

Next is having the evidence identified. That, in turn, means asking that the witness identify it. Dialogue would be something along the lines of "Miss Teaburn, can you identify what has been marked as exhibit 3?" If the answer is "No," the question needs to be asked of another. If the witness says "Yes," then the next request would be, "Please identify exhibit 3 for the jury." She may answer, "This is the letter the victim showed me on September 3." The exhibit should then be handed to the opponent along with dialogue for the record, such as, "Will the record show I am handing exhibit 3 to the defense attorney for identification purposes." The opponent is allowed to examine the object and may question the witness about its identification. The next step is to offer it to the judge by saying, "I offer this into the record as exhibit 3, Your Honor." If there is no objection, he'll accept that. If, on the other hand, the opposing counsel has a problem, there will be some objection, perhaps to its relevance, and any lengthy arguments will take place out of the presence of the jury.

Only after the exhibit has been marked, identified, shown to opposing counsel, and offered up to the judge, will it become an official exhibit. And it is only then that the witness will be given the opportunity to explain it, read from it, or otherwise describe it.

Defense Motion to Dismiss

Picture this: It's the middle of the trial. Say the prosecution has presented its case-in-chief and rested. The defense can make a motion for dismissal, also referred to as a "directed verdict," and ask the judge to rule on whether the prosecution has provided enough evidence to justify a conviction. If the judge believes that the prosecution's case by itself is too weak to support a guilty verdict, he can dismiss the case, which, in essence, is the legal equivalent of an acquittal. The defendant can never be tried for the same crime again. If the motion is denied, the defense proceeds with its case. Since this motion is made in the jury's absence—they may be sent out of the courtroom—there is nothing to lose even if the judge denies the motion.

The granting of this motion is typically based on one of four grounds: The prosecutor failed to show that a crime was committed; he failed to show that the defendant had anything to do with the commission of the crime; prosecution witness testimony was not credible; or the conduct of the prosecutor was improper. Of course, this motion is rarely granted, since prosecutors do not generally take a case to trial unless they believe they can win.

However, there is a minor catch-22 for the judge who is presented with such a request. If the judge refuses to grant the motion, and the defendant is later found guilty, the judge's refusal can be used as an item during an appeal; the defendant simply declares that the judge did not use proper procedural care in making his decision. On the other hand, if the judge grants a directed verdict, he must issue an order finding the defendant not guilty of the charges. And such a motion provides the opportunity for the prosecution to appeal the case—a rare opportunity for the prosecution, who under almost all other circumstances must accept a not-guilty verdict as final.

Defense Motion for Mistrial

If the prosecution has done anything that has trampled the defendant's rights, the defense attorney can make a motion and ask for a mistrial. What he is seeking is a termination of the trial before it reaches a verdict. If the improper conduct cannot be corrected by instructing the jury to disregard, or if the act was so prejudicial as to keep them from making a fair verdict, the judge has no choice but to grant the motion, and the trial will most likely be rescheduled. This span of time then serves to help the defendant by increasing the chance that important evidence will be dissolved, lost, or forgotten. The second trial, though, does not count as double jeopardy because a verdict was never rendered—an important point.

If the misconduct came from a juror or if the jury is in hopeless deadlock, that is also reason for mistrial. In addition, a mistrial ruling could result from illness of a judge or the removal of too many jurors because of an accident, flu epidemic, or something else out of the court's control.

Defendant's Case-in-Chief

Similar to the prosecution, the defense calls its own witnesses. The defense attorney must abide by the same rules of conduct, issuing questions in a Q & A format, refraining from leading the witness, and allowing for cross-examination.

Objections

For an attorney, raising an objection is a delicate *pas de deux* between himself and the judge. To begin, an attorney will put forth an objection when he recognizes that the opposition is about to introduce evidence or testimony that he believes the jury should not see or hear; something that may damage his client or case. It is up to the judge to decide to sustain (approve or consent to) the objection, or overrule (cancel, undo, or decide against) the objection. But the decision to object is fraught with risk, just because that by objecting the attorney may be drawing the jury's attention to a bit of problematic evidence. The trial judge, on the other hand, needs to rule correctly on the objection, in split-second time; a questionable ruling on an objection may be the basis for appeal. And because everything is a matter of record, attorneys often scour the court record for judgment mistakes made in haste. Some examples of objections and what they mean are:

• *Objection! Question assumes facts not in evidence, Your Honor.* There is a way to phrase questions that makes it impossible for a witness to respond, such as saying, "Most people go blank at the sight of a weapon—still, you claim to have been calm when the gunmen entered." This is not a question, and prosecutor is not supposed to testify or assume facts. In lieu of an objection, a savvy defense witness could counter the statement posed by saying, "I can't presume to tell you how other people would or wouldn't react to a gun—I can only tell you I wasn't rattled."

• *Objection, Your Honor. That calls for speculation on the part of the witness.* Similar to the previous statement, an example of this would be, "How many people do you think Edmond would have killed?" No one can tell what was in Edmond's mind, and it is improper to expect a witness to, either.

• *Objection! The prosecutor is misquoting the witness, Your Honor.* Say a witness claims to be in the lounge drinking a beer when the shooting took place. The prosecutor might counter with the inappropriate statement, "So you say that you were a little high when the shots were fired."

• *Objection, Your Honor. That is beyond the scope of the direct examination.* If a witness is being cross-examined, and a question comes up that does not relate to the previous testimony, it is out of bounds. Cross-examination is limited to a scrutiny of the direct examination.

• *Objection. No proper foundation has been laid, Judge.* The opposing attorney uses this objection in order to force his opponent to introduce evidence in its appropriate order. For example, for a gun to be exhibited, some attempt must be made to show that it is the murder weapon or that it has some relation to the crime before it can be traced to an owner.

• *Objection. Asked and answered, Your Honor.* This is to curb the examining attorney from going after the same point, only in another manner. It is a subtle form of harassment.

• *Objection! Irrelevant.* The subject matter has slipped, and the testimony is uncalled for or not relevant to the discourse (perhaps some event or character issue whose relevance has not been specified.)

• *Objection! Immaterial, Judge.* This is another way of restating the previous objection that something is irrelevant; for example, something immaterial is beside the point.

271

FYI—Speak to Me Nice

When addressing the judge, "Your Honor" is the most popular, neutral greeting and the one a judge most likely wants to hear. It is not proper to call him "Sir" or "Ma'am." And judges do expect everyone to stand (or sit in the witness box), address the microphone, speak slowly and clearly, and not talk unless asked. Any talking over or interrupting is considered disrespectful and, if continued and unbridled, is subject to "contempt of court."

Cross-Examination

Cross-examination is the process by which a witness has already been called and has given testimony under direct examination, and the opposing side gets to reexamine or ask questions about that testimony. For a trial attorney, cross-examination is an essential art. The defense attorney will try to put the prosecution's witnesses on trial themselves. This is his opportunity to plant the seeds for an alternative version of the crime; he will have to shine here and know when to push, when to stop. One question too many may kill his case. He will try to unnerve the witnesses and undermine their credibility. Generally, people will not deliberately lie, but they will follow the lead given by the prosecution attorney. And, likewise, the prosecution will try to show inconsistencies between the defense witnesses' testimony in court as juxtaposed against the same statements given over to police during their investigation.

When the defendant asks to testify, he is leaving himself open to cross-examination, and no wily prosecutor will pass up the chance to impeach the defendant (using any prior convictions he's had, pointing out the fact that the defendant has a problem with telling the truth). The prosecutor will hammer the defendant as to his motive to commit the crime—using the defendant's previous mention of debts and bills, for example, the prosecutor might ask him why he took out a life insurance policy on the victim. Or he will question the defendant's physical ability, asking, for example, how he would have been able to see a particular person in the yard so late at night.

A sly trick for the defense to use during cross-examination is the question "Have you discussed your testimony with anyone from the prosecutor's office?" Of course, the answer will be "Yes," but for some reason, it gives the impression of impropriety. Many witnesses think it's wrong to discuss their testimony, so they will stutter, look worried, or attempt to deny it, when it is simply okay. It is not okay to be told what to say, however.

272

Writer's Tip

A good scene is to have the defense attorney preparing the defendant for cross-examination. It would require some role-playing, for example, helping the defendant to see what he is up against by rehearsing what the prosecutor is likely to ask. Later in court, the accused can vent and explain things not previously mentioned, which may serve to cause additional problems.

Rebuttal and Surrebuttal

After the defense rests (has finished presenting its own evidence), the prosecutor has another shot. He can offer rebuttal evidence, which is evidence used to attack what has been offered during the defense case. Two important points: The prosecutor may not use this as a device to rehash his own case-in-chief, nor is he able to put in new evidence that is unrelated to what the defense has shown.

As its name suggests, the surrebuttal is one last shot for the defense to put on evidence after the prosecution's rebuttal. If the prosecution lies low and does not rebut any testimony or evidence, there will be no surrebuttal.

Closing Arguments

A famous credo with up-and-coming defense attorneys follows along these lines: "If you've got a good case, hammer the evidence; if you have a weak one, hammer the people's witnesses; and if you have no case at all, hammer the prosecutor."[121]

Closing arguments, also referred to as "summations," present the prosecutor and defense counsel with an opportunity to convince the jury that the evidence and testimony previously shown supports their individual theories of the case. Again, the prosecutor goes first in most instances and argues his burden-of-proof explanation, and the defense will follow with his version of events. Certain jurisdictions allow the prosecutor another shot at rebutting defense arguments (writers should check their states' particular court guidelines). Judges who allow the prosecutor only one argument often allow the prosecutor to choose whether to argue first or second. Typically, though, the defense has the final word, the last chance to articulate clearly his defendant's "not guilty" posture.

Even though much emphasis is put on the "decision-making process" coming before jurors, some studies show that jurors have already made up their minds before the closing speeches. Just the same, the lawyers will reiterate which law is in question and what the requirements are to convict someone for it; they will remind the jury what was shown and said in testimony; they will evaluate the weight of that evidence and the credibility of the witnesses; and finally, they will make an inference as to how this fits into their version of the case more plausibly than into opposing counsel's version of the case, which was weak and had holes.

The attorneys may even employ the use of emotional pleas, begging either for the jury's mercy (if the defense is speaking) or for justice on behalf of the victim (if the prosecutor is speaking). There is some latitude given over to the defendant if he is representing himself—a *pro se* defense—and the judge will allow such talk as "The prosecutor said the person who did this was an animal. I am not an animal, I am a human being, just like you are."

Some attorneys famous for their elocution may quote from the Bible, Shakespeare, and even contemporary song lyrics in their closing arguments. Others are known for their dramatic narration or emphasis, or for their ability to appeal to the common man through parallel stories or experiences. As one author describes it, "the reworking of a life in a trial is the lawyer's handiwork."[122]

FYI—

What if the defense attorney realizes during the summations that he forgot to offer some important evidence? It happens! Then he can ask the judge to "reopen the case-in-chief." Of course, the evidence must be important and relevant to the case, but it is not out of the realm of possibility that the judge can and will grant such measures within his power to do so.

Judge's Instructions to the Jury

Both the prosecution and the defense attorney meet with the judge out of court to submit their instructions for the jurors. These instructions typically incorporate the legal theories that are routine and drawn from books of approved jury instructions. Sometimes, the instructions are based on appellate court opinions whereby the court justices have defined the crimes or other legal principles, such as how to best explain "beyond a reasonable doubt." The prosecutor or the defense attorney can also craft his own version if he feels the published versions lack appeal or have shortcomings, or if he wants to develop a new instruction for which no preapproved direction exists.

The judge will devise his instructions to the jurors, also called "charging the jury," based on these submissions and on his own take on things. Typically, the jury instructions will contain:
• The definition of crime and the elements needed to convict someone of that crime
• The definition of "reasonable doubt," usually a sticking point among jurors
• The presumption-of-innocence principle
• The fact that the burden of proof is on the prosecution
• Factors the jurors should consider when evaluating the credibility of witnesses
• How to select a foreperson, how the deliberations should be conducted, and rules on returning a verdict
• And, if after considering all the evidence, there remains some reasonable doubt as to the defendant's guilt, how he must be acquitted

Sometimes, judges will also suggest to jurors that anything said by the attorneys is *not* evidence (the attorneys are, technically, never "sworn in") and that if they find a defendant guilty of murder, they must determine as part of the verdict whether they find it to be of the first or second degree. Finally, the judge may also speak about the unanimous agreement required for a decision.

To avoid confusion, the court reporter will often make copies of the judge's instructions so that the jurors will have something to refer to during their deliberations.

Jury Deliberations and Verdict

After the judge has given jurors their instructions, they will retire to the jury room to begin deliberations. Oftentimes, they will have been allowed to take notes during the trial. The only communication available to them now is between the bailiff and themselves. After they get settled, their first order of business is to elect a foreman. The foreman will usually be given a copy of the judge's printed instructions, along with two forms for each crime charged, one for a "guilty" decision, and one for a "not guilty" decision.

Coffee and other drinks are available to them and, if necessary, they may break for lunch, where meals will be provided for them or some other arrangement has been specified within that jurisdiction. Several stipulations are always the same: They are not allowed to discuss the case outside deliberations, read newspaper articles pertaining to the case, or communicate with nonjurors. In addition, they must not attempt to conduct any investigation or experiments pertaining to the case on their own. They are encouraged to judge the worth of testimony and documentation in the light of their own common sense and experience. Generally, the jurors will be allowed to spend their nights at home, but if they have been sequestered—which usually only happens for high-pro-file cases—they be will escorted to dinner and a hotel, where they will remain together until a decision is made. The decision to sequester the jury is left to the discretion of the judge.

During the discussions, which take place in a closed-room environment, they may ask the bailiff to have testimony reread, to view the crime scene, or to look at objects of evidence. Anything they need, even a reiteration or get-ting a written note to the judge, is taken care by the bailiff, who is sworn to take charge of the jurors and their needs. The judge will usually notify the attorneys of any communication between himself and the jurors.

Early on, it is suggested to the jurors that they hold a preliminary "secret ballot" to determine if they are far apart in thinking, or are close to making a decision. They will write a choice on a slip of paper, which will be collected and tallied by the foreman. It is rare that the jury agrees at the first go-round, and discussions about the case and its finer points will take place.

275

A unanimous verdict—everyone agreeing—has been a basic requirement of common law since the fourteenth century. The foreman will notify the bailiff, who in turn tells the judge a decision is in. The judge will reconvene court, the attorneys will come back, and the jurors will enter once again. The foreman will speak on behalf of the jury. The result of their decision is hand-ed to the bailiff, who will give it to the judge, He reads it and hands it back to the bailiff or clerk, who presents it to the foreman for a reading. A guilty ver-dict means the defendant is returned to jail, pending his sentence. A not-guilty decision will be logged by the court clerk, and the defendant will be free to go. Occasionally, one or both of the attorneys will ask for a "polling" of the jury. Each juror will be asked, "Is this your verdict?" or some such question, in order to see if a juror has been intimidated into his decision. In most cases, the juror will restate his vote, and the jury will be dismissed with thanks from the court for their service. If a juror dissents from his vote, the judge will dismiss the panel and declare a mistrial.

Sometimes, though, a jury becomes "hung," meaning its members cannot agree on a verdict. In this instance, a judge will usually encourage them to reconvene and discuss the facts again until they can come to a consensus. Jury deliberations are not subject to fixed time limits, and the judge will sometimes continue to hear other cases. If the jury reports that it is hopelessly deadlocked, the trial judge will declare a mistrial, dismiss these jurors, and new trial pro-ceedings will be scheduled with a new jury, essentially starting the process all over again. It is at this point that many such cases are resolved by the attorneys and the defendant through some type of plea-bargaining.

Juries have been known to disregard the evidence and the judge's instruc-tions on the law and either acquit the defendant or convict him for a lesser offense than charged. This is referred to as "jury nullification."

Over the years, juror misconduct has taken many forms, such as falling

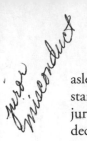
juror misconduct

asleep during testimony, coming into court under the influence of illegal substances or alcohol, lying about backgrounds or allegiance in order to get on a jury panel, discussing the case with counsel, talking to a friend about a verdict decision, and conducting independent investigations. Jurors who fail to obey any admonition from the judge will be removed from the jury, and, upon discussion with the attorneys, may even cause a mistrial.

Post-trial Motion

A convicted defendant frequently files a motion for a new trial. The motion will allege errors committed at trial. Sometimes, the judge will rectify mistakes made during the process and award the defendant a new trial. In reality, though, the motion is a way for the defendant to make open the way—a *pro forma*—to an appeal. At this time, the defendant will also seek bail pending appeal. If the trial judge rules against or disposes these motions, the defendant is up for sentencing.

276

Sentencing

In misdemeanor convictions, sentences usually occur immediately upon conviction and within the guidelines of the statute. The judge will determine and deliver punishment. Nowadays there are many alternatives to incarceration. Community service, monetary fines, boot camp, house arrest—using electronic monitoring bracelets—and probation are some of the options alternative to serving jail time.

THE PRESENCE REPORT: A federal court, as well as many states' courts, is obligated to order a presentence report, sometimes referred to as a presentence investigation (PSI), if the offender is being sentenced as a first-time offender or as a juvenile. Generally, there is a rule that makes the reports available only to the judge, the counsel for the state, the defense, and any experts appointed to the court in order to assist in sentencing, all within the discretion of the sentencing judge. For those who may be sentenced to death, the Supreme Court requires the release of the presentence report to the defendant.

This document details the defendant's criminal history (if he has one), details of the offense, medical history, family background, economic status or tax return, education, employment history, and any interviews conducted by probation officers assigned to the court. The interviews most likely will be with the spouse, employer, or any significant other. There may also be copies of court-ordered physical or mental examinations of the defendant conducted over the course of his entry into the criminal justice system. The idea is for the judge to have a fuller view of the defendant and his circumstances before imposing a sentence.

SENTENCING GUIDELINES: Looking like a mileage grid that comes with most maps, the sentencing guidelines are supposed to standardize criminal sentences and eliminate such factors as race, age, or socioeconomic level. The grid carries the seriousness of the offense, the crime's degree level written in letters (A, B, C class) or numbers (1st degree, 2nd degree, and so forth), and the dangerousness of the offender, the criminal history, or the number of counts on the offense, on the other. Chart the left-hand side of the grid with the opposite axis and find where these two figures meet. This number is the one the judge uses to decide the length of the sentence, whether it is "probationary" or "commitment." It is written as the number of months of sentence applicable, low and high. Points are also given for other areas of misbehavior, such as prior offenses, DWIs, and others, calculated into the total score. Judges do have the authority to deviate from guidelines and impose harsher or lesser sentences when there are factors to justify this change.

THE LONG-AWAITED DAY: The Sentencing Hearing: Sentencing is obviously a critical stage in the defendant's life. After the judge has gone over the presentence report and has weighed evidence offered by either party in the way of aggravation or mitigation of sentence, in most jurisdictions the convicted offender has a right to address the judge personally before any sentence is imposed. This statement on his own behalf is called "allocution," or "the right of allocution." It is simply another way to identify the convicted as a person, and he can plead for mercy, ask for a reduced sentence, a pardon, or leniency, or explain why he did what he did, or take responsibility for his actions.

Recent high-profile death cases have even let the victim's family give victim-impact evidence. This is testimony as to how the murder of a mother, wife, or other family member has affected the family physically, economically, and emotionally.

Moments later, the judge will give a pronouncement of sentence. Felonies are punishable by fines and prison time. The convicted can be sentenced for a determinate term or an indeterminate term, or a combination. Indeterminate sentencing is pretty much outmoded; it was designed to hold a criminal in custody until the prison authorities determined that he was rehabilitated, and then the subject was paroled. Determinate sentencing takes into consideration a variation of the definite sentence, meaning the judge sets a fixed term of years within statutory parameters, and the offender is required to serve that term without possibility of parole. You will also run into a term called "definite sentencing." The idea here is to eliminate discretion, and all offenders who commit the same crimes are punished equally.

MANDATORY MINIMUM SENTENCING: Legislatures have updated many states' statutes, which compel offenders who have committed certain crimes to be sentenced to prison terms for minimum periods. This means that judges have no option with which to place offenders on probation. Most often, mandatory sentences apply to heinous crimes, especially those using firearms.

Also, mandatory sentencing automatically increases the sentence for those convicted of repeated felonies. And a variation of the habitual offender tenet is the "three strikes and you're out" rule. A person convicted of a serious felony or third violent crime would be incarcerated for twenty-five years to life. Currently, the federal government and more than half the states have some form of either the habitual or the three-strikes statute.

FYI—

The state of Virginia has something called the "Twenty-One-Day Rule." The Virginia General Assembly has repeatedly protected Rule 1:1 of the Virginia Supreme Court—an archaic statute that prevents incarcerated individuals from having their guilt or sentencing reviewed on the basis of new evidence that has come forth twenty-one or more days after initial sentencing. Issued to give the citizens of Virginia "finality," this rule prevents the admission of evidence that at the time of sentencing may have appeared inconsequential or inconclusive due to underdeveloped technology or new facts; this rule proves particularly troublesome in light of rape and murder cases for which DNA testing is now available. Expect more head-butting for those seeking to repeal the rule.

CONCURRENT AND CONSECUTIVE SENTENCES: When someone commits multiple crimes and is charged with more than one, he is left open to receiving a separate sentence for each offense. These sentences can run concurrently or consecutively, at the discretion of the trial judge. Serving the terms concurrently means all of the various sentences are served simultaneously. If the judge orders a consecutive sentence, time will be served on the second sentence after the first sentence is completed.

DEATH PENALTY CASES: In states that allow capital punishment, the prosecutor has the initial charging decision on whether to seek the death penalty. He will seek either life without the possibility of parole, or death.

If a prosecutor seeks capital punishment in a jury trial, the jury will make a recommendation to the judge regarding sentencing a defendant to death. This jury recommendation often follows in what's called a separate "penalty phase" hearing. The second phase is where the defendant has already been convicted, and the jury listens to evidence concerning the defendant's background, interviews, and other reported matters. If the jury recommends death, the judge still has the power to impose a lesser sentence. If the jury recommends life without the possibility of parole, however, the judge cannot impose death.

Appeals and the Writ

Appeals are subject to strict time limits. Within seven to ten days after the entry of a final judgment is the most likely window of time to file a paper called a "Notice of Appeal." The appeals process is lengthy, taking many months, and cases may go through two or more levels of appellate courts.

A writ, on the other hand, is an extraordinary remedy and is considered a last-ditch effort. These are usually reserved for cases in which the defendant feels wronged by the actions of a trial judge, or for a concern that goes beyond the trial record, such as an incompetent lawyer charge, any challenge to the legality of the imprisonment, or any new evidence.

Such postconviction proceedings are remedies that must be proven by the defendant in order to overturn a sentence. *Writ of prohibition* is a court order that prevents another court from exercising jurisdiction in a particular case. *Writ of error* occurs when an appellate court seeks to correct an error revealed in the record of a lower-court proceeding. *A writ of certiorari* allows defendant an opportunity to have his case reviewed by the U.S. Supreme Court. Basically, though, a defendant may challenge the trial court's actions or rulings considered to be fundamental errors—pretrial violations of the defendant's rights, trial court rulings or procedural errors made when admitting or excluding evidence, irregularities in the selection or conduct of the jury or their instructions, improper remarks made by the prosecutor, poor interpretations of the law, questionable jurisdiction concerns, evidence that does not meet the burden of proof, and, finally, the voluntariness of a guilty plea.

279

I see the courtroom is going dark for the day. I have presented the facts of law as I see them, and, consequently, any errors are mine—as unintentional as they may be. If you have further queries, comments, or corrections, you may contact me through my Web site, located at *www.andreacampbell.com*. I hope this journey through the criminal law system will add character and verisimilitude to your novels, and if you are further intrigued, I urge you to continue your studies or visit a real courtroom proceeding. Make use of other legal resources, too, whether you choose court reporters, legal libraries, or current cases—the real drama is yours for the taking.

Appendix

After the Trial

Rights of Prisoners After Conviction

• *The right to access the courts.* Prisoners must be given reasonable access to pens, paper, stamps, and items that allow them to correspond with the judicial system. Additionally, inmates cannot be prevented from counseling with each other unless a reasonable substitute is provided, such as a law library.

• *The right of uncensored mail.* Law enforcement cannot exercise broad censorship; however, authorities can censor mail if they can show that such censorship furthers an important government interest and that the inmate's censorship is not broad. For example, guards cannot open legal mail, but if the warden suspects something is awry, he may open it in the convict's presence. Other letters can be scanned to prevent escape plans or contraband.

• *The right to access the press.* Corrections can only place restrictions on this according to the inconvenience or in order to maintain peace.

• *The right to adequate medical care.* This means that deliberate indifference to a serious medical need or condition constitutes cruel and unusual punishment (Eighth Amendment). Simple negligence, however, does not establish deliberate indifference.

The Rights Prisoners Do Not Have

• They don't have the right to do their time in the location of their choice and they may be transferred at any time for any reason.

• They do not have the right to unionize. Prison officials can prohibit prisoners from soliciting other inmates for membership in a prisoner's union and from conducting union-type activities.

• They do not have the right to paroles, serving their time outside the walls.

• Prisoners do not have the right to be free from the consequences of a criminal conviction upon the completion of a prison sentence. Even if a prisoner has paid his debt to society (completed his sentence), a felony conviction is serious. In most states, convicted felons may not possess a firearm. Some jurisdictions permanently disenfranchise convicted felons from the state and federal elections, may terminate parenting rights on the conviction, and permit divorce solely on the grounds of conviction or imprisonment of a felon. Convicted felons often may not be a part of public employment, and they may not serve jury duty. Also, certain states require felons to register as former offenders.

Suggested Steps for Further Writer's Research

- Define the crime
- Find the state or federal statute
- Read some cases pertaining to the offense; look for variations on a theme
- Clip and save all unusual or new case crime stories
- Outline crime from the perpetrator's point of view
- Outline crime from the victim's point of view
- Outline crime from the law enforcement's point of view
- Outline crime from the defense attorney's point of view
- Outline crime from the prosecutor's point of view
- Look for a forensic evidence link
- Interview or consult experts
- Visit a courtroom to observe a trial; take notes
- Watch *Court TV*

Justicia: The Story Behind the Figurehead for Equilibrium and Justice

The best known symbol of the law is the stunning female Justicia, one of the four cardinal virtues. She has also been identified as the eighth enigma of the Tarot, where her personification acts as an allegory for justice.

Tall and imperial-looking, Justicia is usually depicted in a full-faced, symmetrical fashion, in keeping with her symbolic temperament of an exacting and balanced nature. Typically, she wears a red tunic and a blue cloak. In one hand she holds up a pair of scales, representing the balance of good and evil. In her other hand are a law book and a sword, characterizing decisiveness and the Word of God. In Christian art, Emperor Trajan is at her feet. Sometimes, seated on her throne, she wears a crown of fleurons, or iron lances. She is always blindfolded.

Justicia is often referred to as Libra, a sign of the zodiac, and her figure in this context portrays not so much external justice or social legality, but inner judgment, exemplifying the enormity of thought required to determine guilt.

In matters of astronomy, she is Astraea, daughter of Zeus and Themis (the Divine Justice), and after her Golden Age as the star-maiden who lived on Earth and blessed mortals, she was placed among the stars as the constellation Virgo.

Representing harmony and a strict code of behavior, Justicia also has her dark side, signifying restriction, pettiness, and cunning—as an enforcer of the law, Justicia has appeared in some renditions with a severed head in her lap.

Bibliography

Books

American Bar Association, *ABA Standards for Criminal Justice: Prosecution Function and Defense Function*, 3rd ed., 1993. More info at *www.abanet.org*

Bergman, Paul, and Sara J. Berman-Barrett. *The Criminal Law Handbook: Know Your Rights, Survive the System.* Berkeley, California: Nolo Press, 1999.

Boyce, Ronald, and Rollin M. Perkinds. *Cases and Materials on Criminal Law and Procedure*, 8th ed. New York: Foundation Press, 1999.

Burton, William C. *Burton's Legal Thesaurus*, 3rd ed. New York: Macmillan Library Reference, 1998.

Campbell, Andrea. *Forensic Science: Evidence, Clues and Investigation.* Philadelphia: Chelsea House Publishers, 2000.

————. *Rights of the Accused.* Philadelphia: Chelsea House Publishers, 2001.

Chambers, Mortimer, et al. *The Western Experience, Vol. 1: To the Eighteenth Century.* New York: McGraw Hill, 1995.

Dimitrius, Jo-Ellan, and Mark Mazzarella. *Reading People: How to Understand People and Predict Their Behavior—Anytime, Anyplace.* New York: Random House, 1998.

Dix, George E., and M. Michael Sharlot. *Basic Criminal Law: Cases and Materials.* St. Paul, Minnesota: West Publishing, 1987.

Elias, Stephen, and Susan Levinkind. *Legal Research: How to Find and Understand the Law*, 6th ed. Berkeley, California: Nolo Press, 1999.

Elsevier, Reed. *The New American Desk Encyclopedia*, 4th ed. New York: Penguin Putnam, 1997.

Fosdick, Raymond. *American Police Systems.* New York: Century, 1921.

Irons, Peter. *A People's History of the Supreme Court.* New York: Viking, 1999.

Kamisar, Yale, Wayne R. LaFave, and Jerold H. Israel. *Basic Criminal Procedure: Cases, Comments and Questions*, 8th ed. St. Paul, Minnesota: West Publishing, 1994.

Kurland, Michael. *How to Try a Murder.* New York: Macmillan, 1997.

Lazarus, Edward. *Closed Chambers: The Rise, Fall, and Future of the Modern Supreme Court.* New York: Penguin, 1999.

Mullally, David S. *Order in the Court.* Cincinnati, Ohio: Writer's Digest Books, 2000.

Roth, Martin. *The Writer's Complete Crime Reference Book.* Cincinnati, Ohio: Writer's Digest Books, 1990.

Saeger, Michael. *Defend Yourself Against Criminal Charges.* Naperville, Illinois: Sourcebooks, 1997.

Saltzburg, Stephen A., and Daniel J. Capra. *Basic Criminal Procedure*, 2nd ed. St. Paul, Minnesota: West Publishing, 1997.

Scheb, John M, and John M. Scheb II. *Criminal Law and Procedure*. Belmont, California: Wadsworth Publishing, 1999.

Schmidt, Steffen W., et al. *American Government and Politics Today*, 1997–98 ed. Belmont, California: West Publishing, 1997.

Schrager, Sam. *The Trial Lawyer*. Philadelphia: Temple University Press, 2000.

Siegel, Larry J., and Joseph J. Senna. *Juvenile Delinquency, Theory, Practice and Law*. St. Paul, Minnesota: West Publishing, 1997.

Territo, Leonard, James B. Halsted, and Max L. Bromley. *Crime and Justice in America: A Human Perspective*. St. Paul, Minnesota: West Publishing, 1995.

Thibault, A., Lynch, et al., eds. *Proactive Police Management*. Englewood Cliffs, New Jersey: Prentice Hall, 1995

Trojanowicz, Robert, et al. *Community Policing: A Contemporary Perspective*. Cincinnati, Ohio: Anderson, 1990.

Vollmer, August. *The Police and Modern Society*. Montclair, New Jersey: Patterson Smith Reprint Series in Criminology, no. 131, September 1972.

Articles

The American Arbitration Association, "Alternative Dispute Resolution," http://www.lectlaw.com, The'Lectric Law Library.

Editorial, "Case Before High Court Threatens Suspects' Rights," *USA Today* (April 18, 2000).

Hampson, Rick, "Men Run Through Central Park Stripping and Groping Women," *USA Today* (June 12, 2000).

———, "The Supreme Court: The High Court: How It Works," *USA Today* (October 6, 1997).

Methvin, Eugene H., "Will the Supreme Court Arrest Miranda?" *Readers Digest* (May 2000).

Murr, Andrew, and Karen Springen, "Death at a Very Early Age," *Newsweek* (August 28, 2000).

Parker, Laura, and Gary Fields, "Unsolved Killings on the Rise," *USA Today* (February 22, 2000).

Reutter, Mark, "Courts Have Reduced Criminal Defendant's Right to Lawyer," Press release, University of Illinois Urbana-Champaign (April 2000).

Rodger, Will, "Warrants for Online Data Soar," *USA Today* (July 28, 2000).

Willing, Richard, "Justices Appear Split on 'Miranda'," *USA Today* (April 20, 2000).

———, "Prosecutor Often Determines Which Way a Case Will Go," *USA Today* (December 20, 1999).

Government Pamphlets

1999 National Report Series, Juvenile Justice Bulletin. *Children as Victims*, Washington D.C.:U.S. Department of Justice, May 2000, NCJ178257.

Connors, Edward, et. al. *Convicted by Juries, Exonerated by Science: Case Studies in the Use of DNA Evidence to Establish Innocence After Trial*. Washington, D.C.: U.S. Department of Justice, June 1996, NCJ 161258.

Eyewitness Evidence: *A Guide for Law Enforcement*. Washington, D.C.: U.S. Department of Justice, October 1999, NCJ 178240.

Rottman, David B., et al. *State Court Organization 1998*. Washington, D.C.: U.S. Department of Justice, 2000, NCJ 178932.

Webster-Stratton, Carolyn. *The Incredible Years Training Series*. Washington, D.C.: Office of Juvenile Justice and Delinquency Prevention, June 2000, NCJ 173422.

Weisburd, David, and Rosann Greenspan et al. *Police Attitude Toward Abuse of Authority: Findings From a National Study*. Washington, D.C.: U.S. Department of Justice, May 2000, NCJ 181312.

Endnotes

[1] Translated by Robert F. Harper, 1904, language modified. The Western Experience, vol. 1, 6th Ed. (New York: McGraw-Hill, 1995).

[2] Sherman, Dennis, ed., *Western Civilization: Sources, Images, and Interpretations*, 4th ed. (New York: McGraw-Hill, 1995).

[3] West's Fla. Stat. Ann. § 777.04

[4] *Gardner v. State*, 408 A. 2d 1317, 1322 (Md. 1979)

[5] *State v. Schleifer*, 121 A. 805, 809 (Conn. 1923)

[6] *United States v. Singleton*, 144 F.3d 1343 (10th Circuit 1998).

[7] *State v. Bingham*, 40 Wn.App. 553, 699 P.2d 262 (Wash. 1985).

[8] *People v. Roe*, 542 N.E. 2d 610 (NY 1989).

[9] Associated Press, "Bill Making It a Federal Crime to Harm a Fetus in Assault OK'd" (April 2001).

[10] West's Fla. Stat. Ann. § 782.071.

[11] *In re Quinlan*, 355 A.2d 647 (NJ 1976).

[12] *Harod v. State*, 65 Md. App. 128, 499 A 2d 959 (Maryland, 1985).

[13] *West's Ann.* Cal. Penal Code § 203.

[14] *State v. Rooks*, 468 S.E. 2d 354 (Ga. 1996).

[15] Mich Comp. Laws Ann. § 750.520.

[16] McKinney's N.Y. Penal Code § 135.25.

[17] *Commonwealth v. Donovan*, 478 N.E.2d 727 (Mass. 1985).

[18] West's Colo. Rev. Stat. Ann. § 18-4-304.

[19] *Jones v. Commonwealth* 13 Va, App. 566 414 S.E. 2d 193 (Virginia, 1992).

[20] U.S.C.A. § 876.

[21] *People v. Williams* 318 N.W.2d 671(Mich. App. 1982)

[22] *Kennedy v. State* 323 S.E.2d 169 (Ga. App. 1984).

[23] *State v. Tonnisen*, 92 N.J. Super 452, 224 A2d. 21 (N.J. 1966).

[24] Ariz. Rev. Stat. § 13-2002.

[25] Vernon's Tex. Penal Code Ann., § 32.41 (a).

[26] *Griswold v. Connecticut*, 381 U.S. 479, 85 S.Ct. 1678, 14 L.Ed.2d 510 (1965).

[27] Nevada Rev. Stat. §§ 201.380, 201.430, 201.440.

[28] The Mann Act, 18 U.S.C.A. § 2421 et. seq.

[29] *State v. Werner*, 609 So.2d. 585 (Fla. 1992).

[30] *State v. Anonymous*, 377 A.2d 1342 (Conn. Super. 1977).

[31] *Roth v. United States*, 354 U.S. 476, 77 S. Ct. 1304, 1 L.Ed.2d 1498 (1957).

[32] *New York v. Ferber*, 458 U.S. 747, 102 S. Ct. 3348, 73 L.Ed.2d 1113 (1982).

[33] *Knowles v. United States*, 170 F. 409 (8th Cir. 1909).

[34] *Cohen v. California*, supra, 403 U.S. at 25, 91 S. Ct. at 1788, 29 L.Ed.2d at 294.

[35] *Marshall v. State*, 200 S.E. 2d 902 (Ga. App. 1973).

[36] West's Ann. Ind. Code § 35–45–1–1.

[37] *Champlinsky v. New Hampshire*, 315 U.S. 568, 571, 62 S. Ct. 766, 769, 86 L. Ed.1031, 1035 (1942).

[38] 405 U.S. at 162, 92 S. Ct. at 843, 31 L.Ed.2d at 115.

[39] West's Cal. Ann. Vehicle Code § 23152 (a) (b).

[40] *State v. Harrison*, 846 P.2d 1082 (N.M. App. 1992).

[41] M'Naghten's Case, 8 Eng. Rep. 718 (1843).

[42] Durham test: 214 F.2d 862, 876 (D.C. Cir. 1954).

[43] U.S.C.A. § 17 (a).

[44] *Robey v. State*, 456 A, 2d 953 (Md. App. 1983).

[45] Penal Code (Calif.) Sec/ 28-b.

[46] *Montana v. Egelhoff*, 518 U.S. 37 (Montana, 1996) (Certiorari to the S.Ct. of Montana No. 95-566.)

[47] *People v. Merhige*, 180 N.W. 419 (Mich. 1920).

[48] Kan. Stat. Ann § 21-3209.

[49] *State v. Cole*, 403 S.E.2d 117 (S.C. 1991)

[50] *Commonwealth v. Berrigan*, 501 A.2d 226 (Pa. 1985)

[51] *Cleveland v. Municipality of Anchorage*, 631 P.2d 1073, 1078 (Alaska 1981).

[52] *Neal v. State*, 597 P.2d 334, 337 (Okl. Crim. App. 1979).

[53] *State v. Kennamore*, 604 S.W.2d 856, 860 (Tenn. 1980).

[54] *People v. Eatman*, 91 N.E. 2d at 390 (Ill. 1950).

[55] *State v. Grier*, 609 S.W.2d 201, 203 (Mo. App. 1980).

[56] Model Penal Code, Section 3.07 (2)(b)(ii).

[57] 18 U.S.C.A. § 6002.

[58] Page's Ohio Rev. Code Ann. § 2901.13 (A).

[59] *United States v. Armstrong*, 517 U.S. 456, 116 S. Ct. 1480, 134 L. Ed. 2d 687 (1996).

[60] *Rochin v. California*, 342 U.S. 165, 72 S. Ct. 205, 96 L. Ed. 183 (1952).

[61] *United States v. Freitas*, 800 F.2d 1451 (9th Cir. 1986).

[62] 18 U.S.C.A. § 3109.

[63] *United States v. Leon*, 468 U.S. 897, 104 S. Ct. 3405, 82 L. Ed.2d 677 (1984).

[64] 18 U.S.C.A. § 2518 (5).

[65] *United States v. Riley*, 968 F.2d 422 (5th Cir. 1992).

[66] *Michigan v. Tyler*, 436 U.S. 499, 98 S. Ct. 1942, 56 L. Ed.2d 486 (1978).

[67] *Wayne v. United States*, 318 F.2d 295, 212 (D.C. Cir. 1963).

[68] Preponderance of evidence: Evidence is more likely than not to imply guilt.

[69] *Illinois v. Rodriguez* 497 U.S. 177, 110 S. Ct. 2793, 111 L. Ed.2d 148 (1990).

[70] Adapted from Basic Criminal Procedure: American Casebook Series, by Yale Kamisar, et. al.,West Publishing; Illinois v. Rodriguez, p. 353–360.

[71] *Robinson v. United States*, 506 a.2d 572, 575 (DCA. App. 1986).

[72] *Jacobson v. United States*, 503 U.S. 540, (1992).

[73] *State v. Sainz*, 84 N.M. 259, 261, 501 P.2d 1247, 1249 (App. 1972).

[74] ECPA: 18 U.S.C. §§ 2701–11.

[75] *Terry v. Ohio*, 392 U.S. 1, 88 S. Ct. 1868, 20 L.Ed.2d 899 (1968).

[76] *United States v. Watson* 423 U.S. 411, 96 S. Ct. 820, 46 L.Ed.2d 598 (1976).

[77] *Adams v. Williams*, 407 U.S. 143, 92 S. Ct. 1921, 32 L.Ed.2d 612 (1972).

[78] *United States v. Dionisio*, 410 U.S. 1, 93, S. Ct. 764, 35 L.Ed.2d. 67 (1973).

[79] *Rhode Island v. Innis*, 446 U.S. 291, 301, 100 S. Ct. 1682, 1693, 64 L.Ed.2d 297, 308 (1980).

[80] *Hoffman v. United States*, 341 U.S. 479, 71 S. Ct. 814, 95 L. Ed. 1118 (1951).

[81] *Miranda v. Arizona*, 384 U.S. 436, 86 S. Ct. 1602, 16 L.Ed.2d 694 (1966).

[82] *New York v. Quarles*, 467 U.S. 649. 104 S. Ct. 2626, 81 L.Ed.2d 550 (1984).

[83] *People v. Stewart*, 11 Cal. App. 3d 242, September 17, 1970.

[84] *Gideon v. Wainwright*, 372 U.S. 335, 83 S. Ct. 792, 9 L. Ed.2d. 799 (1963).

[85] *Speedy Trial Act*, 18 U.S.C. § 3161.

[86] *Duncan v. Louisiana*, 391 U.S. 145, 88 S. Ct. 1444, 20 L. Ed. 2d. 491 (1968).

[87] *Chambers v. Mississippi*, 410 U.S. 284 (1973).

[88] *Coke v. Georgia*, 433 U.S. 584 97 S. Ct. 2861, 53 L. Ed.2d. 982 (1977).

[89] *United States v. Knotts*, 460 U.S. 276, 103 S. Ct. 1081, 75 L.Ed.2d. 55 (1983).

[90] Title III, Omnibus Crime Control & Safe Streets Act, 18 U.S.C.A. §§ 2510–20.

[91] *United States v. Miller*, 425 U.S. 435, 96 S. Ct. 1619, 48 L.Ed.2d. 71 (1976).

[92] "Police Attitudes Toward Abuse of Authority: Findings from a National Study," NCJ 181312.

[93] *State v. Cayward*, 552 So2d 971 (Fla. App. 1989).

[94] *Gilbert v. California*, 388 U.S. 263, 87 S. Ct. 1951, 18 L. Ed.2d 1178 (1967).

[95] *Manson v. Brathwaite*, 432 U.S. 98, 97 S. Ct. 2243, 53 L.Ed.2d 140 (1977).

[96] Insanity Defense Reform Act of 1984 18 U.S.C.A. § 17 (b).

[97] Title 28 of the United States Code Annotated.

[98] *Gezzi v. State*, 780 P.2d. 972 (Wyo. 1989).

[99] *Frye v. United States* 293 F.1013 (D.C. Cir. 1923).

[100] 18 U.S.C.A. § 1621.

[101] The Federal law for this can be found under 18 U.S.C.A. §§ 981–982.

[102] *United States v. A Parcel of Land*, 507 U.S. 111, 113 S. Ct. 1126, 122 L.Ed.2d 469 (1993).

[103] *Blockberger v. United States*, 284 U.S. 299, 304, 52 S. Ct. 180, 182, 76 L. Ed. 306, 309 (1932).

[104] *Illinois v. Vitale*, 447 U.S. 410, 420, 100 S. Ct. 2260, 2267, 65 L.Ed.2d 228, 238 (1980).

[105] 18 U.S.C.A. §§ 3141–3150.

[106] The prosecution can seek to refile cases dismissed at a prelim, provided there is more information.

[107] 18 U.S.C.A. § 3182.

[108] Illinois Juvenile Court Act of 1899.

[109] *Kent v. United States* (1966).

[110] *Gault v. Arizona* (1967).

[111] *Wheat v. United States*, 486 U.S. 153, 108 S. Ct. 1692, 100 L.Ed.2d 140 (1988).

[112] *Anders v. California*, 386 U.S. 738, 87 S. Ct. 1396, 18 L. Ed.2d 493 (1967).

[113] See the ABA Model Rules of Professional Conduct.

[114] Beware, however, of states that do not yet offer laws allowing preliminary hearings for all defendants. Always remember to research the state in which your novel is set!

[115] *State v. Hall*, 129 Ariz. 589, 633 P.2d 398 (1981).

[116] *Rock v. Arkansas*, 483 U.S. 44, 107 S. Ct. 2704, 97 L.Ed.2d. 37 (1987).

[117] *Strickland v. Washington*, 466 U.S. 668, 104 S. Ct. 2052, 80 L.Ed.2d. 674 (1984). The Supreme Court held that the defendant must make two showings in order to obtain a reversal for ineffective assistance of counsel.

[118] *Swain v. Alabama*, 380 U.S. 202, 85 S. Ct. 824, 13 L.Ed.2d 759 (1965).

[119] Dimitrius, Jo-Ellan. *Reading People: How to Understand People and Predict Their Behavior—Anytime, Anyplace.* New York: Random House, 1998.

[120] ABA Model Rule of Professional Conduct 3.3 (a)(4); 3.4 (e).

[121] Another version of the adage from the old trial lawyers is: If the law is against you, pound the facts; if the facts are against you, pound the law; if both the law and facts are against you, pound the table.

[122] Schrager, Sam. *The Trial Lawyer's Art.* Philadelphia: Temple University Press, 2000.

Index

292

BOOKS FROM ALLWORTH PRESS

The Journalist's Craft: A Guide to Writing Better Stories edited by Dennis Jackson and John Sweeney (paperback, 6 x 9, 240 pages, $19.95)

The Writer's Guide to Queries, Pitches & Proposals by Moira Anderson Allen (paperback, 6 x 9, 288 pages, $16.95)

writing.com: **Creative Internet Strategies to Advance Your Writing Career** by Moira Anderson Allen (paperback, 6 x 9, 256 pages, $16.95)

The Writer's Legal Guide, Second Edition by Tad Crawford and Tony Lyons (paperback, 6 x 9, 320 pages, $19.95)

Marketing Strategies for Writers by Michael Sedge (paperback, 6 x 9, 224 pages, $16.95)

Writing for Interactive Media: The Complete Guide by Jon Samsel and Darryl Wimberly (paperback, 6 x 9, 320 pages, $19.95)

Business and Legal Forms for Authors and Self-Publishers, Revised Edition by Tad Crawford (paperback (with CD-ROM), 8? x 11, 192 pages, $22.95)

The Writer's Guide to Corporate Communications by Mary Moreno (paperback, 6 x 9, 192 pages, $19.95)

How to Write Articles That Sell, Second Edition by L. Perry Wilbur and Jon Samsel (hardcover, 6 x 9, 224 pages, $19.95)

How to Write Books That Sell, Second Edition by L. Perry Wilbur and Jon Samsel (hardcover, 6 x 9, 224 pages, $19.95)

Writing Scripts Hollywood Will Love, Revised Edition by Katherine Atwell Herbert (paperback, 6 x 9, 160 pages, $14.95)

So You Want to Be a Screenwriter: How to Face the Fears and Take the Risks by Sara Caldwell and Marie-Eve Kielson (paperback, 6 x 9, 224 pages, $14.95)

The Screenwriter's Guide to Agents and Managers by John Scott Lewinski (paperback, 6 x 9, 256 pages, $18.95)

The Screenwriter's Legal Guide, Second Edition by Stephen F. Breimer (paperback, 6 x 9, 320 pages, $19.95)

Please write to request our free catalog. To order by credit card, call 1-800-491-2808 or send a check or money order to Allworth Press, 10 East 23rd Street, Suite 510, New York, NY 10010. Include $5 for shipping and handling for the first book ordered and $1 for each additional book. Ten dollars plus $1 for each additional book if ordering from Canada. New York State residents must add sales tax.

To see our complete catalog on the World Wide Web, or to order online, you can find us at *www.allworth.com*.